AF575622

"J. V. Fesko provides a full and helpful treatment of the application of the finished work of Christ culminating in his sending of the Holy Spirit at Pentecost by the work of the Spirit in the salvation of the individual believer and the worship, life, and mission of the church."

**RICHARD B. GAFFIN, JR.**
professor of biblical and systematic theology emeritus,
Westminster Theological Seminary

"'We believe in the Holy Spirit, the Lord, and giver of life' is a crucial tenet of what Christians confess about Trinitarian salvation. And yet, how much confusion throughout church history has there been over the person and work of the Holy Spirit and the comforting benefits that are intended for the believer to enjoy in this life. Thankfully, J. V. Fesko has greatly helped us in combining his experience as a scholar and pastor by writing The Giver of Life, a book that explains our Triune God's work of salvation from beginning to end. Read this book! It will encourage you, as it has me, in explaining the depths of God's love for us in Christ through the work of the Spirit."

**CHRISTOPHER J. GORDON**
senior minister, Escondido United Reformed Church;
host, *Abounding Grace Radio*

"*The Giver of Life* is a comprehensive treatment of the doctrine of the Holy Spirit, providing the reader with exegetical, theological, and pastoral reflections on his person and ministry. J. V. Fesko has captured this historic doctrine beautifully, expressing the 'faith once delivered to the saints' in clear, contemporary terms. Christ's church is enriched by this study."

**JAMES M. RENIHAN**
president and professor of historical theology,
International Reformed Baptist Seminary, Texas

"John Calvin earned his appellation as the Theologian of the Holy Spirit for his unprecedented emphasis on the Spirit's work. Sadly, since Calvin, the doctrine of pneumatology hasn't developed in every arena of theology as it should have. However, J. V. Fesko has put his hand to this task in *The Giver of Life*, which will prove to be a treasure for the church and a standard in systematic theology. Fesko has taken the often neglected, misunderstood, and, to many, mysterious doctrine of the Holy Spirit and showed its connection to every sphere of our theology. His book is thoroughly researched and provides a fair, balanced treatment of the various views on the pertinent issues under this head of theology."

**PETER SAMMONS**
assistant professor of theology, The Master's Seminary

"A spirited soteriological synthesis, gathering up a distinctively Protestant doctrine of salvation under the sign of Nicene pneumatology. Fesko is clear in his decisions, transparent in his method, particular about his (covenantal and Reformed) confession, and generous in his scope. This volume is an exemplary entry in the We Believe series."

**FRED SANDERS**
professor, Torrey Honors College, Biola University

"John Fesko's careful scholarship in a Reformed mode is well known and widely appreciated. In this volume, years of teaching Reformed soteriology bear fruit as we are taken through first the biblical revelation, with a heavy emphasis on the category of covenant, and then historical reflection on that revelation. However, even in the survey of the dogmatic development of these doctrines, the words of Scripture are not left behind. Too often an attempt to recover the resources of 'the great tradition' ends up effectively giving those resources priority over the biblical text. Not so in this book! It is Fesko's determination to keep a clear focus on the teaching of Scripture throughout while taking seriously the contributions of those who have come before us that makes this a refreshing and edifying contribution. I expect to make much use of this volume in my own teaching."

**MARK D. THOMPSON**
principal, Moore Theological College, Sydney

**J. V. FESKO**

is an ordained minister in the Orthodox Presbyterian Church and is the Harriet Barbour Professor of Systematic and Historical Theology at Reformed Theological Seminary in Jackson, Mississippi.

# THE GIVER OF LIFE

## THE BIBLICAL DOCTRINE OF THE HOLY SPIRIT AND SALVATION

# WE BELIEVE

## STUDIES IN REFORMED BIBLICAL DOCTRINE

*We Believe* is a series of eight major studies of the Christian faith's primary doctrines as confessed in the Nicene Creed and guided by the Reformed tradition. In each volume, trusted authors engage a major creedal doctrine in light of its biblical-theological foundations and historical development, drawing out its spiritual, ethical, and missional implications for the church today.

1

**One God Almighty**

The Biblical Doctrine of the Triune God

2

**Maker of Heaven and Earth**

The Biblical Doctrine of Creation and Providence

3

**The Lord Jesus Christ**

The Biblical Doctrine of the Person and Work of Christ

4

**For Us and for Our Salvation**

The Biblical Doctrine of Humanity and Sin

5

**He Will Come Again in Glory**

The Biblical Doctrine of the End

7

**He Spoke through the Prophets**

The Biblical Doctrine of God's Self-Revelation

8

**One, Holy, Catholic, and Apostolic Church**

The Biblical Doctrine of the Church

# THE GIVER OF LIFE

## THE BIBLICAL DOCTRINE OF THE HOLY SPIRIT AND SALVATION

**WE BELIEVE:** STUDIES IN REFORMED BIBLICAL DOCTRINE

VOLUME 6

JOHN MCCLEAN AND MURRAY J. SMITH, SERIES EDITORS

**J. V. FESKO**

*The Giver of Life: The Biblical Doctrine of the Holy Spirit and Salvation*
*We Believe*, edited by John McClean and Murray J. Smith



Lexham Academic, an imprint of Lexham Press
1313 Commercial St., Bellingham, WA 98225
LexhamPress.com



Print ISBN 9781683597490
Digital ISBN 9781683597469
Library of Congress Control Number 2023943146

Lexham Editorial: Todd Hains, Claire Brubaker, Mandi Newell
Cover Design: Joshua Hunt, Sarah Brossow
Typesetting: Anna Fejes, Abigail Stocker

23 24 25 26 27 28 29 / IN / 12 11 10 9 8 7 6 5 4 3 2 1

*Dedicated to*
*James P. Wood,*
*Ray Walker,*
*and*
*Steve Farish*

# CONTENTS

## PART 3: TRUTH FOR WORSHIP, LIFE, AND MISSION

# BIBLICAL EXPOSITIONS

# SERIES INTRODUCTION

*Your word is a lamp to my feet*
*and a light to my path.*
Psalm 119:105

*The unfolding of your words gives light;*
*it imparts understanding to the simple.*
Psalm 119:130

## AN INVITATION TO CONFESSIONAL THEOLOGY

*We Believe* is a series of eight studies of the primary doctrines of the Christian faith as confessed in the Nicene Creed and received in the Reformed tradition. The series marks the 1700th anniversary of the Council of Nicaea (AD 325) by re-affirming and advancing the Church's confession.[1] The title of our series is drawn from the first words of the Creed—the single Greek verb Πιστεύομεν—which introduces what has become the classic confession of the Christian Faith. Since the Church's confession neither began at Nicaea, nor ended with its creed, *We Believe* examines the biblical foundations of the Church's faith, traces its development (especially in the Reformed tradition), and applies its truths to the worship, life, and mission of the Church today. Since true theology begins in prayer and worship of the God who has revealed himself, each volume opens with a theme prayer, shaped by Scripture and the Church's confession. Further,

1. For the history of the Nicene Creed, which received its final form at the Council of Constantinople (ad 381), see D. Fairbairn and R. M. Reeves, *The Story of Creeds and Confessions: Tracing the Development of the Christian Faith* (Grand Rapids: Baker Academic, 2019), 48–79.

since even the deepest truths of the faith need to be simply expounded so they can be clearly grasped and faithfully lived, each volume closes with a series of theses, which summarize the doctrine covered in the book. *We Believe* provides a comprehensive and integrated biblical, theological, and missional treatment of the major doctrines of the Christian faith.

## BIBLICAL REVELATION

The Church's confession is rooted in and ruled by God's revelation in Scripture. The Scriptures are "the Word of God written" and "the rule of faith and life" (Westminster Confession of Faith 1:2). The first part of each study, therefore, is devoted to a fresh examination of biblical revelation.

Fundamentally, our studies are tethered to the text of Scripture, and each volume in the series includes expositions of the primary biblical texts which form the doctrine under consideration.[2] Moreover, since Scripture is the only "infallible rule" for its own interpretation (Westminster Confession of Faith 1:9), our studies seek to interpret Scripture by Scripture, initially by embracing the discipline of Biblical Theology.[3] We begin—where God's people have always begun—with the recognition that Scripture is God's inspired and authoritative Word. We proceed by tracing God's progressive revelation of himself and his purposes in the organically unfolding canon of Scripture, taking full account of its varied forms, while especially recognizing its fundamental, Christ-centered unity. This procedure is one we learn from Scripture itself. The Bible regularly claims that its revelation forms a single coherent narrative climaxing in the gospel of Christ, even as it also indicates that this narrative has many dimensions, and is revealed in a diversity of literary forms.[4] Faithful Christian readings of Scripture—from Irenaeus and Augustine to Calvin and Kuyper—have,

2. For convenience of reference, these biblical expositions are highlighted in text boxes. Several key biblical texts are important for more than one doctrine, but to avoid repetition, these are only treated once in the series.

3. We understand this discipline along the lines sketched by Geerhardus Vos in his 1894 Inaugural Lecture at Princeton Theological Seminary. G. Vos, "The Idea of Biblical Theology as a Science and as a Theological Discipline," in *Redemptive History and Biblical Interpretation: The Shorter Writings of Geerhardus Vos*, ed. R. B. Gaffin (Phillipsburg: P & R, 1980), 3–24; *Biblical Theology: Old and New Testaments* (Grand Rapids: Eerdmans, 1948), 3–18.

4. See, for example: Deut 26:5–11; Josh 24; 1 Sam 12:6–18; Pss 78; 105–6; 136; Neh 9:7-37; Acts 7; 13:13–43; Heb 11.

therefore, always recognized a fundamental unity within the rich diversity of Scripture—a unity which is conceptual (in that the Scriptures speak of the same God relating in consistent ways to the same created world), and narratival (in that the Scriptures narrate a single redemptive-history).[5]

In the first part of each study, then, we look for the organic unfolding of God's revelation from its seed form in the Garden of Eden (Gen 1–2) to its full flowering in the Garden-City of the New Jerusalem (Rev 21–22). As Augustine said, "in the Old Testament the New is concealed, in the New the Old is revealed."[6] So we read Genesis in the light of the Gospels, Exodus in the light of the Epistles, and Ruth in the light of Revelation. We follow the rich network of citations and allusions—the "inner biblical exegesis"—by which Scripture interprets Scripture.[7] We outline the primary biblical themes relevant to each doctrine—God's kingdom and covenant, God's creation and blessing, God's Son and people, God's Spirit and temple—together with their many related sub-themes, as they inform and shape the Church's confession. We use Scripture's own words and categories to trace the drama of redemption from creation to new creation centered on Christ.

Following this approach, we recognize that the Bible fundamentally structures its own unfolding narrative, and organizes all its major themes, around God's two primary covenants with Adam and Christ (Rom 5:12–21; 1 Cor 15:22). Reformed theology came to characterize these as the "covenant of works" and the "covenant of grace," confessing that, from start to finish, God has related to his people and his world by way of covenant (Westminster Confession of Faith 7:1–6).[8] Scripture thus presents each of the major post-fall biblical covenants—God's covenants with Abraham,

---

5. See C. H. H. Scobie, "History of Biblical Theology," in *New Dictionary of Biblical Theology*, ed. T. D. Alexander and B. S. Rosner (Leicester: InterVarsity Press, 2000), 11–20.

6. Augustine, Quaest. in Hept. 2: 73: *Novum Testamentum in Vetere latet, Vetus Testamentum in Novo patet*.

7. The phrase "inner biblical exegesis" was coined by M. A. Fishbane, *Biblical Interpretation in Ancient Israel* (Oxford: Oxford University Press, 1985). See further: G. K. Beale and D. A. Carson, eds., *Commentary on the New Testament Use of the Old Testament* (Grand Rapids: Baker Academic, 2007); G. K. Beale, *Handbook on the New Testament Use of the Old Testament: Exegesis and Interpretation.* (Grand Rapids: Baker Academic, 2012); G. E. Schnittjer, *Old Testament use of Old Testament: A Book-by-Book Guide* (Grand Rapids: Zondervan, 2021).

8. See esp. G. P. Waters, J. N. Reid, and J. R. Muether, eds., *Covenant Theology: Biblical, Theological, and Historical Perspectives* (Wheaton: Crossway, 2020); H. Perkins, *Reformed Covenant Theology: A Systematic Introduction* (Bellingham, WA: Lexham Press, forthcoming).

Israel, David, and the new covenant—as successive administrations of the single covenant of grace: the covenant which was first promised in the garden (Gen 3:15), climactically sealed by the blood of Christ (Matt 26:28 and Mark 14:24 with Exod 24:8), and which ultimately will be fulfilled in the new creation when the triune God comes to dwell with his people at last (Rev 21:3).[9]

Above all—and consistent with the covenant theology we have just sketched—we take Jesus's own word as our guide, and look for him, the Lord Jesus Christ, "in all the Scriptures" (Luke 24:27). Following Jesus and his apostles, we recognize that God "promised...the gospel...beforehand through his prophets in the Holy Scriptures" (Rom 1:3–4; cf. Luke 24:44–49; Gal 3:8; 1 Cor 15:3–5; 1 Pet 1:12). Christ himself—his person, his work, and his kingdom—is the climax and goal of the triune God's gracious plan to redeem his people and his world. Indeed, Christ is the very "substance" of biblical revelation (Col 2:17; cf. John 5:39; Rom 10:4; 1 Cor 10:4; 2 Cor 1:20; 2 Tim 3:15; 1 Pet 1:10–12). The grace of God in Christ was not merely foreshadowed and prophesied in the Old Testament; it was mediated in advance to the saints of old, by the Spirit, through the "promises, prophecies, sacrifices...and other types" given to God's people in that period (Westminster Confession of Faith 7:5–6). We therefore affirm that the Old Testament is *both* Christo-telic (in that it points forward to Christ as its goal), *and* Christo-centric (in that its types and promises really mediated God's grace in Christ, through the Spirit).[10] Thus, with John Calvin, we are right to "seek in the whole of Scripture...truly to know Jesus Christ, and the infinite riches that are comprised in him and are offered to us by him from God the Father."[11]

---

9. For the central covenant promise—"I will be your God and you will be my people" (or variations), see: Gen 17:7–8; 28:15; 31:3, 5, 42; 39:2–6, 21–23; Exod 6:7; 29:45–46; Lev 11:45; 25:38; 26:11–12; Deut 23:15; 26:17–18; 29:12–13; 2 Sam 7:23–24; 1 Chron 17:22; Ps 95:7; Jer 11:4; 24:7; 30:22; 31:1, 33; 32:38; Ezek 14:11; 34:24, 30–31; 36:28; 37:23, 27; Zech 2:11; 8:8; 13:9; Hos 1:8–2:23; Matt 1:23; 18:20; 28:20; 2 Cor 6:16; Rev 21:3.

10. See: P. A. Lillback, ed. *Seeing Christ in All of Scripture: Hermeneutics at Westminster Theological Seminary* (Philadelphia: Westminster Seminary Press, 2016); L. G. Tipton, "Christocentrism *and* Christotelism: The Spirit, Redemptive History, and the Gospel," in *Redeeming the Life of the Mind: Essays in Honor of Vern Poythress*, ed. J. M. Frame, W. A. Grudem, and J. J. Hughes (Wheaton: Crossway, 2018), 129–45.

11. From Calvin's preface to Pierre Olivétan's French translation of the New Testament (1534) in *Calvin: Commentaries*, J.Haroutunian and L.P. Smith, trans. and eds, (Philadelphia: Westminster Press, 1958), 70.

In thus seeking Christ in all the Scriptures, we find that later revelation in Scripture interprets earlier revelation in ways that are consistent with its original meaning; the later revelation shows the "true and full sense" (*sensus plenior*) in light of the fulfillment in Christ (Westminster Confession of Faith 1:9). The New Testament offers no radical reinterpretation, much less correction, of the Old, but unfolds the full meaning of God's inspired Word. As B.B. Warfield put it, the Old Testament is like a room "richly furnished but dimly lighted," such that "the introduction of light [from the New Testament] brings into it nothing which was not in it before," but "brings out into clearer view much of what is in it but was only dimly or even not at all perceived before."[12] As we read the Scriptures as the unfolding narrative of God's redemptive purpose, we learn to see, again and again, that Christ is the center and substance of the Scriptures, and so the center and substance of the Church's faith.

## DOGMATIC DEVELOPMENT

The Church confesses not only what is "expressly set down in Scripture" but what "by good and necessary consequence may be deduced from Scripture" (Westminster Confession of Faith 1:6). The second part of each study in the *We Believe* series, therefore, is devoted to an account of the dogmatic development of the doctrine under consideration. Far from being opposed to each other, Biblical Theology and Systematic and Confessional Dogmatics actually need each other; there is a necessarily reciprocal relationship between the two.[13] While both disciplines deal with God's special revelation in Scripture, they analyze it according to different principles.

12. B. B. Warfield, "The Biblical Doctrine of the Trinity," in *Biblical Doctrines: The Works of Benjamin B. Warfield*, vol. 2 (New York: Oxford University Press, 1932), 141–42.

13. For reflection on the relationship between the two disciples in the Reformed tradition, see esp. Vos, "Idea," 3–24; J. Murray, "Systematic Theology," in *Collected Writings of John Murray, vol. 4. Studies in Theology: Reviews*, ed. I. Murray (Edinburgh: Banner of Truth, 1983), 1–21; R. B. Gaffin, "Systematic Theology and Biblical Theology," *WTJ* 38 (1975–76): 281–99. For review of these contributions and a constructive proposal, see M. Allen, "Systematic Theology and Biblical Theology—Part One," *JRT* 14 (2020): 52–72; "Systematic Theology and Biblical Theology—Part Two," *JRT* 14 (2020): 344–57. Note also: J. McClean, "Of Covenant and Creation: A Conversation between Systematic Theology and Biblical Theology," in *An Everlasting Covenant: Biblical and Theological Essays in Honour of William J. Dumbrell*, ed. J. A. Davies and A. M. Harman, RTR Supplement Series 4 (Doncaster: Reformed Theological Review, 2010), 187–227.

The primary organizing principle for Biblical Theology is history—the organic unfolding of God's work of redemption and his interpretation of the same in his inspired Word. The primary organizing principle of Dogmatics is logic—the rational organization of God's revealed truth. As Geerhardus Vos observes, while Biblical Theology constructs a historical "line," Christian Dogmatics constructs a logical "circle."[14] Thus, while Christian Dogmatics, including the Church's creeds and confessions, generally follow the redemptive-historical shape of biblical revelation, they self-consciously set that redemptive history within the reality of the triune God and his relations to his world as these are revealed in all of Scripture.[15] In the same way, while Christian Dogmatics fundamentally expresses itself using biblical language, it also employs extra-biblical language to summarize and synthesize biblical teaching, especially where Scripture uses a variety of expressions for the same reality, or where this is necessary to refute error.[16] Since "the Word of God is living and active" (Heb 4:12), the God-given language of Scripture remains primary. Faithful Dogmatics rightly recognizes what John Webster calls the "rhetorical sufficiency" of Scripture.[17] Indeed, since "the Old Testament in Hebrew ... and the New Testament in Greek" were "immediately inspired by God," the final court of appeal for all Christian Dogmatics is the words of Scripture in the original languages (Westminster Confession of Faith 1:8). Yet still, the same theological judgment can be expressed in a range of different conceptual and linguistic forms, and the faithful presentation and propagation of biblical truth sometimes requires extra-biblical expression.[18]

There is, moreover, a real history of doctrinal development to be traced through the ages of church history. As the very Word of the living God, the Scriptures possess an inexhaustible depth. As the Church reads and re-reads God's Word in an ever-changing world, we find that there is always more to confess regarding God and his ways in the world, and always more

14. See Vos, "Idea," 23; cf. Murray, "Systematic Theology," 9.

15. Cf. Allen, "Systematic Theology—Part Two," 355–56.

16. Cf. "Systematic Theology—Part Two," 355.

17. J. Webster, "Biblical Reasoning," in *The Domain of the Word: Scripture and Theological Reason* (London: T & T Clark, 2012), 131.

18. See D. S. Yeago, "The New Testament and Nicene Dogma: A Contribution to the Recovery of Theological Exegesis," *ProEccl* 3 (1994): 87–100. Compare B.B. Warfield's comments to this effect on the doctrine of the Trinity (Warfield, "Trinity," 133).

to celebrate in the depths of his "being, wisdom, power, holiness, justice, goodness, and truth" (Westminster Shorter Catechism 4). Herman Bavinck states it well:

> Scripture is not designed so that we should parrot it but that as free children of God we should think his thoughts after him...so much study and reflection on the subject is bound up with it that no person can do it alone. That takes centuries. To that end the church has been appointed and given the promise of the Spirit's guidance into all truth.[19]

As each generation has read the Scriptures, confessed the faith, proclaimed the gospel, instructed children, discipled converts, and refuted errors, the Church—under the oversight of its living Lord, and by the enabling of his Holy Spirit—has deepened in its grasp of biblical truth.[20] The Church has learned again and again that "the Lord hath yet more light and truth to break forth from His Word."[21] The foundational doctrines of God and Christ were fundamentally established in the Church's early centuries, and codified in the ecumenical creeds, such that they received only incremental refinements thereafter. Other doctrines, however, no less crucial to the life of the Church—for example, the doctrines of Scripture and authority—received considerable development in the medieval, Reformation, and modern periods.

Doctrinal development, however—at least where it can be considered faithful—never moves beyond Scripture; it only ever penetrates more deeply into its truth. Faithful Dogmatics is thus not the imposition of a foreign grid onto Scripture, but a complementary means of interpreting Scripture by Scripture. In doing so, we make use of sanctified human reason. For while the Fall has corrupted the human mind (Rom 1:21–23; Eph 4:17–18), that same mind is renewed in Christ and by the Spirit (Rom 12:2; 1 Cor 2:10–13; Eph 4:23), and as such can play the role of servant in the task of theology. Thus Francis Turretin helpfully distinguishes between

---

19. H. Bavinck, *Reformed Dogmatics: Vol. 1—Prolegomena* (Grand Rapids: Baker Academic, 2003), 83.

20. The role of the Spirit in doctrinal development is helpfully emphasized by Murray, "Systematic Theology," 1–21, esp. 6.

21. G. Rawson, "We Limit Not the Truth of God" in *Leeds Hymn Book*, 1853, no. 409.

revelation as the "foundation of faith" and reason as the "instrument of faith," which can serve to "illustrate" and "collate" biblical passages or arguments, to draw out "inferences," and to help assess whether various positions agree or disagree with what has been revealed.[22]

The Church has been at this task for nearly two-thousand years, and there is a great deal to be learned from the wisdom of the ages. For this reason, each volume in the *We Believe* series provides a survey of the historical development of the doctrine under consideration. In charting this development, we give the Church's creeds and confessions pride of place. For while Augustine, Aquinas, Luther, Calvin, Turretin, and Bavinck—among a host of others—have provided significant insight into biblical truth, the Church's creeds and confessions reflect the official teaching of the Church *as* Church or—perhaps better—the common teaching of the Church's elders, that is, the teaching of those appointed by the Spirit, and charged with guarding and promoting the apostolic gospel and, indeed, "the whole counsel of God" (Acts 15:1–35; 16:4; 20:27–28; 1 Tim 3:2; 5:17–18; 2 Tim 2:2; Titus 1:9).[23]

The Church's teaching is always subordinate to Scripture. Scripture is the magisterial authority, the "rule that rules" (*norma normans*); the Church's teaching is a ministerial authority, "the rule that is ruled" (*norma normata*). In the order of authority, "the Supreme Judge, by which all controversies of religion are to be determined, and all decrees of councils, opinions of ancient writers, doctrines of men, and private spirits, are to be examined, and in whose sentence we are to rest, can be no other but the Holy Spirit speaking in the Scripture" (Westminster Confession of Faith 1:10). At the same time, in the order of knowing, there is wisdom in beginning with the Church's confession. We rightly take the Church's teaching as our guide in reading, interpreting, and applying Scripture. We learn the truth from our elders as they teach us the truth from God's Word. This yields an iterative process: the Scriptures form our confession; our Scripturally-formed confession provides the lens through which we read

22. F. Turretin, *Institutes of Elenctic Theology*, trans. G. M. Giger, 3 vols. (Phillipsburg: P&R, 1992–97), §1.8.3, 6–7; 1.12.15.

23. See M. S. Horton, *The Christian Faith: A Systematic Theology for Pilgrims on the Way* (Grand Rapids: Zondervan, 2011), 211–18.

the Scriptures, and; our further reading of the Scriptures further refines our confession.[24]

*We Believe* stands unashamedly in the Reformed confessional tradition, and seeks to defend and advance it. There are, of course, significant differences between the various Christian confessions. While the whole Church receives the doctrine of the ecumenical creeds (the Apostles', Nicene, and Athanasian creeds, together with the definition of Chalcedon), the later confessions present divergent views on a host of significant matters. It is our conviction that the Reformed confessions, especially the Three Forms of Unity and the Westminster Standards, present the best—that is, the most fully biblical—account of Christian truth. That very tradition, however, has always aimed to contend for "the faith that was once for all delivered to the saints" (Jude 3) and has thus championed a kind of Reformed Catholicity.[25] Our approach in the *We Believe* series is therefore eirenic, and ecumenical. We write *from* the perspective of the Reformed tradition, but *for* the Church catholic.

Moreover, while the Reformed confessions of the sixteenth century are a high point in the development of the Church's doctrine, they are not the end point. The body of Christ will not "attain to the unity of the faith and of the knowledge of the Son of God, to mature manhood, to the measure of stature of the fullness of Christ" (Eph 4:13), until Christ fully unites us to himself by his Spirit, when he raises his people from the dead, and perfects us by his glorious presence (1 Cor 15:42–49; Phil 3:20–21). The bride of Christ will not be fully purified, "without spot or wrinkle," until the Lord returns and presents us to himself "in splendour" (Eph 5:27; Rev 21:2, 9). The city of God will not be complete until God himself comes to dwell among us in all his fullness and illumine us with his light (Rev 21:3, 22–23). A Reformed commitment to the creeds and confessions is, therefore, not an end point, but a stimulus to further biblical exposition and dogmatic clarification.[26] As a work in Christian Dogmatics, *We Believe* does

---

24. S. Swain, "A Ruled Reading Reformed: The Role of the Church's Confession in Biblical Interpretation," *IJST* 14 (2012): 177–93.

25. Horton, *Christian Faith*, 30–32. Cf. M. Allen and S. R. Swain, *Reformed Catholicity: The Promise of Retrieval for Theology and Biblical Interpretation* (Grand Rapids: Baker Academic, 2015); *Christian Dogmatics: Reformed Theology for the Church Catholic* (Grand Rapids: Baker Academic, 2016).

26. See Bavinck, *Reformed Dogmatics* 1, 31.

not merely aim to retrieve or to repristinate the Reformed tradition, but to constructively develop it, always under the authority of God's Word. If this series makes a modest contribution to the Church's pilgrimage to maturity in Christ, it will have achieved its goal.

## TRUTH FOR WORSHIP, LIFE, AND MISSION

The Church's maturity in Christ involves far more than doctrinal faithfulness and clarity. The drama of redemption, which forms the Church's doctrine, aims ultimately at discipleship and doxology.[27] The third part of each study in the *We Believe* series, therefore, briefly considers the ways in which the doctrine under consideration shapes the Church's worship, life, and mission. While the discussion here is necessarily indicative rather than exhaustive, we aim to demonstrate how biblical doctrine creates a moral vision for all of life. This includes, at the broadest level, observing the way in which the particular doctrine provides the basis for biblical principles for Christian worship, life, and mission, whether these are given explicitly in the biblical text (e.g. Matt 7:12 the "golden rule"), or summarized from biblical revelation as a whole (e.g. "the sanctity of life").[28] It includes, more sharply, consideration of the way in which Christian doctrine grounds the moral law, summarized in the Ten Commandments, and further summarized in the two great commandments of love for God and neighbor (Westminster Confession of Faith 19.2, 5; see esp. Exod 20:1–17; Deut 5:6–21; Matt 22:37–40; Rom 13:8; Gal 5:14; Jas 2:8). It also includes, further, consideration of the wealth of biblical examples which illustrate—both positively and negatively—the wisdom of life according to God's law. Crucially, since Reformed theology has always emphasized the necessity of the work of the Spirit in enabling faith and renewing those who were lost in sin by uniting them to Christ, this section also considers the way in which each doctrine highlights the gracious work of God in enabling his people "to live and work for his praise and glory" (*A Prayer Book for Australia*).

---

27. For this alliterative summary—"drama, doctrine, doxology, and discipleship"—see Horton, *Christian Faith*, 13–27.

28. See J. Murray, *Principles of Conduct: Aspects of Biblical Ethics* (London: Tyndale Press, 1957), 78–140.

Each of the authors for the series subscribes to one or more of the major Reformed confessions, and shares the general approach to Scripture and theology we have just outlined. At the same time, each author has approached the task in their own way, and—within the rich agreement just sketched—there are differences between us at the level of detail. We have deliberately assembled a company of authors who are experts in either Biblical Theology or Dogmatics on the conviction that in the Reformed tradition scholars must have a facility in both, even while maintaining their own expertise. The books aim to show the necessary integrity of Biblical Theology and Systematic Theology, to introduce students to biblical-confessional theology, and to help enrich and expand Reformed theology, while serving as a resource and reference for pastors, elders, and thoughtful Christians. We're thankful to Lexham Press, and especially our expert editor Dr Todd Hains, for their partnership in this venture. Our hope and prayer is that these eight *Studies in Reformed Biblical Doctrine* might serve to ground the Church more firmly in the truth of God's Word, that together we might "glorify God and enjoy him forever" (Westminster Shorter Catechism 1).

Almighty God, you are enthroned on the praises of Israel,
and all nations will worship and glorify your name.
Grant us counsel, instruct us, and reveal yourself to us,
that we would enjoy and glorify you in heart, soul,
and mind in this life and forever.
Through Jesus Christ our Lord,
who lives and reigns with you
and the Holy Spirit, one God,
now and forever.
Amen.

John McClean
Vice Principal and Lecturer in Systematic Theology and Ethics
Christ College, Sydney

Murray J. Smith
Lecturer in Biblical Theology and Exegesis
Christ College, Sydney

# PREFACE

I HAVE BEEN STUDYING AND teaching the doctrine of salvation for more than thirty years and am thankful for the opportunity to contribute to the We Believe series. I am grateful to Murray Smith and John McClean for recruiting me to this series and for their editorial labors. I owe my thanks to a number of people who helped me along the way in the writing of this book, including my teaching assistant, Levi Berntson, and my colleagues Guy Waters and Blair Smith. I am also grateful especially for my family, my wife, Anneke, and my children, John Jr., Robert, and Carmen. You are a continual source of joy in my life, and you love me in spite of all my faults. You also uphold me in prayer, which is something I needed in great doses as I wrote this book. I had planned to work on this book in what was supposed to be a quiet summer in the midst of the Covid pandemic in 2021. "The plans of the heart belong to man, but the answer of the tongue is from the LORD" (Prov 16:1). My father was diagnosed with cancer and six weeks later died, and then my grandmother died three weeks after that. A summer filled with changed plans, sadness, funerals, and mourning provided an unwanted but well-suited context for reflecting on God's mercy in Christ through the Spirit. It's one thing to write about the blessings of salvation and the hope of the beatific vision, and entirely another to hold your dying father's hand as he enters into the presence of God to enjoy him forever. I pray that this book better equips Christians to know the depths of the riches of God's love in Christ so that we all might glorify God and enjoy him forever.

I dedicate this book to three pastors who were a great influence in my life—men who continually pointed me to Christ. I was fifteen years old and sitting in the new members' class when pastor Jim Wood wrote the TULIP acrostic on the whiteboard. I didn't fully grasp what he was teaching for a number of years, but he planted the seeds of God's sovereignty in salvation in my heart and mind that would later grow. Pastor Wood also helped me with writing my first sermon, which I delivered when I was sixteen years old for Youth Sunday. Pastor Wood's humility left a mark on me that persists to this day, because when people thank me for preaching, I respond, "Praise God!" Pastor Steve Farish taught the Monday night Bible study and regularly mentioned R. C. Sproul, which stirred my interest even more. Steve patiently entertained my objections to God's sovereignty in salvation by pointing me to Romans 9: "Read that chapter every day for the next month, and then come to me if you have any questions. But I don't think you will." I relented and admitted just three days later, "You, Lord, are the Creator, and I am but a creature. You are sovereign and I am not." Steve watered the seed that Pastor Wood planted, and my TULIP grew into a garden in the subsequent years. Throughout my teenage years, another constant in my life was my youth pastor, Ray Walker. Ray spent countless hours with me and my brother at youth events, Bible studies, retreats, and movies, and in small group discipleship. Ray continually pointed my brother and me to Christ. Ray's discipleship was a big factor, I believe, in our growth in God's grace. He also set an example of godliness for us both. Once I saw his T-shirt wrap around the front wheel of his bike, and he flew over the handlebars, his arm and back skidding across the pavement. Despite the ensuing road rash and excruciating pain, Ray never once let a foul word fly. That type of consistent Christian walk in both word and deed left an indelible impression on me to this day. I give thanks to our faithful God to all three of you for pointing me to Christ, and so I dedicate this book to you. I pray that I can do for others what you have done for me and point people to Christ in word and deed. SDG.

J. V. Fesko

# ABBREVIATIONS

| | |
|---|---|
| AB | Anchor Bible |
| *ANF* | *The Ante-Nicene Fathers.* Edited by Alexander Roberts and James Donaldson. 1885–1887. 10 vols. Reprint, Peabody, MA: Hendrickson, 1994 |
| BC | Belgic Confession |
| BECNT | Baker Exegetical Commentary on the New Testament |
| *BBR* | *Bulletin for Biblical Research* |
| CNTC | Calvin's New Testament Commentaries |
| EBC | Expositor's Bible Commentary |
| FC | Fathers of the Church |
| GC | Gallican Confession |
| *GTJ* | *Grace Theological Journal* |
| HC | Heidelberg Catechism |
| *Inst.* | *Institutes of the Christian Religion* |
| *JETS* | *Journal of the Evangelical Theological Society* |
| NICNT | New International Commentary on the New Testament |
| NICOT | New International Commentary on the Old Testament |
| NIGTC | New International Greek Testament Commentary |
| *NPNF*[1] | *The Nicene and Post-Nicene Fathers*, Series 1. Edited by Philip Schaff. 1886–1889. 14 vols. Reprint, Peabody, MA: Hendrickson, 1994 |
| *NPNF*[2] | *The Nicene and Post-Nicene Fathers*, Series 2. Edited by Philip Schaff. 1886–1889. 14 vols. Reprint, Peabody, MA: Hendrickson, 1994 |
| NSBT | New Studies in Biblical Theology |
| NSD | New Studies in Dogmatics |
| PNTC | Pillar New Testament Commentary |

| | |
|---|---|
| *SBET* | *Scottish Bulletin of Evangelical Theology* |
| SD | Studies in Dogmatics |
| *ST* | Thomas Aquinas, *Summa theologica* |
| TOTC | Tyndale Old Testament Commentary |
| *TynBul* | *Tyndale Bulletin* |
| *VT* | *Vetus Testamentum* |
| WBC | Word Biblical Commentary |
| WCF | Westminster Confession of Faith |
| WLC | Westminster Larger Catechism |
| WSC | Westminster Shorter Catechism |
| *WTJ* | *Westminster Theological Journal* |
| WUNT | Wissenschaftliche Untersuchungen zum Neuen Testament |

# A PRAYER FOR THE STUDY OF THE HOLY SPIRIT AND SALVATION

When you send forth your Spirit, they are created,
and you renew the face of the ground.

*Psalm 104:30*

Heavenly Father, we give thanks for your Holy Spirit, the Lord and giver of life, who has opened our eyes and given us faith, so that we might believe in Christ, stand justified in your sight, be ever more conformed day by day to his holy image, and look ever hopefully to our glorification. As we plunge into the depths of your saving work through Christ and the Spirit, we pray that you would grant unto us humility, ears to hear, and eyes to see the marvels and wonders of our salvation. We pray that we would look for the resurrection of the dead and the life of the world to come. In Christ's name we pray, Amen.

INTRODUCTION

# FOR US AND FOR OUR SALVATION

The Nicene Creed historically defended orthodox biblical teaching about the person of Christ, that the Son of God is "begotten from the Father before all ages, God from God, Light from Light, true God from true God, begotten, not made; of the same essence as the Father." These words have been professed for seventeen hundred years by the whole of Christendom, East and West, Protestant and Roman Catholic. As much as the Nicene Creed stakes out important christological truths, it also makes important claims about the doctrine of salvation, a Trinitarian doctrine of salvation no less. The creed confesses that all things were made through the Son and then says that the incarnation was "for us and for our salvation." But Christ does not stand on the stage of redemptive history alone. The creed continues, "And we believe in the Holy Spirit, the Lord, the giver of life. He proceeds from the Father and the Son, and with the Father and the Son is worshiped and glorified." The Nicene Creed therefore sets forth a Trinitarian doctrine of salvation, where the Father sends the Son and the Spirit to create, as "through him" (Christ) "all things were made," and the Holy Spirit is "the Lord, the giver of life." The Son and the Spirit are also the ones whom the Father sends to redeem sinners and to create the new heavens and earth, as the Triune God brings about the "resurrection of the dead, and ... life in the world to come," where the Son rules over his never-ending kingdom. The Father, Son, and Spirit redeem sinners, those who constitute "one holy catholic and apostolic church," and as the recipients of the grace of the Triune God, they take this message into the world so that others may know of the blessings of redemption. The people whom God calls to himself through the gospel are also a *holy* catholic church, a people set apart as those who have received "one baptism for the forgiveness of sins," who manifest their salvation through the gifts of the Spirit and who worship and glorify Father, Son, and Holy Spirit.

This volume in the We Believe series unpacks the scriptural teaching of our Trinitarian salvation, though it does so from the perspective of the Reformed faith. Early Reformed theologians maintained that they were Reformed catholics and not sectarians; they agreed with the Nicene Creed. The Thirty-Nine Articles (1571) state: "The Three Creeds, Nicene Creed, Athanasius's Creed, and that which is commonly called the Apostles' Creed, ought thoroughly to be received and believed: for they may be proved by most certain warrants of Holy Scripture" (8). Likewise, the Gallican Confession (1559) and Belgic Confession (1561) make similar statements: "We willingly accept the three ecumenical creeds—the Apostles', Nicene, and Athanasian—as well as what the ancient fathers decided in agreement with them" (BC 9; see also Gallican Confession 5). The Second Helvetic Confession (1566) also approves and commends the councils of Nicaea, Constantinople, Ephesus, and Chalcedon, along with the Athanasian Creed (11). The Reformers believed that the Nicene Creed was biblical, which is why they included affirmatory statements about it in their confessions of faith. The Nicene Creed and Reformed theology, more specifically soteriology, go hand in hand.

This volume contains three sections. Part 1 treats biblical-theological themes relevant to the doctrine of salvation. Chapter 1 surveys the redemptive-historical foundations of salvation in terms of God's covenant presence through creation and redemption. One of the chief goals of creation and redemption is for God to dwell in the midst of his people. Chapter 2 looks at the nature of God's covenant promises—the blessings he imparts in salvation. Chapter 3 provides an overview of covenant life to show how faith, hope, and love underlie life in the Spirit to fuel the worship, prayer, witness, and mission of the church. Part 2 examines the doctrines of salvation by laying a foundation in chapter 4 with the person and work of the Spirit, which leads to chapter 5 and the union with Christ that the Spirit effects in the regeneration of sinners. The Spirit's effectual call leads to justification (ch. 6), adoption (ch. 7), and sanctification (ch. 8). Chapters 9–11 investigate the nature of the Christian life in terms of faith and repentance (ch. 9), assurance and perseverance (ch. 10), and the gifts of the Spirit, which equip believers for service (ch. 11). Part 3 contains three chapters that explain the nature of true versus counterfeit faith (ch. 12), the pursuit of Christian maturity in the Spirit (ch. 13), and the way in which the Spirit's prophetic revelation equips the church for its witness and mission to the world (ch. 14). The book concludes with summary observations about the Trinitarian character of salvation, a Reformed catholic soteriology that rests on the authority of Scripture and employs the insights of the Nicene Creed.

PART 1

# BIBLICAL REVELATION

1

# COVENANT PRESENCE

## THE SPIRIT OF GOD IN CREATION AND REDEMPTION

One of the Scripture's recurring themes is God dwelling amid his people, whether in the garden-temple of Eden, in the desert tabernacle, in the Solomonic temple, or in the hearts of those united to Christ in the Old Testament and ultimately God's final temple and dwelling place in his people in the new creation. The most iconic expression of this reality comes in God's statement to the Israelites: "I will take you to be my people, and I will be your God, and you shall know that I am the Lord your God, who has brought you out from under the burdens of the Egyptians" (Exod 6:7). This statement entails three key realities. First, God would redeem the Israelites from Egypt and make them his people. This redemption rested on the foundation of God's covenantal promises to the patriarchs: "And God heard their groaning, and God remembered his covenant with Abraham, with Isaac, and with Jacob" (Exod 2:24). Second, God would be their God—he alone would be the sole object of their worship and love, a dynamic captured in Israel's covenantal charter: "Hear, O Israel: The Lord our God, the Lord is one. You shall love the Lord your God with all your heart and with all your soul and with all your might" (Deut 6:4–5). Third, concomitant with the mutually encompassing relationship between Israel and God is the idea that Israel would know God. Exodus 6:7 invokes the covenantal name of God, Yahweh (indicated by the small-caps "Lord" in the English translation). The personal name of God, which he revealed to Moses on Mount Horeb, "I AM WHO I AM" (Exod 3:14) is a name of intimacy and familiarity, a name only for those in covenant with God. When God therefore told his people, "I will be your God," his declaration amounted to a covenantally binding relationship, a marriage between him and his people.

But covenant requires presence and place. Where and by what means, then, does God fellowship with his people? The primary means by which God dwells amid his people is the presence of the third person of the Trinity, the Holy Spirit. This chapter traces this theme throughout preredemptive and redemptive history, from Eden to tabernacle, temple, and church. It then examines the connections between the Spirit and the Son. The chapter subsequently examines the Spirit's role in the new creation.

## THE SPIRIT AND CREATION (LIFE, COMMON GRACE)

THE OPENING WORDS OF THE Bible reveal the Spirit's work in the creation: "The earth was without form and void, and darkness was over the face of the deep. And the Spirit of God was hovering over the face of the waters" (Gen 1:2). The Spirit was an agent of creation, working in concert with Father and Son to create *ex nihilo* (Heb 11:3). Although some believe that the reference to the רוח אלהים refers to the "wind of God," later portions of Scripture reveal that the Spirit was present at creation: "By the word of the LORD the heavens were made, and by the Spirit of his mouth all their host" (Ps 33:6, my trans.).[1] The Nicene Creed captures the Spirit's person and work when it calls him the "Lord and giver of life." The psalmist repeats the idea when he writes: "When you send forth your Spirit, they are created, and you renew the face of the ground" (Ps 104:30). Job attests to the Spirit's role in similar fashion: "By his Spirit [ברוחו] the heaves were made fair" (Job 26:13, my trans.). When Job describes his own creation, he echoes the creation of the first man, Adam. The Genesis narrative memorably states: "Then the LORD God formed the man of dust from the ground and breathed into his nostrils the

1. E.g., E. A. Speiser, *Genesis*, AB (New York: Doubleday, 1962), 3; Nahum M. Sarna, *Genesis*, JPS Torah Commentary (Philadelphia: Jewish Publication Society, 1989), 6. Here the ESV renders וברוח פיו as "by the breath of his mouth," whereas the LXX translates this as τῷ πνεύματι τοῦ στόματος ("by the spirit of his mouth"). See Abraham Kuyper, *The Work of the Holy Spirit*, trans. Henri De Vries (New York: Funk & Wagnalls, 1900), 24.

breath of life [נשמת חיים], and the man became a living creature" (Gen 2:7). Job echoes this when he avers: "The Spirit of God [רוח אל] has made me, and the breath of the Almighty gives me life [ונשמת שדי תחיני]" (Job 33:4).[2] But the creation of Adam and Job communicates more than divine agency. It conveys notions of intimacy and covenantal fellowship.

Genesis 2:7 tells us that God breathed life into Adam's nostrils, but the synonymous parallelism of Job 33:4, which equates God's Spirit with his breath, reveals that God indwelled Adam by his Spirit. God's indwelling presence imparts life, but does so in an intimate way, not from afar but from within. At this stage in preredemptive history, Adam's Spirit-indwelled creation foreshadows the Spirit's work in the new creation. Evocative of Adam's creation, Jesus performed a living parable when he breathed on his disciples: "'Peace be with you. As the Father has sent me, even so I am sending you.' And when he had said this, he breathed on them and said to them, 'Receive the Holy Spirit'" (John 20:21–22).[3] The protological indwelling of the Spirit was the bond of covenantal fellowship, love, and was a gift that Adam was to share with future generations: as George Smeaton writes, "Adam had the Spirit in the state of integrity, not only for himself, but for his seed; and he walked after the Spirit as long as he stood in his integrity."[4] Adam forsook God, and thus sin disrupted his existence. He dissolved the intimate covenantal bond, but this did not mean that the Spirit ceased to uphold the creation.

In the fallen world the Spirit continued to carry out his work as the giver of life, but because of Adam's apostasy the prospect of eschatological life was no longer a possibility, at least not by his labor. Eschatological life would only come by another, by the Son of Man. God exiled Adam from his garden-temple presence, and apart from the Spirit's presence Adam was now subject to the deleterious effects of his sin. Thus he died. The day Adam sinned was the day he died, as God had threatened (Gen 2:16–17). Adam lived East of Eden in a state of exilic death (Num 5:1–4; 12:1–15; 2 Kgs 7:3–8). Adam's exilic death naturally led to his physical death. Adam returned to the dust of the earth as God said he would: "For you are dust,

---

2. Kuyper, *Work of the Holy Spirit*, 61.
3. Kuyper, *Work of the Holy Spirit*, 29, 34.
4. George Smeaton, *The Doctrine of the Holy Spirit* (Edinburgh: T&T Clark, 1882), 11.

and to dust you shall return" (Gen 3:19). In the sin-fallen world, however, the Spirit still upholds the creation and all life even if fallen humans still live east of Eden.

Evidence that the Spirit upholds all existence appears in Job: "If he should set his heart to it and gather to himself his Spirit and his breath, all flesh would perish together, and man would return to dust" (34:14–15, my trans.). All humans still owe their existence to the work of the Holy Spirit, but in the shadow of the fall, such work serves a twofold end. First, the Spirit provides the creation a stay of execution—the final judgment has been postponed. Second, the postponement is not an ad hoc response to the fall but part of the Triune God's foreordained plans laid before the foundations of the world. The judgment postponed provides the needed time to gather the elect, the bride of Christ, from every corner of the earth. Early modern Reformed theologians distinguished between the common and special operations of the Spirit to denote the differences between the Spirit's general work in upholding the creation and the Spirit's special work of redeeming Christ's bride. The Westminster Confession, for example, speaks of the "common operations of the Spirit" but affirms that such acts are insufficient for salvation (10.4). Conversely, within God's providence there is a "special manner" by which he takes "care of his church, and disposeth all things to the good thereof" (5.7). Chief among that special care is the Spirit's work of effectual calling (10.1). In the nineteenth century, Reformed theologians such as Charles Hodge (1797–1878) called the common operations of the Spirit "common grace," which Hodge describes in the following manner:

> The Bible therefore teaches that the Holy Spirit as the Spirit of truth, of holiness, and of life in all its forms, is present with every human mind, enforcing truth, restraining from evil, exciting to good, and imparting wisdom or strength, when, where, and in what measure seemeth to Him good. In this sphere also He divides "to every man severally as He will" (1 Cor 12:11). This is what in theology is called common grace.[5]

5. Charles Hodge, *Systematic Theology* (New York: Scribner, Armstrong, 1876), 2:667.

So even in a fallen world, the Holy Spirit is the author and sustainer of all life, the fount of every virtue (Gen 6:17; 7:15; Pss 33:6; 104:30; 139:2; Job 32:8; Eccl 3:19).[6] But the Spirit's work does not end with merely sustaining life in a sin-fallen world. Rather, the Spirit's work in the creation has a telos in the new creation.

## THE SPIRIT IN THE OLD TESTAMENT AND NEW TESTAMENT: CONTINUITY AND DISCONTINUITY

Geerhardus Vos (1862–1949) makes two key observations regarding special revelation. First, all biblical revelation is progressive. That is, God does not immediately explain and unfold his plan of redemption but instead slowly, progressively, and organically unfolds it from Eden to the new creation. Vos writes, "That part of the knowledge of God which has been revealed to us is so overwhelmingly great and so far transcends our human capacities, is such a flood of light, that it had, as it were, gradually to be let in upon us, ray after ray, and not the full radiancy at once."[7] Second, God's revelation is not merely words but consists of actions. This is what Vos describes as word-act-word revelation. First God gives his revelatory word, he acts in history, and then he reveals a subsequent interpretive word. A microcosmic example of this pattern appears in the creation account. God says, "'Let there be light,' and there was light. And God saw that the light was good" (Gen 1:3–4). God speaks, he acts, and then the subsequent revelation explains that God's act was good: word-act-word.[8] These two principles (progressive and word-act-word revelation) are the prerequisite concepts for understanding the nature of God's presence by the Holy Spirit throughout preredemptive and redemptive history. There is a progressive, organic, unfolding revelation in both word and act that discloses that God's presence through the Holy Spirit lies at the heart of his being the God of his people from Eden to the tabernacle, the temple, the church, and the new creation.

---

6. Herman Bavinck, "Common Grace," trans. Raymond C. Van Leeuwen, *Calvin Theological Journal* 24 (1989): 35–65, here 41. For the most expansive treatment of common grace, see Abraham Kuyper, *Common Grace*, 3 vols. (Bellingham, WA: Lexham Press, 2015–2020).

7. Geerhardus Vos, "The Idea of Biblical Theology as a Science and as a Theological Discipline," in *Redemptive History and Biblical Interpretation: The Shorter Writings of Geerhardus Vos*, ed. Richard B. Gaffin Jr. (Phillipsburg, NJ: P&R, 1980), 3–24, here 7.

8. Geerhardus Vos, *Biblical Theology* (Edinburgh: Banner of Truth, 2014), 7.

*Eden* NATURALLY, TRACING THE THEME OF God's presence through the Holy Spirit begins with the garden of Eden. In the past theologians as diverse as John Calvin (1509–1564) and Gerhard von Rad (1901–1971) characterized the garden of Eden as an ancient Mesopotamian farm.[9] But more recent scholarship rightly notes that Eden is not a farm but the first earthly temple—the first meeting place between God and humans.[10] All of Eden's features point to its status as a temple, and as in subsequent temples, God is present by means of the Holy Spirit. The Spirit, of course, appears in the opening scene of the creation narrative, as noted above. The Spirit's presence continues in the drama in the creation of Adam as well, as he makes an appearance at the climax of the opening scene when God judges Adam and Eve for their sin. As Adam and Eve trembled because they heard God approaching, Genesis says they heard "the sound of the LORD God walking in the garden in the Spirit of the day" (Gen 3:8, my trans.).[11] God came to his temple by the presence of the Holy Spirit to justify or condemn his covenant servant. The Old Testament notes the connection between the Spirit's presence and judgment in several places. For example, the "Spirit of the LORD was upon [Othniel], and he judged Israel" (Judg 3:10). God put his Spirit on his servant, who would "bring forth justice to the nations" (Isa 42:1). In short, in Eden God created a microcosmic version of his macrocosmic creation temple. He established sacred space in the garden and entrusted its sanctity to Adam and the cherubim. Eden was a garden-temple, the place chosen by the Holy Spirit to dwell. The same Spirit who brooded over the chaotic waters of creation now made his dwelling among humans.[12] Adam's sin disrupted the covenantal fellowship between

---

9. John Calvin, *Commentary on Genesis*, trans. James Anderson (Grand Rapids: Baker, 1993), 125; Gerhard von Rad, *Genesis*, Old Testament Library (Philadelphia: Westminster, 1972), 77.

10. G. K. Beale, *The Temple and the Church's Mission: A Biblical Theology of the Dwelling Place of God*, NSBT (Downers Grove, IL: IVP Academic, 2004); J. V. Fesko, *Last Things First: Unlocking Genesis with the Christ of Eschatology* (Fearn, UK: Mentor, 2007), 57–75; L. Michael Morales, *Cult and Cosmos: Tilting toward a Temple-Centered Theology* (Leuven: Peeters, 2014).

11. Meredith G. Kline, *Images of the Spirit* (Eugene, OR: Wipf & Stock, 1999), 97–106; Jeffrey Niehaus, "In the Wind of the Storm: Another Look at Genesis 3:8," *VT* 44, no. 2 (1994): 263–67; see also Christopher L. K. Grundke, "A Tempest in a Teapot? Genesis III 8 Again," *VT* 51, no. 4 (2001): 548–51.

12. Kline, *Images of the Spirit*, 35–37.

God and humans, but in his mercy, God promised to make his dwelling among his people.

*Tabernacle* God heard the cry of his people as they languished in Egypt, and he redeemed them by a mighty hand by delivering them from their bondage. He led them into the wilderness to the foot of Mount Sinai, where he dwelled in their midst atop the mountain shrouded in dark, ominous clouds and attended by peals of thunder and flashes of lightning. The people were terrified of God's presence, but in his mercy, God condescended by means of the desert tabernacle. While there were still procedures for fellowshipping with God, such as sacrifices and especially the protocols of the Day of Atonement (Lev 16), God dwelled amid his people.

God's dwelling was the "tent of meeting" (Exod 27:21). Scholars note that there are verbal parallels between the creation account (Gen 1:1–2:3) and the instructions for constructing the tabernacle (Exod 25–40).[13] In other words, the tabernacle's design mirrored the macrocosmic temple of creation. The seven days of creation inform the speeches concerning the construction of the tabernacle (see Ps 104:2 // Exod 26:7; Gen 1:2 // Exod 26:33; Gen 1:6 // Exod 30:18; Gen 1:14 // Exod 25:31; Gen 1:20 // Exod 25:20; Gen 1:27 // Exod 28:1; Gen 2:1–3 // Exod 39:32, 43).[14] Just as the Spirit hovered over the creation and appeared in the garden-temple of Eden, he also descended on the tabernacle on its completion: "The cloud settled on it, and the glory of the Lord filled the tabernacle" (Exod 40:35). The cloud was a visible revelation of the Holy Spirit that signaled both the Spirit's dwelling in the tabernacle in Israel's midst and his presence leading them through the wilderness: "Throughout all their journeys, whenever the cloud was taken up from over the tabernacle, the people of Israel would set out" (Exod 40:36; Isa 63:10–14).

---

13. E.g., Gordon J. Wenham, "Sanctuary Symbolism in the Garden of Eden Story," in *I Studied Inscriptions from before the Flood: Ancient Near Eastern, Literary, and Linguistic Approaches to Genesis 1–11*, ed. Richard S. Hess and David Toshio Tsumura (Winona Lake, IN: Eisenbrauns, 1994), 399–404, here 403.

14. Peter J. Kearney, "Creation and Liturgy: The P Redaction of Ex 25–40," *Zeitschrift für die alttestamentliche Wissenschaft* 89 (1977): 375–87, here 375–78.

In addition to the Holy Spirit being present in the temple, the Spirit also was involved in its construction. God told Moses, "See, I have called by name Bezalel the son of Uri, son of Hur, of the tribe of Judah, and I have filled him with the Spirit of God, with ability and intelligence, with knowledge and all craftsmanship, to devise artistic designs, to work in gold, silver, and bronze, in cutting stones for setting, and in carving wood, to work in every craft" (Exod 31:1–6). The Spirit sovereignly distributed gifts to facilitate the construction of the dwelling place of God, the meeting place for God and humans. The Spirit's work in this way makes another appearance in his work to make the new creation.

## Numbers 11:24–30

GEERHARDUS VOS DEFINES BIBLICAL THEOLOGY "nothing else than the exhibition of the organic process of supernatural revelation in its historic continuity and multiformity."[15] In the progressive unfolding of supernatural revelation, earlier portions of revelation anticipate later portions. Numbers 11:24–30 foreshadows Pentecost and the descent of the Spirit, which evinces the organic continuity and multiformity that characterizes the progression from Old to New Testament. In this case, Moses is stationed at the tabernacle, the earthly dwelling place of God—the meeting place between God and humans: "Then the LORD came down in the cloud and spoke to him, and took some of the Spirit that was on him and put it on the seventy elders. And as soon as the Spirit rested on them, they prophesied. But they did not continue doing it" (Num 11:25). The cloud presence of the Lord descends and enables the seventy elders to prophesy, but they eventually cease their prophetic activity, which indicates the temporary and provisional nature of the Spirit's anointing.

In the wake of the Spirit's temporary outpouring two men, Eldad and Medad, who did not go out to the tabernacle, nevertheless receive the Spirit and prophesy in the camp (Num 11:27). Joshua is concerned that they might undermine Moses's authority and implores Moses to

15. Vos, "Idea of Biblical Theology," 15.

stop them (Num 11:28). Moses's answer further reinforces the typological character of the Spirit's outpouring: "Are you jealous for my sake? Would that all the LORD's people were prophets, that the LORD would put his Spirit on them!" (Num 11:29). In other words, Moses looks to the future, when God will democratize the outpouring of the Spirit. Note that this outpouring of the Spirit contains the basic elements of the later eschatological outpouring of the Spirit at Pentecost: the anointing of the Spirit, prophecy, the Spirit's presence revealed by a cloud, and the dwelling place of God.

*Temple* ISRAEL'S AMBULATION THROUGH THE WILDERNESS had a telos—the permanent inhabitation of the promised land. Israel would no longer wander through the wilderness and follow the Spirit's cloud-presence; God would establish a permanent dwelling in Israel's midst. Although King David wanted to build a temple for the Lord, God tasked Solomon with this responsibility. As God was progressively unfolding his plan of redemption, he told David he was fulfilling his covenant promises to him: "It is Solomon your son who shall build my house and my courts, for I have chosen him to be my son, and I will be his father" (1 Chr 28:6). This divine word clearly echoes God's covenantal oath to David (2 Sam 7:13–15). God's son would build the temple, but in order to carry out this task, God would anoint him with the Spirit. Once again, we must correlate the construction of God's dwelling place with the Spirit's inhabitation of the temple. Just as God gave Oholiab and Bezalel the Holy Spirit, who equipped them to build the tabernacle, so too God poured the Spirit on Solomon to equip him to build the temple. Solomon, for example, records God's words to him: "If you turn at my reproof, behold, I will pour out my Spirit to you; I will make my words known to you" (Prov 1:23, my trans.). God did in fact pour out the Spirit on Solomon and gave him great wisdom (2 Chr 1:11). Solomon's wisdom was world renowned, such that royalty sought him "to hear his wisdom, which God had put into his mind" (2 Chr 9:22–23). David assured his son that God would be with him "until all the work for the service of the house of the LORD is finished" (1 Chr 28:20). At the climax of the launching of the temple construction, Israel anointed Solomon king a second time (1 Chr 28:22). The Lord's anointed, his Messiah, would build the temple. The anointing oil was symbolic of the anointing of the Spirit—the equipping of the king to carry out the temple-building project.

The temple harked back to both Eden and the tabernacle, God's earlier dwelling places, in its design and architecture. At the completion of the temple, the priests bring the ark of the covenant into the holy of holies, God's throne and symbol of his presence (2 Chr 5:7). When the priests retreat to the outer temple, the Levitical singers and trumpeters break out in song and thanksgiving: "For he is good, for his steadfast love endures forever" (2 Chr 5:13). As at the completion of the desert tabernacle, once again the Spirit of God takes up residence in the Solomonic temple: "The house, the house of the Lord, was filled with a cloud, so that the priests could not stand to minister because of the cloud, for the glory of the Lord filled the house of God" (2 Chr 5:13–14). In the midst of his address before the gathered worshipers, Solomon poignantly asks: "But will God indeed dwell with man on the earth?" (2 Chr 6:18). As Solomon invites God to enter his "resting place" (2 Chr 6:41), "fire came down from heaven and consumed the burnt offering and the sacrifices, and the glory of the Lord filled the temple" (2 Chr 7:1). In all these events a number of different revelatory strands converge and set the stage for future events: the son, messiah, and king, anointed by the Spirit, building a dwelling place for God, the meeting place for God and humans, with God filling the temple with his Spirit, which is visibly manifest in both a cloud and fire from heaven.

## Joel 2:28–32

God's progressive, organic, unfolding self-disclosure continues in one of the more famous Old Testament passages that prophetically foretells of the Spirit's outpouring. There is an organic link between Joel 2:28–32 and the earlier outpouring of the Spirit in Numbers 11:24–30.[16] Hints that God would dispense the Spirit beyond

16. Raymond B. Dillard, "Intrabiblical Exegesis and the Effusion of the Spirit in Joel," in *Creator, Redeemer, Consummator: Festschrift for Meredith G. Kline*, ed. Howard Griffith and John R. Muether (Greenville, SC: Reformed Academic Press, 2000), 87–93; Thomas Edward McComisky, *The Minor Prophets* (Grand Rapids: Baker Academic, 2009), 294–95; also G. K.

the elders of Israel initially appear in that Eldad and Medad, though absent from the tabernacle, nevertheless received the Spirit. Joel reinforces this point when he writes: "I will pour out my Spirit on all flesh; your sons and your daughters shall prophesy, your old men shall dream dreams, and your young men shall see visions. Even on the male and female servants in those days I will pour out my Spirit" (Joel 2:28–29). Unlike the earlier Numbers event, where the Spirit only fell on the elders (including Eldad and Medad), Joel's prophecy is more expansive and reveals that cosmic perturbations will accompany the Spirit's outpouring: "And I will show wonders in the heavens and on the earth, blood and fire and columns of smoke. The sun shall be turned to darkness, and the moon to blood, before the great and awesome day of the LORD comes" (Joel 2:30–31). The eschaton is in Joel's view, given that he sees the day of the Lord on the revelatory horizon; moreover, his cosmic language also suggests that this outpouring will bring both judgment and new creation.

*Church* ALL THE PREVIOUS OLD TESTAMENT revelation regarding God dwelling with his people finds its culmination in the church. This is not to say that the church takes priority over Christ, as only by means of the Son of God, the head, does the church come to life. The relationship between Christ and the church will receive treatment below. We must nevertheless demonstrate the connections between God's earlier dwelling places in Eden, the tabernacle, and temple to establish the church as the eschatological temple and dwelling place of God. The apostle Paul states very succinctly: "Do you not know that you are God's temple and that God's Spirit dwells in you?" (1 Cor 3:16). Collectively, the people of God are the temple of God because the Holy Spirit indwells them. But people are individually also the temple: "Do you not know that your body is a temple of the Holy Spirit within you, whom you have from God?" (1 Cor 6:19). When Paul warns the Corinthians about engaging in idolatry, he asks them: "What agreement has the temple of God with idols? For we are the

Beale, "The Descent of the Eschatological Temple in the Form of the Spirit at Pentecost. Part I: The Clearest Evidence," *TynBul* 56, no. 1 (2005): 73–102, here 94.

temple of the living God; as God said, 'I will make my dwelling among them and walk among them, and I will be their God, and they shall be my people. … I will be a father to you, and you shall be sons and daughters to me, says the Lord Almighty'" (2 Cor 6:16, 18). Paul draws a number of temple-related threads together in this statement from numerous texts across the Old Testament canon, including Leviticus 26:11–12; Ezekiel 37:1–15, 26–28; and 2 Samuel 7:14.[17] In Paul's use of Leviticus and Ezekiel he highlights God's special relationship with his people and the manner in which he carries it out—dwelling in their midst and walking among them, ideas that evoke the original Edenic garden-temple. But Paul also weaves in reference to God's covenantal promise to David, namely that his son would be God's son, which finds its fulfillment in Christ, the son of David, the Son of God (Rom 1:3–4). But now the church, those who believe in Christ and are united to him by the indwelling presence of the Spirit, are also God's sons and daughters—they are part of the royal line.[18]

In addition to Paul's instruction to the Corinthians, there are several other relevant passages that define the church as the Spirit-indwelled temple of God. Paul famously employs temple imagery in Ephesians, where he recognizes the apostle and prophets as the foundation and Christ as the cornerstone, "in whom the whole structure, being joined together, grows into a holy temple in the Lord. In him you are also being built together into a dwelling place for God by the Spirit" (Eph 2:21–22). Likewise, the apostle Peter appeals to this same temple imagery when he states that Christ is "a living stone rejected by men but in the sight of God chosen and precious" and that the individual members of the church are "like living stones being built up as a spiritual house" (1 Pet 2:4–5; see Isa 28:16). Peter and Paul reach into the rich covenantal soil of the Old Testament for handfuls that brim with concepts that go back to Eden: God dwelling with his people by means of the presence of the Holy Spirit, but this time the temple is not a tent or structure built with blocks of stone but is made of living stones—with people.

---

17. G. K. Beale and D. A. Carson, eds., *Commentary on the New Testament Use of the Old Testament* (Grand Rapids: Baker Academic, 2007), 770–71.

18. Beale and Carson, *Commentary on the New Testament Use*, 773.

Christ is the cornerstone of this eschatological temple, as the people constitute the final dwelling place of God. But there are two fundamental elements of this final temple: the Spirit's presence and the Messiah's work. God's dwelling amid his people from Eden, to the desert tabernacle, to the temple finds its fulfillment in Christ, God in the flesh, the one in whom the fullness of deity subsists, dwelling in the midst of his people. The apostle John powerfully captures these truths when he writes: "And the Word became flesh and tabernacled among us, and we have seen his glory, glory as of the only Son from the Father, full of grace and truth" (John 1:14, my trans.). Christ sealed this imagery when he told his disciples he was the temple: "Destroy this temple, and in three days I will raise it up" (John 2:19). Jesus was not speaking of the Herodian temple, as the religious leaders mistakenly believed (John 2:20). Rather, as John parenthetically explains: "He was speaking about the temple of his body" (John 2:21). The progressively unfolding organic Old Testament revelation in both word and act conveys that God will dwell among his people by means of the presence of his Spirit through the work of his Son. This means that the Son and the Spirit work in tandem to establish the final temple.

## THE SPIRIT AND CHRIST (THE WORK OF THE SPIRIT IN THE LIFE OF CHRIST)

That Christ and the Spirit work together for the redemption of the elect is a tree that has roots in the eternal covenant of redemption. The tree's trunk juts through the Old Testament, with many branches that spread throughout the New Testament. In historic iterations of the covenant of redemption, theologians maintain that the when the Father appointed the Son as covenant mediator and surety (Ps 2:7; 110:1; Luke 22:29; Heb 7:22), he swore an oath to equip the Son with the necessary gifts and graces for him to execute his work. The Father therefore promised to anoint the Son with the Spirit without measure.[19] In the big picture from

19. J. V. Fesko, *The Trinity and the Covenant of Redemption* (Fearn, UK: Mentor, 2016), 137–38; Scott Swain, "Covenant of Redemption," in *Christian Dogmatics: Reformed Theology for the Church Catholic*, ed. Michael Allen and Scott Swain (Grand Rapids: Baker Academic, 2016), 78–106.

womb to tomb to throne, the Spirit was the Son's continual companion.[20] In technical terms, the Scriptures reveal the *inseparable operations* of the Trinity.[21] In historic Trinitarian theology, theologians expressed this truth with the aphorism *opera trinitatis ad extra indivisa sunt* ("the external work of the Trinity is indivisible"). Gregory of Nyssa (ca. 335–ca. 395) gives classic expression to this principle:

> But in the case of the Divine nature we do not similarly learn that the Father does anything by Himself in which the Son does not work conjointly, or again that the Son has any special operation apart from the Holy Spirit; but every operation which extends from God to the Creation, and is named according to our variable conception of it, has its origin from the Father, and proceeds through the Son, and is perfect in the Holy Spirit. For this reason the name derived from the operation is not divided with regard to the number of those who fulfil it, because the action of each concerning anything is not separate and peculiar, but whatever comes to pass, in reference either to the acts of His providence for us or to the government and constitution of the universe, comes to pass by the action of the Three, yet what does come to pass is not three things.[22]

The Scriptures are replete with this principle from the creation account in the opening pages.

As God creates, the Spirit broods over the chaotic waters of creation. The New Testament reveals that all things were made through the Word, and "without him was not any thing made that was made" (John 1:3; see Col 1:16; Heb 1:2). The Son and the Spirit were the hands of God, the hands by which he made the creation (Irenaeus, *Against Heresies* 4.20.1, 5.6.1). The coworking of the Son and the Spirit in the creation is the same pattern that unfolds in the new creation. According to the Old Testament, the Son is the Messiah, the *anointed* (Ps 2). Too many have likely lost track of the significance of this title and forget that to be anointed to office was not merely

---

20. Sinclair Ferguson, *The Holy Spirit*, Contours of Christian Theology (Downers Grove, IL: IVP Academic, 1997), 37.

21. Adonis Vidu, *The Same God Who Works All Things: Inseparable Operations in Trinitarian Theology* (Grand Rapids: Eerdmans, 2021), 31–36.

22. Gregory of Nyssa, "On 'Not Three Gods' to Ablabius," *NPNF*[2] 5:334.

ritual but rich symbolism that pointed to the outpouring of the Spirit on the office-bearer. When Samuel anointed David as king, he poured out oil on him, and "the Spirit of the LORD rushed upon David from that day forward" (1 Sam 16:13). In subsequent Old Testament revelation, the prophet Isaiah speaks of the Servant as the one on whom God put his Spirit (Isa 42:1). The prophet again writes: "The Spirit of the Lord GOD is upon me, because the LORD has anointed me to bring good news to the poor; he has sent me to bind up the brokenhearted, to proclaim liberty to the captives, and the opening of the prison to those who are bound" (Isa 61:1). This Isaianic text is relevant because when Christ read the scroll of Isaiah in the Nazarene synagogue, he read from this very passage and then told the congregation, "Today this Scripture has been fulfilled in your hearing" (Luke 4:21).

The anointing of the Spirit has its root in the covenant of redemption, the trunk that extends through the Old Testament with various prophecies and typological acts (such as the anointing of David), and produces its first branch with the conception of Christ, as Mary "was found to be with child from the Holy Spirit" (Matt 1:18). In language evocative of the Spirit's brooding over the primordial waters and the desert tabernacle, the angel Gabriel told Mary: "The Holy Spirit will come upon you, and the power of the Most High will overshadow you; therefore the child to be born will be called holy—the Son of God" (Luke 1:35; see Gen 1:2; Deut 32:1; Exod 40:35; Pss 17:8; 91:4 LXX).[23] As the Spirit of God was active in the creation and formation of Adam, so too the Spirit of God was active in the incarnation of the last Adam. The same cloud that covered Sinai and led the Israelites in the wilderness, that consecrated the temple, and that Isaiah prophesied would cover Mount Zion overshadowed Mary (Exod 19:9; 24:15; 34:5; Deut 4:11–12; 5:22; Exod 13:21; 14:20; 16:10; Num 9:18, 22; 10:34; 14:14; Deut 1:33; Pss 78:14; 105:39; 1 Cor 10:1–2; 1 Kgs 8:10–11; 2 Chr 5:13–14; Ezek 10:4; Isa 4:5).[24]

The next major revelatory event occurred at the baptism of Jesus, the inauguration of his earthly ministry. Christ's baptism was his formal

---

23. Beale and Carson, *Commentary on the New Testament Use*, 260–61; Stephen Wellum, *God the Son Incarnate: The Doctrine of Christ*, Foundations of Evangelical Theology (Wheaton, IL: Crossway, 2016), 238–39.

24. Sally J. Shelton, "Overshadowed by the Spirit: Mary, Mother of Our Lord, Prototype of Spirit-Baptized Humanity" (PhD diss., Regent University, 2016), 106–7.

anointing with the Spirit, as Isaiah 11; 42; and 61 prophesied.[25] Multiple streams of Old Testament revelation converge on this one event, which also reaches back to the initial creation and the Spirit hovering in an avian-like manner over the waters. Layered on top of the creation Spirit imagery are allusions to Psalm 2:7, "You are my son; today I have begotten you"; Isaiah 42:1, "Behold my servant, whom I uphold, my chosen, in whom my soul delights; I have put my Spirit upon him"; and Isaiah 61:1, "The Spirit of the Lord God is upon me, because the Lord has anointed me to bring good news."[26] Unlike Matthew, who takes us back to Abraham in his genealogy (Matt 1:1), Luke traces Christ's genealogy back to Adam, the Son of God (Luke 3:38), and then immediately segues to the Spirit leading Christ into the wilderness as the cloud-presence of the Spirit led Israel of old: "And Jesus, full of the Holy Spirit, returned from the Jordan and was led by the Spirit in the wilderness" (Luke 4:1).

## Luke 3:21–22

God's self-disclosure culminates in the revelation of Jesus Christ, the Son of God. There are two vital contextual elements that link the events of Christ's baptism and the outpouring of the Spirit. First, the previous events of Numbers 11:24–30 and Joel 2:28–32 do not occur as stand-alone events. They unfold within the broader matrix of God's revelation that climaxes in the incarnation of Christ. The concomitant relationship between Christ and the Spirit appears in the Son's office and title, "Christ," משיח, Χριστός. "Christ" is not Jesus's last name but his official title, "Jesus the anointed one," which raises the question, With what is Jesus anointed? As the earlier Numbers 11:24–30 events foreshadow, God would anoint his Son with the Spirit. Isaianic texts make this anointing abundantly clear. The Spirit of the Lord would rest on the Davidic scion, "the Spirit of wisdom and understanding, the Spirit of counsel and might, the Spirit of knowledge and the fear of the Lord" (Isa 11:2). Isaiah later writes: "Behold

25. Vidu, *Same God*, 31.
26. Beale and Carson, *Commentary on the New Testament Use*, 280–81.

my servant, whom I uphold, my chosen, in whom my soul delights; I have put my Spirit upon him; he will bring forth justice to the nations" (Isa 42:1; see also 61:1–2; Luke 4:16–21). When Jesus appeared on the stage of redemptive history, in the fullness of time, his baptism was pregnant with revelatory and eschatological significance as God the Father poured out the Spirit on his Son, who descended in the form of a dove, and God bellowed from the heavens: "You are my beloved Son; with you I am well pleased" (Luke 3:22). Noteworthy are the contextual elements of this event: water, Spirit, and a dove were present—allusions to earlier creation events such as the primeval waters of Genesis, the flood, and the Red Sea crossing, rudiments suggestive of new creation. But the overall significance of Christ's baptism is that the outpouring of the Spirit would first start with the head of the body, Jesus, and then flow to his body, the church, "Like the precious oil on the head running down on the beard, on the beard of Aaron, running down on the collar of his robes!" (Ps 133:2).[27]

In contradistinction to Israel, called God's son (Exod 4:22), Jesus was faithfully obedient to the will of his heavenly Father. Christ's entire earthly ministry was stamped by the presence of the Holy Spirit. Christ resisted Satan's temptation in the wilderness through the Spirit (Mark 1:12–13; Matt 4:1–11; Luke 4:1–13). Christ performed his ministry in the power of the Spirit as the Isaianic prophesies foretold. Christ exorcised demons in the authority of the Holy Spirit, evident by the fact that the religious leaders accused him of casting out demons by the power of Beelzebub. Christ countered that they were blaspheming against the Holy Spirit by leveling such a charge. In other words, Christ performed exorcisms in the power of the Spirit (Mark 3:22–30; Matt 12:24–32; Luke 11:15–23). Christ also "through the eternal Spirit offered himself without blemish to God" (Heb 9:14). Christ was raised by the power of the Spirit (Rom 1:3–4; 8:11; 1 Pet 3:18).[28]

---

27. David Dickson, *A Brief Explication of the Last Fifty Psalmes, from Ps. 100 to the End* (London: T. R. and E. M., 1654), 281.

28. Vidu, *Same God*, 32.

Christ carried out his ministry in the power and anointing of the Spirit, and this anointing was the means by which the Father equipped the Son for his work: "The Spirit of the LORD shall rest upon him, the Spirit of wisdom and understanding, the Spirit of counsel and might, the Spirit of knowledge and the fear of the LORD" (Isa 11:2). This means that the Spirit defined the God-man: "Christ's earthly sonship appears to be constituted throughout by the Spirit, such that there is no aspect of Christ's life, ministry, and passion that is not under the direct auspices of the Spirit."[29] Theologians throughout the history of the church have acknowledged the Spirit's role in the work of Christ. St. Augustine (354–430), for example, writes: "The Lord Jesus Christ Himself not only gave the Holy Spirit as God, but also received it as man, and therefore He is said to be full of grace [John 1:14], and of the Holy Spirit [Luke 2:52; 4:1]. And in the acts of the Apostles it is more plainly written of Him, 'Because God anointed Him with the Holy Spirit' [Acts 10:38]."[30] Reformation-era confessional documents echo the idea of the Spirit's anointing of Christ. Calvin's Geneva Catechism (1541) asks the question: "With what kind of oil was [Jesus] anointed?" It responds: "Not with visible oil as was used for ancient kings, priest, and prophets, but this anointing was the grace of the Holy Spirit, who is the reality signified by that outward anointing made in time past" (q. 36). Later, high orthodox confessions of faith such as Westminster (1646) intertwined Christology and pneumatology in its statements about Christ:

> The Lord Jesus, in his human nature thus united to the divine, was sanctified, and anointed with the Holy Spirit, above measure, having in him all the treasures of wisdom and knowledge; in whom it pleased the Father that all fullness should dwell; to the end that, being holy, harmless, undefiled, and full of grace and truth, he might be thoroughly furnished to execute the office of a mediator, and surety. Which office he took not unto himself, but was thereunto called by his Father, who put all power and judgment into his hand, and gave him commandment to execute the same. (8.3)

---

29. Vidu, *Same God*, 32.

30. Augustine, *On the Holy Trinity* 15.26.46, *NPNF*[2] 3:224.

The Confession also connects the Spirit's anointing to Christ's crucifixion: "The Lord Jesus, by his perfect obedience, and sacrifice of himself, which he, through the eternal Spirit, once offered up unto God, hath fully satisfied the justice of his Father" (8.5).

Westminster divine Thomas Goodwin (1600–1680) provides some context for a more detailed understanding of what the confession's statements about Christ and the Spirit mean. Goodwin argues that the Spirit sanctified Christ by anointing him and imparting all his graces (Isa 11:2). "The graces of Christ, as man, are attributed to this Spirit, as the immediate author of them; so although the Son of God dwelt personally, in the humane nature, and so advanced that nature above the ordinary rank of creatures, and raised it up to dignity and worth; yet all his habitual graces, which even his soul was full of, were from the Holy Ghost; the Holy Spirit is therefore said to be *given him without measure*."[31] Thus, Christ received the virtues of wisdom, counsel, and might from the Spirit and in this way constitutes the antitypical counterpart to Solomon, on whom the Spirit poured out wisdom and other virtues. But Christ did not receive the anointing to keep the gifts and graces of the Spirit to himself.

## John 3:1–8

When Jesus speaks with Nicodemus under the dark cover of night and shows him the nature of the Spirit's work, he speaks in terms of water and Spirit, invoking themes connected with new creation. He tells Nicodemus, "Unless one is born again he cannot see the kingdom of God" (John 3:3). When Nicodemus does not understand, Jesus tells him: "Unless one is born of water and the Spirit, he cannot enter the kingdom of God. That which is born of the flesh is flesh, and that which is born of the Spirit is spirit. ... The wind blows where it wishes, and you hear its sound, but you do not know where it comes from or where it goes. So it is with everyone who is born of the Spirit" (John 3:5–6, 8). Christ's comments are noteworthy on three fronts. First,

31. Thomas Goodwin, *Of the Work of the Holy Ghost*, in *The Works of Thomas Goodwin D.D.* (Edinburgh: James Nichol, 1863), 6:50.

water, Spirit, and wind draw readers' attention back to the creation narrative, as the Spirit hovered over the primeval waters of creation and as God sent a wind (רוח) over the earth after the flood to cause the waters to subside and a new creation emerged.[32] Second, Jesus tells Nicodemus that one must be born of the Spirit in order to see the kingdom of God, which undoubtedly has reference to the kingdom of God's anointed, his Messiah (Ps 2). In other words, the Spirit and kingdom will come to fruition through the work of the Messiah. Third, Jesus implicitly refers to the two major epochs of redemptive history when he places "flesh" and "spirit in antithesis" (see Rom 5:12–21; 1 Cor 2:14–16; 15:20–28; 15:44–46). Flesh can only give birth to flesh, and the Spirit can only give birth to spirit, that is, to the citizens of the eschatological messianic kingdom.

## THE SPIRIT OF CHRIST (THE SPIRIT AS THE GIFT, PRESENCE, AND POWER OF THE RISEN CHRIST)

One of the briefest but nevertheless crucial verses that reveals the nexus between the Spirit, Christ, and the church is 1 Corinthians 15:45, "Thus it is written, 'The first man Adam became a living being'; the last Adam became a life-giving Spirit" (my trans.). Here different ideas converge: Adam's Spirit-animated enlivening, one of the pinnacles of the first creation, and Paul calling Jesus the *last Adam*. This Adam–last Adam nexus reveals that the new, or eschatological, creation unfolds in a similar manner to the first.[33] Nevertheless, there is a stark contrast between the two Adams, as Paul writes: "But it is not the spiritual that is first but the natural, and then the spiritual." Adam never achieved eschatological life through the covenant of works because of his apostasy, but the last Adam was faithful and thus attained eschatological life and the right to dispense it by the outpouring of the Spirit. Peter's sermon at Pentecost fleshes out Paul's terse statement in 1 Corinthians 15:45. Peter tells the gathered crowd:

---

32. Similarly, Beale and Carson, *Commentary on the New Testament Use*, 435.

33. Geerhardus Vos, *The Pauline Eschatology* (Phillipsburg, NJ: P&R, 1994), 10, 184.

> Being therefore exalted at the right hand of God, and having received from the Father the promise of the Holy Spirit, he has poured out this that you yourselves are seeing and hearing. For David did not ascend into the heavens, but he himself says,
>
> "The Lord said to my Lord,
>
> 'Sit at my right hand,
> until I make your enemies your footstool.' " (Acts 2:33–35)

This statement contains numerous threads bound together: implicit reference to Christ's Spirit-empowered resurrection, his exaltation to the right hand of God to exercise his kingly office, that Christ himself received the promised Spirit, and an allusion to the various Isaianic prophecies (Isa 11:2; 42:1; 61:1).[34] But Peter explains that, though David wrote about these realities (Pss 2:7; 110:1), they were ultimately about Jesus. What did Jesus do when he ascended the throne? He "poured out" the Spirit.

## Acts 2:1–36

When the disciples are gathered for Pentecost, as noted above, the Spirit descends on them in the form of rushing wind and tongues of fire resting on each individual, which signifies the tabernacle presence of God now resting on his people rather than on a tent or temple. The people of God are now his eschatological dwelling place. Two aspects of this text signal that the events of Pentecost were the fulfillment of long-awaited promises. First, when Peter explains the significance of the Spirit's presence, he appeals to the prophecy of Joel 2:28–32. Noteworthy, however, is that Peter slightly alters Joel's prophecy. Joel begins his prophecy with the words, "And it shall come to pass afterward [והיה אחרי כן // Καὶ ἔσται μετὰ ταῦτα]," which Peter arguably clarifies by saying, "And in the last days [ἐν ταῖς ἐσχάταις ἡμέραις]" (Acts 2:17).[35] In other words, Peter amplifies or clarifies Joel's prophecy to highlight that the eschaton is dawning. Second, as noted

34. Beale and Carson, *Commentary on the New Testament Use*, 540–42.
35. Beale and Carson, *Commentary on the New Testament Use*, 534.

above, Peter connects the outpouring of the Spirit to the agency of both the Father and the Son: "Being therefore exalted at the right hand of God, and having received from the Father the promise of the Holy Spirit, he has poured out this that you yourselves are seeing and hearing" (Acts 2:33).

Christ, who had earlier received the anointing of the Spirit, now pivoted to impart the Spirit to the church so that they could continue the gospel ministry that he started.[36] God promised that he would give his Son the Spirit both to equip him for the task of saving his bride and to save and equip the church to carry the gospel message into the world. Christ became the "life-giving Spirit" because he gives the Spirit to the church as the consequence and blessing of his completed work. Recall that when John was conducting his ministry at the Jordan, he told the crowds that he baptized with only water but that the Messiah would baptize "with the Holy Spirit and fire" (Luke 3:16).[37] Fulfillment of John's prophecy appeared in the events at Pentecost: "And suddenly there came from heaven a sound like a mighty rushing wind, and it filled the entire house where they were sitting. And divided tongues as of fire appeared to them and rested on each one of them. And they were all filled with the Holy Spirit and began to speak in other tongues as the Spirit gave them utterance" (Acts 2:2–4). Luke mentions the basic elements that appear in John's prophecy: the outpouring of the Spirit and the presence of tongues of fire. But Luke's description of these events has roots that go back to the Old Testament and God dwelling amid his people.

The Gospels clearly record Jesus identifying himself as the end-time temple (John 2:19–22), and Paul explains that the church is the latter-day temple of the Holy Spirit (2 Cor 6:16), but there is seemingly no explicit statement regarding the formation of the church as the eschatological temple and dwelling place of God.[38] Christ's outpouring of the Spirit at Pentecost constitutes the formal declaration of making the church his

36. F. F. Bruce, *The Book of Acts*, NICNT (Grand Rapids: Eerdmans, 1988), 67.

37. James D. G. Dunn, *Baptism in the Holy Spirit* (Louisville: Westminster John Knox, 1970), 40.

38. Beale, "Descent of the Eschatological Temple," 72.

end-time temple.[39] Elements in Luke's description of the outpouring of the Spirit confirm this claim. Luke states that "a sound like a mighty rushing wind" and "tongues of fire ... rested on each one of them." The elements of wind and fire hark back to God's descent on Mount Sinai and his theophanic presence in the form of thunder, flashes of lightning, and thick, dark clouds of smoke (Exod 19:16–20; 20:18). Deuteronomy 33:2 describes God's descent on Sinai as being flanked by "ten thousands" of angels and "with flaming fire at his right hand."[40] Exodus 19 and 24 present Sinai as a tabernacle where God's revelatory presence resided.[41] When Isaiah describes the theophanic temple-presence of God, he describes him as "burning with his anger, and in thick rising smoke," with lips "full of fury" and a tongue "like a devouring fire" (Isa 30:27). Isaiah's language echoes Exodus's Sinai theophany (see Isa 66:15).[42] Equally relevant are the psalmist's description of God's fiery words that emanate from his cloud-shrouded temple: "He made darkness his covering, his canopy around him, thick clouds dark with water. Out of the brightness before him hailstones and coals of fire broke through his clouds. The LORD also thundered in the heavens, and the Most High uttered his voice, hailstones and coals of fire" (Ps 18:11–13). The psalmist again writes: "The voice of the LORD flashes forth flames of fire" from "his temple" (Ps 29:7, 9).[43] But what we must note is that the descent of God's theophanic presence is a manifestation of the Holy Spirit.

In the Exodus account a cloud descended on Sinai: "On the morning of the third day there were thunders and lightnings and a thick cloud on the mountain" (Exod 19:16), and the text describes this action as the descent of the Lord (Exod 19:11). When Nehemiah reflects on these events he writes: "By a pillar of cloud you led them in the day, and by a pillar of fire in the night to light for them the way in which they should go. You came down on Mount Sinai and spoke with them from heaven and gave them right rules and true laws, good statutes and commandments" (Neh 9:12–13). Nehemiah then explicitly connects the Spirit with this cloud: "The pillar of cloud to lead them in the way did not depart from them by day, nor the pillar of

---

39. Beale, "Descent of the Eschatological Temple," 74.
40. Beale, "Descent of the Eschatological Temple," 76–77.
41. Beale, "Descent of the Eschatological Temple," 82.
42. Beale, "Descent of the Eschatological Temple," 84, 86.
43. Beale, "Descent of the Eschatological Temple," 87.

fire by night to light for them the way by which they should go. You gave your good Spirit to instruct them" (Neh 9:19–20). Nehemiah's words echo the events of Numbers 11:24–30, when Moses gathered the seventy elders at the tabernacle and the Lord came down in the form of a cloud and took some of the Spirit that was on Moses and put it on the elders: "And as soon as the Spirit rested on them, they prophesied" (Num 11:25).[44] When Christ, therefore, poured out the Spirit at Pentecost, the Spirit's presence signaled both the fulfillment of Old Testament typological prophecies at Sinai and the later temple, and that in the last days God's Spirit would descend on the eschatological temple. That there was the sound of loud rushing wind and tongues of fire resting on each of the disciples signaled that God had formally established his end-time dwelling place through the presence of his Spirit.

The Scriptures characterize the descent of the Spirit and formation of the eschatological temple under the rubric of two different ideas, namely, the Spirit as gift and outpoured love. One of the most insightful explanations of the Holy Spirit as gift and love comes from St. Augustine. The bishop of Hippo reflects on John's statement: "Beloved, let us love one another, for love is from God, and whoever loves has been born of God and knows God. Anyone who does not love does not know God, because God is love" (1 John 4:7–8). Augustine rightly presupposes that John speaks of the triune God of the Bible—Father, Son, and Holy Spirit. He also observes two important points in John's statement. First, "love is from God" (ἡ ἀγάπη ἐκ τοῦ θεοῦ ἐστιν), but at the same time he states, "God is love" (ὁ θεὸς ἀγάπη ἐστίν). Therefore God is love, and love is from God.[45] These statements elicit a specific question, namely, Does John refer to the Son or the Spirit when he writes of the love that comes *from* God? In the verses that follow John writes: "In this the love of God was made manifest among us, that God sent his only Son into the world, so that we might live through him. In this is love, not that we have loved God but that he loved us and sent his Son to

44. Beale, "Descent of the Eschatological Temple," 81, 94; see also William N. Wilder, *Echoes of the Exodus Narrative in the Context and Background of Galatians 5:18* (New York: Peter Lang, 2001), 121–74.

45. Augustine, *The Trinity*, trans. Stephen McKenna, FC (Washington, DC: Catholic University of America Press, 1963), 451–70.; Matthew Levering, *Engaging the Doctrine of the Holy Spirit: Love and Gift in the Trinity and the Church* (Grand Rapids: Baker Academic, 2016), 51ff.

be the propitiation for our sins" (1 John 4:9–10). God clearly sends his love through the Son, as he is the expiation for our sins, but the "love ... from God" does not cease with the Son.

John continues: "Beloved, if God so loved us, we also ought to love one another. No one has ever seen God; if we love one another, God abides in us and his love is perfected in us" (1 John 4:11–12). As God sends his love through the Son, the only way that Christians can love one another is by the abiding presence of God in believers (note that God's abiding presence overlaps with themes of believers constituting the final dwelling place of God, his temple). By what means does God abide in believers? John states: "By this we know that we abide in him and he in us, because he has given us of his Spirit" (1 John 4:13). Augustine rightly concludes, then, that the whole Triune God is love, but when the Triune God sends love, the Father sends his love through the Son, and by the work of the Spirit he applies it to the lives of believers. In short, as the Second Person of the Trinity has the proper name of "Son," the Third Person of the Trinity has the proper names of Love and Gift. Further confirmation of this conclusion appears in 1 John 4:16, "God is love, and whoever abides in love abides in God, and God abides in him." As 1 John 4:13 assures us, we know that we abide in God and that he abides in us because he gives us the Holy Spirit. This means that the Spirit's abiding presence and God's love are the same.[46] Thus, when John says that love is from God, he has the Holy Spirit ultimately in view.

The apostle Paul similarly connects the themes of gift and love to the person and work of the Spirit. Echoing creation imagery, Paul likens the Spirit to water when he writes that there is one Lord, one faith, and one baptism (Eph 4:6). He then writes: "But grace was given to each one of us according to the measure of Christ's gift" (Eph 4:7). Paul echoes both creation themes and Christ's own characterization of the gift of the Holy Spirit: "Whoever believes in me, as the Scripture has said, 'Out of his heart will flow rivers of living water.' Now this he said about the Spirit, whom those who believed in him were to receive, for as yet the Spirit had not been given, because Jesus was not yet glorified" (John 7:38–39). This statement parallels what Jesus told the Samaritan woman at the well: "If you knew the gift of God, and who it is that is saying to you, 'Give me a drink,' you

46. Levering, *Engaging the Doctrine*, 56.

would have asked him, and he would have given you living water" (John 4:10). Paul reinforces the idea of the Spirit as gift when he cites Psalm 68:18, "Therefore it says, 'When he ascended on high he led a host of captives, and he gave gifts to men'" (Eph 4:8).[47] Ephesians is not the only place where Paul employs these themes, as they also appear in this epistle to the Romans. "Gift," "love," and "outpouring," terms reminiscent of Pentecost, appear: "God's love has been poured into our hearts through the Holy Spirit who has been given to us" (Rom 5:5).

## John 14:18–27; 15:26–27

WHAT LIES IMPLICIT IN CHRIST's statements to Nicodemus regarding the connections between the Messiah, his kingdom, and the dispensation of the Spirit becomes explicit in latter portions of John's Gospel. Christ tells his disciples that he will ascend to his Father's right hand but that he will not leave them as orphans (John 14:18), a promise that invokes Moses's parting words to Israel: "The LORD ... will not leave you or forsake you" (Deut 31:6; see also Josh 1:5).[48] Christ promises to send another: "But the Helper, the Holy Spirit, whom the Father will send in my name, he will teach you all things and bring to your remembrance all that I have said to you" (John 14:26). There are two noteworthy features concerning Christ's promise. First, the Spirit is the παράκλητος ("helper," NAS, ESV; "comforter," KJV; "counselor," NIV), and in this role the Spirit teaches the people of God—he brings to remembrance all the things that Christ taught the church. The Spirit is the means of the Son's presence. Second, Christ imparts peace through the Spirit's presence: "Peace I leave with you; my peace I give to you" (John 14:27). Peace is the consequence of a right relationship with God, most powerfully captured in the Aaronic blessing: "The LORD bless you and keep you; the LORD make his face to shine upon you and be gracious to you; the LORD lift up his countenance upon you and give you peace" (Num 6:24–26). At the same time Christ's communication of peace through the Spirit's presence

47. Levering, *Engaging the Doctrine*, 61.

48. Beale and Carson, *Commentary on the New Testament Use*, 490.

rests on a bedrock of Old Testament messianic promises, namely that the Messiah is the "Prince of Peace" (Isa 9:6) who will "speak peace to the nations" (Zech 9:10) and will proclaim peace and salvation (Isa 52:7). The Old Testament promised that God would make a "covenant of peace" with his people (Ezek 37:26).[49]

When Jesus again speaks of the Spirit, he tells his disciples: "But when the Helper comes, whom I will send to you from the Father, the Spirit of truth, who proceeds from the Father, he will bear witness about me. And you also will bear witness, because you have been with me from the beginning" (John 15:26–27; cf. 16:7). Jesus specifically explains that both he and the Father will send the Spirit, a promise that harks back to the anticipation of the outpouring of the Spirit and the inauguration of the eschatological kingdom (see Isa 11:1–10; 32:14–18; 42:1–4; 44:1–5; 61:1–2; Jer 31:31–34; Ezek 11:17–20; 36:24–27; 37:1–14; Joel 2:28–32). Christ highlights the imminent in-breaking of eschatological realities when he says, "The hour is coming" (John 16:2; see Isa 39:6; Jer 7:32; 9:25; 16:14; 31:31, 38; Zech 14:1).[50] While we can say that the kingdom and eschaton dawned with the birth of the Messiah—with the advent of the king, the kingdom is present—the fulfillment of Christ's words awaits the heady day of Pentecost.

We come full circle to the incredible events of Pentecost and Christ's outpouring of the Spirit. On the heels of Peter's sermon, the people cried out and asked what they had to do to be saved, to which Peter responded: "Repent and be baptized every one of you in the name of Jesus Christ for the forgiveness of your sins, and you will receive the gift of the Holy Spirit" (Acts 2:38). God would freely give the gift of the Spirit by his grace, though Simon Magus erroneously thought he could purchase "the gift of God with money" (Acts 8:20). Simon specifically sought to receive the Holy Spirit (Acts 8:19). Later in the book of Acts Luke shows that the final temple of God consisted of both Jews and gentiles, as Peter was amazed "because the gift of the Holy Spirit was poured out even on the Gentiles" (Acts 10:45). As Peter

---

49. Beale and Carson, *Commentary on the New Testament Use*, 490–91.

50. Beale and Carson, *Commentary on the New Testament Use*, 495.

came to grips with the gentile reception of the Spirit, he told the disciples: "God gave the same gift to them as he gave to us when we believed in the Lord Jesus Christ" (Acts 11:17).[51] In short, the Holy Spirit is the means by which God establishes his eschatological dwelling place among his people, and as such, the Spirit is both God's love and gift to fallen but redeemed sinners.

Augustine was not the only one to recognize that the Spirit is both the love of God between Father and Son and the outpoured gift on redeemed sinners. John Owen (1616–1683) beautifully reflects on both the ontology of the Trinity and the economy of redemption as he describes the way Father, Son, and Holy Spirit love one another and then pour out their love on sinners in their redemption:

> The Father Loves us, and "chose us before the Foundation of the world;" but in the pursuit of that love, "he blesseth us with all spiritual blessings in heavenly places in Christ," Eph. 1. 3, 4. From his love, he sheds, or pours out the Holy Spirit richly upon us, through Jesus Christ our Saviour, Tit. 3.6. In the pouring out of his love, there is not one drop that falls besides the Lord Christ. The holy anointing oil, was all poured on the head of Aaron: Psa. 133.2. and thence went down to the skirts of his clothing. Love is first poured out on Christ; and from him, it drops as the dew of Hermon upon the souls of his saints. The Father will have him to have "in all things the pre-eminence," Col. 1.18; "it pleased him that in him all fulness should dwell," verse 19; that "of his fulness we might receive, and grace for grace," John 1.16. Though the love of the Father's purpose and good pleasure have its rise and foundation in his mere grace and will, yet the design of its accomplishment is only in Christ. All the fruits of it are first given to him; and it is in him only that they are dispensed to us. So that though the saints may, nay, do, see an infinite ocean of love unto them in the bosom of the Father, yet they are not to look for one drop from him but what comes through Christ. He is the only means of communication. Love in the Father, is like *honey in the flower*; it must be in the comb, before it be for our use. Christ must extract and prepare this honey for us. He draws

51. Levering, *Engaging the Doctrine*, 62.

> this water from the fountain through union and dispensation of fullness;—we by faith, from the wells of salvation that are in him.[52]

Love originates in the Trinity among Father, Son, and Holy Spirit, and the Father pours out the Spirit on the Son, and both in turn pour out the Spirit on the church—a gift of love.

## THE SPIRIT IN THE NEW CREATION

One final theme is the Spirit as the agent of new creation. This idea has roots in the opening words of Scripture when the Spirit (רוח) hovered over the primeval waters (Gen 1:2). The creation emerged from beneath the miry waters—dry land, beasts of the earth, and of course, the crown of the creation, human beings. Water, Spirit, and new-creation themes occur in different subsequent Old Testament events. Genesis 1:2 describes the Spirit hovering like a bird over the waters; in fact, the term "hover," or רחף, in the *piel* stem occurs in only one other place in the Old Testament: "Like an eagle that stirs up its nest, that flutters over its young, spreading out its wings, catching them, bearing them on its pinions" (Deut 32:11). This avian imagery informs the flood narrative, when God remembered Noah and sent a רוח ("wind") to blow over the waters (Gen 8:1). A different form of the image appears to describe when Noah sent out a dove over the floodwaters (Gen 8:10), which recalls the Spirit's hovering over the creation waters and also anticipates the Spirit's descent on Christ, the last Adam, at his baptism in the form of a dove (Luke 3:22). Water and Spirit materialized when Israel crossed the Red Sea, led by the Spirit in the form of a cloud by day and pillar of fire by night (Exod 13:21–22; 14:24). Subsequent intracanonical reflection on the Red Sea crossing reveals that it was an act of new creation by means of water and Spirit. The prophet Isaiah writes: "Then he remembered the days of old, of Moses and his people. Where is he who brought them up out of the sea with the shepherds of his flock? Where is he who put in the midst of them his Holy Spirit?" (Isa 63:11). When Paul comments on the crossing he explains that the "fathers were all under the cloud, and all passed through the sea" (1 Cor 10:1).

---

52. John Owen, *Communion with God*, in *The Works of John Owen*, ed. William H. Goold (Edinburgh: Banner of Truth, 1966), 2:27.

These different types converged at Pentecost, when Christ baptized the church in the Spirit, an event that Paul describes as a regeneration: "But when the goodness and loving kindness of God our Savior appeared, he saved us, not because of works done by us in righteousness, but according to his own mercy, by the washing of regeneration and renewal of the Holy Spirit, whom he poured out on us richly through Jesus Christ our Savior" (Titus 3:4–6). While this statement has created questions about baptismal regeneration, Paul's statements are not about baptism per se but first and foremost about the Spirit's role in the new creation. There is only one other occurrence of the term "regeneration" (παλιγγενεσία), namely, Matthew 19:28, "Truly, I say to you, in the new world [ἐν τῇ παλιγγενεσίᾳ], when the Son of Man will sit on his glorious throne, you who have followed me will also sit on twelve thrones, judging the twelve tribes of Israel."[53] When Christ poured out the Spirit, the Spirit began the process of creating the new heavens and earth, and the first parts of the new creation appeared in the eschatological temple, the church. When Christ poured out the Spirit on the church and inaugurated the new creation, this divine act flowed out of heaven and reached the church, both corporately and individually. Paul writes of this reality when he says we are "buried therefore with him by baptism into death, in order that, just as Christ was raised from the dead by the glory of the Father, we too might walk in newness of life" (Rom 6:4). "Newness of life" is an existence empowered by the "powers of the age to come," namely, the Holy Spirit (Heb 6:5).[54]

The Spirit's new-creation presence has its locus in the eschatological temple, as Paul, for example, notes in several places: "Do you not know that you are God's temple and that God's Spirit dwells in you?" (1 Cor 3:16; also 1 Cor 6:19). Paul reiterates ideas that Christ himself taught when Jesus told the multitude gathered for the Feast of Tabernacles: "Whoever believes in me, as the Scripture has said, 'Out of his heart will flow rivers of living water'" (John 7:38). John parenthetically explains: "Now this he said about the Spirit, whom those who believed in him were to receive, for as yet the Spirit had not been given, because Jesus was not yet glorified" (John 7:39).

---

53. Vos, *Pauline Eschatology*, 50.

54. Douglas Moo, *The Epistle to the Romans*, NICNT (Grand Rapids: Eerdmans, 1996), 361; also, Geerhardus Vos, "Eschatology and the Spirit in Paul," in *Biblical and Theological Studies* (New York: Charles Scribner's Sons, 1912), 211–59, here 216.

The idea of the Spirit flowing from God's dwelling place into the hearts and lives of his people and throughout the new creation appears in the prophet Ezekiel where he prophesies of water issuing forth from beneath the threshold of the temple door and flooding the creation. But rather than bringing destruction, as in the Noachian flood, it brings life in its wake (Ezek 47:1–12).[55]

## CONCLUSION

God's covenant with his people requires both presence and place—that is, by what means and where does God fellowship with his people. The primary means that God dwells amid his people is through the presence of the Holy Spirit in the various temples throughout preredemptive and redemptive history. The Spirit's presence in Eden finds its culmination in his indwelling presence in the people of God—the final temple. God's presence through the Spirit is a blessing both because he abides with his people and because of the promises he makes, which is the subject of the next chapter.

### FURTHER READING

Augustine. *The Trinity*. FC. Translated by Stephen McKenna. Washington, DC: Catholic University Press of America, 1963. One of the great classics of Western Christianity, a foundational text for understanding biblical trinitarianism.

Beale, G. K. *The Temple and the Church's Mission: A Biblical Theology of the Dwelling Place of God*. Downers Grove, IL: InterVarsity Press, 2004. A broader survey regarding the concept of the temple in the Old Testament but nevertheless an excellent study that touches on the Spirit's dwelling amid the people of God from Eden to the new creation.

Kline, Meredith G. *Images of the Spirit*. Eugene, OR: Wipf & Stock, 1999. An insightful, though at times challenging to read, book on the Holy Spirit in the Old Testament.

55. G. K. Beale, *The Book of Revelation*, NIGTC (Grand Rapids: Eerdmans, 1999), 1104.

Kuyper, Abraham. *The Work of the Holy Spirit*. Translated by Henri De Vries. New York: Funk & Wagnalls, 1900. An excellent treatment of the doctrine of the Holy Spirit that was part of the renewed interest in pneumatology in the nineteenth century. Kuyper covers the person and work of the Spirit in exegetical, redemptive-historical, and theological detail.

Smeaton, George. *The Doctrine of the Holy Spirit*. Edinburgh: T&T Clark, 1882. Another work, this one by a Scottish Presbyterian theologian, that comes from the context of the nineteenth-century pneumatology revival. Conversative theological works from this period sought to set forth a biblical pneumatology to counter the views of G. W. F. Hegel and his idea of the Spirit. Smeaton's work is worth the read.

11

# COVENANT PROMISE

## BLESSING AND REDEMPTION

"THE MOST BEAUTIFUL PART OF every picture is the frame," G. K. Chesterton (1874–1936) once observed, and the same is true of God's dealings with his people.[1] The frame of the doctrine of the covenant is perhaps one of the most beautiful parts of the picture of God's relationship with his people. As Robert Rollock (ca. 1555–1599) insightfully notes, "God says nothing to man apart from the covenant."[2] The frame of covenant provides the context in which God reveals his blessings to his people—the positive consequences of dwelling in God's presence: "I will walk among you and will be your God, and you shall be my people" (Lev 26:12). The covenant is the chief place where God blesses his people, where he imparts a covenantal inheritance to future generations. This chapter therefore examines the blessings of the covenant, sonship and inheritance, and the blessings of redemption, including righteousness and forgiveness (justification), a new heart (sanctification), and protection (glorification).

1. G. K. Chesterton, "The Toy Theatre," in *On Lying in Bed and Other Essays*, ed. Alberto Manguel (Calgary, Alberta: Bayeux Arts, 2004), 141–46, here 144.

2. Robert Rollock, *A Treatise of Our Effectual Calling*, in *Select Works of Robert Rollock*, ed. William M. Gunn (Edinburgh: Wodrow Society, 1844), 1:33. See also Geerhardus Vos, "The Doctrine of the Covenant in Reformed Theology," in *Redemptive History and Biblical Interpretation*, 234–67, here 239.

**BLESSING** Blessing leaps off the first pages of the Bible in the creation account as God covenanted with Adam. God's first recorded words to his image-bearers are blessing: "And God blessed them. And God said to them, 'Be fruitful and multiply and fill the earth and subdue it, and have dominion over the fish of the sea and over the birds of the heavens and over every living thing that moves on the earth'" (Gen 1:28). In his blessing, God gave to Adam and Eve both dominion over the creation and the gift of all of the earth's vegetation for food (Gen 1:29). God's intention was to bless his image-bearers, though we must observe the sobering truth that God's revelation is always double-edged: "For the word of God is living and active, sharper than any two-edged sword, piercing to the division of soul and of spirit, of joints and of marrow, and discerning the thoughts and intentions of the heart" (Heb 4:12). Blessing is one-half of the covenantal administrative formula. The second half lies in the specter of covenantal sanction—the penalty for violating the terms of the covenant: "And the Lord God commanded the man, saying, 'You may surely eat of every tree of the garden, but of the tree of the knowledge of good and evil you shall not eat, for in the day that you eat of it you shall surely die'" (Gen 2:16–17). In the redemptive context, God's chief aim and purpose is blessing, a feature that appears in his subsequent covenants throughout redemptive history.

The initial outbreaking of grace and blessing occurs immediately on the heels of the fall. When God appeared in the garden in the "Spirit of the day" (Gen 3:8) to justify or condemn his covenant servant, he had every right to bring the full weight of his just condemnation on Adam's head.[3] But rather than give Adam the just deserts of his disobedience, he held out mercy, forgiveness, and restoration by promising to redeem both him and his wife by the seed of the woman (Gen 3:15). In lieu of the hastily gathered fig leaves to cover their nakedness, God clothed Adam and Even in animal skins, which foreshadowed future blessing and restoration to God's benevolent presence (Gen 3:21). Their divine investiture represented the "future consummate inheritance as kings of the earth."[4]

---

3. Kline, *Images of the Spirit*, 97–115.

4. G. K. Beale, *A New Testament Biblical Theology: The Unfolding of the Old Testament in the New* (Grand Rapids: Baker Academic, 2011), 41; also William N. Wilder, "Illumination and Investiture: The Royal Significance of the Tree of Wisdom," *WTJ* 68 (2006): 56–69.

Covenant blessing and promise continue in the pages of Genesis as God speaks to humans by way of covenant, in this case in the Abrahamic covenant. When God casted the bonds of his covenantal promises around Abraham, Adam's failure still loomed large over the narrative. But in the darkness of Adam's sin the light of God's grace shone all the more brilliantly as he raises other Adam-like figures to whom he gives blessings: "Now the Lord said to Abram, 'Go from your country and your kindred and your father's house to the land that I will show you. And I will make of you a great nation, and I will bless you and make your name great, so that you will be a blessing' " (Gen 12:1–2).[5] The narrative invokes the covenantal name of God (יהוה) and couples it with blessing. The divine blessings echo the original Adamic blessing of the covenant of works, where God enjoined on Adam the responsibility of procreating image-bearers and filling the earth with them. In this case, however, the blessing is no longer a command but a promise. God will bless Abraham, make his name great, so that he will be blessing—so that he will become a great nation.

When God repeats this covenantal blessing on the heels of the Aqedah ("binding"), God tells Abraham: "I will surely bless you, and I will surely multiply your offspring as the stars of heaven and as the sand that is on the seashore. And your offspring shall possess the gate of his enemies, and in your offspring shall all the nations of the earth be blessed, because you have obeyed my voice" (Gen 22:17–18). God told Adam and Eve to be fruitful and multiply, and now God says *he* will multiply Abraham's offspring; God told Adam and Eve to subdue the earth, and now God promises that Abraham will possess the gate of his enemies. God told Adam to fill the whole earth, and now God promises that "all the nations of the earth" (LXX πάντα τὰ ἔθνη τῆς γῆς) will be blessed through Abraham.[6] The narrative quietly whispers that God continues the blessings of the covenant of works, but they are no longer commands but promises. God does not change the blessings of the Adamic covenant but will himself ensure their fulfillment through the seed of the woman.[7] God repeats these promissory blessings

---

5. Beale, *New Testament Biblical Theology*, 46.

6. Beale, *New Testament Biblical Theology*, 48.

7. Similarly, N. T. Wright, *The New Testament and the People of God* (Philadelphia: Fortress, 1992), 263; William Dumbrell, *Covenant and Creation: A Theology of the Old Testament Covenants*, 2nd ed. (Milton Keynes, UK: Authentic Media, 2002), 63–68.

throughout subsequent covenants with Isaac, Jacob, and Israel (Gen 47:27; 48:3–4; Exod 1:7, 12; 20; Num 23:10–11; Lev 26:9; Deut 7:13; 15:4, 6; 28:11–12 LXX; 30:16; 2 Sam 7:29).[8] But though these blessings have Adamic hues, one must read them through the lens of God's promise to deliver Adam's descendants through the seed of the woman, the seed of Abraham, Isaac, and Jacob, and the seed of David. In other words, the covenantal blessings find their fulfilment in the Messiah. Blessing comes only in covenant with God, but the focal point of those blessings is the Son of God.

## Genesis 12:1–3

God's call of Abraham is one of the chief foundation stones in the cathedral of God's unfolding plan of redemption, a stone that rests on his promise to redeem Adam's offspring through the seed of the woman (Gen 3:15). As noted above, this text begins to take the blessings of the covenant of works that were given to Adam as a command and transforms them into a promise. The apostle Paul's interpretation of this text, however, sheds greater light on its significance. As Paul unpacks the doctrine of justification, he reaches back to Genesis 15:6 to prove that God credited or imputed righteousness to Abraham by faith alone: "Just as Abraham 'believed God and it was counted to him as righteousness' " (Gal 3:6). Paul then pivots to show the Judaizers that, gentile or not, those who place their faith in Jesus are "sons of Abraham" (Gal 3:7). The double strand of covenant and sonship appears—God's covenant with Abraham produces the promised offspring that are as numerous as the sands of the sea and stars of the sky through faith in the Messiah. Paul highlights the global extent of the Abrahamic covenant when he writes: "And the Scripture, foreseeing that God would justify the Gentiles by faith, preached the gospel beforehand to Abraham, saying, 'In you shall all the nations be blessed'" (Gal 3:8). Here Paul combines the Septuagint's Genesis 12:3, ἐνευλογηθήσονται ἐν σοὶ πᾶσαι αἱ φυλαὶ τῆς γῆς ("in you all the tribes of the earth will be blessed"), with Genesis 18:8, ἐνευλογηθήσονται

8. Beale, *New Testament Biblical Theology*, 48–49.

ἐν αὐτῷ πάντα τὰ ἔθνη τῆς γῆς ("in him all the nations of the earth will be blessed").[9]

There are two important aspects of Paul's authoritative interpretation of Genesis 12:3. First, his exegesis underscores the continuity between the Old and New Testaments. Paul states that the Scriptures "preached the gospel beforehand" (προευηγγελίσατο).[10] There are not two plans of redemption but only one. Second, in a sin-fallen world there is only one way to enter the new heavens and earth: by believing in the person and work of the Messiah, Jesus. Immediately after he cites Genesis 12:3, Paul explains the nature of justification by juxtaposing the only two paths to eschatological life: either perfect obedience through the law, hence his quotation of Leviticus 18:5, "The one who does them shall live by them" (Gal 3:12), or faith in Jesus, hence his quotation of Habakkuk 2:4, "The righteous shall live by faith" (Gal 3:11).[11] In other words, salvation either comes by faith in the Messiah or by perfect obedience to the law—not both. "The law is not of faith" (Gal 3:12)—in justification, either you do the law or believe the gospel. Or, as Paul writes: "For if righteousness were through the law, then Christ died for no purpose" (Gal 2:21).

## SONSHIP/INHERITANCE (ADOPTION)

Covenant and sonship are two revelatory strands that converge in God's redemptive promises, strands that find their roots in the covenant of works. From the outset, God blessed Adam and Eve and commanded them to fill the earth with more divine image-bearers. God created Adam and Eve in his image and likeness (Gen 1:26), and as the subsequent narrative explains, image-bearing and sonship go hand in hand, connections that Genesis makes explicit: "When God created man, he made him in the likeness of God. Male and female he created them, and he blessed them and named them Man when they were created. When Adam had lived 130 years, he fathered a son in his own likeness, after his image, and named him Seth" (Gen 5:1–3). God made Adam and Eve in his

9. Beale and Carson, *Commentary on the New Testament Use*, 794.
10. Beale and Carson, *Commentary on the New Testament Use*, 795.
11. Beale and Carson, *Commentary on the New Testament Use*, 800–804.

own image, and then Adam fathered a son in his own image and likeness. To be an image-bearer is to be a son.

The double strand of covenant and sonship continues in subsequent covenantal administrations as God repeatedly cuts or ratifies covenants with his people and their offspring, whether in the Noachian, Abrahamic, Mosaic, Davidic, or new covenant (Gen 6:18; 17:9; Num 18:19; 2 Chr 21:7; Jer 31:31–34; 32:38–40; Acts 2:39). But the promises do not fall immediately on God's covenant people but must first come through the seed of the woman, the Messiah. The Old Testament gradually and progressively reveals that the Messiah comes through the seed of the woman, Seth, Abraham, Isaac, Jacob, Judah, and especially David. The anointed king sought to build God a permanent temple, but God told him that one of his heirs would have this task: "When your days are fulfilled and you lie down with your fathers, I will raise up your offspring after you, who shall come from your body, and I will establish his kingdom. He shall build a house for my name, and I will establish the throne of his kingdom forever" (2 Sam 7:12–13). The words that follow draw on the themes of covenant and sonship: "I will be to him a father, and he shall be to me a son" (2 Sam 7:14).

This language is an adoption formula that appears elsewhere in the Old Testament. When Moses was born under the shadow of Pharaoh's genocidal edict to eradicate male Israelite babies, his mother placed him in a tiny ark and set him in a river where Pharaoh's daughter came to bathe. Pharaoh's daughter found Moses, took pity on him, and paid Moses's mother to nurse him, and when he grew older Moses's mother "brought him to Pharaoh's daughter, and he became her son" (Exod 2:10; see Acts 7:21). Note the adoption formula, "he became her son" (ויהי לה לבן). This is the same formula we find in 2 Samuel 7:14, "He shall be to me a son" (יהיה לי לבן). The intracanonical interpretation of God's promise to David also describes it as a covenant: "You have said, 'I have made a covenant with my chosen one; I have sworn to David my servant: "I will establish your offspring forever, and build your throne for all generations"'" (Ps 89:3–4). Paul appeals to this pattern and connects covenant, sonship, and promise: "They are Israelites, and to them belong the adoption [υἱοθεσία], the glory, the covenants, the giving of the law, the worship, and the promises" (Rom 9:4).[12]

12. On this OT concept of adoption, see James Scott, *Adoption as Sons of God: An Exegetical Investigation into the Background in the Pauline Corpus* (Tübingen: Mohr Siebeck, 1992).

Covenant, promise, and sonship congregate around the Messiah in the psalmist's reflection on these realities when he famously writes: "The LORD said to me, 'You are my Son; today I have begotten you.' Ask of me, and I will make the nations your heritage, and the ends of the earth your possession" (Ps 2:7–8). The psalmist recognizes the Messiah as God's Son, who is at the same time the Davidic covenantal scion, who receives the nations as his inheritance (נחלה; κληρονομία). The inheritance has the same global scope as the Adamic and Abrahamic covenant, but the only way the blessings come to "all the nations of the earth" (Gen 22:18) is through the Son of God. The psalmist casts further light on the Davidic covenant when he writes in terms evocative of Psalm 2:

> He shall cry to me, "You are my Father,
> my God, and the Rock of my salvation."
> And I will make him the firstborn,
> the highest of the kings of the earth.
> My steadfast love I will keep for him forever,
> and my covenant will stand firm for him.
> I will establish his offspring forever
> and his throne as the days of the heavens.
> If his children forsake my law
> and do not walk according to my rules,
> if they violate my statutes
> and do not keep my commandments,
> then I will punish their transgression with the rod
> and their iniquity with stripes,
> but I will not remove from him my steadfast love
> or be false to my faithfulness.
> I will not violate my covenant
> or alter the word that went forth from my lips.
> Once for all I have sworn by my holiness;
> I will not lie to David.
> His offspring shall endure forever,
> his throne as long as the sun before me. (Ps 89:26–36)

In verses 26–27, the psalmist echoes 2 Samuel 7:14, "I will be to him a father, and he shall be to me a son," when he writes, "'You are my Father, my God and the Rock of my salvation.' And I will make him the firstborn, the highest of the kings of the earth."

The psalmist sheds light on how God will discipline the Davidic scion. God initially told David of his heir: "I will be to him a father, and he shall be to me a son. When he commits iniquity, I will discipline him with the rod of men, with the stripes of the sons of men, but my steadfast love will not depart from him" (2 Sam 7:14–15). How can the Messiah potentially be guilty of sin such that God would discipline him with the rod of men? Would not sin invalidate his intercessory work? The answer to this question comes in Psalm 89:29–34.

The psalmist does not explain it, but he writes of an irrefragable bond between the Davidic heir and his children, literally "his sons" (בניו; οἱ υἱοὶ αὐτοῦ, Ps 89:30). If the heir's sons disobey God's rules and statutes, he will discipline them as a father disciplines his children, but he will not curse them—the blessings of the covenant on the heir's sons are irrevocable.

Covenant, sonship, and inheritance come to fruition in the seemingly mundane and pedestrian New Testament genealogies. Matthew opens his Gospel with a string on which he places five beautiful pearls: "The book of the genealogy of Jesus Christ, the son of David, the son of Abraham" (Matt 1:1). First, that Matthew presents a genealogy places the reader within the matrix of fathers and sons, those who are the image and likeness of their fathers. Matthew's genealogy evokes the opening chapters of the Bible with the use of the phrase "the book of the genealogy," which occurs in Genesis 2:4 and 5:1 (LXX). Second, he states that this is the genealogy of Jesus (Ἰησοῦς), which is the Greek form of the Old Testament name Joshua. But more importantly, the Hebrew name Joshua, or alternatively Jehoshua or Jeshua, means "Yahweh saves," as it is a combination of the name of God, Yahweh, or יה, and the term ישע, "he saves" (see Josh 1:1; Zech 3:1; Ezra 2:2). The Old Testament invests names with significance—your name is who you are. Thus, when Matthew calls the Savior "Jesus," he says this person embodies the fulfillment of Yahweh's promises to save.[13]

13. Thomas Weinandy, *Jesus Becoming Jesus: A Theological Interpretation of the Synoptic Gospels* (Washington, DC: Catholic University of America Press, 2018), 8–11.

Third, that Matthew attributes the title "Messiah" to Jesus of Nazareth means that the carpenter's son is the Lord's anointed of Psalm 2. Fourth, he confirms Jesus's status as the Messiah when he says Jesus is the son of David, the long-prophesied heir of 2 Samuel 7:12–15 and Psalm 89. Fifth, Matthew drives Jesus's genealogy back to Abraham.[14] Not only are we in the context of father and son, image-bearers, but even though Matthew does not invoke the term, covenant looms large. God gave promises of blessings that would come through the seed of Abraham and David in terms of his covenants with them. We can gloss the opening statement from Matthew's Gospel as: "The fulfillment of Genesis, the one by whom Yahweh saves, Yahweh's anointed, the son and fulfillment of the Davidic covenant, and the son and fulfillment of the Abrahamic covenant." Equally relevant is that Luke pushes Jesus's genealogy all the way back to Adam (Luke 3:38). In other words, Jesus is not merely the Messiah and savior for the Jews, but he is the long-awaited seed of the woman, the savior of both Jew and gentile—the one through whom the Adamic blessings of the dominion mandate will be fulfilled.

The second person of the Trinity, the Son of God, is also the Messiah, the son of David, and the son of Abraham. In keeping with the theme of fruitful offspring, whether in the Adamic command-blessing or in the subsequent Abrahamic and Davidic promise-blessings, Matthew connects the Abrahamic benediction that he will be a blessing to "all the nations" (πάντα τὰ ἔθνη, Gen 22:18) to Christ's Great Commission: "All authority in heaven and on earth has been given to me. Go therefore and make disciples of all nations [πάντα τὰ ἔθνη], baptizing them in the name of the Father and of the Son and of the Holy Spirit, teaching them to observe all that I have commanded you" (Matt 28:18–20).[15] The Abrahamic covenant, and its promise of blessing and multiplied offspring as numerous as the stars of heaven and the sand of the seashore, comes to fruition through the Messiah and the Great Commission.

As Paul reflects on the sweep of redemptive history, God gives him a revelatory glimpse of the inner life of the Godhead before the foundation of the world, which enables him to write: "He predestined us for adoption

14. Beale and Carson, *Commentary on the New Testament Use*, 2.

15. D. A. Carson, *Matthew: Chapters 13–28*, EBC 2 (Grand Rapids: Zondervan, 1995), 594.

through Jesus Christ, according to the purpose of his will" (Eph 1:5). Likewise, he writes: "In Christ Jesus you are all sons of God, through faith" (Gal 3:26). Christ restores sinners back to the relationship that Adam had with God, but to a heightened eschatological state. Christ does not return us to the garden but instead plants us firmly in him, the one who reigns as the last Adam in the new heavens and earth. Thus, Paul writes: "For you did not receive the spirit of slavery to fall back into fear, but you have received the Spirit of adoption as sons, by whom we cry, 'Abba! Father!'" (Rom 8:15). The intimacy we have with God is greater than that enjoyed by any other Old Testament saint. No Old Testament saint ever personally called God "Father." Israel was collectively God's son, and thus the nation could refer to God as their Father. But because anyone in Christ is a son of God, all may call on him as Father, Abba.[16] In short, we are all sons in the Son, but we must distinguish our adoption from Christ's status as Son.

Strictly speaking, the Second Person of the Trinity is the natural Son of God, whereas the redeemed are the adopted sons of God. Thomas Aquinas (1224–1275) distinguishes between natural and adopted sons of God. The Son is the natural Son because he is "begotten not made," which is the language of the Nicene Creed. Think, for example, of Psalm 2:7: "You are my Son," declares the Father to the Son. Conversely, Scripture says of the redeemed: "He gave the right to become children of God" (John 1:12). Thus, the redeemed are the adopted sons of God (*ST* IIIa, q. 23, art 2). Aquinas makes this distinction to fend off the Arian heresy, which taught that Jesus was a mere human being whose piety commended him to God, who then adopted him as his son.[17] We may speak of Christ's adoption if we have in view the adoption formula in 2 Samuel 7:12–15, "I will be to him a father, and he shall be to me a son," but these words do not address ontology but economy—they deal with the Son's mission, not his eternal filiation; these words apply to the God-man.[18] The adoption formula in 2 Samuel 7:12–15

---

16. "Abba" does not mean "daddy" but is the term that any adult would call their father. The term is not an affectionate name that a child utters but instead a respectful term of intimacy. Evidence of this is immediately evident in how Paul translates the Aramaic term *Abba*, "Father" (ὁ πατήρ; Rom 8:15). See James Barr, "Abba Isn't 'Daddy,'" *JTS* 39, no. 1 (1988): 28–47.

17. Michael Bird, *Jesus the Eternal Son: Answering Adoptionist Christology* (Grand Rapids: Eerdmans, 2017).

18. David B. Garner, *Sons in the Son: The Riches and Reach of Adoption in Christ* (Phillipsburg, NJ: P&R, 2016), 195–218; Michael Allen, *Sanctification*, NSD (Grand Rapids: Zondervan, 2017),

finds its fulfillment in Psalm 2:7, "You are my Son; today I have begotten you." When the New Testament appeals to this text, economy and resurrection are in view, not the Son's ontology (Acts 13:33). Paul draws on this web of texts when he writes: "Concerning his Son, who was descended from David according to the flesh and was declared to be the Son of God in power according to the Spirit of holiness by his resurrection from the dead, Jesus Christ our Lord" (Rom 1:3–4). Paul specifically connects the fulfillment of the Davidic covenant with Christ's resurrection from the dead, which constituted his legal declaration as the Son of God.

## RIGHTEOUSNESS AND FORGIVENESS (JUSTIFICATION)

As God's sons in the Son, believers lay hold of the inheritance that was promised to the Messiah (Ps 2:7–8): "The Spirit himself bears witness with our spirit that we are children of God, and if children, then heirs—heirs of God and fellow heirs with Christ" (Rom 8:16–17). As co-heirs with Christ, believers possess "an inheritance that is imperishable, undefiled, and unfading, kept in heaven" (1 Pet 1:4). But sin is an obstacle to the reception of this inheritance that must be remedied by the Son. The catena of God's promises of blessing, sonship, and inheritance therefore address the obstacle of sin. When Abraham looked on himself and his wife, Sarah, he remembered God's promise that God would make him a great nation, but he gazed on his and Sarah's withering bodies and wondered when God would fulfill his promise (Gen 12:1–2; 15:1–2). God promised him an heir, and so Abraham believed God. The Genesis narrative records some of the most important words in all of Scripture: "And he believed the Lord, and he counted it to him as righteousness" (Gen 15:6).

Paul explains that Abraham did not work to receive his justified status but rather believed in the promise of God: "And to the one who does not work but believes in him who justifies the ungodly, his faith is counted as righteousness" (Rom 4:5). Paul's statement communicates two earth-shattering truths. First, Abraham was ungodly. Second, despite his ungodliness, Abraham's belief in God's promise meant that God declared him

134; see also Trevor J. Burke, *Adopted into God's Family: Exploring a Pauline Metaphor* (Downers Grove, IL: InterVarsity Press, 2006), 105–7, 199–200.

righteous—he was now in full conformity with the law (see Deut 6:25). God issued a forensic verdict over Abraham and declared him righteous in his sight. God's verdict overcame Abraham's sinful condition. But how could this be? How could God declare ungodly Abraham righteous?

Within the immediate context of Genesis 15, God instructed Abraham to gather animals and cut them in half (Gen 15:7–11). This was the common ancient Near Eastern practice of making a covenant. Covenantal parties cut animals in two, walked between the severed animal halves, and swore self-maledictory oaths confirming their agreement. If either party violated the terms of the covenant, then the offending party received covenant sanction. The prophet Jeremiah captures this covenant-making activity: "The men who transgressed my covenant and did not keep the terms of the covenant that they made before me, I will make them like the calf that they cut in two and passed between its parts" (Jer 34:18). What stands out in Genesis 15 is that God put Abraham into a deep sleep and then he alone, represented by a "flaming torch," passed between the severed animals (Gen 15:12, 17). In effect, God told Abraham, "If I violate the covenant, I will suffer the curse," but he also amazingly said, "If *you* violate the covenant, I will suffer the curse."[19]

## Psalm 103:1–19

PSALM 103 IS ONE PLACE where a number of different themes of covenant life converge, including worship, salvation, revelation, God's covenant love, and the covenant love of his servants. Words of praise and worship punctuate David's psalm: "Bless the LORD, O my soul, and all that is within me, bless his holy name!" (v. 1). David praises God for his acts of redemption, such as the forgiveness of David's sins (vv. 2–3), God's covenant love (חסד; vv. 4, 8), the strength that God provides (v. 5), and his ethical purity (v. 6). Following the word-act-word pattern of revelation, David writes: "He made known his ways to Moses, his acts to the people of Israel" (v. 7). In other words,

19. Delbert R. Hillers, *The History of a Biblical Idea* (Baltimore: Johns Hopkins University Press, 1969), 103; Vos, *Biblical Theology*, 69, 257; Meredith G. Kline, *By Oath Consigned: A Reinterpretation of the Covenant Signs of Circumcision and Baptism* (Grand Rapids: 1968), 45.

both God's words and acts are forms of revelation. In his self-disclosure, God reveals himself to his people as a merciful Father, which echoes the idea that Israel was God's firstborn son (Exod 4:22; Hos 11:1): "As a father shows compassion to his children, so the LORD shows compassion to those who fear him" (Ps 103:13; see vv. 17–18). But as God showers his people with his covenant love, he does so to elicit their reciprocal love—his desire is for his people to fear him. As John Calvin writes, such a response is not a servile fear, but a fear of filial respect, honor, and love.[20] The way that God brings sinful people into covenant fellowship with him is by forgiving their sins: "As far as the east is from the west, so far does he remove our transgressions from us" (Ps 103:12).[21]

God therefore does not ignore the sins of his people but steps into the breach in the person of his Son. But the Son's work as Messiah does not merely remedy the violation of the Adamic and Mosaic covenants; the Son also fulfills the original Adamic vocation. God does not rewrite Adam's vocation to be fruitful, multiply, fill all the earth, and subdue it, but instead sends a Son, one like Adam, the Son of Man, who will faithfully fulfill it. God provides the fulfillment of the original Adamic vocation by crediting Christ's perfect law-keeping and suffering to those who are united to him by faith. Paul weaves the themes of covenant, blessing, sonship, and justification together when he writes: "But when the fullness of time had come, God sent forth his Son, born of woman, born under the law, to redeem those who were under the law, so that we might receive adoption as sons" (Gal 4:4–5). Correlatively, Paul places Adam and Christ in parallel to explain the relative effects of their (dis)obedience: "For as by the one man's disobedience the many were constituted sinners, so by the one man's obedience the many will be constituted righteous" (Rom 5:19, my trans.). As Francis Turretin (1623–1687) succinctly explains: "We are constituted sinners in Adam in the same way in which we are constituted righteous in Christ."[22]

---

20. Calvin, *Inst.* 3.2.27.

21. Derek Kidner, *Psalms 73–150*, TOTC (Downers Grove, IL: IVP Academic, 1981), 363–67.

22. Francis Turretin, *Institutes of Elenctic Theology*, trans. George Musgrave Giger, ed. James T. Dennison Jr. (Phillipsburg, NJ: Presbyterian and Reformed, 1992–1997), 9.9.16.

One of the covenantal blessings believers receive in the promise of Christ is his imputed righteousness, evidence that God "constitutes" (καθίστημι) people either as sinners or as righteous based on the federal headship of either Adam or Christ.[23]

## Luke 18:9–14

Even though some New Testament scholars have tried to pit the apostle Paul against Jesus, we find the same Pauline antithesis between faith and works in justification in the teaching of Jesus. In Luke 18:9–14 Christ gives the parable of the Pharisee and the tax collector.[24] The context of the parable is crucial for grasping its intent: "He also told this parable to some who trusted in themselves that they were righteous, and treated others with contempt" (Luke 18:9). Many first-century Jews understood how the law functioned. Deuteronomy 6:25 presents the principle that obedience yields righteousness: "And it will be righteousness for us, if we are careful to do all this commandment before the Lord our God, as he has commanded us." Righteousness is conformity to a moral or ethical standard, in this case, conformity to God's law. The Gospels record different instances where people approached Jesus with this proper understanding of the law: "And a ruler asked him, 'Good Teacher, what must I do to inherit eternal life?'" (Luke 18:18 // Mark 10:17; see Matt 19:16). While many understood the nature of the law, they had a defective anthropology—they believed they could fulfill the law in spite of their sinfulness. They also had an erroneous Christology—they believed they did not need the Messiah to fulfill the law on their behalf. Thus, when Jesus preached the parable of the Pharisee and the tax collector, he took aim at those "who trusted in themselves" (Luke 18:9), those who thought they could sufficiently obey the law.

---

23. Charles Hodge, *Romans* (Edinburgh: Banner of Truth, 1989), 173–74; Ben C. Dunson, *Individual and Community in Paul's Letter to the Romans* (Tübingen: Mohr Siebeck, 2012), 148–54; John Murray, *The Imputation of Adam's Sin* (Phillipsburg, NJ: Presbyterian and Reformed, 1977).

24. On this parable, see Klyne R. Snodgrass, *Stories with Intent: A Comprehensive Guide to the Parables*, 2nd ed. (Grand Rapids: Eerdmans, 2018), 462–76.

Law-keeping confidence appears in Christ's parable when he describes the Pharisee's prayer: "God, I thank you that I am not like other men, extortioners, unjust, adulterers, or even like this tax collector" (Luke 18:11). The Pharisee then lists the ways in which he keeps the law: "I fast twice a week; I give tithes of all that I get" (Luke 18:12). By contrast, tax collectors were despised in first-century Israel because they had a reputation of being extortioners and thieves.[25] The Pharisees, for example, accuse Christ of associating with lowlifes, with "tax collectors and sinners" and gluttons and drunkards, as evidence of his supposed immorality (Matt 9:10–11; 11:19). In spite of the tax collectors' ungodly reputation, Christ characterizes him very differently: "But the tax collector, standing far off, would not even lift up his eyes to heaven, but beat his breast, saying, 'God be merciful to me, a sinner!'" (Luke 18:13). The tax collector has no confidence in his own law-keeping but casts himself entirely on the mercy of God. The message is implicit, but it is that the tax collector is looking to God's covenant promises, not to the law. Christ and Paul, therefore, speak with one voice—the law is not of faith, but the righteous shall live by faith. For this reason, Christ concludes his parable, "I tell you, this man went down to his house justified, rather than the other. For everyone who exalts himself will be humbled, but the one who humbles himself will be exalted" (Luke 18:14).

Though the parable ends, there are two important contextual points that prove the unanimity of Paul and Jesus. First, after the parable Luke records that people brought infants to Jesus, but the disciples tried to prevent this (Luke 18:15). Jesus nevertheless mildly rebukes his disciples and says: "Let the children come to me, and do not hinder them, for to such belongs the kingdom of God. Truly, I say to you, whoever does not receive the kingdom of God like a child shall not enter it" (Luke 18:16–17). Set against the backdrop of the parable, the message is clear: Do not think that your law-keeping will save you. Rather, you must have the faith of a child (Matt 18:3; Mark 10:14). Second, Luke records Christ's encounter with the ruler

25. Jacob Neusner, *First-Century Judaism in Crisis: Yohanan ben Zakkai and the Renaissance of Torah* (Eugene, OR: Wipf & Stock, 2006), 29.

who asked him, "What must I do to inherit eternal life?" (Luke 18:18). In parallel with Paul, Jesus presents the demands of the law: "You know the commandments" (18:20). The ruler, like the Pharisee in Christ's parable, claims, "All these I have kept from my youth" (Luke 18:21). So Jesus challenges him to sell all he owns and give it to the poor, which makes the ruler very sad because he has great wealth (Luke 18:22–23). In this instance, Christ presses the demands of the law and uncovers the ruler's hidden idolatry of mammon. But in another similar circumstance when a lawyer asks Christ what he has to do to inherit eternal life, Jesus again points to the law. The lawyer rattles off Deuteronomy 6:4 and Leviticus 19:18, and Christ responds, "You have answered correctly; do this, and you will live" (Luke 10:28). In the case of the lawyer's question, Jesus simply acknowledges that obedience to the law yields eternal life with his quotation of Leviticus 18:5, which again parallels Paul's use: "The law is not of faith, rather 'The one who does them shall live by them'" (Gal 3:12; Lev 18:5).

## Romans 3:21–26

The Bible presents two paths to justification and everlasting life: perfect obedience to the law or faith in Jesus Christ, evident in Jesus's and Paul's appeal to the function of the law and their interpretation of Leviticus 18:5. When Paul therefore writes of the universal condemnation of all people under the law, whether in its Adamic or Mosaic form, he introduces a prepositional phrase with eschatological significance in Romans 3:21, Νυνὶ δὲ ("But now"). These two small words signal a shift in redemptive history from the present era to the dawning of the eschaton, from the Mosaic to the new covenant.[26] Thus, note the redemptive historical shift that occurs with the advent of Christ: "But now the righteousness of God has been manifested apart from the law, although the Law and the Prophets bear witness to it" (Rom 3:21). In contrast to the affirmation of Leviticus 18:5, that the

26. D. A. Carson, "Atonement in Romans 3:21–26," in *The Glory of the Atonement: Biblical, Historical, and Practical Perspectives. Essays in Honor of Roger Nicole*, ed. Charles E. Hill and Frank A. James III (Downers Grove, IL: InterVarsity Press, 2004), 119–39, here 121.

person who obeys the law will secure eternal life, Paul says that the righteousness of God has been revealed χωρὶς νόμου ("apart from the law"). In other words, a person cannot become righteous by means of the law, or the Mosaic covenant, but rather his righteousness must come through Christ, which is why he says that the Mosaic covenant and the Prophets bear witness to it—they foretell of Christ.[27]

The law and the prophets bear witness to the δικαιοσύνη θεοῦ ("righteousness of God") that comes apart from the law. The δικαιοσύνη θεοῦ is a contested theolegoumenon. Interpreters are split on whether it should be read as a subjective or objective genitive: Is the righteousness of God his own (i.e., his covenant faithfulness), as N. T. Wright contends, or is it the righteousness that God gives to believers? Space prohibits extensive exposition and argumentation, but others have ably engaged the issues and satisfactorily argued that the disputed theolegoumenon is an objective genitive. Paul therefore writes, "The righteousness of God through faith in Jesus Christ for all who believe" (Rom 3:22).[28] The righteousness of God does not come to people through the law but through faith in Jesus.

Paul makes the point that what God has done through Jesus is of universal and global significance, given that he says, "For there is no distinction: for all have sinned and fall short of the glory of God" (Rom 3:22–23). Building off the universal sinfulness of both Jew and gentile in Romans 1:18–3:19, Paul writes that all people fall short of God's glory. Paul does not invoke specific language of the blessing of the covenant of works, but that he places the whole human race under a blanket condemnation reminds us that Jesus, the last Adam, is the divine remedy for the failures of the first Adam. In fact, Paul says "all ... fall short of the glory of God," a reference to the glory of

27. Carson, "Atonement in Romans 3:21–26," 121–23.

28. Carson, "Atonement in Romans 3:21–26," 125–27; see also Moisés Silva, "Faith versus Works of Law in Galatians," in *Justification and Variegated Nomism*, ed. D. A. Carson, Peter T. O'Brien, and Mark Seifrid (Grand Rapids: Baker Academic, 2004), 2:217–48; Charles Lee Irons, *The Righteousness of God*, WUNT (Tübingen: Mohr Siebeck, 2015), 280–89; contra N. T. Wright, "Romans and the Theology of Paul," in *Pauline Theology*, vol. 3, *Romans*, ed. David M. Hay and E. Elizabeth Johnson (Minneapolis: Fortress, 1995), 30–67, here 38–39. *Pace* Murray Smith, "God's Righteousness, Christ's Faith/fulness, and 'Justification by Faith Alone' (Romans 3:21–26)," in *Romans and the Legacy of St. Paul*, ed. Peter G. Bolt and James R. Harrison (Macquarie Park, NSW: SCD, 2019), 181–254, esp. 202; see also Irons, *Righteousness of God*, 61–83.

the image of God that he impressed on humans at their creation, an image now distorted and twisted by sin.[29] Two factors commend this interpretation. First, Paul says πάντες γὰρ ἥμαρτον ("for all have sinned"), which is virtually the same lexeme he employs when talking about the significance of Adam's sin, πάντες ἥμαρτον ("all ... sinned," Rom 5:12).[30] Second, when Paul writes that all have sinned and fall short τῆς δόξης τοῦ θεοῦ ("of the glory of God"), he has in view the image of God. When Paul speaks of δόξα ("glory"), he often has God's own glory in view but also at times speaks of the glory God gave to humans through his image: "And we all, with unveiled face, beholding the glory of the Lord, are being transformed into the same image from one degree of glory to another" (2 Cor 3:18). Note especially: "Man ... is the image and glory of God" (1 Cor 11:7).[31] Thus, Jesus remedies humanity's lack of glory because they have sullied the Adamic image of God through both Adam's sin and their own personal sins.[32] But as Paul elsewhere writes: "As was the man of dust, so also are those who are of the dust, and as is the man of heaven, so also are those who are of heaven. Just as we have borne the image of the man of dust, we shall also bear the image of the man of heaven" (1 Cor 15:48–49).

God remedies the sinful human condition by two means. First, Paul writes that "all who believe ... are justified by his grace as a gift, through the redemption that is in Christ Jesus" (Rom 3:22, 24). God sent his Son as a gift of his grace, and redemption, freedom from slavery to sin, comes through Jesus. God declares that sinners are in perfect conformity to the standard of the law because of the redemption through Jesus.[33] Second, Paul describes the redeeming work of Christ as "a propitiation by his blood, to be received by faith" (Rom 3:25). What is a ἱλαστήριον ("propitiation")? The short answer is, this

---

29. Dane Ortlund, "What Does It Mean to Fall Short of the Glory of God? Romans 3:23 in Biblical-Theological Perspective," *WTJ* 80 (2018): 121–40, here 124.

30. Ortlund, "What Does It Mean," 125.

31. Ortlund, "What Does It Mean, 129; see also Sigurd Grindheim, "A Theology of Glory: Paul's Use of *Doxa* Terminology in Romans," *Journal of Biblical Literature* 136, no. 2 (2017): 451–65.

32. Ortlund, "What Does It Mean," 130–31.

33. Carson, "Atonement in Romans 3:21–26," 128.

term originates in the Septuagint and the Day of Atonement, when God would appear in a cloud over the ark and the priest would pour sacrificial blood over the mercy seat, the ark's cover (Lev 16:2, 14). This is how Hebrews 9:5 uses the term when it describes the ark: "Above it were the cherubim of glory overshadowing the mercy seat." Paul therefore presents Jesus as the fulfillment of the mercy seat, the one through whom sinners can receive the forgiveness of sins.[34] God has done this wonderful work of redemption "to show his righteousness at the present time, so that he might be just and the justifier of the one who has faith in Jesus" (Rom 3:26).

## NEW HEART (SANCTIFICATION)

A SECOND COVENANT PROMISE IS that God will give his people a new heart. Ever since Adam and Eve ate the forbidden fruit, the dark cloud of sin has hung low over the world. Some of the saddest words written about human beings come to us from the preflood history: "The LORD saw that the wickedness of man was great in the earth, and that every intention of the thoughts of his heart was only evil continually" (Gen 6:5). Despite the flood judgment against humanity, water alone does not eradicate sin from the heart of sinful human beings. Even on the ark, the seed of the serpent was present and slithered back on the stage of redemptive history when the floodwaters resided. Ham sinned against Noah and polluted the sanctified creation once again (Gen 9:22). Just as God cursed the serpent for his role in the fall, so too Noah cursed Ham's son, Canaan, for his sin.[35] Echoing the Law, Psalms, and Prophets in their indictments against all people, both Jew and gentile, the apostle Paul famously writes:

> "None is righteous, no, not one;
> no one understands;
> no one seeks for God.

34. Carson, "Atonement in Romans 3:21–26," 129–30.

35. Meredith G. Kline, *Kingdom Prologue: Genesis Foundations for a Covenantal Worldview* (Eugene, OR: Wipf & Stock, 2006), 265–66; Kline, *God, Heaven, and Har Magedon: A Covenantal Tale of Cosmos and Telos* (Eugene, OR: Wipf & Stock, 2006), 95.

> All have turned aside; together they have become worthless;
> no one does good,
> not even one."
> "Their throat is an open grave;
> they use their tongues to deceive."
> "The venom of asps is under their lips."
> "Their mouth is full of curses and bitterness."
> "Their feet are swift to shed blood;
> in their paths are ruin and misery,
> and the way of peace they have not known."
> "There is no fear of God before their eyes." (Rom 3:10–18; see Ps 13:1, 3; Eccl 7:20; Deut 29:18; Pss 5:9; 140:3b; 10:7; Isa 59:7; Prov 1:16; Isa 59:7–8; Ps 36:1)[36]

God promised to bless his people covenantally, therefore, by declaring them righteous in in their justification. But their justification only addresses their legal standing vis-à-vis the law; this is where God's promise of a new heart, or sanctification, enters the picture.

God continually calls his people to be holy: "You shall be holy, for I the Lord your God am holy" (Lev 19:2). In the shift from the Mosaic to the new covenant, God still calls his people to holiness: "But as he who called you is holy, you also be holy in all your conduct, since it is written, 'You shall be holy, for I am holy'" (1 Pet 1:15–16). For Old and New Testament saints alike, being in covenant with God means belonging exclusively to him, and thus that covenantal relationship shapes our moral and ethical behavior.[37] The whole book of Leviticus is about the purity and sanctity of God's people as distinct from the surrounding gentile nations. The prohibition against wearing clothing of mixed fabrics is not a fashion statement but is about moral purity (Lev 19:19). But the only way that sinful humans can give up their corrupt and idolatrous ways is if God gives them a new heart. In the face of their stubbornness and hard-heartedness, Moses commanded Israel to circumcise the foreskins of their hearts (Deut 10:16), which was the divine call to renew their hearts. God knew they were incapable of doing

---

36. Beale and Carson, *Commentary on the New Testament Use*, 615–18.

37. Beale and Carson, *Commentary on the New Testament Use*, 1017–18.

this and therefore promised to do it for them: "And the LORD your God will circumcise your heart and the heart of your offspring, so that you will love the LORD your God with all your heart and with all your soul, that you may live" (Deut 30:6). While the language is slightly different, Moses presents the first promise of the prophet Jeremiah's new covenant.[38]

Jeremiah and Ezekiel pick up these Deuteronomic themes in their own prophecies. Like Moses calling on Israel to circumcise their hearts, Ezekiel preaches: "Cast away from you all the transgressions that you have committed, and make yourselves a new heart and a new spirit! Why will you die, O house of Israel?" (Ezek 18:31). Yet, like Deuteronomy 30:6, Ezekiel holds out the promise of God: "I will give you a new heart, and a new spirit I will put within you. And I will remove the heart of stone from your flesh and give you a heart of flesh. And I will put my Spirit within you, and cause you to walk in my statutes and be careful to obey my rules" (Ezek 36:26–27).[39] Likewise, Jeremiah calls Judah to repentance: "Circumcise yourselves to the LORD; remove the foreskin of your hearts, O men of Judah and inhabitants of Jerusalem" (Jer 4:4).[40] God meets Judah's inability with his miraculous ability and promises them a new heart: "For this is the covenant that I will make with the house of Israel after those days, declares the LORD: I will put my law within them, and I will write it on their hearts. And I will be their God, and they shall be my people" (Jer 31:33).

God will create holiness and sanctity within the hearts of his people by means of the Messiah's outpouring of the Spirit.[41] God will write his law on the hearts of his people, and given that the law plumbs the depths of our hearts in terms of whom we worship, respect, protect, and even what we desire, this means that God promises that his holiness will pervade the redeemed sinner's entire life. But Jeremiah also joins the promise of a new heart to concepts connected with the covenant of works. Jeremiah explains that God's promise of a new covenant and heart for his people will unfold in the "latter days" (30:24), which in Jeremiah 31:33 he writes of "after those days," that is, the latter days. In this context Jeremiah echoes the blessing

---

38. John Sailhamer, *The Pentateuch as Narrative: A Biblical-Theological Commentary* (Grand Rapids: Zondervan, 1992), 473.

39. Beale, *New Testament Biblical Theology*, 910.

40. Vos, *Biblical Theology*, 89–90.

41. Vos, *Biblical Theology*, 300.

of the covenant of works: "I will multiply them, and they shall not be few; I will make them honored, and they shall not be small" (Jer 30:19).[42] The New Testament picks up this thread in a number of different places, such as Romans 2:29, where Paul describes circumcision as being "a matter of the heart, by the Spirit, not by the letter," and says that believers are those who "have become obedient form the heart" (Rom 6:17). Here Paul is arguably echoing Jeremiah and Ezekiel, but the author of Hebrews becomes explicit as he quotes Jeremiah 31:31–34 (Heb 8:8–12; 10:16–17).

## Romans 8:1–27

PAUL CONTINUES TO EXPOUND THE significance of Christ's work in Romans 8:1–27, in which he presents at least four key insights. First, Paul once again invokes his eschatological adverb when he writes: "There is therefore *now* no condemnation for those who are in Christ Jesus" (Rom 8:1). We can gloss Paul's statement as, "There is therefore now justification for those who are in Christ Jesus." Jesus has fulfilled the law and suffered its curse on behalf of those who believe in him. "For God has done what the law, weakened by the flesh, could not do. By sending his own Sin in the likeness of sinful flesh and as a sin offering, he condemned sin in the flesh, in order that the righteous requirement of the law might be fulfilled in us, who walk not according to the flesh but according to the Spirit" (Rom 8:3–4, my trans.). Common explanations of these opening verses claim that Paul's point is that Jesus has freed sinners to fulfill the law through their obedience by his intercessory work.[43] But Paul does not have sanctification and the obedience of believers in view but rather realm transfer.

Those who are in Christ have been taken out from under the aegis of the first Adam and placed under the rule of the last Adam (see Rom 5:12–21). How has God accomplished this? Through Christ's fulfillment of the law and serving as a sin offering. Romans 8:3–4 is not, therefore, about what redeemed sinners might do but about what God has done

42. Beale, *New Testament Biblical Theology*, 106.

43. N. T. Wright, *Romans*, New Interpreter's Bible Commentary 10 (Nashville: Abingdon, 2002), 577–81.

in Christ. Christ entered into the sinful human condition, he came in the "likeness of sinful flesh ... in order that the righteous requirement of the law might be fulfilled in us" (Rom 8:3–4). In other words, God imputes Christ's representative suffering and obedience to believers. Some might object to this reading, however, because of Paul's concluding clause, "that ... the law might be fulfilled in us." There are two factors that mitigate against understanding Paul's statement as addressing the obedience of believers: (1) Paul uses an aorist passive subjunctive verb, πληρωθῇ ("might be fulfilled"), which indicates that this is not something that believers do but that has been done for them; and (2) given the strict demands of the law, how can a believer's imperfect obedience constitute a δικαίωμα τοῦ νόμου ("righteous requirement of the law")? Note how Paul elsewhere uses this term: "Therefore, as one trespass led to condemnation for all men, so one act of righteousness [δικαιώματος] leads to justification and life for all men" (Rom 5:18; see also Rom 1:32). Paul therefore speaks of what God has done in Christ and his work as the last Adam.[44]

Second, Christ's work unleashes the eschatological outpouring of the Spirit: "the Spirit is life because of righteousness" (Rom 8:10). When believers receive their justification from Christ by faith in him, it brings the whole range of redemptive blessings in its train.[45] In Christ believers receive the covenant promises and blessings of justification, adoption, sanctification, and glorification. As noted above, Paul characterizes Christ's outpouring of the Spirit as the means by which God adopts sinners as his sons, which means we are also heirs: "For you did not receive the spirit of slavery to fall back into fear, but you have received the Spirit of adoption as sons, by whom we cry, 'Abba! Father!' The Spirit himself bears witness with our spirit that we are children of God, and if children, then heirs—heirs of God and fellow heirs with Christ, provided we suffer with him in order that we may also be glorified with him" (Rom 8:15–17).

44. Turretin, *Institutes of Elenctic Theology* 16.3.19.

45. Herman Bavinck, *Reformed Dogmatics*, ed, John Bolt, trans. John Vriend (Grand Rapids: Baker Academic, 2003–2008), 4:249.

Third, the blessings of redemption in Christ and the dawn of the eschaton unfold in the middle of the present evil age. "There is therefore now no condemnation for those who are in Christ Jesus" (Rom 8:1), but at the same time the creation and believers "groan inwardly as we wait eagerly for adoption as sons, the redemption of our bodies" (Rom 8:23). The eschatological outpouring of the Spirit initiates our salvation through our effectual calling, the gift of faith, and our justification, which is "*now*," but we must in the present live by the Spirit and "put to death the deeds of the body" as "we wait eagerly for ... the redemption of our bodies," the resurrection of the dead (Rom 8:1, 13, 23). There are aspects of our salvation that are *already* (faith and justification, initiated sanctification, and adoption) and other aspects that are *not yet* (completed sanctification, resurrection—which Paul designates as our "adoption as sons," Rom 8:23—and glorification).

Fourth, as we eagerly await the redemption of our bodies, we are not alone. As Christ tells us, "And, lo, I am with you always, even unto the end of the world" (Matt 28:20 KJV). Christ is with us through the outpouring of the Spirit.[46] Here Paul characterizes the Spirit as the ἀπαρχὴ ("firstfruits"), which is a term from the Feast of the Firstfruits (Lev 23:1–2, 9–14 LXX), where Israel celebrated the harvest of their fields on the first day of the week by bringing the very best part of the harvest in sacrifice to God. The firstfruits were representative of what was ready to be harvested. Thus, we receive a dispensation of the Spirit that is but a foretaste of a greater outpouring of the Spirit that is yet to come at the consummation. In the meantime, as we seek to put to death the deeds of the flesh and eagerly await the redemption of our bodies, "the Spirit helps us in our weakness" by interceding "for us with groanings too deep for words" when we pray (Rom 8:26). The Spirit intercedes for us in our prayers so that we pray "according to the will of God" (Rom 8:27).

46. Douglas B. Farrow, *Ascension and Ecclesia: On the Significance of the Doctrine of Ascension* (Edinburgh: T&T Clark, 1999), 15–40.

## PROTECTION AND GLORIFICATION

God's promises of a new heart come within the context of the in-breaking new creation. This means that the redeemed people of God will shed their old Adamic natures and receive a new nature suited for the eschaton—God will re-create them through Christ and the Spirit in the image of the last Adam. God will eternally protect and heal his people. In the wake of the fall, God pronounced covenant sanctions on the serpent, the woman, and the man. For their part in the fall, God told Adam and Eve that the consequence of their rebellion was death: "By the sweat of your face you shall eat bread, till you return to the ground, for out of it you were taken; for you are dust, and to dust you shall return" (Gen 3:19). But when God clothed Adam and Eve in animal skins, they were exiled from God's presence with the hope of a return from exile—the seed of the woman was going to crush the head of the serpent (Gen 3:15). If dwelling in the presence of God means life, then living east of Eden means death. But the prospects of returning once again to dwelling in the presence of God meant restoration, healing, and glorification.

The Adamic return from exile finds its typological counterpart in Israel's promised return from exile. When Israel stood at the threshold of the promised land Moses prophesied of their coming apostasy and exile but also held out the prospect of restoration: "The Lord your God will restore your fortunes and have mercy on you, and he will gather you again from all the peoples where the Lord your God has scattered you" (Deut 30:3). Within the immediate context, Moses characterizes God's re-creation of Israel in terms of his power as the Great Physician: "'See now that I, even I, am he, and there is no god beside me; I kill and I make alive; I wound and I heal; and there is none that can deliver out of my hand" (Deut 32:39). Later Old Testament revelation portrays Israel's exile in terms of their death—they lie expelled from God's presence in an exilic graveyard—they are a pile of dry bones.[47] God instructed Ezekiel to prophesy to the dry bones and to raise them from the dead. But like Adam's lifeless body in the garden, Israel did not live until God to breathed life into Israel: "Prophesy to the breath; prophesy, son of man, and say to the breath, Thus says the Lord

47. Stephen G. Dempster, *Dominion and Dynasty: A Theology of the Hebrew Bible* (Downers Grove, IL: InterVarsity Press, 2003), 126, 153.

GOD: Come from the four winds, O breath, and breathe on these slain, that they may live" (Ezek 37:9; see Gen 2:7).[48] This resurrection from the dead and return to the land was not one more repetition of an endless cycle of apostasy and restoration, as unfolds in the book of Judges. Rather, the events of Ezekiel's prophecy constitute the inauguration of the eschaton—pivotal events of the dawning new creation.

Daniel has a series of visions where a heavenly messenger comes to Daniel to help him understand what is to happen to Israel "in the latter days" (Dan 10:14). Daniel 11–12 comprises the content of this eschatological revelation, which culminates in Israel's final historical tribulation and a subsequent resurrection from the dead of the righteous and wicked:

> At that time shall arise Michael, the great prince who has charge of your people. And there shall be a time of trouble, such as never has been since there was a nation till that time. But at that time your people shall be delivered, everyone whose name shall be found written in the book. And many of those who sleep in the dust of the earth shall awake, some to everlasting life, and some to shame and everlasting contempt. And those who are wise shall shine like the brightness of the sky above; and those who turn many to righteousness, like the stars forever and ever. (Dan 12:1–3)[49]

Like in Ezekiel's prophecy, God revealed to Daniel that he would reverse the Adamic curse and re-create those who had returned to the dust. The righteous would eternally shine like stars, language that evokes the promises of the Abrahamic covenant (Gen 15:5; 22:17; 26:4). The prophecies of Ezekiel and Daniel constitute covenantal promises of irrevocable, irreversible, and immutable healing and restoration.

As with all the other covenant promises, final healing and glorification come only through the work of the Messiah. When Job languished in stricken state, he nevertheless looked to a time when God would heal him: "If a man dies, shall he live again? All the days of my service I would wait, till my renewal should come" (Job 14:14). When Job later reflected on his renewal, he looked to the idea of resurrection: "For I know that my

---

48. Beale, *New Testament Biblical Theology*, 561.

49. Beale, *New Testament Biblical Theology*, 111.

Redeemer lives, and at the last he will stand upon the earth. And after my skin has been thus destroyed, yet in my flesh I shall see God, whom I shall see for myself, and my eyes shall behold, and not another" (Job 19:25–27). He knew that God himself would be the means of his resurrection and restoration, or glorification. There are two revelatory tracks on which the Old Testament places the resurrection of the Messiah as the means by which God resurrects the people of God. First, one of the overarching typological threads that runs from Genesis to Revelation is the story of God's sons. Adam is God's son, but he was unfaithful and did not love his heavenly Father (Luke 3:38). Israel was God's son, but he, too, was unfaithful and did not love his heavenly Father (Exod 4:22; Hos 11:1). When God revealed his only begotten Son, he declared out of the heavens, "This is my beloved Son, with whom I am well pleased" (Matt 3:17). In contrast to Israel's rebellious wandering in the wilderness for forty years as the Spirit led them, Jesus was faithful in the wilderness for forty days as he was led by the Spirit (Matt 4:1–11).[50] All of this means: Jesus is the Israel of God.[51] Thus, Ezekiel's prophecy of Israel's resurrection is, first and foremost, about the resurrection of Jesus.

Second, there are small but powerful statements about the Messiah's resurrection in the Old Testament. In Isaiah's fourth Servant Song, the prophet waxes eloquently about the Servant's suffering. The prophet speaks of the Messiah bringing the blessing of justification and imputation: "Out of the anguish of his soul he shall see and be satisfied; by his knowledge shall the righteous one, my servant, make many to be accounted righteous, and he shall bear their iniquities" (Isa 53:11). In the latter half of this verse the prophet clearly has justification and imputation in view when he writes of the servant as the righteous one making many "to be accounted righteous." In Isaiah 53:12 the prophet writes: "Because he poured out his soul to death and was numbered with the transgressors [καὶ ἐν τοῖς ἀνόμοις ἐλογίσθη]." The prophet again invokes imputation language, which is the same terminology that the apostle Paul employs in his discussions of justification and imputation (Rom 4:1–8). But the prophet also bundles the

50. On the Adam-Israel-Jesus connections, see Brandon D. Crowe, *Last Adam: A Theology of the Obedient Life of Jesus in the Gospels* (Grand Rapids: Baker Academic, 2017).

51. Beale, *New Testament Biblical Theology*, 406–22.

servant's resurrection together with justification and imputation: "Out of the anguish of his soul he shall see and be satisfied" (Isa 53:11). The imagery may at first seem vague, but Isaiah conveys that the servant was going to suffer death but would then be resurrected. The Septuagint clarifies this when it adds one interpretive word to Isaiah's text: ἀπὸ τοῦ πόνου τῆς ψυχῆς αὐτοῦ, δεῖξαι αὐτῷ φῶς ("out of the anguish of his soul, to show him light"). The Septuagint adds the word φῶς ("light"); "to see light" is a metaphor for life (Pss 36:9; 49:19; Job 3:16; 33:28–30).[52] No wonder, then, that we find these same themes in Romans 4—justification, imputation, and resurrection: "It will be counted to us who believe in him who raised from the dead Jesus our Lord, who was delivered up for our trespasses and raised for our justification" (Rom 4:24–25; see Isa 53:11–12 LXX).[53]

The revelatory threads of healing, restoration, and resurrection appear in Paul's succinct statement in Romans 8:29–30: "For those whom he foreknew he also predestined to be conformed to the image of his Son, in order that he might be the firstborn among many brothers. And those whom he predestined he also called, and those whom he called he also justified, and those whom he justified he also glorified." Several different covenantal strands unite in Paul's statement, such as Jesus as God's image and being firstborn among many brothers. When Paul calls Jesus the "firstborn," he refers to his resurrection, not a temporal ontological genesis. Both Paul and John call Jesus the "firstborn from the dead" (Col 1:18; Rev 1:5). Christ's resurrection brings the resurrection of many other image-bearers, many other sons, in its wake. Echoing Isaianic themes of justification and resurrection, Paul leaps from predestination, to calling, to justification, and lands on glorification. That Paul places glorification immediately after justification apart from any explanation of their exact relation means that justification results in the final resurrection and glorification of those united to Christ.[54]

---

52. Otfried Hofius, "The Fourth Servant Song in the New Testament Letters," in *The Suffering Servant: Isaiah 53 in Jewish and Christian Sources*, ed. Bernd Janowski and Peter Stuhlmacher (Grand Rapids: Eerdmans, 2004), 163–88, here 180–81.

53. Beale, *New Testament Biblical Theology*, 490–92.

54. Beale, *New Testament Biblical Theology*, 500–501.

## 1 John 1:5–2:2; 3:1–3

THE SAME THEMES OF BLESSING, sonship, righteousness, sanctification, and glorification appear in John's epistles. John opens with the testimony of the reality of the flesh-and-blood Messiah, whom he and the apostles all heard, saw with their eyes, and touched with their hands (1 John 1:1). However, there are two contextual elements that mark John's first epistle. First, he alludes to the creation themes of light and darkness to characterize the ministry and gospel of Christ (1 John 1:5). John employs the light-and darkness imagery to convey that the darkness of the old creation is passing away as the light of the new creation dawns (see Gen 1; Isa 60:1–3; John 1:1–10; 2 Cor 4:4–6; Eph 5:8–9, 13–14).[55] Second, the term "covenant" never appears in the Johannine epistles, but the idea is prominent throughout. John repeatedly writes of "abiding" (μένω), for example:

> Whoever says he abides in him ought to walk in the same way in which he walked. (1 John 2:6)
>
> If what you heard from the beginning abides in you, then you too will abide in the Son and in the Father. (1 John 2:24)
>
> Whoever keeps his commandments abides in God, and God in him. And by this we know that he abides in us, by the Spirit whom he has given us. (1 John 3:24)

JOHN USES THE TERM "ABIDE" twenty-six times throughout his epistles (1 John 2:6, 10, 14, 17, 24, 27, 28; 3:6, 9, 14–15, 17, 24; 4:12–13, 15–16; 2 John 2, 9). How does this term connect to covenant?

The term "abide" alludes to Old Testament covenant promises regarding God's indwelling and abiding presence. God promises Israel that he will put his Spirit in them and will cause them to walk in his statutes and keep his judgments: "You shall dwell in the land that I gave to your fathers, and you shall be my people, and I will be

55. Beale, *New Testament Biblical Theology*, 332.

your God" (Ezek 36:28). The prophet Isaiah characterizes the blessings of the covenant in terms of abiding in God: "Therefore the Lord waits to be gracious to you, and therefore he exalts himself to show mercy to you. For the Lord is a God of justice; blessed are all those who wait for him [οἱ ἐμμένοντες ἐν αὐτῷ]" (Isa 30:18 LXX). Conversely, the term is also reminiscent of curses for those who do not abide in the words of the law: "'Cursed be anyone who does not confirm [ἐμμενεῖ] the words of this law by doing them.' And all the people shall say, 'Amen'" (Deut 27:26 LXX).[56] Thus, John casts his reflections on the work of Christ in terms of new creation and covenant fulfillment.

Within this context, John exhorts his recipients to walk in the light of the new creation—to walk in the light of the Triune God that shines forth in the new creation, a reality that comes about through the "blood of Jesus," which "cleanses us from all sin" (1 John 1:7). Jesus the Righteous One has wrought this redemptive work, that is, Jesus, has fulfilled the law and paid the penalty for its fracture. Jesus is both the Righteous One and "the propitiation for our sins," not just the sins of Jews but of gentiles as well, "the sins of the whole world" (1 John 2:2).[57] John deals in global terms given that he writes in the tones of old versus new creation. Christ redeems in global, Adamic terms—people from every tribe, tongue, and nation (Rev 14:6). At the same time, John also recognizes the already-but-not-yet-nature of our redemption when he casts redemption in terms of adoption and sonship: "See what kind of love the Father has given us, that we should be called children of God; and so we are" (1 John 3:1). John looks at the present eschatological status of God's people by virtue of their union with Christ—we are God's children *now*. But John also draws attention to the not-yet of our salvation: "Beloved, we are God's children now, and what we will be has not yet appeared; but we know that when he appears we shall be like him, because we shall see him as he is" (1 John 3:2). John plays the same Christ-hymn as Paul, but

56. Edward Malatesta, *Interiority and Covenant: A Study of* εἶναι ἐν *and* μένειν *In the First Letter of Saint John* (Rome: Biblical Institute Press, 1978), 58–64; Sherri Brown, *Gift upon Gift: Covenant through Word in the Gospel of John* (Eugene, OR: Pickwick, 2010), 3.

57. J. Ramsey Michaels, "Atonement in John's Gospel and Epistles," in Hill and James, *Glory of the Atonement*, 106–18, here 116–17.

does so in a different key. We are God's children *now*, just as there is *now* no condemnation for those in Christ Jesus (Rom 8:1). "What we will be has not yet appeared," just as we "wait eagerly for adoption as sons, the redemption of our bodies" (Rom 8:23). Christ will "transform our lowly body to be like his glorious body" (Phil 3:21), just as when Christ "appears we shall be like him, because we shall see him as he is" (1 John 3:2).

## CONCLUSION

COVENANT PROVIDES THE CONTEXT FOR all of the blessings that come to God's people—his indwelling presence as well as the numerous benefits of redemption: sonship and inheritance, righteousness and forgiveness (justification), a new heart (sanctification), and protection (glorification). The ever-familiar words of the Twenty-Third Psalm capture these blessings: "Surely goodness and mercy shall pursue me all the days of my life, and I shall dwell in the house of the LORD forever" (Ps 23:6, my trans.). God relentlessly loves and pursues us until we dwell eternally in his presence fully conformed to the image of his Son. Oh "that I may dwell in the house of the LORD all the days of my life, to gaze upon the beauty of the LORD" (Ps 27:4).

## FURTHER READING

Crowe, Brandon D. *Last Adam: A Theology of the Obedient Life of Jesus in the Gospels*. Grand Rapids: Baker Academic, 2017. An excellent treatment of the idea that Jesus is the last Adam and how his obedience addresses the disobedience of the first Adam.

Dempster, Stephen G. *Dominion and Dynasty: A Theology of the Hebrew Bible*. Downers Grove, IL: InterVarsity Press, 2003. An important study that demonstrates the narrative structure of the Hebrew order of the Old Testament canon.

Vos, Geerhardus. "The Doctrine of the Covenant in Reformed Theology." In *Redemptive History and Biblical Interpretation: The Shorter Writings of Geerhardus Vos*, edited by Richard B. Gaffin Jr., 234–67. Phillipsburg: NJ, Presbyterian and Reformed, 1980. A helpful essay that surveys the history of the doctrine of the covenant in the early modern Reformed tradition, specifically in the sixteenth and seventeenth centuries.

III

# COVENANT LIFE

## HOLINESS, WISDOM, AND WITNESS

God redeemed Israel out of Egypt and called them to a life of holiness as they dwelled in his presence. They left the furnace of Egypt for the land flowing with milk and honey. The blueprint for Israel's sanctity lay in God's covenant law—a code that called them to live lives marked by faith, hope, and love. But God did not call them to produce these virtues under their own steam but to find their source in his covenant promises and to use his law as a guide to show them their need for repentance. In reliance on his promises to save them through the seed of the woman, he called Israel to love, to worship him, and to manifest his wisdom. They were not, however, supposed to keep the light of God's love for themselves but carry the message of salvation to the nations. This chapter therefore examines the nature of covenant life by surveying the three theological virtues of faith, hope, and love across the canvas of redemptive history. It then looks at the nature of repentance and how God expected Israel to be faithful and obedient to his law. The chapter then explores the worship and prayer life to which God called his people. But what if God's law did not address specific circumstances? The chapter consequently examines the wisdom to which God called Israel. Finally, the chapter examines Israel's mission of witness to the world. This chapter observes the trajectory and path of covenant life, noting that Israel was not the final stage of God's plan of redemption; rather, covenant life ultimately culminates in Christ and new covenant.

## FAITH, HOPE, AND LOVE

God covenanted with Israel and called them to a life of holiness, a vocation codified in the book of Deuteronomy, which has been called Israel's covenantal charter—their Magna Carta.[1] God gave Israel his laws with the aim of ordering their lives to reflect his holiness and righteousness, lives marked by faith, hope, and love. This triad of virtues famously appears in the apostle Paul's poetic reflection on love: "So now faith, hope, and love abide, these three; but the greatest of these is love" (1 Cor 13:13). The apostle did not invent these virtues de novo but mined them from the Old Testament. From the earliest pages of Holy Writ, the Old Testament underscores that faith in the covenantal promises of God is supposed to mark the people of God. God delivered Abraham, the great patriarch of Israel, from Ur of the Chaldees and entered a covenant relationship with him. He promised to make him a great nation, to bless him, and bless all the families of the earth through him (Gen 12:1–2). God made these promises, and the Scriptures quietly remark: "So Abram went, as the Lord had told him" (Gen 12:4). Abraham responded in faith—he trusted in the word of God. What lay implicit in Abraham's initial response to God's call becomes explicit in the subsequent narrative, when he looks on the withered bodies of himself and Sarah, beholds his heirless state, and asks God whether one of his servants will be his heir (Gen 15:2). God promises him again: "Your very own son shall be your heir" (Gen 15:4). God shows him the stars of the heavens and challenges Abraham to number them: "So shall your offspring be" (Gen 15:5). Abraham responds to this promise: "And he believed the Lord, and he counted it to him as righteousness" (Gen 15:6).

Genesis 15:6 is, of course, a *sedes doctrinae* ("seat of doctrine") for the doctrine of justification. The apostle Paul appeals to this verse in his explanation of justification in both Galatians and Romans (Gal 3:10–14; Rom 4:1–8). God declares us righteous before the divine bar through faith alone in

---

1. E.g., Scott Hahn, *Kinship by Covenant: A Canonical Approach to the Fulfillment of God's Saving Promises* (New Haven: Yale University Press, 2009), 71; for the significance of Deuteronomy on the overall structure of the OT canon, see Meredith G. Kline, *The Structure of Biblical Authority* (Eugene, OR: Wipf & Stock, 1997).

Christ alone by God's grace alone. As crucial as this verse is for the doctrine of justification, it also underscores that faith is a way of life for those who are covenanted with the God of Israel. God justifies sinners by faith alone, and those same justified sinners then continue to live by faith in the gospel promises of God. Later Old Testament revelation confirms this connection when the prophet Habakkuk echoes Genesis 15:6 in his own prophecy: "Behold, his soul is puffed up; it is not upright within him, but the righteous shall live by his faith" (Hab 2:4).[2] In Habakkuk's own context, the prophet looked on the impending Babylonian invasion with horror: "You who are of purer eyes than to see evil and cannot look at wrong, why do you idly look at traitors and remain silent when the wicked swallows up the man more righteous than he?" (Hab 1:13). How could God sweep away the wicked and the righteous, and by the lawless hands of gentile pagans, no less? The prophet looks on Israel and beholds an apparent covenantal sterility, very much like Abraham and Sarah's withered bodies and childless state.

As he looked on the prospects of invasion and exile, Habakkuk invoked the necessity of a God-ward Abrahamic faith: "The righteous shall live by his faith" (Hab 2:4). In the face of trial and uncertainty, the person who trusted in Christ for his salvation was at the same time one who lived by faith in God's promises: "Though the fig tree should not blossom, nor fruit be on the vines, the produce of the olive fail and the fields yield no food, the flock be cut off from the fold and there be no herd in the stalls, yet I will rejoice in the LORD; I will take joy in the God of my salvation" (Hab 3:17–18). Habakkuk's understanding of faith anticipates Paul's similar statements: "I have learned in whatever situation I am to be content. I know how to be brought low, and I know how to abound. In any and every circumstance, I have learned the secret of facing plenty and hunger, abundance and need. I can do all things through him who strengthens me" (Phil 4:11–13). Life in the covenant is one lived by faith in the promises of God, a point the author of Hebrews emphatically makes in his famous great "hall of faith" when he lists Abel, Enoch, Noah, Abraham, Sarah, Jacob, Moses, Israel, Rahab, Gideon, Barak, Samson, Jephthah, David, Samuel, the prophets, and many others as those who lived by faith (Heb 11).

---

2. O. Palmer Robertson, *The Books of Nahum, Habakkuk, and Zephaniah*, NICOT (Grand Rapids: Eerdmans, 1990), 178–79.

The second great covenantal virtue is hope, a characteristic that goes hand in hand with faith. That God made many promises to his people meant that they had to hold on to his word and look forward to the fulfillment of those promises. The author of Hebrews gives classic expression to this truth when he writes: "Now faith is the assurance of things hoped for, the conviction of things not seen" (Heb 11:1). Faith looks to and hopes in the promises of God, especially in the face of adversity and trial. The Old Testament wisdom literature is replete with calls for the faithful to find their hope in the God of Israel. Job cries out, "O that I might have my request, and that God would fulfill my hope" (Job 6:8). The psalmist likewise avers: "Behold, the eye of the Lord is upon us, even as we hope in you" (Ps 33:22). In times of suffering, the psalmist repeatedly asks, "Why are you cast down, O my soul, and why are you in turmoil within me? Hope in God; for I shall again praise him, my salvation" (Pss 42:5, 11; 43:5). The psalmist casts his hope on God (Ps 71:14), his rules (Ps 119:43), word (Ps 119:74), salvation (Ps 119:81), and promises (Ps 119:116). Throughout the Christian life, God leads his people through trial and tribulation to produce the virtue of hope. As Paul writes: "We rejoice in hope of the glory of God. Not only that, but we rejoice in our sufferings, knowing that suffering produces endurance, and endurance produces character, and character produces hope, and hope does not put us to shame, because God's love has been poured into our hearts through the Holy Spirit who has been given to us" (Rom 5:2–5).

But Israel's was not a generic virtue focused on God but on his promises, and the chief promise and hope of Israel was the anointed, the Messiah. The pinnacle of Old Testament revelation comes in the advent of Christ. The entire Old Testament economy looked forward to the revelation of a "better hope ... through which we draw near to God" (Heb 7:19). The apostle Peter writes: "Blessed be the God and Father of our Lord Jesus Christ! According to his great mercy, he has caused us to be born again to a living hope through the resurrection of Jesus Christ from the dead" (1 Pet 1:3). But even though the people of God found the goal and source of their hope in the revelation of Christ, this does not mean that their need for hope evaporated with the dawn of the light of the Son. As the people of God continue to pilgrim in this present evil age, they look with hope at the horizon in anticipation of the second advent of Christ: "Therefore, preparing your minds for action, and being sober-minded, set your hope fully on the grace that will be brough to you at the revelation of Jesus Christ" (1 Pet 1:13). Moreover, as we live in the midst of the sin-darkened world, we must always be prepared to "make a defense to anyone who asks you for a reason for the hope that is in you" (1 Pet 3:15).

Love is the third of the trinity of virtues and is the one characteristic from which all of the other virtues flow. If God is love (1 John 4:8), and he has made humans in his image, it stands to reason that image-bearers are supposed to be marked, above all else, by love. Love therefore stands at the heart of Israel's covenantal charter: "Hear, O Israel: The Lord our God, the Lord is one. You shall love the Lord your God with all your heart and with all your soul and with all your might" (Deut 6:4–5). First and foremost, Israel was supposed to love God—their faithful covenant Lord, redeemer, and sustainer. When Moses asked to see God, the Lord passed before him and proclaimed: "The Lord, the Lord, a God merciful and gracious, slow to anger, and abounding in steadfast love and faithfulness" (Exod 34:6). God's covenant was the place of his "steadfast love" (חסד), or covenant faithfulness.[3] Love abounds within the Godhead among Father, Son, and Holy Spirit and overflows to his covenant people, and in turn God's people are supposed to love him. The chief manifestation of love toward God is not merely an affection or feeling but concrete action, namely, obedience.[4] More will be said about obedience below.

As God poured out his love on his people, they were supposed to love him and one another: "You shall love your neighbor as yourself: I am the Lord" (Lev 19:18). Love flowed in vertical (reciprocally between God and humans) and horizontal (communally among humans) directions within his covenant. God's covenant was a realm of love, even for those gentiles who lived in Israel's midst: "You shall treat the stranger who sojourns with you as the native among you, and you shall love him as yourself, for you were strangers in the land of Egypt: I am the Lord your God" (Lev 19:34). As Israel received God's love when he delivered them from bondage in

3. Nelson Glueck, *Hesed in the Bible* (New York: Ktav, 1975), 35–37, 39, 51–52, 86–87; Gordon R. Clark, *The Word Hesed in the Hebrew Bible* (Sheffield: JSOT Press, 1993), 259–61, 267–68; Katherine Doob Sakenfeld, *The Meaning of Hesed in the Hebrew Bible* (Missoula, MT: Scholars Press, 1978), 233–39.

4. William L. Moran, "The Ancient Near Eastern Background of the Love of God in Deuteronomy," *Catholic Biblical Quarterly* 25, no. 1 (1963): 77–87, esp. 78.

Egypt, so Israel was supposed to demonstrate love to the gentiles in their midst. But this love was exclusive to Israel and the covenant, because outside the covenant God instructed Israel to take a martial stance toward the surrounding nations. Israel was God's instrument of judgment against the Canaanites, Hittites, Amorites, Perizzites, Hivites, and Jebusites (Exod 3:17). With the advent of Christ, the new covenant, and a redemptive scope that extended throughout the earth, the command to love one's neighbor was no longer restricted to the promised land but was to reach to the ends of the earth. Jesus expanded the scope of God's covenant love when he received the question from a lawyer, "Who is my neighbor?" (Luke 10:29). Jesus responded with the parable of the good Samaritan.

In his parable Jesus speaks of a man who was traveling from Jerusalem to Jericho and fell among robbers, who stripped, beat, and left him for dead.[5] A priest came upon him and passed by on the other side. A Levite also found and passed him by. But a Samaritan, a despised class of individual because of his mixed Israelite and Assyrian descent (John 4:9), saw and had compassion on the assaulted man. He bound his wounds, cared for him, and found him shelter. Jesus asks his interlocutor, "Which of these three, do you think, proved to be a neighbor to the man who fell among the robbers?" (Luke 10:36). The lawyer responds, "The one who showed him mercy." And so Jesus responds, "You go, and do likewise" (Luke 10:37). St. Augustine (354–430) explains,

> It is clear that we should understand by our neighbor the person to whom an act of compassion is due if he needs it or would be due if he needed it. It follows from this that a person from whom an act of compassion is due to us in our turn is also our neighbor. For the word "neighbor" implies a relationship: one can only be a neighbor to a neighbor. Who can fail to see that there is no exception to this, nobody to whom compassion is not due?[6]

We must love everyone, including our enemies: "Love your enemies and pray for those who persecute you, so that you may be sons of your Father who is in heaven" (Matt 5:44–45). The apostle Paul echoes Christ's teaching

---

5. Snodgrass, *Stories with Intent*, 338–62, esp. 348–50, 357–59.

6. Augustine, *On Christian Teaching*, trans. R. P. H. Green (Oxford: Oxford University Press, 1997), 1.30.31 (p. 23).

when he quotes the sixth, seventh, ninth, and tenth commandments, sums up the law by quoting Leviticus 19:18, "You shall love your neighbor as yourself" (Rom 13:9), and then comments: "Love does no wrong to a neighbor; therefore love is the fulfilling of the law" (Rom 13:10). Augustine therefore concludes, "All people must be reckoned as neighbors, because evil must not be done to anyone."[7] Alternatively stated, the seed of love grows in the covenantal soil of Israel and expands throughout the whole earth in the new covenant. Christ commands his people to love everyone.

## Galatians 5:16–26

FAITH, HOPE, AND LOVE ARE marks of covenant life, and the source of these virtues is Christ's outpouring of the Spirit on the church.[8] The Spirit's work in the life of the church was first typified in the garden-temple of Eden, as Adam and Eve were in a temple environment that was full of fruit-bearing trees created by the Father by the Son and through the Spirit. Old Testament passages hint at the Spirit's work when the psalmist, for example, likens the righteous man to a fruit-bearing tree that both produces fruit in season and does not wither (Ps 1:3). "The righteous flourish like the palm tree" (Ps 92:12), and godly men will have wives who are like fruitful vines and children like olive shoots (Ps 128:3). This fruit imagery feeds into prophecies about the Messiah: "There shall come forth a shoot from the stump of Jesse, and a branch from his roots shall bear fruit" (Isa 11:1). Through the seed of David, "in days to come Jacob shall take root, Israel shall blossom and put forth shoots and fill the whole world with fruit" (Isa 27:6). God also promised to make Israel fruitful through the work of the Spirit:

> For the palace is forsaken,
> the populous city deserted;
> the hill and the watchtower
> will become dens forever,

7. Augustine, *On Christian Teaching* 1.30.31–33 (p. 23).

8. G. K. Beale, "The Old Testament Background of Paul's Reference to the 'Fruit of the Spirit' in Galatians 5:22," *BBR* 15 (2005): 1–38.

> a joy of wild donkeys,
> a pasture of flocks;
> until the Spirit is poured upon us from on high,
> and the wilderness becomes a fruitful field,
> and the fruitful field is deemed a forest.
> Then justice will dwell in the wilderness,
> and righteousness abide in the fruitful field.
> And the effect of righteousness will be peace,
> and the result of righteousness, quietness and trust forever.
> (Isa 32:14–17; see also 44:2–4)

God pledged to anoint his Son with the Holy Spirit, and the Son was tasked with pouring out the Spirit on the people of God. The outpouring of the Spirit promised to produce the fruit of righteousness and peace. The prophet elsewhere writes of these same blessings through Christ and the Spirit: "Shower, O heavens, from above, and let the clouds rain down righteousness; let the earth open, that salvation and righteousness may bear fruit; let the earth cause them both to sprout; I the Lord have created it" (Isa 45:8). Through the outpouring of the Spirit, God returns Israel to Eden: "For the Lord comforts Zion; he comforts all her waste places and makes her wilderness like Eden, her desert like the garden of the Lord; joy and gladness will be found in her, thanksgiving and the voice of song" (Isa 51:3).

These Old Testament prophecies constitute the foundation for Paul's exposition of the fruit of the Spirit. Paul contrasts the fruit of the Spirit with the works of the flesh: sexual immorality, impurity, sensuality, idolatry, sorcery, enmity, strife, jealousy, fits of anger, rivalries, dissensions, divisions, envy, drunkenness, and orgies constitute the mores of Adam's fallen kingdom, the ethics of the "present evil age" (Gal 1:4). When Christ poured out the Spirit at Pentecost, it was to both eschatological and soteriological ends. The outpouring of the Spirit was an event prophesied in the Old Testament, and Peter confirms this when he quotes Joel 2:32, "And in the last days it shall be, God declares, that I will pour out my Spirit on all flesh" (Acts 2:17).[9]

9. Beale and Carson, *Commentary on the New Testament Use*, 533–34.

Christ's outpouring of the Spirit signaled that the last days had begun and the age to come had dawned with the ministry of Christ (see 1 Cor 10:11; Eph 1:21). In this vein, the Spirit is the power of the age to come (Heb 6:5).

The outpouring of the Spirit is both an eschatological and soteriological phenomenon; stated alternatively, the salvation of God's people is an eschatological event. Christ's outpouring of the Spirit therefore soteriologically transforms the redeemed. In contrast to those who walk according to the flesh and produce sinful works, the long-promised fruit of the Spirit marks the bride of Christ: love, joy, peace, patience, kindness, goodness, faithfulness, gentleness, and self-control (Gal 5:22–23). The redeemed manifest the ethics of the new creation in the midst of the old creation, which is passing away. In action, the redeemed follow Christ's teaching on the Sermon on the Mount (Matt 5–7), the ethical charter of the new covenant, a charter that rests on the foundation of the Old Testament and the Decalogue.

God planted the seeds of faith, hope, and love through his gospel promises to Israel. God revealed himself to Israel and dwelled in their midst as the sole object of their faith, but with the definitive revelation of God in Christ, the object of their faith was more fully revealed. In the words of Hebrews, "God spoke to our fathers by the prophets, but in these last days he has spoken to us by his Son" (Heb 1:1–2). Or in the words of Christ, "Whoever has seen me has seen the Father" (John 14:9). Correlatively, the psalmist repeatedly preaches to his own heart to hope in God (e.g., Pss 42:5, 11; 43:5; 62:5; 69:6; 78:7; 146:5). With the advent of Christ, God has unfurled hope through Christ and the Spirit (Rom 5:5). Scripture tells us that "God is love" (1 John 4:16), and Israel knew of his love both by his gracious presence and through the giving of the law, the means by which God called his people to love him (Deut 6:4–6), but in the New Testament Paul tells us, "God shows his love for us in that while we were still sinners, Christ died for us" (Rom 5:8). Christ embodies our object of faith, the anchor of our hopes, and the pinnacle of God's love for his people.

## REPENTANCE

God calls his people to faith, hope, and love, but stepping onto this threefold path of virtue requires beginning with repentance—turning from one's own sin. Ezekiel describes what repentance looks like and its effect: "But if a wicked person turns away from all his sins that he has committed and keeps all my statutes and does what is just and right, he shall surely live; he shall not die. None of the transgressions that he has committed shall be remembered against him; for the righteousness that he has done he shall live" (Ezek 18:21–22). Here Ezekiel uses a common Old Testament word for the concept of repentance, שׁוּב, or literally "turning away." If a sinner walks toward the west, then repentance (or turning) means that the sinner does a 180-degree turn toward the east.

There are several things we should note about repentance. First, repentance is a universal need for every human being. On the heels of the fall God saw "that every intention of the thoughts of [man's] heart was only evil continually" (Gen 6:5). Even after God judged the world and began with a new creation and new Adam in Noah and his family, sin still reared its ugly head. This means that, in order to enter into a covenantal relationship with God, people must repent of their sin. God is holy, and sin is an impediment to covenantal fellowship with him. In one sense, the entire sacrificial system of Israel represents a call to repentance. In his catena of Old Testament quotations, the apostle Paul levels a universal indictment against all humans: "None is righteous, no, not one; no one understands; no one seeks for God. All have turned aside; together they have become worthless; no one does good, not even one" (Rom 3:10–12; see also vv. 13–18; Pss 14:1–3; 53:1–3; Eccl 7:20; Deut 29:18; Pss 5:9; 140:3; 10:7; Prov 1:16; Isa 59:7–8; Ps 36:1).[10]

Second, sinful human beings are incapable of repenting under their own moral steam. As the previous chapter explained, God spoke to Israel through Moses and called them to repent of their sin: "Circumcise therefore the foreskin of your heart, and be no longer stubborn" (Deut 10:16). Israel was incapable of circumcising their hearts, and thus exile from the land was an inevitability. God promised to gather them from the nations and circumcise their hearts. Through this divine act of mercy, God would

10. Beale and Carson, *Commentary on the New Testament Use*, 614–18.

enable his people to love him with all of their heart and soul (Deut 30:6). God continually called through the prophets for Israel to repent of her sin: "Repent and turn away from your idols, and turn away your faces from all your abominations" (Ezek 14:6). But they refused to repent (Jer 5:3). God reiterated his promise to give his people the ability to repent in the promise of the new covenant: "For this is the covenant that I will make with the house of Israel after those days, declares the Lord: I will put my law within them, and I will write it on their hearts" (Jer 31:33). Concerning the new covenant, the prophet Ezekiel writes: "I will give you a new heart, and a new spirit I will put within you. And I will remove the heart of stone from your flesh and give you a heart of flesh. And I will put my Spirit within you, and cause you to walk in my statutes and be careful to obey my rules" (Ezek 36:26–27). God through his Spirit enables the people of God to turn away from sin and walk in obedience. With the advent of Christ and the dawn of the new covenant, Jesus continued the call for Israel's repentance with his well-known cry, "Repent, for the kingdom of heaven is at hand" (Matt 4:17). But Israel persisted in her impenitence, a hard-heartedness that culminated in the crucifixion of Christ. Jesus predicted their lack of repentance when he contrasted the first-century wicked generation to the people of Nineveh, who "repented at the preaching of Jonah" (Luke 11:32). Christ's message of repentance, however, was not solely for Israel but the whole world. When Paul addressed the philosophers at Mars Hill he told them, "The times of ignorance God overlooked, but now he commands all people everywhere to repent" (Acts 17:30).

Third, if repentance is something only God grants by his grace by circumcising the sinner's heart, or removing the heart of stone and replacing it with a heart of flesh through the work of the Spirit, then repentance is not a cause of salvation but one of the firstfruits and evidences of a person's saved state. As the Westminster Shorter Catechism states, "Repentance unto life is a saving grace, whereby a sinner, out of a true sense of his sin, and apprehension of the mercy of God in Christ, doth, with grief and hatred of his sin, turn from it unto God, with full purpose of, and endeavor after, new obedience" (q. 87).

Repentance is a phenomenon that stretches across the canon of Scripture. Adam repented when he renamed the woman "Eve," an action that revealed that he believed in God's promise to crush the head of the serpent through the seed of the woman, as she would be "the mother of all living" (Gen 3:20). David's repentance on the heels of his sin against Bathsheba and Uriah the Hittite captures the grieving and mourning that marks one whom the Spirit has convicted: "Against you, you only, have I sinned and done what is evil in your sight" (Ps 51:4). And Peter's great shame at recognizing his sin animated his repentance: "Depart from me, for I am a sinful man, O Lord" (Luke 5:8). Yet, even though the saints have repented from their sin from the first until the last sin, believers in the New Testament have both a clearer testimony of God's law through the Scriptures and greater dispensation of the Spirit, who convicts of sin. Moreover, in the Old Testament the Spirit's activity largely centered on the tabernacle (and later the temple), and one might be exiled from the camp for sin, thus David's fear: "Cast me not away from your presence, and take not your Holy Spirit from me" (Ps 51:11). In the New Testament, however, the presence of God through the Spirit is not in a building such as the temple but rather in the hearts of believers (John 14:17; Rom 8:9; 1 Cor 3:16; Eph 2:22; 2 Tim 1:14). Thus for New Testament believers, there is no sense in which God will take his Spirit from the believer. This is not to say that believers may sin with reckless abandon, as Christians can "fall under God's fatherly displeasure, and not have the light of his countenance restored unto them, until they humble themselves, confess their sins, beg pardon, and renew their faith and repentance" (WCF 11.5).

### Ephesians 4:17–24

This passage showcases both the eschatological and soteriological. Paul calls on the Ephesians to walk in a manner befitting their union with Christ—not to walk with darkened understanding, alienated from the life of God (Eph 4:17–18). Rather, Paul writes: "Put off your old man, which belongs to your former manner of life and is corrupt through deceitful desires, and to be renewed in the spirit of your minds, and to put on the new man, created after the likeness of God in true righteousness and holiness" (Eph 4:22–24, my trans.). The key to understanding Paul's paraenesis is to remember that his ethical imperatives in Ephesians 4–6 rest on the theological indicatives of Ephesians 1–3. Paul's call to put off the old and put on the new man is not a summons to muster one's ethical might but to seek ethical change through Jesus, the last Adam. To put off one's old man is to turn away from one's existence in Adam and to look by faith to the last Adam, Jesus. Only seeking transformation by Christ through the Spirit brings conformity to his holy and righteous image, an image adorned by the fruit of the Spirit.[11]

## FAITHFULNESS AND OBEDIENCE

The virtues of faith, hope, and love mark the repentant life, entailing that the saved person lives a life of covenant faithfulness and obedience. Once again, covenant faithfulness originates in God, first objectively and second subjectively. Objectively, God displays his steadfast love (חסד) by his covenant promises; he manifests his faithfulness (אמת) to his covenant promises. When Abraham sent his servant to find a wife for Isaac, his servant prayed to God: "Blessed be the Lord, the God of my master Abraham, who has not forsaken his steadfast love and his faithfulness [חסדו ואמתו] toward my master" (Gen 24:27). These are the same attributes that God proclaimed to Moses as he sheltered in the cleft of the rock and beheld the glory of God (Exod 34:6), and to David (1 Kgs 3:6), and they comprise the continual refrain of the psalmist in his praise of God (Pss 25:10; 26:3; 36:5; 40:10–11; 57:10; 61:7, 13; 85:10, 15; 88:11; 92:2; 100:5; 108:4; 115:1; 138:2). The psalmist repeatedly invokes these attributes to describe God's actions in his covenant with David (Ps 89:1–2, 14, 33, 49).

If God objectively exhibits these attributes, then his image-bearers were created to do the same. In a sin-fallen world, the prophets excoriated Israel for their lack of faithfulness and love: "There is no faithfulness or steadfast love, and no knowledge of God in the land" (Hos 4:1). Thus, faithful kings and prophets exhorted Israel to adorn themselves with these godly virtues: "Let not steadfast love and faithfulness forsake you; bind them around your neck; write them on the tablet of your heart" (Prov 3:3). As image-bearers, the confederated people of God were supposed to manifest

11. S. M. Baugh, *Ephesians*, Evangelical Exegetical Commentary (Bellingham, WA: Lexham Press, 2016), 354–79, esp. 369–77.

steadfast love toward both God and their fellow human beings. In the wake of the demise of Saul's house, David asked whether there was anyone in Saul's line to whom he could show "the steadfast love [חסד] of God" (2 Sam 9:3, my trans.). As God showed his steadfast love to him, David pivoted to his fellow human beings to show them steadfast love. The chief recipient, however, of steadfast love and ultimately obedience was supposed to be God. God rebuked Israel: "For I desire steadfast love and not sacrifice, the knowledge of God rather than burnt offerings" (Hos 6:6). In the context of Hosea's prophecy, "knowledge" (דעת) is a metonym for "obedience," evident in the following statement: "My people are destroyed for lack of knowledge; because you have rejected knowledge, I reject you from being a priest to me. And since you have forgotten the law of your God, I also will forget your children" (Hos 4:6). Hosea places "knowledge" in parallel with God's law, as the law is the embodiment of knowledge and truth (Rom 2:20). Forgetting God's law is to disobey it. For the covenant people, steadfast love and obedience are supposed to go hand in hand.[12]

God intended that, chief among his people, the king of Israel would embody all these virtues: "Steadfast love and faithfulness preserve the king, and by steadfast love his throne is upheld" (Prov 20:28). Yet, with a few outliers, Israel's history well attests to the decadence, disobedience, and disloyalty of her kings to God. God therefore sent a king to remedy Israel's royal failings: "Then a throne will be established in steadfast love, and on it will sit faithfulness in the tent of David one who judges and seeks justice and is swift to do righteousness" (Isa 16:5). In this promise, God manifested his own faithfulness to Jacob and steadfast love to Abraham, his sworn covenant promises to the patriarchs (Mic 7:20).

The New Testament fulfillment of steadfast love (חסד) and faithfulness (אמת) is revealed mostly clearly in the Son of God. When God promised to redeem Israel, he told them: "And I will betroth you to me forever. I will betroth you to me in righteousness and in justice, in steadfast love [חסד] and in mercy. I will betroth you to me in faithfulness [באמונה]. And you shall know the Lord" (Hos 2:19–20). Here אמונה is a cognate term for אמת and can also be translated "truth." We find this cluster of terms surrounding

12. Willem A. VanGemeren, *Interpreting the Prophetic Word: An Introduction to the Prophetic Literature of the Old Testament* (Grand Rapids: Zondervan, 1990), 111.

John's description of the incarnation: "And the Word became flesh and tabernacled among us, and we have seen his glory, glory as of the only begotten of the Father, full of grace and truth [χάριτος καὶ ἀληθείας]" (John 1:14, my trans.). For John χάριτος ("grace") and ἀλήθεια ("truth") are the New Testament counterparts to חסד ("steadfast love") and אמת ("faithfulness").[13] God in the person of his Son stepped on to the stage of redemptive history to give his people the steadfast love and faithfulness they failed to render under God. The incarnation was at the same time a manifestation of his steadfast love and faithfulness to his people, and the representative obedience and love that the people of God failed to give to God. The only way that God's people can embody steadfast love, faithfulness, and obedience is through the redemptive work of the Messiah.

If we raise the issue of obedience and steadfast love, the question naturally arises, What is the standard by which God determines obedience? The answer is God's law. One of the common pairings in Scripture is covenant and law. God administers his laws, rules, statutes, and decrees within the context of his covenants. In the big picture, God made a covenant with Israel and gave them his laws and statutes, both after the exodus (Exod 20:1–17) and on the threshold of entering the promised land (Deut 5:6–21). The Decalogue is familiar to most and contains a summary of the morality that God requires of his people:

1. "You shall have no other gods before me" (Exod 20:3).
2. "You shall not make for yourself a carved image, or any likeness of anything that is in heaven above, or that is in the earth beneath, or that is in the water under the earth" (Exod 20:4).
3. "You shall not take the name of the LORD your God in vain" (Exod 20:7).
4. "Remember the Sabbath day, to keep it holy" (Exod 20:8).
5. "Honor your father and your mother" (Exod 20:12).
6. "You shall not murder" (Exod 20:13).

---

13. George Eldon Ladd, *A Theology of the New Testament*, rev. ed., ed. Donald A. Hagner (Grand Rapids: Eerdmans, 1993), 302.

7. "You shall not commit adultery" (Exod 20:14).
8. "You shall not steal" (Exod 20:15).
9. "You shall not bear false witness" (Exod 20:16).
10. "You shall not covet" (Exod 20:7).

But God also gave two other sets of laws to his people, which we can initially label the Covenant Code (or Book of the Covenant) and the Levitical laws.

The Covenant Code (Exod 20:22–23:19) follows the Decalogue and provides Israel with a series of case laws, that is, what to do in the event of various circumstances if people committed wrongs against one another. The code covers topics as diverse as idolatry and worship (20:22–26; 22:20), slaves (21:1–11), assault (21:12–15), human trafficking (21:15–16), respect for authority (21:17), quarreling (21:18–19), homicide (21:20–25), retribution (21:26–36), theft (22:1–15), sexual assault (22:16–17), witchcraft (22:18), bestiality (22:19), treatment of aliens (22:21–24; 23:9), usury (22:25–27), reviling (22:28), tithing (22:29–30), diet (22:31), deception and honesty (23:1–6), agriculture (23:10–11), Sabbath observance (23:12), and observance of festivals (23:13–19). The Covenant Code differs from the Levitical laws, which deal with the protocols of the tabernacle and the different types, purposes, and procedures for the various sacrifices. Historically, theologians have observed the different types of laws that appear in the Old Testament and placed them under three different rubrics: the moral, ceremonial, and judicial laws.

Thomas Aquinas gives classic expression to this threefold distinction, though the distinction substantively goes back as far as Augustine (see *Reply to Faustus the Manichean* 6.2). The Decalogue consists of moral commands, precepts by which God directs human actions and virtues toward himself. God directs humans to himself first by interior acts of the mind, which are faith, hope, and love, and second by external works, whereby humans profess their subjection to God. These acts belong to divine worship, and this worship has gone under the term "ceremony"; thus the ceremonial laws, the Levitical laws that govern Israel's worship (*ST* Ia IIae, q. 99, arts 2–3). The judicial commands dictate conduct among humans. Both the moral and judicial laws aim at the ordering of human life (*ST* Ia IIae,

q. 99, art 4).[14] This is the same threefold distinction that appears in early modern Reformed theology, such as in the Westminster Confession (19.3–4). But just because theologians divided the law into these three categories does not mean that they saw them as disconnected silos that have nothing to do with one another.

## Matthew 5:17–20

The religious authorities perceived that Jesus was trying to do away with the Mosaic law. Jesus dismissed this misunderstanding: "Do not think that I have come to abolish the Law or the Prophets; I have not come to abolish them but to fulfill them" (Matt 5:17).[15] First, Christ does not come to abolish the Law or the Prophets. In other words, he was not destroying or doing away with them. Second, he came to fulfill them. In other words, Christ was using the common terms for two-thirds of the Hebrew Bible, the Torah (Law) and the Nevi'im (Prophets). Even though he does not mention the Ketuvim (the Writings), elsewhere he states that the whole Old Testament looks to him. On the road to Emmaus Jesus instructed his disciples: "These are my words that I spoke to you while I was still with you, that everything written about me in the Law of Moses and the Prophets and the Psalms must be fulfilled" (Luke 24:44).[16] The Law, or Pentateuch, which includes the Decalogue, points to Christ in some form or fashion. Thus, Christ rebuked the religious leaders: "For if you believed Moses, you would believe me; for he wrote of me" (John 5:46).[17] The prophets find their fulfillment in Christ, whether in terms of their predictions about the coming Messiah (e.g., Isa 11:1; 52:13–53:12; Mic 5:2; Acts 7:52) or in that the prophets were types that foreshadowed Jesus: "The Lord your God will raise up for you a prophet

14. See Stephen J. Casselli, "The Threefold Division of the Law in the Thought of Aquinas," *WTJ* 61, no. 2 (1999): 175–207.

15. D. A. Carson, *Matthew*, EBC 1 (Grand Rapids: Zondervan, 1995), 140–47.

16. Darrell L. Bock, *Luke 9:51–24:53*, BECNT (Grand Rapids: Baker Academic, 1996), 1935–37.

17. D. A. Carson, *The Gospel according to John*, PNTC (Grand Rapids: Eerdmans, 1990), 266.

like me from among you, from your brothers—it is to him you shall listen" (Deut 18:15; see Matt 17:6; Mark 9:7; Luke 9:35; John 1:21; 5:46; Acts 7:38).[18] Jesus is the fulfillment of the Writings, as they too look for his advent: the Psalms anticipate Christ (e.g., Pss. 1–2); Proverbs is about the pursuit of wisdom and finds its telos in Christ, God's wisdom incarnate (1 Cor 1:24); and Job is about a righteous man who nevertheless suffers, a shadowy image of Jesus.

Given Christ's relationship to the Old Testament, he forbade the relaxation of "one of the least of these commandments" (Matt 5:19). He said, "For truly, I say to you, until heaven and earth pass away, not an iota, not a dot, will pass from the Law until all is accomplished" (Matt 5:18).[19] Paul states this same truth in another way when he writes: "For Christ is the end of the law for righteousness to everyone who believes" (Rom 10:4). Christ fulfills the law, which means he is the reality to which the law points—the law is the promise, and Christ is the fulfillment. Christ also fulfills the law in that he obeys it perfectly, as his righteousness exceeded that of the scribes and Pharisees (Matt 5:20), which means that through his obedience and suffering he opened the way for sinners to enter the kingdom of God (Gal 4:4–5). But recall that there are three different types of laws: moral, ceremonial, and judicial. Christ fulfills the moral law through his obedience and suffering—he suffers the penalty of the law on behalf of sinners and positively fulfills it on their behalf. He fulfills the law as a covenant, which means that he presents his personal, perfect, and perpetual obedience to the law to redeem sinners. His fulfillment of the law does not mean, however, that believers are utterly free from the moral law. Rather, believers are free from the law as a *covenant*, but it still functions as a *rule*, as a guide and standard for the Christian life (WCF 19.6). Christ fulfills the ceremonial law in that he is the one perfect sacrifice to which the whole sacrificial system looks (Heb 8–10). Christ fulfills the judicial laws in that

18. Beale and Carson, *Commentary on the New Testament Use*, 55–56, 187, 312, 419, 420, 443, 563–64.

19. Carson, *Matthew*, 145–46.

he is the King of Israel, and Israel's typical judicial laws find their fulfillment in his eschatological, antitypical kingly rule.

There are five observations to note regarding God's laws. First, law is a focal point in Israel's covenantal narratives, evident by the fact that God delivered Israel from Egypt, brought them to Sinai, and gave them his law.[20] As Israel stood on the threshold of the promised land, God once again issued his law suited for their tenure in the land, as they were no longer a wandering, nomadic people. Moses told the people that "two tablets of the testimony" were "written with the finger of God" (Exod 31:18) and that the law was "the voice of the LORD" (Deut 30:10). Second, given that all of God's laws are his commands, all his precepts have a moral dimension. Just because a law is ceremonial, for example, does not mean that Israel should ignore or disobey it. Israel had to obey all of God's commands. Similarly, the moral law can have ceremonial aspects. The fourth commandment to observe the Sabbath, for example, has a moral substance (worship God one day a week), with a positive ceremonial accident (the Sabbath, the last day of the week). With the advent of Christ, the moral substance remains the same (worship God), but the positive accident changes (we worship on the first, not the last, day of the week). Third, the moral law is binding on all people, whether in the form of natural law or the Torah.[21] Paul explains that God has written the works of the law on the hearts of all people, and he distinguishes the natural form of the law from the law revealed at Sinai. The "gentiles," writes Paul, "who do not have the law, by nature do what the law requires" (Rom 2:14).[22]

Fourth, the moral law is universally binding on all people, but the ceremonial and judicial laws are peculiar to Israel. Concerning the ceremonial laws, for example, we read: "For since the law has but a shadow of the good things to come instead of the true form of these realities, it can never,

---

20. Stephen A. Kaufman, "The Structure of the Deuteronomic Law," *Maarav* 1, no. 2 (1979): 105–58, esp. 109–11, 145–47.

21. Moo, *Epistle to the Romans*, 149; C. John Collins, "Echoes of Aristotle in Romans 2:14–15: Or, Maybe Abimelech Was Not So Bad After All," *Journal of Markets and Morality* 13, no. 1 (2010): 123–73, here 129–30.

22. Contra, e.g., S. J. Gathercole, "A Law unto Themselves: The Gentiles in Romans 2.14–15 Revisited," *Journal for the Study of the New Testament* 85 (2002): 27–49.

by the same sacrifices that are continually offered every year, make perfect those who draw near" (Heb 10:1).[23] Here the author speaks of the sacrifices as being but a shadow of the good things to come. The same shadow-reality pattern holds true for the judicial laws. Paul instructs the Colossians not to let anyone pass judgment on them regarding a festival, new moon, or Sabbath, which refer to laws in both the Decalogue and the Book of the Covenant; worshiping on the Sabbath is a ceremonial aspect of the moral law that passes away along with the requirements of the celebration of festivals with the advent of Christ. Paul explains: "These are a shadow of the things to come, but the substance belongs to Christ" (Col 2:17).[24] This means, fifth, that all the laws (moral, ceremonial, and judicial) find their fulfillment in Christ. As Paul writes, "For Christ is the end of the law for righteousness to everyone who believes" (Rom 10:4).[25] Christ fulfills the whole law in all its aspects, but this does not mean that the law is no longer binding on the redeemed.

From the very outset of Israel's constitution, God intended for law and love to go hand in hand, a point evident in that the first and greatest *commandment* is to love God with one's whole being and the second *commandment* is to love one's neighbor as oneself (Matt 22:37–38). That love and law go together appears when Joshua exhorts Israel: "Only be very careful to observe the commandment and the law that Moses the servant of the LORD commanded you, to love the LORD your God, and to walk in all his ways and to keep his commandments and to cling to him and to serve him with all your heart and with all your soul" (Josh 22:5). The longest chapter in the Bible is a hymn dedicated to the law of God, where the psalmist punctuates his verse with declarations of his love of God's law: "Oh how I love your law! It is my meditation all the day" (Ps 119:97; also vv. 113, 163, 165). The same estimation of the law persists in the New Testament when Paul and James both commend the law as a manifestation of love: "Owe no one anything, except to love each other, for the one who loves another has fulfilled the law" (Rom 13:8). Paul, in fact, sums up the law in one small

---

23. Thomas R. Schreiner, *Commentary on Hebrews*, Biblical Theology for Christian Proclamation (Nashville: Holman Reference, 2015), 290–91.

24. Douglas J. Moo, *The Letters to the Colossians and to Philemon*, PNTC (Grand Rapids: Eerdmans, 2008), 222–23.

25. Moo, *Epistle to the Romans*, 636–43, esp. 642–43.

statement: "You shall love your neighbor as yourself" (Gal 5:14). Likewise, James writes: "If you really fulfill the royal law according to the Scripture, 'You shall love your neighbor as yourself,' you are doing well" (Jas 2:8).

The love of the law and the Christian life are eminently compatible. Christians must therefore love God's law because it is a reflection of his being and attributes, and thus is worthy of praise as a merciful revelation of the moral duties required of his image-bearers. It ultimately points to Christ, the one who has fulfilled the law on behalf of sinners. Christians must also seek to fulfill the law, but the Christian's precise relationship to the law requires careful observation of the distinction between the moral, ceremonial, and judicial laws. While Christ fulfills the whole law in all its aspects, the ceremonial and judicial laws are no longer binding on the church. Evaluating the moral law necessitates acknowledgment of the ways in which Christ fulfills the moral law but also the ways in which it is still binding on believers. To say that the moral law is no longer binding on Christians is to fall into the error of antinomianism, and conversely to say that Christ has somehow not fulfilled the law for believers invites legalism, or neonomianism. Both are serious errors and must be rejected. But how one avoids antinomianism and neonomianism awaits detailed explanation in chapter 8, on sanctification.

## WORSHIP AND PRAYER

It is no exaggeration to say that Old Testament life was centered on worship and prayer and fellowshipping with God, the covenant Lord. Worship lies at the heart of the Shema, to love God with one's heart, soul, and strength (Deut 6:4). In the Old Testament there are several terms associated with the worship of God. Recall that God created Adam "to work … and keep" (לעבדה ולשמרה) the garden, the first earthly temple (Gen 2:15). These terms are associated with the priestly labors in the temple and with worship contexts.[26] Adam's whole priestly existence, therefore, was geared toward the worship of God.[27] Another term is "bow," or "worship" (חוה), which typically denotes the act of paying homage to someone: "The man bowed [וישתחו] his head and worshiped the Lord" (Gen 24:26). An added factor

26. Beale, *Temple and the Church's Mission*, 66–70.

27. Kline, *Structure of Biblical Authority*, 62–63.

revolves around the inclusion of psalms in the Old Testament, which constitute Israel's songs of worship and prayers to God. Israel's psalms are not confined to the book of Psalms but appear in various places throughout the Old Testament (e.g., Exod 15; Judg 5; 1 Sam 2; 2 Sam 22; Hab 3).[28] In short, God created humans to enter his presence, worship, sing praises, and pray to him, but they instead sought to worship themselves, which created an impediment to worship.

Sin is the great obstruction to covenant worship and communion. The obstacle of sin stands out in the earliest recorded instance of worship, when Cain and Abel brought their sacrifices to God: "And the Lord had regard for Abel and his offering, but for Cain his offering he had no regard" (Gen 4:4–5). The book of Hebrews explains that Abel offered his sacrifice "by faith," which made his offering more acceptable than Cain's (Heb 11:4). Cain worshiped God with the trappings of formalism but not with faith in his covenant promises to redeem by means of the seed of the woman.[29] His sin kept him from worshiping God in an acceptable manner. Cain and Abel serve as microcosms of the rest of Scripture as two different ways of worshiping God: coming to him in faith and offering acceptable sacrifice and praise versus approaching with mere formalism. The former way accounts for sin and the need for a divine remedy, whereas the latter discounts sin and approaches God in self-directed manner, what the Puritans called "will worship."[30]

When God delivered Israel from bondage in Egypt, one of the stated purposes of their liberation was to free them to worship him. God instructed Moses to tell Pharaoh: "Let my people go, that they may hold a feast to me in the wilderness" (Exod 5:1). When Israel arrived at Sinai, God summoned their elders into his presence to worship him, but down the mountain, like Adam, Israel engaged in idolatry (Exod 24:1; 32:8). The continual refrain throughout the Old Testament is whether Israel will worship their covenant Lord or the gods of the land. Embedded, for example, in the first table of the law are precepts that govern worship. The first command instructs

28. Timothy M. Pierce, *Enthroned on Our Praise: An Old Testament Theology of Worship* (Nashville: B&H Academic, 2008), 4.

29. Pierce, *Enthroned on Our Praise*, 36.

30. E.g., William Ames, *A Fresh Suit against Human Ceremonies in God's Worship* (Amsterdam: Giles Thorp, 1633).

Israel *whom* they are to worship—the one, true, living God, Yahweh (Exod 20:3). The second command teaches Israel *how* to worship God (Exod 20:4). The third command protects the sanctity of God's name in relationship to Israel's confession and worship (Exod 20:5–7). Israel must treat God's name as holy, not as a profane thing. And the fourth command tells Israel *when* they are supposed to worship God (Exod 20:8–11).[31] These commands convey that God is holy, and like Adam in the garden, Israel must approach God in the manner of his instruction, not according to their own desires. When God tabernacled in Israel's midst, he revealed himself in the pillar of cloud, and the people worshiped (Exod 33:10).

In the act of worship, Israel entered a dialogue with God by means of his divine revelation and their response. God revealed his word to Israel either through Moses or through the reading of the law (e.g., Exod 12:14–28; Neh 9:3). But recall Geerhardus Vos's observations about God's word-act-word revelation. God first speaks, then he acts, and then he interprets his previous words and acts with a subsequent word. God spoke to Moses and commanded him to lead Israel to walk through the Red Sea. He told Moses that he would harden the hearts of the Egyptians so that they would pursue them and God would receive glory (Exod 14:17–18). This is God's preparatory revelatory word. The angel of God acted as a rear guard, which allowed Israel to pass through the sea, and but when God removed the angel, the Egyptians gave chase. Moses stretched out his hand, and the sea returned, and "the LORD threw the Egyptians into the midst of the sea" (Exod 14:27). Israel's deliverance and Egypt's judgment is God's revelatory act. God then followed both the preparatory word and revelatory act with an interpretive word, which appears in the Song of Moses (Exod 15:1–26). The song explains that Israel's deliverance was not fortuitous, a chance occurrence, caused by natural events, or executed by Moses and Israel; rather, their deliverance was wrought by God in accordance with his promise. The song rehearses Israel's Red Sea deliverance but also extols the attributes of God: "Who is like you, O LORD, among the gods? Who is like you, majestic in holiness, awesome in glorious deeds, doing wonders?" (Exod 15:11). The word-act-word pattern of revelation frequently appears in Israel's worship, evident in the psalmist's refrain, "Sing to him a new song" (Ps 33:3; also 96:1; 98:1;

31. John I. Durham, *Exodus*, WBC 3 (Nashville: Thomas Nelson, 1987), 284–90.

144:9; 148:1). When God acted in mighty ways, the psalmist called on Israel to respond with a new song. Mighty acts of redemption warrant and invite new songs of praise to and worship of the God who saves. These same patterns of worship, song, and prayer continue in the New Testament.

Worship and prayer still lie at the heart of the new-covenant community, but they focus on the Messiah, the Son of God. From the moment of Christ's birth, the angels heralded his advent, and gentile magi came to worship him as the King of the Jews (Luke 2:13–15; Matt 2:2). When his disciples saw Jesus walk on water, they "worshiped him, saying, 'Truly you are the Son of God'" (Matt 14:33). As Jesus entered Jerusalem on a colt, the crowds ran out to meet him and cried out: "Hosanna to the Son of David! Blessed is he who comes in the name of the Lord! Hosanna in the highest!" (Matt 21:9). And when Jesus was raised from the dead and presented himself to his disciples, they worshiped him (Matt 28:9). Beyond Christ's earthly ministry, the New Testament continues to call on Christians to worship Jesus (Phil 3:3), the culmination of which comes in the book of Revelation, when the four living creatures and the twenty-four elders "fell down before the Lamb ... and they sang a new song, saying, 'Worthy are you to take the scroll and to open its seals, for you were slain, and by your blood you ransomed people for God from every tribe and language and people and nation, and you have made them a kingdom of priests to our God, and they shall reign on earth'" (Rev 5:8–10). God has revealed his anticipatory word, acted in the revelation of his Son, and now the subsequent interpretive word-revelation comes in a new song explaining the significance of the work of Christ.

At the heart of Christ's work lies his obedience to his Father's will, which means that, like no other, Jesus did not engage in idolatry but worshiped his heavenly Father. When Jesus began his public ministry, John baptized him in the Jordan, and then the Spirit led Christ into the wilderness, where he was tempted by devil, who promised to give him all the kingdoms of the world: "All these I will give you, if you will fall down and worship me" (Matt 4:9). The devil tempted the last Adam like he did the first—seek to grasp equality with God by cutting your own path, choosing your own way, and giving your worship to someone other than God. But Jesus responded: "Be gone, Satan! For it is written, 'You shall worship the Lord your God and him only shall you serve'" (Matt 4:10). Jesus was faithful—obedience and worship go hand in hand.[32] But not only did Jesus refuse to worship the devil; he also regularly prayed to his heavenly Father (e.g., Luke 3:21; 11:1; Matt 26:36). Christ's most famous prayer, of course, is his high-priestly prayer (John 17). Christ's faithful worship, obedience, and prayers constitute both the foundation for our salvation and the paradigm to which God calls all believers.

## Matthew 6:9–13

When the disciples ask Jesus how to pray, Jesus teaches them a brief paradigmatic prayer that presents three vital truths about covenant life. First, through Christ we have a new, more intimate, relationship with God. In the Old Testament no individual Israelite referred to God as "father."[33] The entire nation could make this claim, as God called Israel his firstborn son (Exod 4:22; Hos 11:1). But when Jesus starts his prayer with the words "Our Father," it reveals that through union with the only begotten Son of God, all believers enjoy a unique filial relationship with God that entitles them individually to call God "Father." This is a term of intimacy that Christ himself enjoyed with his heavenly Father: "Abba, Father, all things are possible for you. Remove this cup from me. Yet not what I will, but what you will" (Mark 14:36). This is an expression of intimacy that believers may also invoke: "For you did not receive the spirit of slavery to fall back into fear, but you have received the Spirit of adoption as sons, by whom we cry, 'Abba! Father'" (Rom 8:15; also Gal 4:6)!

Second, Jesus subtly reveals that the Christian life is one of pilgrimage, the final exodus.[34] Different elements of the passage point to the exodus as the narrative subtext of the Lord's Prayer. Jesus teaches believers to call God "Father," which, as noted above invokes

---

32. Crowe, *Last Adam*, 23–54.

33. Carson, *Matthew*, 169.

34. Brant Pitre, "The Lord's Prayer and the New Exodus," *Letter & Spirit* 2 (2006): 69–96, here 70. Pitre cites the less researched but nonetheless thought-provoking essay by N. T. Wright, "The Lord's Prayer as a Paradigm of Christian Prayer," in *Into God's Presence: Prayer in the New Testament* (Grand Rapids: Eerdmans, 2002), 132–54.

the father-son relationship that God had with Israel (Exod 4:22).[35] We pray that God would establish his kingdom on earth as it is in heaven, a key feature of the exodus narrative, as God's deliverance constituted Israel as a kingdom (Exod 19:6). As God fed his people in the wilderness with a daily provision of manna from heaven, the church prays that God would provide them with "daily bread" (Matt 6:11).[36] Jesus's prayer instructs his disciples to seek the forgiveness of their sins as they also forgive others. In contrast to Luke, who uses the term ἁμαρτία ("sin"), Matthew uses the term ὀφείλημα ("debt"); the terms are synonyms (see Luke 7:41–43; Col 2:13–14). Nevertheless, against the backdrop of the Old Testament, Matthew's term harks back to Jubilee, an event laden with the exodus motif. The Jubilee was supposed to happen once every forty-nine years, after seven "weeks" of years (Lev 25:1–55). During the Jubilee Year, slaves were set free and debts were forgiven (Lev 25:25–38, 39–40). The Jubilee was also a time when people were supposed be restored to their land (Lev 25:24, 28). There is a link, therefore, between the Jubilee and the exodus, as the exodus was the event that triggered God's gift of the land to Israel. Christ launched the eschatological Jubilee with his own ministry (Isa 61:1–2); hence he teaches his disciples to forgive debtors as God forgave their debts in Christ.[37] Finally, the prayer concludes with a request for preservation against temptation, a key exodus theme, as Israel regularly succumbed to temptation and sin. As Jesus recapitulated Israel's postexodus forty-year wilderness wanderings in his forty-day probation, he rebuffed the temptations of the evil. So, through this prayer Jesus calls the church to the same obediential fidelity.

Third, the Christian life exists amid the tension of the already-but-not-yet. This prayer signals that the kingdom of God has come with the advent of Christ, and therefore believers must pray for the return of Christ and the consummation of the age. What many do not realize is that this aspect of the Lord's Prayer stands with the

---

35. W. D. Davies and D. C. Allison, *Matthew 1–7*, International Critical Commentary (London: T&T Clark, 1988), 602; Joachim Jeremias, *The Prayers of Jesus* (Philadelphia: Fortress, 1967), 11–56.

36. Jeremias, *Prayers of Jesus*, 100–101.

37. Davies and Allison, *Matthew*, 611; Carson, *Matthew*, 172; Pitre, "Lord's Prayer," 88–89.

imprecatory psalms, those psalms that call for judgment on God's enemies. When believers pray for the coming of the kingdom, they also pray for God's will to be done on earth as it is in heaven. That is, we pray either that people will repent of their sins and kiss the Son (Ps 2:12), or that Christ's judgment will fall on them for their impenitence. Then "every knee should bow, in heaven and on earth and under the earth, and every tongue confess that Jesus Christ is Lord, to the glory of God the Father" (Phil 2:10–11). That the church takes this prayer on its lips also means that we live between Christ's advents; covenant life is one of pilgrimage, and thus we pray for faithfulness along the way.

Even though Christ has fulfilled the Old Testament sacrificial system, this does not mean that New Testament believers cease from worshiping God through sacrifice. As new-covenant priests by virtue of their union with Christ, they share in his priestly office and therefore continue Adam's work of serving in God's temple, the church: "To him who loves us and has freed us from our sins by his blood and made us a kingdom, priests to his God and Father, to him be glory and dominion forever and ever" (Rev 1:5–6). As new-covenant priests, we join the heavenly host in their perpetual worship of God when we gather on earth. Through faith in Christ we

> come to Mount Zion and to the city of the living God, the heavenly Jerusalem, and to innumerable angels in festal gathering, and to the assembly of the firstborn who are enrolled in heaven, and to God, the judge of all, and to the spirits of the righteous made perfect, and to Jesus, the mediator of a new covenant, and to the sprinkled blood that speaks of a better word than the blood of Abel. (Heb 12:22–24)

As we gather, we "offer to God acceptable worship, with reverence and awe" (Heb 12:28).[38] No longer do God's people offer sacrificial animals, but, like Christ, they offer up their own lives: "I appeal to you therefore, brothers, by the mercies of God, to present your bodies as a living sacrifice, holy and

38. Schreiner, *Commentary on Hebrews*, 406–7.

acceptable to God, which is your spiritual worship" (Rom 12:1).[39] The worship-filled lives of God's people stand in contrast to the idolatrous ways of the unbelieving nations (e.g., Rev 13:4; 16:2; 19:20).

As with the Old Testament saints, prayer is a cardinal feature of New Testament worship and life. After Christ's ascension, the disciples devoted themselves to prayer (Acts 1:14) and regularly interceded on behalf of the church (e.g., Rom 15:30; Col 1:3; 4:12). In the New Testament, however, the Spirit takes on a more prominent role in the prayers of the saints. In the Old Testament there was no democratized outpouring of the Holy Spirit, as there was at Pentecost. Certain individuals received anointings of the Spirit for specific tasks, such as Samson battling a lion or the enemies of Israel (Judg 14:5–6, 19; 15:14), Balaam prophesying blessings on Israel (Num 24:2), Saul and his men prophesying (1 Sam 10:10; 19:20), or Ezekiel prophesying (Ezek 11:5). The Spirit also assisted people when they were in the precincts of the temple, the location of God's earthly presence. Jesus explained the difference between Old and New Testament worship to the Samaritan woman at the well, that true worship would no longer be restricted to a specific place, such as Jerusalem, where the temple was located, but that "true worshipers will worship the Father in Spirit and truth, for the Father is seeking such people wo worship him. God is spirit, and those who worship him must worship in spirit and truth" (John 4:23–24). Jesus told the woman that people had to worship in the power of the Holy Spirit and according to the truth, that is, according to Jesus Christ, the only way, truth, and life (John 14:6).[40]

The pillar of cloud and fire no longer rests over the tabernacle or temple but, since the outpouring of the Spirit at Pentecost, now rests on individual believers. This means we have greater access to the Spirit's intercessory work in prayer. The apostle Paul explains: "Likewise the Spirit helps us in our weakness. For we do not know what to pray for as we ought, but the Spirit himself intercedes for us with groanings too deep for words. And he who searches hearts knows what is the mind of the Spirit, because the Spirit intercedes for the saints according to the will of God" (Rom 8:26–27).[41]

39. Moo, *Epistle to the Romans*, 748–754.

40. Carson, *Gospel according to John*, 224–26, 490–92.

41. Moo, *Epistle to the Romans*, 522–27.

If saints have access to the throne of God by means of Christ's high-priestly mediation and the Spirit's intercessory work in prayer, then it is unsurprising that Paul exhorts the church to pray "at all times in the Spirit, with all prayer and supplication" (Eph 6:18).[42] Moreover, given that song in worship is a form of prayer, Paul also instructs us not to get drunk with wine but to be filled with the Spirit and to address "one another in psalms and hymns and spiritual songs, singing and making melody to the Lord with your heart, giving thanks always and for everything to God the Father in the name of the Lord Jesus Christ" (Eph 5:19–20).[43]

## Hebrews 10:19–25

As much as we must highlight the democratization of the indwelling of the Spirit and the donation of his fruit in the life of all believers, an individuated soteriology must never lose sight of its corporality. While the Spirit applies the saving work of Christ to individuals, he saves those individuals to be part of a corporate body, the church. Another way to understand the individual-corporate connection is to remember that all Christians are saved by the blood of Jesus, the "great priest over the house of God" (Heb 10:21). We cannot love the head but reject his body; we cannot love Jesus and rebuff his church. Christ is the cornerstone, "in whom the whole structure, being joined together, grows into a holy temple in the Lord." "In him," writes Paul, "you also are being built together into a dwelling place for God by the Spirit" (Eph 2:20–22).

In light of this fact, we must "hold fast the confession of our hope without wavering, for he who promised is faithful" (Heb 10:23). In other words, every individual must hold fast to Christ, our great high priest and head of the church. Conversely, since we share in the bond of the Spirit, we must hold fast to one another. We must "consider how to stir up one another to love and good works" (Heb 10:24), which means that as we make pilgrimage to the heavenly Jerusalem,

42. Baugh, *Ephesians*, 558.

43. Baugh, *Ephesians*, 454–61.

we do so as a body. As a body we stand together and seek to manifest the fruit of the Spirit. One of the chief ways we stir up one another to love and good works is through meeting together for corporate worship and prayer (Heb 10:25).[44] If salvation is covenantal, then it is inherently communal. In the church's covenant life, therefore, we encourage one another to love and good works until the return of Christ and the consummation of the age.

**WISDOM** The Holy Spirit assists beyond the confines of worship and prayer, as he also grants his aid for covenant life by giving the wisdom of Christ. The law of God is itself a manifestation of his wisdom, as Deuteronomy attests about God's commands: "Keep them and do them, for that will be your wisdom and your understanding in the sight of the peoples, who, when they hear all these statutes, will say, 'Surely this great nation is a wise and understanding people'" (Deut 4:6). The psalmist likewise observes: "The law of the Lord is perfect, reviving the soul; the testimony of the Lord is sure, making wise the simple" (Ps 19:7). The links between law and wisdom reveal that wisdom is therefore a covenantal category. In short, the way of wisdom is the way of covenant.[45] Beyond the law, in the face of life's vexing questions and challenges, wisdom literature takes center stage: Proverbs, Job, Ecclesiastes, various psalms, and Song of Songs.[46] Wisdom literature recognizes that there are difficult circumstances in life where the law does not give clear guidance.

In other words, not all situations and life are black and white but are often gray. Priests, for example, had to rely on the Urim and Thummim (Exod 28:30) to reveal the will of God when circumstances were unclear.[47] When Saul engaged the Philistines in battle, to secure his victory he swore a self-maledictory oath that anyone who ate food until evening would be cursed if he did not defeat his enemies (1 Sam 14:24). Saul's son Jonathan did not know that his father made this curse-oath and ate some honey

44. Baugh, *Ephesians*, 201–5.

45. J. S. Thompson, *Deuteronomy*, TOTC (Downers Grove, IL: InterVarsity Press, 1974), 103.

46. Kline, *Structure of Biblical Authority*, 64–66.

47. Cornelis Van Dam, *The Urim and Thummim: A Means of Revelation in Ancient Israel* (Winona Lake, IN: Eisenbrauns, 1997).

(1 Sam 14:27). When Saul inquired of the Lord as to whether he should attack the Philistines later that night, God did not answer him (1 Sam 14:37). Saul suspected someone had violated his oath-curse; when no one admitted to breaking his oath, he resorted to the Urim and Thummim to reveal the transgressor: "'O LORD God of Israel, why have you not answered your servant this day? If this guilt is in me or in Jonathan my son, O LORD, God of Israel, give Urim. But if this guilt is in your people Israel, give Thummim.' And Jonathan and Saul were taken, but the people escaped" (1 Sam 14:41).[48] Saul used the Urim and Thummim to reveal God's will when there was no apparent course of action.

Things were very different when King Solomon faced his own perplexing situation. When Solomon ascended his father David's throne, he knew he was unequal to the task, and so he prayed to God: "Give your servant therefore an understanding mind to govern your people, that I may discern between good and evil, for who is able to govern this your great people?" (1 Kgs 3:9).[49] Solomon did not employ the specific term, but he was seeking wisdom. Eve faced the same dilemma in the garden when she gazed at the tree of the knowledge of good and evil and saw that it was "good for food, and that it was a delight to the eyes, and that the tree was to be desired to make one wise" (Gen 3:6).[50] Both Solomon and Eve desired wisdom, but unlike Eve, Solomon pursued it in accordance with God's will. God answered Solomon's prayer: "Because you have asked this ... I give you a wise and discerning mind" (1 Kgs 3:11–12). The means by which God gave Solomon wisdom was through the Holy Spirit: "If you turn at my reproof, behold, I will pour out my Spirit to you; I will make my words known to you" (Prov 1:23, my trans.; see Exod 31:3; 11:2–3).[51] With the anointing of the Spirit, Solomon was able to face challenging situations without consulting the Urim and Thummim. Rather, to determine which one of two prostitutes was the mother of a child, Solomon employed his Spirit-given

48. Ralph W. Klein, *1 Samuel*, WBC (Nashville: Thomas Nelson, 2000), 140–41.

49. Simon J. DeVries, *1 Kings*, WBC (Waco, TX: Word Books, 1985), 52–53.

50. Gordon J. Wenham, "Sanctuary Symbolism in the Garden of Eden Story," in Hess and Tsumura, *I Studied Inscriptions from before the Flood*, 399–404; also J. A. Davies, "'Discerning between Good and Evil': Solomon as a New Adam," *WTJ* 73 (2011): 39–57.

51. Tremper Longman III, *Proverbs*, Baker Commentary on the Old Testament Wisdom and Psalms (Grand Rapids: Baker Academic, 2006), 112–13.

wisdom: "And all Israel heard of the judgment that the king had rendered, and they stood in awe of the king, because they perceived that the wisdom of God was in him to do justice" (1 Kgs 3:28).

Solomon was a type of Christ, the one on whom the Spirit of the Lord would rest, a "Spirit of wisdom and understanding, the Spirit of counsel and might, the Spirit of knowledge and the fear of the Lord" (Isa 11:2). Christ is the one on whom God poured out his Spirit in his baptism at the Jordan (Matt 4:16–17), who then turned and baptized the church in the Spirit at Pentecost (Acts 2:33; Mark 1:8; Matt 3:11; Luke 3:16; John 1:33). Among many blessings, the baptism of the Spirit brings the gift of wisdom. Unlike human wisdom, Christ sends the Spirit to teach the church so they can understand spiritual truths (1 Cor 2:13). The Spirit gives believers utterances of wisdom and knowledge (1 Cor 12:8), and so, like Solomon, Christians should pray that God would give us "the Spirit of wisdom and of revelation in the knowledge of him" (Eph 1:17).[52] Paul says that Christ is the power and wisdom of God (1 Cor 1:24), the one "in whom are hidden all the treasures of wisdom and knowledge" (Col 2:3; see Prov 2:1–8).[53] So, while God's law does not address every conceivable ethical scenario in the Christian life, God through Christ pours out his Spirit of wisdom on the church so that it can discern good from evil.

## WITNESS AND MISSION

The covenant people of God are the recipients of his love in the forgiveness of their sins; right standing before the divine bar; the Spirit's blessings of faith, hope, and love; and the privilege of worshiping the triune God, calling on him in prayer, and receiving God's wisdom in Christ through the Spirit. Thus, their desire should be to share this love with the rest of the world. God never intended to restrict the blessings of the covenant to the geographic boundaries of Old Testament Israel. Recall that Adam's original covenantal labor had global scope—he was supposed to be fruitful, multiply, fill all the earth, and subdue it (Gen 1:28). After the fall, God took up the failed Adamic vocation and transformed it into a promise. He told Abraham: "I will bless those who bless you, and him who dishonors you

52. Baugh, *Ephesians*, 117.

53. Moo, *Letters to the Colossians*, 169–71.

I will curse, and in you all the families of the earth shall be blessed" (Gen 12:3). The Old Testament prophets foresaw a time when the gentiles would pour into Jerusalem to worship the one true God:

> It shall come to pass in the latter days
> that the mountain of the house of the LORD
> shall be established as the highest of the mountains,
> and shall be lifted up above the hills;
> and all the nations shall flow to it,
> and many peoples shall come, and say:
> "Come, let us go up to the mountain of the LORD,
> to the house of the God of Jacob,
> that he may teach us his ways
> and that we may walk in his paths."
> For out of Zion shall go forth the law,
> and the word of the LORD from Jerusalem. (Isa 2:2–3)

God gave his people a mission to give witness to the saving love of God, evident in that, as a nation, they were a "kingdom of priests and a holy nation" (Exod 19:6).[54] They were supposed to be ambassadors of the good news of God's salvation to the nations. But Israel was sinful and rejected their priestly calling. Jesus's indictment against the misuse of God's temple testifies against Israel: "Is it not written, 'My house shall be called a house of prayer for all the nations'? But you have made it a den of robbers" (Mark 11:17).[55]

The task of witnessing to the nations fell on God himself: "The LORD has bared his holy arm before the eyes of all the nations, and all the ends of the earth shall see the salvation of our God" (Isa 52:10; see 51:4–6).[56] Zion would turn into a "herald of good news" and cry out, "Behold your God!" (Isa 40:9). The message of salvation would come through the Lord's Messiah: "The Spirit of the Lord GOD is upon me, because the LORD has anointed me to bring good news to the poor; he has sent me to bind up the brokenhearted, to proclaim liberty to the captives, and the opening of

---

54. Durham, *Exodus*, 263.

55. R. T. France, *The Gospel of Mark*, NIGTC (Grand Rapids: Eerdmans, 2002), 445.

56. J. Alec Motyer, *The Prophecy of Isaiah: An Introduction and Commentary* (Downers Grove, IL: IVP Academic, 1993), 420.

the prison to those who are bound" (Isa 61:1).[57] God has accomplished and continues to carry out the mission of spreading the good news through Jesus: "Go therefore and make disciples of all nations, baptizing them in the name of the Father and of the Son and of the Holy Spirit, teaching them to observe all that I have commanded you. And behold, I am with you always, to the end of the age" (Matt 28:19). Unlike Adam and Israel, the last Adam has been, is, and will be faithful to carry out the mission of heralding the good news of salvation. Eve was Adam's helpmate to accomplish his earth-filling labor, and now the church is the bride of Christ, the last Eve to the last Adam, who assists him in carrying out his mission of evangelizing the nations.

## CONCLUSION

Israel's covenant life bears the marks of the gospel and the virtues of faith, hope, and love, but the Mosaic covenant was a parenthesis in redemptive history—a rough sketch of the kingdom of Christ, a foreshadow and type. Israel's covenant life was a play within a play, like the play *Murder of Gonzago* within Shakespeare's *Hamlet*. God was setting the stage for the new covenant and his definitive self-disclosure in Christ and salvation in its fullest sense, which the next section unpacks.

## FURTHER READING

Beale, G. K. "The Old Testament Background of Paul's Reference to the 'Fruit of the Spirit' in Galatians 5:22." *BBR* 15 (2005): 1–38. An important essay that shows the Isaianic Old Testament background to the apostle Paul's fruit of the Spirit in Galatians.

Carson, D. A. *Praying with Paul: A Call to Spiritual Reformation*. 2nd ed. Grand Rapids: Baker Academic, 2015. An excellent study on the prayers of the apostle Paul.

Collins, C. John. "Echoes of Aristotle in Romans 2:14–15: Or, Maybe Abimelech Was Not So Bad after All." *Journal of Markets and Morality* 13, no. 1 (2010): 123–73. Persuasively shows textual

57. Motyer, *Isaiah*, 504–5.

parallels between the apostle Paul and Aristotle on the topic of works of the law, which shows at minimum that Paul was appealing to ideas that were common to first-century life and at maximum that he had read and borrowed concepts from Aristotle.

Fesko, J. V. *The Rule of Love: Broken, Fulfilled, and Applied*. Grand Rapids: Reformation Heritage Books, 2009. A brief devotional study of the Ten Commandments that explores each commandment within its original historical context, how Christ fulfills the commandment, and how the commandment applies to the lives of believers.

———. *Where Wisdom Is Found: Christ in Ecclesiastes*. Grand Rapids: Reformation Heritage Books, 2010. A brief devotional study of the book of Ecclesiastes that treats the topic of wisdom and the Christian life. The book examines each chapter and connects its ponderings on wisdom to Christ, then shows how Christians can live out this Christ-shaped wisdom.

Kline, Meredith G. *The Structure of Biblical Authority*. Eugene, OR: Wipf & Stock, 1997. Shows how Deuteronomy is a key book for understanding the Old Testament as a covenant document rather than a ragbag collection of disparate books.

PART 2

# DOGMATIC DEVELOPMENT

IV

# THE PERSON AND WORK OF THE HOLY SPIRIT

## PROCESSION AND MISSION

EXEGESIS LAYS THE FOUNDATION FOR theology, but the first stone in the cathedral of soteriology is the doctrine of the Holy Spirit.[1] We must account for the agent of salvation, which in this case is the Triune God. But more specifically, the members of the Godhead have distinct missions in the economy of salvation. The Father sends the Son, the Son serves as mediator and covenant surety, and the Spirit applies the work of the Son in the salvation of the elect. Thus, a complete account of soteriology includes both the subjective reception of salvation, the *ordo salutis*, and its objective agent, the person and work of the Spirit. A right understanding of the person and work of the Spirit requires the proper contexts: the context of the Triune God and the economy of redemption. Therefore, this chapter first briefly sets forth the doctrine of the Trinity and then delves into the person of the Holy Spirit. Understanding how the Spirit relates to the Trinity establishes the Spirit's ontology and his relationship to the Father and Son. Or in technical terms, the Spirit's relationship to Father and Son establishes his procession, the *opera ad intra* ("internal work"). Second, the

1. For a survey of the history of the doctrine of the Holy Spirit, see Anthony C. Thiselton, *The Holy Spirit—In Biblical Teaching, through the Centuries, and Today* (Grand Rapids: Eerdmans, 2013), 163–467. For an older survey, see Smeaton, *Doctrine of the Holy Spirit*, 256–368. For a list of key Reformed works on the Holy Spirit, see Kuyper, *Work of the Holy Spirit*, xiii–xiv.

chapter explores the Spirit's work, or mission, the *opera ad extra* ("external work"). Two related contextual factors connect to the Spirit's work. The chapter demonstrates that the Spirit's mission is covenantal, in terms of both the originating intra-Trinitarian covenant of redemption and its execution in the covenant of grace. The chapter also underscores that the Spirit's soteriological mission is primarily eschatological. This means that to discuss the Spirit's mission is to cover soteriology, and the Spirit's soteriological mission is eschatological. Pneumatology, soteriology, and eschatology do not stand in separate silos undisturbed by the other doctrinal loci but operate in concert.

## PERSON OF THE HOLY SPIRIT: PROCESSIONS

The Niceno-Constantinopolitan Creed (381) confesses belief in one God, who consists of God the Father and the Son of God, who is "begotten from the Father before all ages, God from God, Light from Light, true God from true God, begotten, not made," who is "of the same essence as the Father." The Spirit is the "Lord, the giver of life," who "proceeds from the Father and the Son, and with the Father and the Son is worshipped and glorified." The creed also affirms that the Spirit "spoke through the prophets." The creed argues that the one true God therefore exists in three persons, who are all equally God. In this vein, the creed makes three major claims regarding the Holy Spirit. First, the Holy Spirit is God, given that it denominates him as "Lord" and states that he should be worshiped together with the Father and the Son. Second, the Holy Spirit is a divine person, and as the Third Person of the trinity, he proceeds from the Father and the Son.[2] Third, the creed attributes two major works to the Spirit: (1) he is the "giver of life," which means he is both creator and re-creator, and (2) he is the one who spoke through the prophets, which means he inspired the Scriptures.[3]

---

2. On the Reformed explanation of the *filioque*, see Richard A. Muller, *Post Reformation Reformed* (Grand Rapids: Baker, 2003), 4:373–76. See also Marc A. Pugliese, "How Important Is the Filioque for Reformed Orthodoxy?," *WTJ* 66, no. 1 (2004): 159–77. For a history of the *filioque*, see A. Edward Siecienski, *The Filioque: History of a Doctrinal Controversy* (Oxford: Oxford University Press, 2010).

3. Gregg R. Allison and Andreas J. Köstenberger, *The Holy Spirit*, Theology for the People of God (Nashville: B&H Academic, 2020), 237–38.

The Scriptures record a number of statements that confirm these doctrinal claims. One of the most important claims appears in the apostle Peter's interaction with Ananias and Sapphira, who sold their property and held back some of the money but wanted to give the impression that they gave all of the proceeds to the church, so they lied. Peter confronted their deception: "Ananias, why has Satan filled your heart to lie to the Holy Spirit and to keep back for yourself part of the proceeds of the land? ... You have not lied to man but to God" (Acts 5:3–4). When Peter confronted Sapphira, he asked her: "How is it that you have agreed together to test the Spirit of the Lord?" (Acts 5:9). The lexeme πειράσαι τὸ πνεῦμα κυρίου ("test the Spirit of the Lord") is an Old Testament expression for sinning against Yahweh: "Why do you test the LORD?" (Exod 17:2; also, e.g., Deut 6:16; Ps 78:18, 41, 56).[4] This Acts passage alone therefore confirms that the Holy Spirit is God. In addition to this Acts passage, however, are other passages that confirm the deity of the Spirit. The Bible affirms the omnipresence of the Spirit: "Where shall I go from your Spirit? Or where shall I flee from your presence? If I ascend to heaven, you are there! If I make my bed in Sheol, you are there!" (Ps 139:7–8).[5] The Spirit also possesses wisdom, understanding, counsel, might, and knowledge (Isa 11:2). Paul attributes omniscience to the Spirit: "For the Spirit searches everything, even the depths of God. For who knows a person's thoughts except the spirit of that person, which is in him? So also no one comprehends the thoughts of God except the Spirit of God" (1 Cor 2:10–11).[6] The Scriptures ascribe immensity to the Spirit: "Who has measured the Spirit of the LORD?" (Isa 40:13). These passages reveal that the Spirit possesses the same attributes as Yahweh and thus is God.

Other passages of Scripture reveal that the Spirit is a member of the Godhead with both the Father and the Son. In the opening chapter of the Bible, the Spirit hovers over the primordial waters (Gen 1:2), and the Godhead deliberates over the creation of human beings: "Then God said, 'Let us make man in our image, after our likeness'" (Gen 1:26).[7] At the baptism of the Son, the Father thunders his approbation out of the heavens for his Son,

---

4. Allison and Köstenberger, *Holy Spirit*, 239–40.

5. Allison and Köstenberger, *Holy Spirit*, 240.

6. Smeaton, *Doctrine of the Holy Spirit*, 111.

7. Christopher J. H. Wright, *Knowing the Holy Spirit through the Old Testament* (Downers Grove, IL: InterVarsity Press, 2006), 13–18; Thomas Goodwin, *The Work of the Holy Ghost in*

and the Spirit descends on him in the form of a dove (Matt 3:16–17). In the Great Commission Jesus commands the church to baptize into the name of the Triune God: "All authority in heaven and on earth has been given to me. Go therefore and make disciples of all nations, baptizing them in the name of the Father and the Son and of the Holy Spirit" (Matt 28:18–19). Likewise, the apostle Paul presents Trinitarian benedictions in his epistles: "The grace of the Lord Jesus Christ and the love of God and the fellowship of the Holy Spirit be with you all" (2 Cor 13:14).[8]

These passages confirm both the deity of the Spirit and the existence of the Triune God. But how exactly do we understand the Spirit's ontological relationship to the Father and the Son?

The church has historically spoken of the Triune God sharing in one divine essence or substance. They use this *terminus technicus* ("technical term") to refer to the various places that the Bible attributes divinity to each member of the godhead: Father (John 1:18), Son (John 1:1–4), and Spirit (Acts 5:3–4; see *ST* Ia, qq. 33–38).[9] On the other hand, Father, Son, and Holy Spirit are distinct persons within the Godhead, to whom the church has applied the term *hypostases* or *subsistences* (*ST* Ia, q. 29, arts 1–2).[10] We must therefore recognize the unity of the Godhead (that all three persons are God and share the same divine essence), which is a rejection of tritheism—we do not worship three gods. Or, as Herman Bavinck (1854–1921) observes: In "each of the three persons, we might say, the divine being is completely coextensive with being the Father, Son, and Spirit."[11] In more technical terms, theologians have referred to *perichoresis*, which is the "mutual indwelling of the three persons of the Trinity in the one being of God."[12]

*Our Salvation* 1.7, in *The Works of Thomas Goodwin* (Eureka, CA: Tanski, 1996), 6:49; John Owen, *Pneumatologia* 1.3, in *Works of John Owen* 3:75.

8. Allison and Köstenberger, *Holy Spirit*, 241–42.

9. See Gilles Emery, *The Trinitarian Theology of St. Thomas Aquinas* (Oxford: Oxford University Press, 2010); Emery, *The Trinity: An Introduction to the Catholic Doctrine of the Triune God* (Washington, DC: Catholic University of America Press, 2011), 83–110.

10. See also Richard A. Muller, *Dictionary of Latin and Greek Theological Terms: Drawn Principally from Protestant Scholastic Theology*, 2nd ed. (Grand Rapids: Baker Academic, 2017), s.v. *hypostasis* and *subsistentia* (155, 346).

11. Bavinck, *Reformed Dogmatics* 2:305.

12. Robert Letham, *The Holy Trinity: In Scripture, History, Theology, and Worship* (Phillipsburg: NJ: P&R, 2004), 501.

Scripture speaks of this when Christ states: "I am in the Father and the Father is in me" (John 14:10). John of Damascus (ca. 675–749) explains:

> The abiding and resting of the Persons in one another is not in such a manner that they coalesce or become confused, but, rather, so that they adhere to one another, for they are without interval between them and inseparable and their mutual indwelling is without confusion. For the Son is in the Father and the Spirit, and the Spirit is in the Father and the Son, and the Father is in the Son and the Spirit, and there is no merging or bleeding or confusion.[13]

Conversely, we recognize the three persons without collapsing them into the essence lest we promote unitarianism, modalism, or monarchianism (i.e., that there is only one person in the Godhead). As St. Anselm (1033–1109) succinctly states: "The unity should never lose its consequences except when a relational opposition stands in the way" (see also *ST* Ia, q. 34, art 1).[14] In other words, Father, Son, and Holy Spirit are all God, but the Father is neither the Son nor the Spirit, the Son is neither the Father nor the Spirit, and the Spirit is neither the Father nor the Son.

The church has distinguished the different members of the Godhead in terms of both their unique names (e.g., Father, Son, and Holy Spirit) and their intra-Trinitarian personal relations, or what theologians have designated the *opera ad intra* ("internal work").[15] The church has further distinguished the essence and persons of the Godhead through the idea of a *notion*, which is a proper idea whereby we know a divine person. The person of the Father is not from another, and thus he possesses the notion of *innascibility*. The Father can be known in two other ways. Because the Son is from him, the Father is known by the notion of *paternity*, and since the Spirit is from the Father he is also known by the notion *spiration*. The Son is begotten by the Father and thus possesses the notion of *filiation*, but since the Spirit is also from the Son, the Son also possesses the notion of *spiration*. The Spirit is from another and is thus known by the notion of *procession*,

---

13. John of Damascus, *An Exact Exposition of the Orthodox Faith*, in *Saint John of Damascus*, trans. Frederic H. Chase Jr., FC 37 (Washington, D.C.: Catholic University of America Press, 1958), 1.14.

14. St. Anselm, *On the Procession of the Holy Spirit* 6, in *Anselm of Canterbury: The Major Works*, ed. Brian Davies and G. R. Evans (Oxford: Oxford University Press, 1998), 393.

15. Muller, *Dictionary*, s.v. *opera ad intra* (244).

as he proceeds from both the Father and the Son. There are therefore five notions: innascibility, paternity, filiation, spiration, and procession (*ST* Ia, q. 32, art 3). In the simplest terms, the notions are another way of saying Father, Son, and Holy Spirit. Still yet another way of expressing the notions comes to us in the Athanasian Creed: "The Father was neither made nor created nor begotten from anyone. The Son was neither made nor created; he was begotten from the Father alone. The Holy Spirit was neither made nor created nor begotten; he proceeds from the Father and the Son." The two processions within the Godhead are therefore the Son's eternal begetting and the Spirit's eternal proceeding. We distinguish between the two types of processions, filiation versus spiration, to differentiate between the Son and Spirit (Gregory of Nazianzus, *Oration* 5.8).[16]

The Belgic Confession (1561) echoes both the Trinitarian notions and the Athanasian Creed when it explains the nature of the Spirit's deity: "We believe and confess also that the Holy Spirit proceeds eternally from the Father and the Son—neither made, nor created, nor begotten, but only proceeding from the two of them. In regard to order, the Spirit is the third person of the Trinity—of one and the same essence, and majesty, and glory, with the Father and the Son, being true and eternal God, as the Holy Scriptures teach us" (11). The Belgic Confession affirms the full deity of the Spirit, thus highlighting the shared divine essence, when it states that the Spirit is neither made nor created and that he is of one and the same essence as the Father and Son. But the confession equally stresses the Spirit's person when it distinguishes his proceeding from begetting, which is unique to the Son.[17]

Since soteriology specifically deals with the work of the Spirit, we will focus on the Spirit's names and procession. The Third Person of the Trinity possesses the name "Holy Spirit," as numerous places in the Old Testament and Gospels attest (e.g., Ps 51:1; Isa 63:10–11; Matt 1:18, 20; 3:11; 12:32; 28:19; Mark 1:8; 3:29; 13:11; Luke 1:35, 41, 67; 2:25; 3:16; 3:22; 4:1; 10:21; 11:13; 12:10; 12:12; John 1:33; 14:26; 20:22). In addition to this, the Scriptures also call the

16. See also Augustine, *Trinity*, 518.

17. For a survey of the doctrine of the Holy Spirit in early modern confessional Reformed theology, see Yuzo Adhinarta, *The Doctrine of the Holy Spirit in the Major Reformed Confessions and Catechisms of the Sixteenth and Seventeenth Centuries* (Cambridge: Langham, 2012); also see Smeaton, *Doctrine of the Holy Spirit*, 312–13.

Spirit "love," "gift," and "comforter" or "helper." As noted in chapter 1, "God is love" (1 John 4:7–8), but "love is from God."[18] God sends his love through both his Son and the Spirit: "By this we know that we abide in him and he in us, because he has given us of his Spirit" (1 John 4:13). The Spirit is the means by which the Father applies his love in the Son.[19] As Paul writes: "Hope does not put us to shame, because God's love has been poured into our hearts through the Holy Spirit who has been given to us" (Rom 5:5). But the Spirit is also gift, which is another proper name of the Spirit. As Peter states in his Pentecost sermon: "Repent and be baptized every one of you in the name of Jesus Christ for the forgiveness of your sins, and you will receive the gift of the Holy Spirit" (Acts 2:38; see also 8:19; 10:45; 11:17; *ST* Ia, qq. 37–38).[20] Perhaps one of the best-known names for the Holy Spirit is παράκλητος ("comforter" or "helper"). Although Scripture calls Jesus our "advocate" (παράκλητον, 1 John 2:1), Jesus gives the Spirit this name because, as the Helper or Advocate, the Spirit brings to the church's remembrance the teachings of Christ (John 14:26).[21] He also assists believers when they pray as he "intercedes for us with groanings too deep for words" (Rom 8:26).

## WORK OF THE HOLY SPIRIT: MISSIONS

The intra-Trinitarian processions lead to the Trinitarian missions.[22] Alternatively stated, ontology leads to economy.[23] In the simplest of terms, our salvation reflects the nature and attributes of our Triune God. In this case, there are different passages of Scripture that reveal that the Father sends the Son (e.g., John 6:44, 57; 8:16, 42; 10:36; 12:49; 14:24; 17:21, 25; 20:21) and that the Father and the Son send the Spirit (John 14:26; 15:26). Theologians have designated these sendings as Trinitarian *missions*. A mission implies a kind of procession of the one sent from the sender, such as when a master sends a servant (*ST* Ia, q. 43, art 1).

18. Augustine, *Trinity*, 451–528.

19. Levering, *Engaging the Doctrine*, 56.

20. Levering, *Engaging the Doctrine*, 61–62.

21. Carson, *Gospel according to John*, 505.

22. Christopher R. J. Holmes, *The Holy Spirit*, NSD (Grand Rapids: Zondervan, 2015), 74–75; also Smeaton, *Doctrine of the Holy Spirit*, 105–15; Goodwin, *Work of the Holy Ghost* 1.1 (*Works of John Owen* 6:5); Owen, *Pneumatologia* 1.3–4, 2.5 (*Works of John Owen* 3:92, 116–17, 198–99).

23. Holmes, *Holy Spirit*, 76.

With respect to the missions of the Son and Spirit, they are temporal, which stands in contrast to the eternal ontological processions. The Son, for example, proceeds eternally from the Father as his only begotten Son, but he temporally was born in human nature according to his visible mission (*ST* Ia, q. 43, art 2). The Spirit eternally proceeds from the Father and the Son, and the Father and Son temporally send the Spirit in a visible manner as the agent of sanctification. The Spirit as the love of God is the gift of sanctification (*ST* Ia, q. 43, art 7). The eternal processions lead to the visible missions—ontology grounds economy. But we must factor three important elements regarding the processions and missions concerning the link between ontology and economy.

First, as the introduction noted, we must keep the *pactum salutis* ("covenant of redemption") in view to frame rightly the Trinitarian missions. The Triune God only comes to human beings by way of covenant. In this case, the Father, Son, and Holy Spirit covenant among themselves to elect, create, and redeem a people.[24] The Scriptures clearly reveal that from all eternity the triune God decreed to create and redeem a people (Eph 1:4–7; 3:11; 2 Thess 2:13; 2 Tim 1:9; Jas 2:5; 1 Pet 1:2). The Scriptures present the elements of this decree in terms of a covenantal agreement. Jesus told his disciples: "I covenant to you, as my Father has covenanted to me, a kingdom" (ἀγὼ διατίθεμαι ὑμῖν καθὼς διέθετό μοι ὁ πατήρ μου βασιλείαν; Luke 22:29, my trans.). The Father swore a covenantal oath to the Son: the Son "was made a priest with an oath by the one who said to him: 'The Lord has sworn and will not change his mind, "You are a priest forever"'" (Heb 7:21; see Pss 110:4; 105:8–10, esp. v. 9). The author of Hebrews explains that the Father made the Son the covenant guarantor, or surety, of a better covenant by means of his covenantal oath (Heb 7:22).[25] The Son's references to his Father's covenantal commission appear when he repeatedly says the Father sent him (John 5:30, 43; 6:38–40; 17:4–12). The Father covenantally commissions the Son to create and redeem a people. But given the ontology of the Trinity, namely that the Triune God always works in concert, we must naturally factor the Spirit's role in the covenant of redemption.

24. For an exposition of the covenant of redemption, see Fesko, *Trinity and the Covenant*, 129–42.

25. For a fuller treatment of Ps 110:4 and Heb 7:21–22, see Fesko, *Trinity and the Covenant*, 95–106.

Just as the Son testifies to his covenantal commission by speaking of the Father sending him, the Son also confirms the Spirit's mission: "But the Helper, the Holy Spirit, who the Father will send in my name, he will teach you all things and bring to your remembrance all that I have said to you" (John 14:26). Here Jesus reveals that the Father will send the Spirit. Jesus also says that he will send the Spirit: "But when the Helper comes, whom I will send to you from the Father, the Spirit of truth, who proceeds from the Father, he will bear witness about me" (John 15:26). As the Father sends the Son, so too the Father and Son send the Spirit; correlatively, the Holy Spirit does not send himself. That the Son and Spirit are sent means that both voluntarily go. This does not mean, of course, that the will of the Triune God is split but rather the single will of God applies to the members of the Trinity in different ways. In more technical terms, the will of the Triune God does not negate the important distinction of the divine appropriations. As John Owen explains: "The will of God as to the peculiar actings of the Father in this matter is the will of the Father, and the will of God with regard unto the peculiar actings of the Son is the will of the Son; not by a distinction of sundry wills, but by the distinct application of the same will unto its *distinct acts* in the persons of the Father and the Son."[26] The covenant of redemption is the context where the Triune God defines these Trinitarian missions. The Trinitarian missions naturally follow the intra-Trinitarian processions; or, the economy of redemption reflects the ontology of the Trinity.

Second, both the ontology of the Trinity and the covenant of redemption inseparably unite the work of the Son and Spirit in creation and redemption. Creation and redemption do not unfold in a sequential manner, where the Father first steps on the stage of history, followed by the Son, and finally succeeded by the Spirit, where the three only unite on stage for the final curtain call to take a bow.[27] Or stated another way, the persons of the Godhead do not act independently in either creation or redemption. The Triune God always works in concert, or, in words attributed to St. Augustine: *opera trinitatis ad extra indivisa sunt*, "the external works of

---

26. John Owen, "Exercitation XXVIII: Federal Transactions between the Father and the Son," in *Works of John Owen* 19:87–88.

27. Kuyper, *Work of the Holy Spirit*, 46–47.

the trinity are indivisible."[28] The Father is active in creation and redemption because he sends both the Son and the Spirit to create and redeem. The Son and the Spirit are the two hands of the Father by which he creates and redeems (Irenaeus, *Against Heresies* 4.20.1, 5.6.1). The Scriptures clearly attest to the Son's and Spirit's agency in creation. The Spirit hovered over the primordial waters (Gen 1:2), and the Father consulted the Son when he said, "Let us make man in our image, after our likeness" (Gen 1:26; see, e.g., Ambrose, *Exposition of the Christian Faith* 1.7.53, 1.17.111; John Chrysostom, *Homilies on Genesis* 14.16). The New Testament also reveals that all things were made through the Son, and without him was not any thing made that was made (John 1:3; Col 1:16; Heb 1:3). That the Son and Spirit continue to work in concert in redemption is evident from a number of passages, but Pentecost features prominently, where upon his exaltation to the right hand of the Father, the Son poured out the Holy Spirit (Acts 2:33). In this vein the eternal Son fulfills his temporal mission as the eschatological Adam by becoming the "life-giving Spirit" (1 Cor 15:45, my trans.). The Son's outpouring of the Spirit gives rise to the lexeme "the Spirit of Christ" (Acts 16:7; Rom 8:9; Gal 4:6; Phil 1:19).[29]

The Son and the Spirit work together in redemption both in the Son's temporal mission of his life, death, and resurrection and in the application of redemption to the elect. The Westminster Confession of Faith (1647) captures the united nature of the Son's and Spirit's work when it recounts that the Son was incarnate by the "power of the Holy Ghost, in the womb of the virgin Mary, of her substance" (8.2). He was "sanctified, and anointed with the Holy Spirit, above measure, having in him all the treasures of wisdom and knowledge" (8.3), he offered himself up by his "perfect obedience, and sacrifice" "through the eternal Spirit" (8.5), and he applies and communicates his purchased redemption by "effectually persuading them by his Spirit to believe and obey." He governs "their hearts by his Word and Spirit" (8.8). Christology is therefore intrinsically pneumatological,

28. Cornelis van der Kooi and Gijsbert van den Brink, *Christian Dogmatics: An Introduction*, trans. Reinder Bruinsma and James D. Bratt (Grand Rapids: Eerdmans, 2017), 97; see also Smeaton, *Doctrine of the Holy Spirit*, 108.

29. Owen, *Pneumatologia* 1.2 (*Works of John Owen* 3:60–64).

and conversely pneumatology is inherently christological.[30] Salvation is fundamentally Trinitarian.

Third, the Spirit applies the salvation wrought by the Son by uniting the elect to the Son. The Old Testament presents salvation in terms of Israel's marital union with Yahweh, a relationship parabolically captured in the prophet Hosea's marriage to Gomer, an adulterous woman (Hos 1:2). The same marital-union imagery appears in Ezekiel (16:8–21). As this imagery progressively sharpens with the revelation of God in Christ, Paul connects the marriage relationship between Adam and Eve to the church's marital union with Christ: "'Therefore a man shall leave his father and mother and hold fast to his wife, and the two shall become one flesh.' This mystery is profound, and I am saying that it refers to Christ and the church" (Eph 5:31–32; see Gen 2:24). The Holy Spirit is the agent who unites sinners to Christ to affect their redemption because the blessings of salvation come only from Christ. Only by union with Christ can a sinner lay hold of his perfect obedience and satisfaction. But the Triune God who saves sinners continues to work in a Trinitarian fashion. In other words, the processions and covenantal missions shape the *ordo salutis* ("order of salvation").

The eternal Trinitarian processions are the basis for the missions of the Son and Spirit, which first become manifest in the covenant of redemption.[31] The Son's mission as covenant surety takes priority to the Spirit's work of application because his mission is logically (in the covenant of redemption) prior to the Spirit's mission. There is no outpouring of the Spirit apart from the Son's completed work as surety: "The Spirit is life because of righteousness" (Rom 8:10). Thus, the basis for the priorities of the *ordo salutis* lies in the covenant of redemption, which ultimately rests in the Trinitarian processions.[32] Justification (the legal, forensic aspect of our union with Christ) takes logical priority to sanctification (the transformative aspect of our union with Christ) because of the logical priority

30. Smeaton, *Doctrine of the Holy Spirit*, 116–36; Wright, *Knowing the Holy Spirit*, 112–15; Kuyper, *Work of the Holy Spirit*, 85–120; Goodwin, *Work of the Holy Ghost* 1.3, 8, 10 (6:10–13, 49–50, 66); Owen, *Pneumatologia* 2.3–4 (*Works of John Owen* 3:159–88).

31. Geerhardus Vos, *The Self-Disclosure of Jesus: The Modern Debate about the Messianic Consciousness*, 2nd ed., ed. J. G. Vos (Phillipsburg, NJ: P&R, n.d.), 189–90.

32. Geerhardus Vos, "The Covenant in Reformed Theology," in *Redemptive History and Biblical Interpretation*, 248; also Owen, *Pneumatologia* 1.6 (*Works of John Owen* 3:94).

of the Son's mission as covenant surety to the Spirit's mission as the agent of sanctification.

## CONCLUSION

Even though the Holy Spirit is the agent of the application of salvation, the Spirit always works in concert with the whole Triune God. The Father, Son and Spirit do not pass the baton of salvation as each takes their turn running on the track of redemptive history. Rather, the Father sends the Son, who accomplishes his covenantal mission in the anointing and power of the Spirit, and the Father and Son both send the Spirit to apply the life-saving work of the Son. The Heidelberg Catechism captures the Trinitarian nature of salvation when it asks, "What do you believe concerning 'the Holy Spirit'?" The catechism responds: "First, that the Spirit, with the Father and the Son, is eternal God. Second, that the Spirit is given also to me, so that, through true faith, he makes me share in Christ and all his benefits, comforts me, and will remain with me forever" (q. 53).

### FURTHER READING

Allison, Gregg R., and Andreas J. Köstenberger. *The Holy Spirit*. Theology for the People of God. Nashville: B&H Academic, 2020. One of the most recent full-fledged treatments of the doctrine of the Holy Spirit.

Emery, Gilles. *The Trinitarian Theology of St. Thomas Aquinas*. Oxford: Oxford University Press, 2010. Explains Aquinas's doctrine of the Trinity, which is a vital component to the historic Reformed understanding of the doctrine, as it is part of the Reformed tradition's catholic (universal church, not Roman Catholic) heritage.

Goodwin, Thomas. *The Work of the Holy Ghost in Our Salvation*. In *The Works of Thomas Goodwin*, vol. 6. Eureka, CA: Tanski, 1996. An often overlooked work on the person and work of the Holy Spirit written by a Westminster divine. This work is on par with John Owen's *Pneumatologia* and is required reading.

Gregory of Nazianzus. *On God and Christ: The Five Theological Orations and Two Letters to Cleodonius*. Yonkers, NY: St. Vladimir's Seminary Press, 2002. A classic work from one of the Cappadocian fathers who was instrumental in shaping the doctrine of the Nicene Creed over against false anti-Trinitarian teachings. This is required reading for any serious student of Scripture.

Kuyper, Abraham. *The Work of the Holy Spirit*. New York: Funk & Wagnalls, 1900. A contemporary classic on the work of the Holy Spirit that was written in the wake of the negative influence of G. W. F. Hegel on Protestant theology. Kuyper's work is in dialogue with historical sources but also addresses more recent concerns and issues.

Owen, John Owen. *Pneumatologia*. In *The Works of John Owen*, vol. 3, edited by William H. Goold. Edinburgh: Banner of Truth, 1994. A Reformed classic on the person and work of the Holy Spirit that is at the same time exegetical, historical, and theological. Owen's work is required reading.

V

# UNION WITH COMMUNION WITH CHRIST IN GRACE

## ELECTION AND APPLICATION

GREGORY OF NAZIANZUS (329–90) FAMOUSLY STATES that what the Son "has not assumed He has not healed; but that which is united to His Godhead is also saved."[1] Within the context of the fourth-century christological controversies, Gregory stressed the importance of the full humanity of Christ. If Christ was not fully human, then human beings could not be saved—the unassumed is unhealed. The Son therefore assumed a human nature in order to redeem fallen sinners. But Christ's assumption of a human nature is only part of the salvation equation. As Gregory avers, God must unite fallen sinners to Christ in order to save them. Whether in Christology or soteriology, the unassumed is unhealed. The doctrine of union with Christ is therefore a focal point of soteriology. Only union with the incarnated and resurrected Son of God grants sinners access to the blessings of redemption. Through union with Christ redeemed sinners then enjoy communion and fellowship with the Triune God. As John Owen has explains: "Our communion, then, with God consists in his communication of himself unto us with our return unto him of that which he requires and accepts, flowing from that union which Jesus Christ we have with him."[2] The means by

1. Gregory of Nazianzus, "Against Apollinarius," *NPNF*² 7:440.
2. Owen, *Communion with God*, 8–9. Archaic English in this quote has been contemporized.

which the Triune God unites sinners to the Son is the applicatory work of the Holy Spirit. According to William Perkins (1558–1602), the Spirit is the bond of the believer's union with Christ by means of his gift of faith and indwelling presence.[3] John Calvin gives classic expression to this idea in the opening words of book 3 of his *Institutes*: "So long as we are without Christ and separated from him, nothing which he suffered and did for the salvation of the human race is of the least benefit to us. To communicate to us the blessings which he received from the Father, he must become ours and dwell in us."[4]

God's work of uniting elect sinners to the Son has multiple facets, being effected through a series of acts and processes, which have historically been set forth in the *ordo salutis* ("order of salvation"): predestination, effectual calling, faith, justification, adoption, sanctification, and glorification.[5] These are all distinct elements in our union with Christ that cannot be confused with the other. Predestination, for example, is not sanctification, and glorification is not justification, but they are all part of our union with Christ. In his wisdom and grace, God has assigned an order to the application of the different aspects of our union with Christ.[6] Contrary to the claims of some, union with Christ and the *ordo salutis* are not incompatible.[7] To speak of union with Christ is to observe the forest, and to discuss the *ordo salutis* is to notice the individual trees. In other words, to discuss the *ordo salutis* is to speak of union with Christ. Technically, the first step of our union with Christ comes in predestination, which is evident when

---

3. William Perkins, *A Golden Chaine, or The Description of Theologie, Containing the Order of the Causes of Salvation and Damnation, According to Gods Word* (Cambridge: John Legate, 1597), 36 (p. 139).

4. Calvin, *Inst.* 3.1.1.

5. Geerhardus Vos, *Reformed Dogmatics*, 5 vols., ed. Richard B. Gaffin Jr. (Bellingham, WA: Lexham Press, 2014–16), 4:1–2.

6. John Murray, *Redemption Accomplished and Applied* (Grand Rapids: Eerdmans, 1955), 79–80.

7. E.g., William B. Evans, *Imputation and Impartation: Union with Christ in American Reformed Theology* (Milton Keynes, UK: Paternoster, 2008), 43–83, 264–66, esp. 265; G. C. Berkouwer, *Faith and Justification*, SD (Grand Rapids: Eerdmans, 1954), 30–32; Otto Weber, *Foundations for Dogmatics*, trans. Darrell L. Guder (Grand Rapids: Eerdmans, 1983), 2:337–40; Karl Barth, *Theology of the Reformed Confessions*, trans. Darrell L. Guder and Judith J. Guder (Louisville: Westminster John Knox, 2002), 151–52; Garner, *Sons in the Son*, 219–55, 287–314. For an engagement of criticisms and defense of the *ordo salutis*, see J. V. Fesko, "Romans 8.29–30 and the Question of the *Ordo Salutis*," *Journal of Reformed Theology* 8 (2014): 35–60.

Paul writes: "He chose us in him [ἐν αὐτῷ]," in Christ, "before the foundation of the world" (Eph 1:4).[8] In election God unites sinners to the Son by means of the decree of election, which theologians have called the union of the decree.[9]

The union of application, when the Spirit unites elect sinners to Christ by faith, begins with the sinner's effectual calling.[10] Effectual calling is the work of the Holy Spirit whereby he invites and draws sinners to Christ by his regenerating work and word by enlightening their minds and renewing their wills, which enables them to receive Christ by faith (WLC, q. 67). This effectual call initiates the sinner's union with Christ. The Westminster Larger Catechism, for example, explains: "The union with the elect have with Christ is the work of God's grace, whereby they are spiritually and mystically, yet really and inseparably, joined to Christ as their head and husband; which is done in their effectual calling" (q. 66; see qq. 64–69). Heinrich Heppe (1820–1879) likewise observes: "According to its real nature the calling of the elect is thus an *insitio in Christum* ["grafting in Christ"] or *unio cum Christo* ["union with Christ"], a real, wholesale, spiritual and indissoluble union of the person of the elect with the divine-human person of the Redeemer, so that for the former the latter is exactly the same as soul is for body."[11] In order to have a better understanding of effectual calling, this chapter first unpacks the biblical data about the Spirit's effectual call. Second, the chapter constructs the doctrine by comparing and contrasting the biblical data with other competing views. Third and finally, the chapter concludes with summary observations about the nature of the Spirit's effectual call.

## BIBLICAL DATA

There are a number of passages of Scripture that underscore the power of God's word in both creation and redemption as the Spirit applies it to the work of the Triune

---

8. Constantine R. Campbell, *Paul and Union with Christ: An Exegetical and Theological Study* (Grand Rapids: Zondervan, 2012), 177, 330, 354.

9. E.g., Herman Witsius, *Conciliatory, or Irenical Animadversions on the Controversies Agitated in Britain, Under the Unhappy Names of Antinomians and Neonomians*, trans. Thomas Bell (Glasgow: W. Lang, 1807), 6.1 (p. 67).

10. Witsius, *Animadversions* 6.4 (pp. 68–69).

11. Heinrich Heppe, *Reformed Dogmatics: Set Out and Illustrated from the Sources*, trans. G. T. Thomson, ed. Ernst Bizer (London: George and Unwin, 1950), 511.

God. In the beginning, when there was nothing but the Triune God, he spoke the creation into existence by the power of his word: "And God said, 'Let there be light,' and there was light" (Gen 1:3).[12] Isaiah comments on the life-giving and effectual nature of God's word: "For as the rain and the snow come down from heaven and do not return there but water the earth, making it bring forth and sprout, giving seed to the sower and bread to the eater, so shall my word be that goes out from my mouth; it shall not return to me empty, but it shall accomplish that which I purpose, and shall succeed in the thing for which I sent it" (Isa 55:10–11). The psalmist writes: "By the word of the Lord the heavens were made, and by the breath of his mouth all their host" (Ps 33:6). God's creative word is also redemptive, a point Paul captures when he describes Abraham's salvation in creation language: "'I have made you the father of many nations'—in the presence of the God in whom he believed, who gives life to the dead and calls into existence the things that do not exist" (Rom 4:17).[13] Paul draws his Old Testament text from Genesis 17:5 (LXX), which expounds God's promise to Abraham in Genesis 15:5. As much as God's promise focuses on Abraham, Paul sees something larger at work—God's effectual call (*verbum efficax*) to Abraham brought Abraham into existence, he who was dead in his sins and trespasses. God's call brought into existence things that did not exist, a redemptive act that clearly echoes the opening creative acts of God.[14]

The effectual call of God appears powerfully in Ezekiel's valley of dry bones as Spirit and word work in concert to bring about redemption. The prophet portrays Israel as lying in an exilic graveyard, and to emphasize their macabre state he describes the nation as a valley of dry bones (Ezek 37:1–3; see Jer 8:1–3).[15] God then commanded the prophet: "Prophesy over these bones, and say to them, O dry bones, hear the word of the Lord. Thus says the Lord God to these bones: Behold, I will cause breath to enter you, and you shall live" (Ezek 37:4–5). God told Ezekiel that his prophetic word

12. Michael S. Horton, *Covenant and Salvation: Union with Christ* (Louisville: Westminster John Knox, 2007), 216–42.

13. Hughes Oliphant Old, *The Reading and Preaching of the Scriptures in the Worship of the Christian Church* (Grand Rapids: Eerdmans, 1998), 1:228.

14. Beale and Carson, *Commentary on the New Testament Use*, 636.

15. Daniel I. Block, *The Book of Ezekiel: Chapters 25–48*, NICOT (Grand Rapids: Eerdmans, 1998), 373–79.

would cause the valley of dry bones to come to life (Ezek 37:6). Ezekiel prophesied over the dry bones, and they rattled and assembled, sinews began to form, and flesh covered the bones, but like Adam in his initial creation by God, "there was no breath in them" (Ezek 37:8). Echoing the Spirit's in-breathing of life into Adam's nostrils, God commanded Ezekiel: "Prophesy to the breath; prophesy, son of man, and say to the breath, Thus says the Lord God: Come from the four winds, O breath, and breathe on these slain, that they may live" (Ezek 37:9; see Gen 2:7; John 20:22).[16] So, Ezekiel prophesied again, and the bones "lived and stood on their feet, an exceedingly great army" (Ezek 37:10). God's redemptive word brought Israel to life—his word resurrected people dead in sin.

The redemptive power of God's word appears especially in the context of resurrection, such as when, after Lazarus had been dead in his tomb for four days, Jesus commanded that the stone be moved away, prayed, and then cried: "Lazarus, come out" (John 11:43). Lazarus came to life and emerged from his tomb still bound in burial cloths (John 11:44). Jesus explicitly connected the resurrection of the saints with the power of his word: "Truly, truly, I say to you, an hour is coming, and is now here, when the dead will hear the voice of the Son of God, and those who hear will live" (John 5:25; see 6:63, 68; 11:43; Isa 55:3; Ezek 37:1–10).[17] The Scriptures therefore attribute creation and redemption to the word of God, whether in terms of God's effectual call as that which raises people from spiritual death to life, or the voice of Christ as that which raises the dead from their graves to everlasting life. Herman Bavinck makes the connection between Ezekiel's valley of dry bones and the resurrecting power of Christ's word: "The preaching of the prophet was nevertheless the route whereby and the occasion when God revealed His life-giving power in the dry and dead bones. Similarly, it was not the outward sound of Jesus' voice that made Lazarus rise from the dead; nonetheless, the dead Lazarus came forth at the moment when Jesus called with a loud voice, 'Lazarus, come forth!'"[18]

But the Bible also links the word of God to the ongoing work of redemption in sanctification. Paul, for example, praises the Thessalonians because

16. Block, *Ezekiel*, 379.

17. Carson, *Gospel according to John*, 256.

18. Herman Bavinck, *Saved by Grace: The Holy Spirit's Work in Calling and Regeneration*, trans. Nelson D. Kloosterman (Grand Rapids: Reformation Heritage Books, 2012), 159.

they received the word of God through apostolic preaching and teaching and because they did not receive it as the word of men, and he also characterizes the word of God as that "which is at work in you believers" (1 Thess 2:13). The apostolic preaching and teaching was not a *nuda verbum*: "Our gospel came to you not only in word, but also in power and in the Holy Spirit and with full conviction" (1 Thess 1:5). In other words, the Holy Spirit works through the word to effect redemption, which begins with the initial effectual call. Throughout all of preredemptive and redemptive history, God speaks, and the Spirit applies his word to reveal his will. God's word therefore brings about what he declares, which is the truth that lies behind the doctrine of effectual calling.

## DOCTRINAL CONSTRUCTION

The biblical data shapes doctrinal formulation in a manner that precludes certain views.[19] The Roman Catholic Church maintains that regeneration, or being raised from spiritual death to life, the raising of the inner man, occurs through baptism. Baptism, not God's effectual call, regenerates *ex opere operato* ("by the work performed").[20] Some Lutheran theologians have advocated a view of baptismal regeneration. Johannes Quendstedt (1617–1688), for example, argues: "The Spirit acts efficaciously in, with and by the water of Baptism, works faith, regeneration, and renovation in those who do not strive against God."[21] Remonstrant theologians such as Jacob Arminius (1560–1609) move effectual calling away from the word of God and place it under the locus of divine providence. Through divine providence God dispenses "supernatural gifts, and elevation of dignities … according to the right use of both nature and grace," which means that all people have the ability and capacity to accept or reject Christ.[22] In other words, the power of regeneration does not lie within the

---

19. For the structure of what follows, see Louis Berkhof, *Systematic Theology: New Combined Edition* (repr., Grand Rapids: Eerdmans, 1996), 451–52, 458–59.

20. *Catechism of the Catholic Church*, 2nd ed. (New York: Doubleday, 2003), §§1265–66.

21. As cited in Heinrich Schmid, *The Doctrinal Theology of the Evangelical Lutheran Church*, trans. Charles A. Hay and Henry E. Jacobs (Philadelphia: Lutheran Publication Society, 1876), 557.

22. Jacob Arminius, *Private Disputations* 28.5, in *The Works of James Arminius*, ed. James Nichols and William Nichols (Grand Rapids: Baker Book House, 1996), 2:367; also Arminius, "Disputation XVI: On the Vocation of Men to Salvation," in *Works* 2:230–31; see J. V. Fesko,

scope of God's efficacious call, but because of the providential dispensation of prevenient grace, the ability to believe lies within the human will.

Rationalist accounts, for instance the theology of Pelagius (360–420) or Charles Finney (1792–1875), attribute regeneration entirely to the human mind apart from the work of the Holy Spirit.[23] Such views make regeneration an entirely autonomous human act of moral reformation. Finney, for example, explains that since humans are not inherently sinful, they do not require a regenerating act of the Spirit: "No such change is needed, as the sinner has all the faculties and natural abilities requisite to render perfect obedience to God. All he requires is to be induced to use these powers and attributes as he ought."[24] The Spirit merely presents the truth; humans must actively embrace it on their own.[25] Roman Catholic, Lutheran baptismal regeneration, and rationalist views do not align with the biblical data on the Spirit's effectual call and should therefore be set aside, especially in the case of Pelagius and Finney because their views are heretical.

Among Reformed theologians, there have been two different trends that warrant examination, the views of Louis Berkhof (1873–1957) and those of Michael Horton. Berkhof maintains what is largely a traditional Reformed view of effectual calling, though he believes that one should separate effectual calling and regeneration. He acknowledges that the tradition has historically treated effectual calling and regeneration as interchangeable. He instead argues that regeneration "is that act of God by which the principle of new life is implanted in man, and the governing disposition of the soul is made holy." Conversely, effectual calling "is teleological, [and] draws out the new life and points it in a God-ward direction. It secures the exercises of the new disposition and brings the new life into action." According to Berkhof, there are therefore two distinct acts: God effectually calls a person through the word and points them in a God-ward direction, but

*Arminius and the Reformed Tradition: Grace and the Doctrine of Salvation* (Grand Rapids: Reformation Heritage Books, forthcoming), ch. 3.

23. See Pelagius, "To Demetrias," in *The Letters of Pelagius and His Followers*, trans. B. R. Rees (Rochester, NY: Boydell & Brewer, 1991), 40; Charles G. Finney, *Lectures on Revivals of Religion*, ed. William G. McLoughlin (Cambridge: Harvard University Press, 1960), 33.

24. Charles G. Finney, *Finney's Systematic Theology: The Complete and Newly Expanded 1878 Edition*, ed. Dennis Carroll, Bill Nicely, and L. G. Parkhurst Jr. (Minneapolis: Bethany House, 1994), 271–72.

25. Finney, *Finney's Systematic Theology*, 276.

regeneration is the hyperphysical act of the Spirit whereby he implants the principle of new life within the sinner.[26]

Horton, on the other hand, takes issue with historic understandings of effectual calling that posit the infusion of habits to effect regeneration, which means that Berkhof's understanding falls under Horton's critique. Horton engages Petrus Van Mastricht (1630–1706), who claims that regeneration and effectual calling work in concert but that regeneration is distinct. According to Van Mastricht, regeneration sows the seeds of grace that give a sinner the capacity positively to receive the call of God.[27] Horton believes Van Mastricht's idea is aligned with the earlier views of Thomas Aquinas and avers: "We do not need infused habits prior to speech, since God's speech itself comes from the Father in the Son and reaches its appointed goal through the Spirit."[28] Rather than posit two distinct acts, regeneration and the effectual call, Horton maintains we need only God's performative word, by which he effectually calls sinners to himself. Horton writes:

> Why do we need an immediately infused *habitus* to intervene between these mediated events? Why not just say that the Spirit regenerates through the proclaimed gospel ... just as the Reformed confessions and catechisms affirm? Do we really need to appeal to the medieval category of infused habits, however revised in content, in order to refute synergism?[29]

Berkhof and some Reformed theologians therefore conceive of two distinct acts: regeneration, by which God infuses a new habit or disposition into a person to make them receptive to the gospel, and the effectual call of the Spirit. Horton, on the other hand, eliminates regeneration as the infusion of a new habit and posits the need for only God's effectual call—his call is a regenerating call apart from the infusion of any habit. How do we proceed in the face of these differences of opinion? How do we formulate

26. Berkhof, *Systematic Theology*, 469, 471.

27. Petrus Van Mastricht, *A Treatise on Regeneration*, ed. Brandon Withrow (Morgan, PA: Soli Deo Gloria, 2002), 24, 26.

28. Horton, *Covenant and Salvation*, 227; see also Michael Horton, *The Christian Faith: A Systematic Theology for Pilgrims on the Way* (Grand Rapids: Zondervan, 2011), 608–11.

29. Horton, *Covenant and Salvation*, 239.

the doctrine of effectual calling? The biblical data provides us with three principles necessary for the doctrine.

First, we can distinguish between regeneration (the change that occurs within the sinner) and the Spirit's effectual call, but we should not separate them as Berkhof does.[30] Whether in creation or redemption, the Bible clearly reveals the powerful nature of God's word—he calls into existence things that do not exist. Thus the Westminster Confession rightly presents the effectual call as a regenerating call: "This effectual call is of God's free and special grace alone, not from anything at all foreseen in man, who is altogether passive therein, until, being quickened and renewed by the Holy Spirit, he is thereby enabled to answer this call, and to embrace the grace offered and conveyed in it" (10.2).[31] God effectually calls people through the word and Spirit, "which is at work in you believers" (1 Thess 2:13). The words of the gospel are the "power of God for salvation" (Rom 1:16; see 10:17; 1 Thess 2:5). Thus, effectual calling and regeneration are interchangeable terms and refer to the same act of God.

Second, as much as we need to account for the performative character of God's word, we must also explain the effect of God's word on the sinner. In biblical terms, God's word raises a sinner from spiritual death to life, what some passages refer to as the new birth (e.g., John 3:3, 7; 1 Pet 1:3, 23).[32] In the prophetic idiom, Moses speaks of the new birth as the circumcision of the heart (Deut 30:6) and Ezekiel as replacing the heart of stone with a heart of flesh (Ezek 36:26). Especially relevant in this regard is the seed imagery that the New Testament employs. Peter speaks of both the power of the word *and* the implanting of seed in connection with the new birth: "You have been born again, not of perishable seed but of imperishable, through the living and abiding word of God" (1 Pet 1:23). In this context the seed is God's word, which has been implanted in the believer.[33] John similarly writes: "No one born of God makes a practice of sinning,

30. For those who see effectual calling and regeneration as interchangeable, see Vos, *Reformed Dogmatics* 4:3; Johannes Wollebius, *Christiana Theologia Compendium* (Amsterdam: Johannes Jansonius, 1633), 38.1–2; Johannes Polyander et al., *Synopsis Purioris Theologiae / Synopsis of a Purer Theology*, ed. Dolf te Velde et al. (Leiden: Brill, 2014–20), 3:208–27.

31. So Horton, *Covenant and Salvation*, 235.

32. Vos, *Reformed Dogmatics* 4:30–31.

33. Karen H. Jobes, *1 Peter*, BECNT (Grand Rapids: Baker Academic, 2005), 124–25.

for God's seed abides in him; and he cannot keep on sinning, because he has been born of God" (1 John 3:9). In John's epistle "seed" takes on a slightly different nuance and refers not to the word but to the "divine principle of life which abides in the believer."[34]

The Spirit-empowered application of the word effects a change in the sinner, which the New Testament describes in terms of implanting a seed. The Westminster Confession and Westminster Larger Catechism capitalize on this language and speak of the "seed of God within" redeemed sinners as one of the sources of perseverance in salvation (17.2) and that even in the face of besetting sin, no believer is ever "utterly destitute of that seed of God" (18.4). Conversely, while the Westminster Standards reject the concept of infused grace in justification (11.1), they maintain the concept for the doctrine of sanctification: "God in justification imputeth the righteousness of Christ; in sanctification his Spirit infuseth grace, and enableth to the exercise thereof" (q. 77). The Standards do not invoke the specific term, but "infused grace" and "implanted seeds" are interchangeable with "infused habits."[35] Similarly, the Canons of Dort speak in this manner. When the Spirit effectually calls sinners, he "penetrates into the inmost being, opens the closed heart, softens the hard heart, and circumcises the heart that is uncircumcised. God infuses new qualities into the will, making the dead will alive, and evil one good, the unwilling one willing, and the stubborn one compliant" (3/4.11; see also 10–17).[36]

*Pace* Horton, the concept of an infused habit is a useful confessional metaphysical distinction to assist in explaining what occurs in the Spirit's effectual call.[37] When we invoke the category of an *infused* habit, we are saying that this is something that is received from without, not from within. God, for example, infuses the soul into the body at Adam's creation (Gen 2:7). The effectual call creates an infused habit within the sinner, which stands in stark contrast to an *acquired* habit, which is something that a

---

34. I. Howard Marshall, *The Epistles of John*, NICNT (Grand Rapids: Eerdmans, 1978), 186–87.

35. On the interchangeability of "seed" and "habit," see the work of Westminster divine Goodwin, *Work of the Holy Ghost* 5.i–5 (6:187–216).

36. Vos, *Reformed Dogmatics* 4:3, 55; also see Turretin, *Institutes of Elenctic Theology* 15.4.13–17.

37. Allen, *Sanctification*, 246–55.

person creates on their own through repetition.[38] To say that something is *infused* merely differentiates between what is natural to fallen human beings versus what God supernaturally gives. When we speak of an infused *habit*, we simply mean that we receive a divinely given disposition toward a particular end. As fallen sinners we have a natural disposition toward sin, but when God redeems us through the Spirit's effectual call, he implants his seed within us, which is a habitual disposition of grace toward righteousness. Such a distinction guards against rationalist claims that effectual calling is an entirely natural process (Canons of Dort 3/4, rejection of errors §6).[39] In this case, the Spirit of God effectually calls people through the word; the Spirit infuses a habit in the person to ensure the positive reception of the word. While Reformed theologians may speak of God first preparing a person for the reception of the word by the infusion of habit, they typically speak in terms of the order of nature, not of time. That is, the infusion and effectual call occur simultaneously, as the effectual call is the cause of the sinner's transformation. But in terms of the order of nature, that is, the logical relationship between the call and infusion, they speak first of preparation and then of reception.[40] To borrow imagery from Christ's parable of the sower, preachers sow the seed of the gospel, but the Spirit must first cultivate and prepare the soil where the seed lands to ensure that it grows and produces fruit (Matt 13:1–23; Luke 8:4–15; Mark 4:1–20).[41]

---

38. Bernard Wuellner, *Dictionary of Scholastic Philosophy* (Fitzwilliam, NH: Loreto, 2012), 161.

39. Within the historic Reformed tradition Claude Pajon (1626–1685), professor at the Academy of Saumur, caused a controversy with his novel doctrine of effectual calling. Pajon argued that God's call was effectual because it was persuasive, not because of the regenerating work of the Spirit. His views were rejected, but there has been an effort to retrieve them. For the history of the controversy, see Albert Gootjes, *Claude Pajon (1626–1685) and the Academy of Saumur: The First Controversy over Grace* (Leiden: Brill, 2013). For the retrieval, see Jonathan Hoglund, *Called by Triune Grace: Divine Rhetoric and the Effectual Call*, Studies in Christian Doctrine and Scripture (Downers Grove, IL: IVP Academic, 2016); see also Vos, *Reformed Dogmatics* 4:38.

40. E.g., Robert Rollock, *A Treatise of Our Effectual Calling*, in *Select Works of Robert Rollock*, ed. William M. Gunn (Edinburgh: Wodrow Society, 1844); Thomas Halyburton, "Whether Regeneration or Justification Has the Precedency in the Order of Nature," in *The Works of the Rev. Thomas Halyburton* (London: Thomas Tegg & Son, 1835), 547–59; James Buchanan, *The Office and Work of the Holy Spirit* (New York: Robert Carter, 1847), 75; also see Vos, *Reformed Dogmatics* 4:29.

41. For more detailed argumentation, see J. V. Fesko, "Aquinas's Doctrine of Justification and Infused Habits in Reformed Soteriology," in *Aquinas among the Protestants*, ed. Manfred

Third, a biblical doctrine of effectual calling must account for the performative nature of God's word but must nevertheless distinguish between the *vocatio externa et interna* ("the external and internal call"). When preachers herald the gospel, the word of God goes forth and falls on all within earshot. This is the *vocatio externum*, or the universal call. Due to humanity's fallen state, apart from the Spirit's sovereign work the external call is of no avail for salvation. When the Spirit applies the external call with the *vocatio internum*, or the special call, then the sinner receives the word of God for salvation.[42] Once again, with effectual calling we must distinguish but not separate the internal and external call. As Johannes Heidegger (1633–1698) observes: "The word is the same which man preaches and which the Spirit writes on the heart. There is strictly one calling, but its cause and medium is twofold: instrumental, man preaching the word outwardly; principal, the Holy Spirit inwardly writing it on the heart."[43] For this reason, the Spirit's call is irresistible and always effectual. If, however, the Spirit does not effectually apply the call of the word by means of the internal call, this does not mean that God's word has returned void.

We must always remember that God's word is double-edged and that he wields his word for both salvation and judgment (Heb 4:12). In the event that the external call goes forth apart from the internal call, God's intention is often judgment. The other possibility is that God exposes a person to the external call of the gospel but reserves his effectual call for a later time. In the total absence of the internal call, the external call is ineffectual for one's salvation but effectual for condemnation. Recall the Kohathite rebellion; Korah and his motley band challenged Moses's authority, and so God revealed that Moses was his chosen servant, which was a vindication for Moses and judgment for Korah, his family, and followers (Num 16:28–33). Korah and his followers received the external word of God apart from the internal work of the Spirit, and thus it was judgment for them. When God commissioned Isaiah, he did not accompany the prophet's message with the

Svenson and David VanDrunen (Oxford: Wiley-Blackwell, 2018), 249–66; see also Horton, *Christian Faith*, 608–12.

42. Calvin, *Inst.* 3.34.8; also Bavinck, *Reformed Dogmatics* 4:378–79.

43. Johannes Heidegger, *Corpus Theologiae* (Zurich, 1700), 21.22, as cited in Heppe, *Reformed Dogmatics*, 518.

Spirit's internal call, as the prophet's mission was one of judgment. Isaiah was supposed to preach until the cities of Israel were razed (Isa 6:10–11).

A microcosm of God's double-edged revelation appears in the crucifixion of Christ. Luke records the single event—crucifixion, Savior, and thieves flanking Christ—yet one thief received the word unto salvation and the other unto condemnation; one thief received the internal call and the other only the external call (Luke 23:39:43). In the words of Paul, "For we are the aroma of Christ to God among those who are being saved and among those who are perishing, to one a fragrance from death to death, to the other a fragrance from life to life. Who is sufficient for these things?" (2 Cor 2:15–16). In other words, Paul recognized the burden and weight of preaching, knowing that he heralded only the external call, which when joined with the Spirit's sovereign internal call could bring life, but if absent of the Spirit's work would bring death. As Charles Hodge observes: "The word of God is quick and powerful either to save or to destroy. It cannot be neutral. If it does not save, it destroys."[44]

## CONCLUSION

THE SPIRIT'S EFFECTUAL CALL IS the first step in the application of redemption, the means by which the Triune God unites fallen sinners to Christ. Even as rain falls on the earth and makes it fruitful, so the Spirit applies the word to human hearts. Through the Spirit's effectual call, the word has the power to fulfill its ideas and to transform those ideas into reality. The word of promise creates the future; word and Spirit are the means by which God calls into existence things that do not exist—the means by which the Triune God makes the new heavens and earth.[45] Effectual calling highlights both the powerful nature of God's word and Spirit and the cruciality of preaching as the chief means by which God calls sinners to himself. For this reason, the Second Helvetic Confession states: "The preaching of the Word of God is the Word of God" (1). In other words, wherever preachers lawfully called herald God's word, there God audibly speaks to his people. "How is the word made effectual to salvation?" asks the Westminster Larger Catechism (q. 155).

---

44. Charles Hodge, *An Exposition of the Second Epistle to the Corinthians* (New York: Robert Carter, 1866), 46.

45. Bavinck, *Saved by Grace*, 157.

"The Spirit of God maketh the reading, but especially the preaching of the word, an effectual means of enlightening, convincing, and humbling sinners; of driving them out of themselves, and drawing them unto Christ; of conforming them to his image, and subduing them to his will" (see HC, q. 65).

## FURTHER READING

Bavinck, Herman. *Saved by Grace: The Holy Spirit's Work in Calling and Regeneration*. Translated by Nelson D. Kloosterman. Grand Rapids: Reformation Heritage Books, 2012. An important work that discusses the doctrine of effectual calling written by Dutch Reformed theologian Herman Bavinck. He specifically engages and critiques the baptismal-regeneration views of Abraham Kuyper in this work.

Billings, J. Todd. *Union with Christ: Reframing Theology and Ministry for the Church*. Grand Rapids: Baker Academic, 2011. A brief but well-informed treatment of union with Christ that also addresses practical, ministry-related issues. Billings's work is informed by careful historical study on Calvin's doctrine of union with Christ.

Campbell, Constantine R. *Paul and Union with Christ: An Exegetical and Theological Study*. Grand Rapids: Zondervan Academic, 2012. An exhaustive study on all of the lexemes that relate to union with Christ. Campbell carefully explains the significance of Paul's usage of various phrases such as "in him" and "in Christ." Think of this book like an exegetical commentary on union-with-Christ phrases.

McCaskill, Grant. *Living in Union with Christ: Paul's Gospel and Christian Moral Identity*. Grand Rapids: Baker Academic, 2019. A helpful exploration of the doctrine of union with Christ regarding the Christian's moral life. McCaskill's emphasis on union with Christ as the source of the Christian life is a welcomed theme, given that many seek to live their lives under their own moral steam. One weakness of the book is McCaskill's uncritical use of the term "identity," which has a very fluid meaning in contemporary culture.

Zanchi, Girolamo. *The Spiritual Marriage between Christ and His Church and Every One of the Faithful*. Translated by Patrick O'Banion. Grand Rapids: Reformation Heritage Books, 2021. Perhaps one of the most important books on union with Christ from the sixteenth century. Very few early modern theologians devoted a specific locus to the doctrine of union with Christ, which makes this work a standout. Zanchi's work originated as a doctrinal locus on his commentary on Ephesians, and it was extracted as a standalone work. His work is exegetical, catholic, and distinctly Reformed.

VI

# JUSTIFICATION

## DECLARED RIGHTEOUS

"The article of justification is said to be the article of the standing or falling of the church," writes Reformed theologian Johan Heinrich Alsted (1588–1638).[1] Alsted believed this along with countless others in the church throughout the ages. In the Epistle to Diognetus, which dates back to the second century, the author reflects on God's mercy in Christ: "In his mercy he took upon himself our sins; he himself gave his own Son as a ransom for us, the holy one for the lawless, the guiltless for the guilty, the just for the unjust, the incorruptible for the corruptible, the immortal for the mortal. For what else but his righteousness could have covered our sins?" The author then describes these truths in terms that sound as if they came from Martin Luther (1483–1546): "In whom was it possible for us, the lawless and ungodly, to be justified, except in the Son of God alone? O the sweet exchange, O the incomprehensible work of God, O the unexpected blessings, that the sinfulness of many should be hidden in one righteous person, while the righteousness of one should justify many sinners."[2]

---

1. Johann Heinrich Alsted, *Theologia Scholastica Didactica: Exhibens Locos Communes Theologicos Methodo Scholastica* (Hanau: Eifridus, 1618), 711: "Articulus iustificationis dicitur articulus stantis & cadentis Ecclesiae" (trans. mine); see also Alister McGrath, *Iustitia Dei: A History of the Christian Doctrine of Justification*, 2nd ed. (Cambridge: Cambridge University Press, 1998), 188, 448n3.

2. Epistle to Diognetus 9.2–5, in *The Apostolic Fathers: Greek Texts and English Translation*, 3rd ed., ed. and trans. Michael W. Holmes, J. B. Lightfoot, and J. R. Harmer (Grand Rapids:

For centuries Christians have taken shelter in the glorious exchange that comes to us in the doctrine of justification. The Westminster Shorter Catechism gives a definition of justification as "an act of God's free grace, wherein he pardoneth all our sins, and accepteth us as righteous in his sight, only for the righteousness of Christ imputed to us, and received by faith alone" (q. 33; WCF 11; BC 22–23; HC, qq. 56, 59–64; Canons of Dort 3/4:10–17). This simple statement embodies why justification is the article of the church's standing or falling and why theologians from the early church to Luther and beyond call it the glorious exchange. Condemned sinners who place their faith in Jesus Christ receive a divine verdict of righteous, a forensic declaration that does not rest on their own obedience or worthiness but on the obedience and satisfaction of Jesus Christ.

God's verdict over sinners, however, comes to them only in Christ through the Spirit. God pronounced his verdict of righteous over his Son by the Spirit. Paul's succinct but powerful words capture this truth when he writes that Jesus "was manifested in the flesh, justified by the Spirit, seen by angels, proclaimed among the nations, believed on in the world, taken up in glory" (1 Tim 3:16, my trans.).[3] Christ's justification by the Spirit is the source of our justification when we lay hold of Christ by faith. Since our justification comes in Christ by the Spirit, this verdict is pregnant with eschatological meaning: the Son is the last, or eschatological, Adam, the "life-giving Spirit," and the Spirit is the "power of the age to come" (1 Cor 15:45, my trans.; Heb 6:4). That is, the doctrine of justification is laden with both soteriological and eschatological weight.

In order to grasp the doctrine of justification, this chapter first explains its nature, its protological provenance, and its eschatological significance. Second, this chapter examines its elements, namely, the imputed active and passive obedience of Christ, and faith as its instrumental cause, which brings righteousness and forgiveness. Third, the chapter surveys the recent challenges presented by the New Perspective on Paul and explains why the New Perspective on Paul fails to overturn what we may call the old

Baker Academic, 2007), 710–11; Martin Luther, "Sermon on Matt. 3:13–17," in *Sermons*, ed. Jaroslav Pelikan, LW 51 (Philadelphia: Fortress, 1959), 313–30, here 316.

3. Allen and Swain, *Christian Dogmatics*, 275.

perspective on Paul. The chapter then concludes with summary observations about the article of the church's standing or falling.

## NATURE

TRACING THE ORIGINS OF JUSTIFICATION is necessary for a proper understanding of the doctrine.[4] Most theological excavations of the doctrine's provenance go back to Genesis 15 and Abraham's profession of faith, since this is the Old Testament text that Paul appeals to in Romans 4.[5] Genesis 15 is obviously a crucial passage, but justification goes further back, to the opening chapters of the Bible. To justify is to declare that a person is in conformity with the demands of the law: "Keep far from a false charge, and do not kill the innocent and righteous, for I will not justify the wicked" (Exod 23:7, my trans.). In the New Testament, for example, the verb δικαιόω means "to declare [a person] righteous"—to say that they are in conformity with the law (Acts 13:38–39).[6] Conversely, if a person is not in conformity with the law, he merits the verdict of condemnation: "Who shall bring any charge against God's elect? It is God who justifies. Who is to condemn?" (Rom 8:33–34).

If justification is a declaration that a person is in conformity with the law, then the first instance where the opportunity occurs for God to justify a person is in the garden of Eden. When God commanded Adam to be fruitful, to multiply, to fill all the earth, to subdue it, and not to eat from the tree of the knowledge of good and evil (Gen 1:28; 2:16–17), he gave him the opportunity to be either in or out of conformity to his command, to be justified or condemned.[7] On the heels of Adam's sin, the Holy Spirit arrived to exercise his judicial prerogative as Creator: "And they heard the sound of the LORD God walking in the garden in the Spirit of the day, and the man and his wife hid themselves from the face of the LORD God

---

4. For the structural categories of *nature* and *elements* of justification, see Berkhof, *Systematic Theology*, 510–15.

5. Brian Vickers, *Justification by Grace through Faith: Finding Freedom from Legalism, Lawlessness, Pride, and Despair*, Explorations in Biblical Theology (Phillipsburg, NJ: P&R, 2013), 13–23.

6. Vos, *Reformed Dogmatics* 4:136.

7. E.g., Thomas Brooks, *Paradise Opened*, in *The Complete Works of Thomas Brooks* (Edinburgh: James Nichol, 1867), 5:296; Samuel Rutherford, *The Covenant of Life Opened* (Edinburgh: Robert Broun, 1654), 1.7 (p. 46); John Murray, "The Adamic Administration," in *The Collected Writings of John Murray*, vol. 2, *Systematic Theology* (Edinburgh: Banner of Truth, 1991), 47; Vos, *Reformed Dogmatics* 4:138.

among the trees of the garden" (Gen 3:8, my trans.).[8] God condemned and cursed Adam, but had he been obedient, God would have justified him. The doctrine of justification thus has protological origins.

At the same time, the doctrine of justification is eschatological in nature. When God gave Adam his work to fill and subdue the earth and not eat from the tree of knowledge, there was a telos or goal for his labors. There would have been a time when he either completed his probation and/or fulfilled his work. This means there was an endpoint, an eschatological hope. The weekly Sabbath-day rest was supposed to be Adam's foretaste of God's eschatological Sabbath rest.[9] Each Sabbath Adam would have rested from his labors and enjoyed a foretaste of God's eternal rest, and upon the completion of his labors he would have entered that eternal rest. God would have declared Adam righteous, which would have ushered in the eschaton, the new heavens and earth. As the apostle Paul writes: "The Spirit is life because of righteousness" (Rom 8:10; see 5:21).[10] But since Adam failed his divinely given covenantal vocation, God sent another Adam, who would faithfully fulfill the work. Jesus as the "last Adam" became the life-giving Spirit (1 Cor 15:45). He was obedient to the commands of his Father, and thus he was "justified by the Spirit" (1 Tim 3:16). By means of Spirit's work in resurrecting him, the Father declared Jesus to be "the Son of God in power" (Rom 1:4).[11] God justified his Son—he declared him righteous—and Christ's work and justification poured out the eschatological Spirit on the creation.

Thus, justification is a judicial verdict where God declares a person in conformity with his law, and it has protological origins and is laden with eschatological significance. In the covenant of grace God does not grant us anything beyond what he would have given Adam had he been faithful. The covenant of grace does not differ from the covenant of works in its eschatological goal, only in the road taken: Adam's obedience versus Christ's.[12] In the simplest of terms, there was an eschatology before the fall;

8. Kline, *Images of the Spirit*, 102–5, 115–20.

9. Vos, *Biblical Theology* , 140.

10. Douglas J. Moo, *The Letter to the Romans*, 2nd ed., NICNT (Grand Rapids: Eerdmans, 2018), 513–15.

11. Geerhardus Vos, "The Eschatological Aspect of the Pauline Conception of the Spirit," in *Redemptive History and Biblical Interpretation*, 91–125, esp. 103–5.

12. Bavinck, *Reformed Dogmatics* 2:577.

eschatology is older than soteriology. Justification is older than salvation.[13] Adam's justification was supposed to be on the basis of his obedience, but Christ secured his justification by his obedience. Christ's obedience is then the foundation for our justification. Adam's justification was by obedience, but now in a fallen world our justification can only be by faith in Christ—by trusting in the obedience of the last Adam. Justification is therefore either by works or by faith alone in Jesus's works.[14]

## ELEMENTS

THE CHIEF ELEMENTS OF THE doctrine of justification fall under two categories: the objective work of Christ and the subjective appropriation of these benefits by believers. We can further subdivide Christ's objective work into negative and positive aspects—negative in the sense that Christ's work takes away our guilt and sin, and positive in the sense that his work credits righteousness and holiness to sinners.

### *Active and Passive Obedience*

THE NEGATIVE AND POSITIVE ELEMENTS rest in the distinction between the *active* and *passive* obedience of Christ.[15] The active obedience of Christ is his fulfillment of the law in its entirety, what Paul describes as "one act of righteousness" (δικαιώματος), or the "one man's obedience" by which the "many are appointed righteous" (δίκαιοι κατασταθήσονται οἱ πολλοί; Rom 5:18–19, my trans.).[16] Conversely, the passive obedience is Christ's suffering the penalty of the law on behalf of sinners: "Christ redeemed us from the curse of the law by becoming a curse for us—for it is written,

13. Vos, *Pauline Eschatology*, 325n1.

14. On the debated question of *pistis Christou* and whether it should be translated as an objective ("faith in Christ") vs. a subjective ("faith of Christ") genitive, see Kevin W. McFadden, *Faith in the Son of God: The Place of Christ-Oriented Faith within Pauline Theology* (Wheaton, IL: Crossway, 2021).

15. On the origins and history of the distinction, see Heber Carlos de Campos, *Doctrine in Development: Johannes Piscator and Debates over Christ's Active Obedience* (Grand Rapids: Reformation Heritage Books, 2017).

16. David VanDrunen, "To Obey Is Better Than Sacrifice: A Defense of the Active Obedience of Christ in the Light of Recent Criticism," in *By Faith Alone: Answering the Challenges to the Doctrine of Justification*, ed. Gary L. W. Johnson and Guy P. Waters (Wheaton, IL: Crossway, 2006), 127–46; Vos, *Reformed Dogmatics* 4:164.

'Cursed is everyone who is hanged on a tree'" (Gal 3:13).[17] Christ's passive obedience is not merely what he suffered on the cross because he was passive—he allowed the Roman soldiers to crucify him. This misunderstanding of Christ's passive obedience focuses on the crucifixion.[18] Christ offers his passive obedience (from the Latin *passio*, "suffering") throughout the entirety of his life in his state of humiliation. From the moment that he was born and placed in a manger rather than a royal cradle, the pain he suffered in his circumcision, the ridicule, reviling, and rejection from his countrymen, hunger and fatigue, and especially the *via Dolorosa*, his arrest, trial, beating, crucifixion, death, and burial—this is the complex of Christ's passive obedience.

There is an important qualification we must note regarding the distinction between Christ's active and passive obedience. Some have criticized the distinction because it supposedly rends the seamless garment of Christ's obedience in two.[19] Yet, we must remember the all-important theological point that something can be distinct but not separate. Charles Hodge explains: "The active and passive obedience of Christ, however, are only different phases or aspects of the same thing. He obeyed in suffering. His highest acts of obedience were rendered in the garden, and upon the cross. Hence this distinction is not so presented in Scripture as though the obedience of Christ answered one purpose, and his sufferings another and a distinct purpose."[20] We must distinguish Christ's active and passive obedience, but they are inseparably bound together.

---

17. Brandon Crowe, "The Passive *and* Active Obedience of Christ: Retrieving a Biblical Distinction," in *The Doctrine on Which the Church Stands or Falls*, ed. Matthew Barrett (Wheaton, IL: Crossway, 2019), 441–68.

18. For this misunderstanding of the active and passive obedience, see Anselm, *Why God Became Man*, 9.

19. E.g., Johannes Piscator, *A Learned and Profitable Treatise on Man's Justification* (London: 1599), 20; Emil Brunner, *The Christian Doctrine of Creation and Redemption*, trans. Olive Wyon, Dogmatics 2 (Philadelphia: Westminster, 1952), 282.

20. Hodge, *Systematic Theology* 3:143; see also Berkhof, *Systematic Theology*, 379–80; Murray, *Redemption Accomplished and Applied*, 20–22. Here Hodge says the active and passive obedience are "phases or aspects," where "aspect" is the preferred term since "phases" might imply a succession of moments. Christ's active and passive obedience run concurrently during his life.

*Imputation* A SECOND KEY ISSUE IS the manner by which God communicates Christ's obedience to sinners. What is the bridge by which sinners receive Christ's work? The bridge is twofold: imputation and faith. In his discussion of justification Paul cites Genesis 15:6, "Abraham believed God, and it was counted to him as righteousness" (Rom 4:3). Paul's statement stands in stark contrast to one path to righteousness in the Old Testament: "If a person does them [the commandments], he shall live by them" (Lev 18:5; see Luke 10:28; Gal 3:12; Rom 10:5). Deuteronomy 6:25 says something similar: "And it will be righteousness for us, if we are careful to do all this commandment before the LORD our God, as he has commanded us."[21] Paul juxtaposes achieving a status of righteous by obedience versus faith when he says that Abraham *believed* God, and God *counted* (ἐλογίσθη) righteousness to him: "Now to the one who works, his wages are not counted as a gift but as his due. And to the one who does not work but believes in him who justifies the ungodly, his faith is counted as righteousness" (Rom 4:4–5). Paul contrasts justification by obedience versus by faith. Either a person personally fulfills the law, or Christ fulfills it for him. To put these principles in covenantal terms, one lays hold of eternal life through either the covenant of works or the covenant of grace. We can also state this principle in terms of the difference between law and gospel—you either obey the law for salvation or believe in the gospel.[22] There is no middle ground; there is no alchemy whereby a person can smelt the grace of God with his own obedience in the hopes of producing the gold of justification and salvation.

Imputation ("accrediting," "accounting," "counting," "crediting," "reckoning") is the means by which God communicates the obedience of Christ to sinners. Imputation does not stand alone on the stage of redemptive history as an abstract mechanism by which God gives sinners Christ's righteousness. Rather, imputation is part and parcel of covenant theology, how God communicates the representative actions of the first and last Adams.

---

21. John Calvin, *Sermons on Deuteronomy*, trans. Arthur Golding (London: Henry Middleton, 1583), sermon 172 (p. 1066).

22. Calvin, *Inst.* 3.11.14; Zacharias Ursinus, *Larger Catechism*, q. 36, in *An Introduction to the Heidelberg Catechism: Sources, History and Theology*, ed. Lyle D. Bierma et al. (Grand Rapids: Baker Academic, 2005), 168–69; Thomas Cartwright, *Christian Religion, Substantially, Methodicallie, Plainlie, and Profitablie Treatised* (London: Felix Man, 1611), 64–65; Bavinck, *Reformed Dogmatics* 4:448–55.

The most succinct presentation of imputation appears in Romans 5, where Paul contrasts the respective consequences of the (dis)obedience of Adam and Christ: "Therefore, as one trespass led to condemnation for all men, so one act of righteousness leads to justification and life for all men. For as by the one man's disobedience the many were appointed sinners, so by the one man's obedience the many will be appointed righteous" (Rom 5:18–19). God imputes Adam's sin to those whom he represents and thus appoints (καθίστημι) them as sinners; conversely, God imputes the obedience of Christ in order to appoint sinners as righteous.[23] The imputation of the representative (dis)obedience of the first and last Adams lies at the heart of covenant theology, or federal representation.

Beyond Romans 4 and 5, imputation appears throughout the Scriptures and warrants a brief reconnaissance to establish the broad attestation of the doctrine. The Day of Atonement (Lev 16) showcases imputation in the hand-laying ceremony, where the high priest placed his hands over the scapegoat and confessed Israel's sins over the nation (Lev 16:21). When he did so he transferred the nation's sins to the goat, and thus "the goat shall bear all their iniquities on itself to a remote area" (Lev 16:22). God imputed or credited Israel's sins to the goat—the goat bore their sins.[24] The protocols of the Day of Atonement reappear in the Old Testament as Isaiah speaks of the suffering servant's work in Levitical terms: "Yet he bore the sin of many, and makes intercession for the transgressors" (Isa 53:12). Just as the goat bore (נשא) Israel's sins, now the suffering servant bears the sin of many.[25] Within this context, the prophet expands on this imputation theme and reveals that God will impute the sins of the many to his servant, and conversely he will impute the servant's righteousness to the many: "Out of the anguish of his soul he shall see and be satisfied; by his knowledge shall the righteous one, my servant, make many to be accounted righteous, and he shall bear their iniquities" (Isa 53:11). It is important to note how the Septuagint translates Isaiah's statements. The Septuagint therefore, "Out of

23. Here in Rom 5:18–19 English translations render καθίστημι as "made" (ESV), "result(ed)" (NIV, NAS), "came" (KJV), "led to / leads to" (NRSV), yet the term "appoint" best captures its meaning (see Matt 24:45, 47; 25:21, 23; Luke 12:14; Acts 6:3; 7:10, 27, 35). See Thomas Schreiner, *Romans*, 2nd ed., BECNT (Grand Rapids: Baker Academic, 2018), 293.

24. Jacob Milgrom, *Leviticus*, AB (New Haven: Yale University Press, 1991), 1043.

25. John Goldingay, *The Message of Isaiah 40–55: A Literary-Theological Commentary* (London: T&T Clark, 2005), 510–11.

the anguish of his soul he shall see light," which is a common idiom for resurrection (Job 3:16; Pss 36:9; 49:19; Job 3:16; 33:28–30).[26] Additionally, Isaiah says that the servant will be "numbered [מנה] with the transgressors," (Isa 53:12), which the Septuagint translates as λογίζομαι ("number" or "count").[27]

The Levitical and Isaianic texts serve as the bedrock for Paul's statements about imputation. Justification and resurrection appear in the heart of Paul's discussion: "It will be counted [λογίζεσθαι] to us who believe in him who raised from the dead Jesus our Lord, who was delivered up for our trespasses and raised for our justification" (Rom 4:24–25).[28] In fact, within this Romans 4 context Paul uses λογίζομαι eleven times to highlight that we receive Christ's righteousness by imputation (Rom 4:3, 4, 5, 6, 8, 9, 10, 11, 22, 23, 24). This is no mere sidelight in Paul's argument, as some have erroneously claimed, but lies at the heart of the doctrine of justification.[29] Moreover, Paul's point also runs against the grain of Roman Catholic claims that justification is on the basis of an infused righteousness.[30] In other words, God does not implant righteousness into sinners and then, on the basis of this inherent righteousness, declare them righteous. That the Scriptures speak of justification by imputed righteousness underscores that it is an *iustitia aliena* ("alien righteousness"), that is, that it is Christ's righteousness—something that is *extra nos* ("outside us").[31] In more technical terms, Christ's good works, not ours, constitute the material cause of our justification.[32] Imputation lies at the heart of the glorious exchange between Christ and sinners: "For our sake he made him to be sin who knew no sin, so that in him we might become the righteousness of God" (2 Cor 5:21). Christ wears the tattered and stained garments of our sin and gives us his pure, royal robes of righteousness (Zech 3:1–5; Isa 61:10).

---

26. Hoffius, "Fourth Servant Song," 180.

27. E. J. Young, *The Book of Isaiah* (Grand Rapids: Eerdmans, 1972), 2:356–58.

28. Moo, *Letter to the Romans*, 313–15; Hoffius, "Fourth Servant Song," 181n68.

29. Wright, *Romans*, 491.

30. Council of Trent, "Sixth Session, January 13, 1547," canons, 9, 11, in *The Creeds of Christendom*, ed. Philip Schaff (repr., Grand Rapids: Baker Books, 1990), 2:112–13.

31. See, e.g., Zacharias Ursinus, *The Commentary of Dr. Zacharias Ursinus on the Heidelberg Catechism* (1852; Phillipsburg: P&R, n. d.), 329; Ursinus, *Corpus Doctrinae Orthodoxae, sive Catecheticarum Explicationum* (Heidelberg: Ionas Rhodius, 1616), 330.

32. Calvin, *Inst.* 3.14.17.

*Faith* How do we receive the righteousness of Christ if not by infusion, as Rome contends? God justifies sinners by faith alone in Christ alone. There are several different terms for "faith" or "believe" in the Old and New Testaments. In the Old Testament the most common word for "believe" is the *hiphil* form אמונה, which the Septuagint translates as πίστις: "Behold, his soul is puffed up; it is not upright within him, but the righteous shall live by his faith" (Hab 2:4). In the New Testament, the term πίστις appears in contexts that reveal the need for a confident trust in Christ with a view to salvation. We receive the "righteousness of God through faith in Jesus Christ" (Rom 3:22).[33] Or, Paul elsewhere writes: "We know that a person is not justified by works of the law but through faith in Jesus Christ, so we also have believed in Christ Jesus, in order to be justified by faith in Christ and not by works of the law, because by works of the law no one will be justified" (Gal 2:16).[34] Paul brings Abraham front and center as the paradigmatic New Testament believer—the one whom God justified by faith, not by works. As a case in point, Paul uses the terms πίστις ("faith") or πιστεύω ("believe") in Romans 4 sixteen times to emphasize the point that our good works play no role in our justification and that justification comes only by faith in Christ (Rom 4:3, 5, 9, 11, 12, 13, 14, 16, 17, 19, 20, 22, 23). In short, faith is the state of being fully convinced that God is able to do what he has promised in Christ (Rom 4:21).

The Westminster Larger Catechism describes how faith justifies in the sight of God: "Faith justifies a sinner in the sight of God, not because of those other graces which do always accompany it, or of good works that are the fruits of it, nor as if the grace of faith or any act thereof, were imputed to him for his justification; but only as it is an instrument by which he receiveth and applieth Christ and his righteousness" (q. 73). The catechism highlights an important exegetical nuance that helps us distinguish between Christ's work as the material cause of our justification and faith as the *instrumental* case. When Paul writes of justifying faith, he reveals that justification is "by" or "through" (ἐκ or διὰ πίστεως; e.g., Rom 3:27–30;

33. McFadden, *Faith in the Son*, 60–64, 69–76.

34. See Michael Allen, *The Christ's Faith: A Dogmatic Account* (London: T&T Clark, 2009); Smith, "God's Righteousness, Christ's Faith/fulness"; Silva, "Faith versus Works of Law," 217–48, esp. 228–34.

5:1; 9:30, 32; Gal 2:16; 3:5, 8, 11; 24; Eph 2:8).[35] In other words, faith is not the material cause of our justification; it does not constitute the "stuff" that justifies us. Rather, saving faith lays hold of the work of Christ. The Westminster Confession explains that "the principal acts of saving faith are accepting, receiving, and resting upon Christ alone for justification, sanctification, and eternal life, by virtue of the covenant of grace" (14.2). Faith is the instrument, not the ground or basis, of our justification, and thus the Westminster divines write of faith in passive terms: accepting, receiving, and resting. We accept and receive the obedience and satisfaction of Christ—we rest in his finished work.

### *Righteousness and Forgiveness*

When sinners trust in the completed work of Christ, they receive two chief benefits through their justification: the status of righteous as concerns the law and the forgiveness of their sins. God through Christ and the work of the Spirit constitutes believers as righteous (Rom 5:1–19). Even though a person has broken God's law, both in terms of original and actual sin, when they trust in Christ for their salvation God justifies them—declares them righteous with respect to the law. Some of the most amazing words in all of Scripture speak of this truth: "And to the one who does not work but believes in him who justifies the ungodly, his faith is counted as righteousness" (Rom 4:5). God looks on the ungodly as if they were righteous, as if they were in complete conformity to his holy law. In addition to the imputation of Christ's righteousness, God also forgives those who trust in Christ: "Blessed are those whose lawless deeds are forgiven, and whose sins are covered; blessed is the man against whom the Lord will not count his sin" (Rom 4:7–8). In the giving of righteousness and the forgiving of sins, God both imputes or credits (λογίζομαι) righteousness to the sinner (Rom 4:3, 5, 9, 11) and does not impute or credit (μὴ λογίσηται) sin (Rom 4:8). Imputation and nonimputation are at work in God's justification of the sinner.

God forgives covenantal transgressions, both original and actual, so that when he looks on the sinner, he only sees his Son's righteousness and holiness. In the words of the psalmist, "As far as the east is from the west, so far

35. McFadden, *Faith in the Son*, 97.

does he remove our transgressions from us" (Ps 103:12). The Heidelberg Catechism summarizes the blessings of justification when it asks the question, "How are you righteous before God?" The catechism responds:

> Even though my conscience accuses me of having grievously sinned against all God's commandments, of never having kept any of them, and of still being inclined toward all evil, nevertheless, without any merit of my own, out of sheer grace, God grants and credits to me the perfect satisfaction, righteousness, and holiness of Christ, as if I had never sinned nor been a sinner, and as if I had been as perfectly obedient as Christ was obedient for me. All I need to do is accept this gift with a believing heart. (q. 60)

The catechism explains that sinners who trust in Christ receive his satisfaction, righteousness, and holiness in justification, and thus God only sees Christ's perfections when he looks on the sinner.

The imputed righteousness, satisfaction, and holiness of Christ have eschatological significance for the believer. The Protestant understanding of the doctrine of justification stands in stark contrast to Roman Catholic and neonomian views. The former understand justification as the in-breaking of the verdict of the final judgment in the present and therefore conceive of justification as irreversible, immutable, and indefectible.[36] By contrast, Roman Catholic and neonomian views construe justification as reversible, mutable, and defectible, and hence it is not truly eschatological. The apostle Paul powerfully testifies to this fact when he writes: "There is therefore now no condemnation for those who are in Christ Jesus" (Rom 8:1). God has irrevocably removed the curse of the law for anyone who is in Christ—for anyone who has received the imputed righteousness, satisfaction, and holiness of Christ by faith alone. Since Christ has both fulfilled the law and secured eschatological life through his obedience and has suffered the curse of the law, he has both undergone the final judgment and inaugurated the new heavens and earth *in the middle of history*.[37] As Christ stood at the threshold of his crucifixion he announced: "Now is

---

36. Vos, *Reformed Dogmatics* 4:139.

37. Brian Vickers, *Jesus' Blood and Righteousness: Paul's Theology of Imputation* (Wheaton, IL: Crossway, 2006), 62–63.

the judgment of this world; now will the ruler of this world be cast out" (John 12:31).[38] This is why Paul writes that for those who believe in Christ there is *now* no condemnation.

Luther famously captures the eschatological character of justification through his aphorism that we are *simil iustus et peccator* ("at the same time righteous and a sinner").[39] This aphorism is Luther's way of capturing the already-but-not-yet of salvation. The Christian is already declared righteous in Christ but still struggles with sin. The Christian nevertheless lives from the future—the verdict of the final judgment has been pronounced over Christ in the present. Believers share in Christ's justification by faith alone and through the reception of his imputed righteousness, satisfaction, and holiness. Believers' good works play no role whatsoever in justification.[40] This understanding of justification is different from Roman Catholic and neonomian views that posit a twofold justification: a justification in the present that rests on the work of Christ and a second or final justification in the future that rests on the Spirit-produced works of the believer.[41] In Roman and neonomian formulations, the believer's status is uncertain because justification is a process that awaits the final judgment. Not all of those who are initially justified may be finally justified. Roman Catholic and neonomian views de-eschatologize justification and turn it into a reversible verdict that does not rest wholly on the perfect righteousness, satisfaction, and holiness of Christ.

## THE NEW PERSPECTIVE ON PAUL

The doctrine of justification has always been under assault, even from the earliest days of the church. Paul confronted the Judaizers, Augustine debated Pelagius, the Reformers challenged Rome,

38. Carson, *Gospel according to John*, 440.

39. Martin Luther, *Lectures on Galatians (1535): Chapters 1–4*, LW 26 (St. Louis: Concordia House, 1963), 232.

40. Vos, *Reformed Dogmatics* 4:143, 166–74.

41. E.g., Council of Trent, "Sixth Session, January 13, 1547," ch. 10, in Schaff, *Creeds of Christendom* 2:99; Jacob Arminius, *Works* 2:405–7; Richard Baxter, *Confession of His Faith: Especially Concerning the Interest of Repentance and Sincere Obedience to Christ, in Our Justification and Salvation* (London: 1654), 52, 296. N. T. Wright makes similar statements; for reference to those places in his corpus, see M. J. Smith, "Paul in the Twenty-First Century," in *All Things to All Cultures: Paul among Jews, Greeks and Romans*, ed. M. Harding and A. Nobbs (Grand Rapids: Eerdmans, 2013), 1–33.

and in eighteenth-century Scotland the Marrowmen engaged neonomians. In the present, we may add the New Perspective on Paul as the latest challenge to the gospel and the doctrine of justification more narrowly. The New Perspective on Paul arose within the late twentieth-century New Testament guild, among other reasons, as a response to traditional Reformation readings of Paul. N. T. Wright claimed that Protestants had created a Paul of faith rather than exegeting the Paul of history.[42] The New Perspective on Paul is not a monolithic movement. Nevertheless, there are three key claims that conflict with historic Protestant teaching on justification that pertain to (1) works of the law, (2) righteousness, and (3) justification.

First, the New Perspective claims Protestants have misunderstood Paul's teaching on justification because they have an erroneous understanding of the lexeme ἔργων νόμου ("works of the law"): "For by works of the law no human being will be justified in his sight, since through the law comes knowledge of sin" (Rom 3:20). Historic Protestant exegesis claims that Paul opposes works-righteousness by this lexeme, but New Perspective scholars contend that Paul has the narrower idea of the Jewish food laws, circumcision, and Sabbath observance in view.[43] In other words, Paul's chief concern was to combat Jewish fears about gentiles joining Israel apart from the traditional national boundary markers—those markers that delineated Jew from gentile.[44] According to New Perspective proponents, faith is the new boundary marker, not circumcision, food laws, or Sabbath observance.[45]

Second, New Perspective proponents argue that Protestants have misunderstood Paul's concept of righteousness. Righteousness can have one of four domains, according to N. T. Wright: right behavior, the law court, covenant, or the cosmos.[46] In other words, righteousness can refer to a person's conduct, the verdict that a judge delivers in the law-court setting,

---

42. N. T. Wright, "The Paul of History and the Apostle of Faith," *TynBul* 29 (1978): 61–88.

43. Wright, *New Testament and the People*, 238, 334; N. T. Wright, *Jesus and the Victory of God* (Minneapolis: Fortress, 1996), 384, 388.

44. Wright, *Jesus and the Victory*, 381.

45. James D. G. Dunn, *Jesus, Paul, and the Law: Studies in Mark and Galatians* (Louisville: Westminster John Knox, 1990), 196; Wright, *Jesus and the Victory*, 381.

46. N. T. Wright, *Paul and the Faithfulness of God*, 2 vols. (Minneapolis: Fortress, 2013), 796–97.

covenant fidelity, or God's broader activity in the creation. Given these four different layers, one cannot easily summarize Paul's use of the term in his letters. Regarding the lexeme δικαιοσύνη θεοῦ (Rom 3:21; see also Rom 1:17; 3:5; 3:22; 10:3; 2 Cor 5:21; Phil 3:9), Wright claims that it refers to God's own righteousness, his faithfulness to his promises, and not a status that he imputes or gives to humans.

Third, when Wright combines his concept of righteousness with his doctrine of justification, he claims that "justification is all about being declared to be a member of God's people." The declaration of justification is about defining the family of Abraham, not about being saved.[47] In his view, justification is first and foremost about ecclesiology, not soteriology. Justification does, of course, have connections to ecclesiology; those whom God declares righteous become a part of the church, the people of God. However, justification is primarily soteriology, that is, being "justified in his sight" (Rom 3:20), and secondarily about ecclesiology.

The literature exchanged between advocates of the Old and New Perspectives is legion, but there are nevertheless salient observations to make about each of these contentions.[48] Regarding the meaning of ἔργων νόμου ("works of the law"), the New Perspective on Paul is not so new in its claim that Paul supposedly refers only to boundary markers. Early modern Roman Catholic theologians similarly argued that Paul only had the ceremonial, not the moral, law in view.[49] In fact, some New Perspective scholars such as James D. G. Dunn (1939–2020) argue that Paul does not argue

---

47. Wright, *Paul and the Faithfulness*, 856, 859.

48. For works in favor of the New Perspective on Paul, see, e.g., James D. G. Dunn, *The New Perspective on Paul*, 2nd ed. (Grand Rapids: Eerdmans, 2007); N. T. Wright, *Paul: In Fresh Perspective* (Minneapolis: Fortress, 2006); Don Garlington, *In Defense of the New Perspective on Paul: Essays and Reviews* (Eugene, OR: Wipf & Stock, 2005). For works that critique the New Perspective on Paul , see, e.g., Stephen Westerholm, *Perspectives Old and New on Paul: The "Lutheran" Paul and His Critics* (Grand Rapids: Eerdmans, 2003); D. A. Carson, Peter T. O'Brien, and Mark A. Seifrid, eds., *Justification and Variegated Nomism*, 2 vols. (Grand Rapids: Baker Academic, 2001–2004); Guy Prentiss Waters, *Justification and the New Perspectives on Paul: A Review and Response* (Phillipsburg, NJ: P&R, 2004); Robert J. Cara, *Cracking the Foundation of the New Perspective on Paul: Covenantal Nomism vs. Reformed Covenantal Theology* (Fearn, UK: Mentor, 2017). For surveys of the New Perspective literature and issues, see Kent Yinger, *The New Perspective: An Introduction* (Eugene, OR: Cascade Books, 2011); Smith, "Paul in the Twenty-First Century."

49. E.g., John Calvin, *Galatians, Ephesians, Philippians, and Colossians*, ed. David W. Torrance and T. F. Torrance, trans. T. H. L. Parker, CNTC (Grand Rapids: Eerdmans, 1996), on Gal 2:15 (p. 38).

against works-righteousness, and this is therefore evidence that Paul did not write Ephesians, because it mentions works-righteousness: "For by grace you have been saved through faith. And this is not your own doing; it is the gift of God, not a result of works, so that no one may boast" (Eph 2:8–9).[50] Setting aside the question of Paul's authorship of Ephesians for the sake of brevity (although Paul *is* the author of Ephesians), if first-century Jews were not guilty of believing in works-righteousness, then why would Ephesians address this issue? The simplest solution to this issue is to recognize that when Paul writes of the works of the law, or simply "works," he has works-righteousness in view.[51] Paul makes this abundantly clear when he juxtaposes faith and works throughout his letters: "For we hold that one is justified by faith apart from works of the law" (Rom 3:28). What else can Paul mean when he writes, "And to the one who does not work but believes in him who justifies the ungodly, his faith is counted as righteousness" (Rom 4:5)? Paul does not have some narrower subset of the law in view when he pits faith against works in justification.

Does δικαιοσύνη θεοῦ ("the righteousness of God") refer only to God's faithfulness? Wright recognizes that righteousness has other referents, such as right conduct, and he even draws attention to Genesis 38:26 and the dispute between Judah and Tamar: "She is more righteous than I." He rightly argues that righteousness can refer to the moral character of either the defendant or plaintiff in a judicial case, and that it can also refer to the status that a person has after the judge has pronounced a verdict.[52] However, this aspect of righteousness does not feature in Wright's doctrine of justification. Moreover, he does not ask the question, What defines a person's moral character as righteous? What is the moral standard that the judge employs to determine a person's innocence or guilt? The simple answer to these questions is the law of God. The law is the index to determine whether a person is righteous or unrighteous. And there are only two ways that a person can be declared righteous vis-à-vis the law: either by perfectly obeying it or by having Jesus perfectly obey it in their stead.

---

50. James D. G. Dunn, *The Theology of Paul the Apostle* (Grand Rapids: Eerdmans, 1998), 354.

51. See, e.g., Silva, "Faith versus Works of Law."

52. Wright, *Paul and the Faithfulness*, 797. For a critique of Wright's position on righteousness, see Irons, *Righteousness of God*.

Paul, for example, states: "Let it be known to you therefore, brothers, that through this man [Jesus] forgiveness of sins is proclaimed to you, and by him everyone who believes is justified from everything from which you could not be justified by the law of Moses" (Acts 13:38–39, my trans.).[53] Justification and the law work in concert, and there are only two ways to secure the verdict of righteous: faith or works. This is the whole point of Paul's argument in Galatians 3:10–14. "For all who rely on works of the law are under a curse, 'Cursed be everyone who does not abide by all things written in the Book of the law, and do them'" (Gal 3:10). We have to do πᾶσιν ("all things") written in the book of the law; Paul has the whole law in view, not merely boundary markers. Paul then shows the impossibility of such a feat: "Now it is evident that no one is justified before God by the law, for 'the righteous shall live by faith.' But the law is not of faith, rather 'The one who does them shall live by them'" (Gal 3:11–12). The contrast is justification by doing the law or by believing in the gospel.

Finally, while there is undoubtedly an ecclesial dimension to the doctrine of justification (i.e., Jews relating to gentiles), the issue that stands prominently in the foreground is soteriological. Justification is primarily about one's salvation. The Philippian jailer made this abundantly clear when he asked Paul and Silas: "What must I do to be saved?" (Acts 16:30). The jailer's concern was not about ecclesiology, about belonging to the family of Abraham, but about his sin disqualifying him from salvation. "To be saved" (σωθῶ) in this context refers to deliverance from sin, ruin, guilt, punishment, and most importantly, the wrath of God.[54] Likewise, Paul writes: "For with the heart one believes and is justified, and with the mouth one confesses and is saved" (Rom 10:10).

## CONCLUSION

The Belgic Confession expresses the only hope that sinners have as they stand before the divine bar: "We believe that our blessedness lies in the forgiveness of our sins because of Jesus Christ, and that in it our righteousness before God is contained." We do not claim a thing for ourselves or our merits but lean and rest wholly

53. Joseph Addison Alexander, *The Acts of the Apostles Explained* (London: James Nisbet, 1857), 2:34–35.

54. Alexander, *Acts of the Apostles*, 125.

on the sole obedience of Christ crucified. His obedience and satisfaction is "enough to cover all our sins and to make us confident, freeing the conscience from the fear, dread, and terror of God's approach" (23). We share in the judicial verdict passed over the last Adam and with him are justified in the Spirit. We go to the final judgment with confidence and hope, knowing that we do not go to meet the Judge of the cosmos but our heavenly Father, and that our Elder Brother, Jesus, is our Advocate who has obeyed the law perfectly in our stead and has suffered the curse of the law. We rest in Christ's finished work as we stand before the throne of grace dressed in his robe of righteousness. Such truth imparts peace, hope, and assurance.

## FURTHER READING

Allen, R. Michael. *Justification and the Gospel: Understanding the Contexts and Controversies*. Grand Rapids: Baker Academic, 2013. A wonderful volume that situates justification in recent exegetical and theological discussions and also relates justification to sanctification.

Barrett, Matthew. *The Doctrine on Which the Church Stands or Falls: Justification in Biblical, Theological, Historical and Practical Perspective*. Wheaton, IL: Crossway, 2019. An excellent edited volume with contributions from a wide array of scholars addressing numerous disciplines and issues related to the doctrine of justification.

Buchanan, James. *The Doctrine of Justification: An Outline of Its History in the Church, and of Its Exposition from Scripture*. Edinburgh: T&T Clark, 1867. A classic exposition of the doctrine of justification written by Scottish Presbyterian minister James Buchanan in the nineteenth century. Buchanan's work was published by Banner of Truth but is now out of print, though it is available through independent publishers and online as a free PDF. This work is an excellent historical overview of the doctrine followed by exegesis and doctrinal formulation. It is must-reading to understand the historic Protestant doctrine up to the nineteenth century.

Buzenitz, Nathan. *Long before Luther: Tracing the Heart of the Gospel from Christ to the Reformation*. Chicago: Moody, 2017. An accessible history of the doctrine of justification that showcases the evidence for the existence of justification *sola fide* prior to the sixteenth-century Reformation. The Protestant doctrine is not a sixteenth-century innovation but has roots in the teaching of the ancient and medieval church.

Carson, D. A., Peter T. O'Brien, and Mark A. Seifrid, eds. *Justification and Variegated Nomism*, vol. 2, *The Paradoxes of Paul*. Grand Rapids: Baker Academic, 2004. A technical engagement of issues related to the New Perspective on Paul that is must-reading, though knowledge of Greek and Hebrew is a prerequisite for the most profitable reading of this volume.

Fesko, J. V. *Justification: Understanding the Classic Reformed Doctrine*. Phillipsburg, NJ: P&R, 2007. A work that surveys the history of the doctrine and address issues related to the New Perspective on Paul.

Waters, Guy Prentiss. *Justification and the New Perspectives on Paul: A Review and Response*. Phillipsburg, NJ: P&R, 2004. An important response to the various challenges presented by the New Perspective on Paul. Waters gets into the issues, but he writes in an accessible manner.

VII

# ADOPTION

## SONS OF GOD, ALL

FROM THE VERY OUTSET OF creation God made humans, male and female, and he made them in his image (Gen 1:27). As the subsequent narrative makes clear, image-bearing is akin to sonship; sons share their father's image: "When God created man, he made him in the likeness of God. Male and female he created them, and he blessed them and named them Man when they were created. When Adam had lived 130 years, he fathered a son in his own likeness, after his image, and named him Seth" (Gen 5:1–3). All human beings are therefore the children of God. This is a truth that even unbelievers have discerned from general revelation. When he debated the philosophers at Mars Hill, the apostle Paul quoted Aratus (ca. 215–240 BC) and his poem *Phaenomena*: "As even some of your own poets have said, 'For we are indeed his offspring'" (Acts 17:28).[1] Yet in a fallen world sin has disrupted the filial relationship that all humans have with God, and thus apart from Christ we are all God's estranged sons. Paul spells this fact out in no uncertain terms: we are "by nature children of wrath" (Eph 2:3). Blessedly, through the redemption that comes through Christ and union with him, estranged children of wrath become sons of God through the Son.

The doctrine of adoption has been taught throughout the ages. Irenaeus (ca. 130–ca. 202) writes: "For it was for this end that the Word of God was

1. Darrell L. Bock, *Acts*, BECNT (Grand Rapids: Baker Academic, 2007), 568.

made man, and He who was the Son of God became the Son of man, that man, having been taken into the Word, and receiving the adoption, might become the son of God."[2] Martin Luther writes of the "inestimable grace and glory that we have in Christ, that we miserable sinners, by nature children of wrath (Eph 2:3), may arrive at this honor, that through faith in Christ we are made children and heirs of God and fellow heirs with Christ (Rom 8:17), lords of heaven and earth."[3] Likewise, the Westminster Larger Catechism explains: "The communion in grace which the members of the invisible church have with Christ, is their partaking of the virtue of his mediation, in their justification, adoption, sanctification, and whatever else, in this life, manifests their union with him" (q. 69). What does adoption entail? What blessings does adoption impart to the believer? This chapter answers these questions first by showing how this blessing was foreshadowed in the Old Testament and finds its fulfillment in Christ. Second, it defines adoption and explains its benefits. Third, the chapter explains adoption's relationship to the rest of the order of salvation. Finally, the chapter concludes with summary observations about the doctrine of adoption.[4]

## ADOPTION FORESHADOWED AND FULFILLED

The Old Testament foreshadows adoption in God's relationship to Israel; the exodus was the event where God adopted his people. God told Moses to inform Pharaoh that Israel was his "firstborn son" (Exod 4:22), and Hosea paints God's relationship to Israel in filial terms: "When Israel was a child, I loved him, and out of Egypt I called my son" (Hos 11:1). Paul characterizes this relationship in terms of adoption: "They are Israelites, and to them belong the adoption [υἱοθεσία], the glory, the covenants, the giving of the law, the worship, and

2. Irenaeus, *Against Heresies* 3.19.1, in *ANF* 1:448.

3. Luther, *Lectures on Galatians (1535)*, 352.

4. For a brief overview of the history of the doctrine of adoption, see Tim J. R. Trumper, "The Theological History of Adoption I: An Account," *SBET* 20, no. 1 (2002): 4–28; Trumper, "The Theological History of Adoption II: A Rationale," *SBET* 20, no. 2 (2002): 177–202; Joel R. Beeke, *Heirs with Christ: The Puritans on Adoption* (Grand Rapids: Reformation Heritage Books, 2008).

the promises" (Rom 9:4).[5] Israel's sonship finds its primary fulfillment in the incarnation of the Son of God. God announced the advent of his Son at four key moments during his incarnation. He announced the forthcoming birth of his Son to Mary (Luke 1:35), he declared from the heavens that Jesus was his Son at his baptism (Luke 3:22), he proclaimed that Jesus was his Son on the Mount of Transfiguration (Luke 9:35), and the Father declared that Jesus was his Son through his resurrection from the dead (Rom 1:3–4). Jesus is the true Israel of God, and the one to whom Israel's sonship points.[6]

Israel's adoption finds its secondary fulfillment in the redemption of God's people. Paul writes of the blessings of adoption unfolding before the foundation of the world: "He predestined us for adoption through Jesus Christ, according to the purpose of his will" (Eph 1:5). When the Triune God executes his decree of election, the Father sends the Son to redeem a people, and the Spirit applies the Son's work to those elected before the foundation of the world. The Spirit effectually calls, justifies, and adopts the elect as God's sons. Paul, for example, writes: "For you did not receive the spirit of slavery to fall back into fear, but you have received the Spirit of adoption as sons, by whom we cry, 'Abba! Father!'" (Rom 8:15). This adoptive status comes only through union with Christ. Paul writes: "For in Christ Jesus you are all sons of God, through faith. For as many of you as were baptized into Christ have put on Christ" (Gal 3:26–27). All people, male or female, are God's sons through faith in and union with the Son. This does not mean that redemption negates the differences between male and female. Rather, just as women are God's sons, so too men are the bride of Christ. Sonship is but one aspect of a rich redemption that we have in Christ that no one benefit can exhaust; this rich redemption requires a host of doctrines and metaphors to explain.

One of the chief purposes of Christ's ministry was to restore God's estranged sons to the family of God. Paul writes:

---

5. Moo, *Letter to the Romans*, 580–82. For the OT background to the doctrine of adoption, see Scott, *Adoption as Sons*.

6. Hans K. LaRondelle, *The Israel of God in Prophecy: Principles of Prophetic Interpretation* (Berrien Springs, MI: Andrews University Press, 1983); O. Palmer Robertson, *The Israel of God: Yesterday, Today, and Tomorrow* (Phillipsburg, NJ: P&R, 2000).

> In the same way we also, when we were children, were enslaved to the elementary principles of the world. But when the fullness of time had come, God sent forth his Son, born of woman, born under the law, to redeem those who were under the law, so that we might receive adoption as sons. And because you are sons, God has sent the Spirit of his Son into our hearts, crying, "Abba! Father!" So you are no longer a slave, but a son, and if a son, then an heir through God. (Gal 4:3–7)

Paul notes the estrangement and rebellion that marks fallen human beings—we were enslaved children—in bondage to the elementary principles of the world and under the yoke of the law. But Jesus was born under the law to redeem us out from under its yoke to be adopted as God's sons. Through Christ we are no longer slaves but sons, and if sons, then we are heirs with Christ and have a degree of intimacy with the Father that estranged children of God do not possess.

## ADOPTION DEFINED AND EXPLAINED

Given this biblical data, the doctrine of adoption has been defined as "an act of the free grace of God, in and for his only Son Jesus Christ, whereby all those that are justified are received into the number of his children, have his name put upon them, the Spirit of his Son given to them, are under his fatherly care and dispensations, admitted to all the liberties and privileges of the sons of God, made heirs of all the promises, and fellow-heirs with Christ in glory" (WLC q. 74). Within this definition there are several blessings, including becoming a son of God, bearing the name of Christ, receiving the Spirit of God, being under the fatherly care of God, and becoming co-heirs with Christ.

### *A New Name*

That God puts his name on his sons comes from passages such as Revelation 22:4, "They will see his face, and his name will be on their foreheads." This is an Old Testament notion that conveys intimate fellowship with God. Israel's high priest, for example, had God's name written on his forehead (Exod 28:36–38). Isaiah speaks of a time when God will give his people new names: "The nations shall see your righteousness, and all the kings your glory, and you shall be called by a new name that the mouth of the LORD will give" (Isa 62:2). John speaks of the people of God receiving a new name (Rev 2:17; 3:12; 7:2–3). They receive the name of Christ and the Father (Rev 14:1). Embedded in receiving the name of God is the idea of adoption and that we are God's children: "Beloved, we are God's children now, and what we will be has not yet appeared; but we know that when he appears we shall be like him, because we shall see him as he is" (1 John 3:2). Image-bearing is sonship, and sonship is name bearing, and name bearing means reflecting the character of God.[7] When God adopts us, he not only gives us a new name but a new nature, heart, temper, and disposition.[8]

*Spirit of Adoption* WHEN GOD ADOPTS US AS his sons, he gives the Spirit of Christ, which is the means by which he maintains his paternal intimacy with us. The Spirit of adoption enables us to cry out to God as Abba, Father (Rom 8:15). "Abba" does not mean "daddy" and is not a child's word. "Abba" is a word adults used and that Paul translates from Aramaic as "father," ὁ πατήρ. The term is not the lisping of a child but instead conveys intimacy that no Israelite before Christ knew. The nation collectively referred to God as Father, but not individually (e.g., Isa 63:16; 64:8; Jer 31:9; Ps 103:13).[9] Jesus uniquely addressed God as Father because he was the eternal only begotten Son of God and thus had a matchless relationship with God. But as the Father unites us to the Son by the Spirit, in the Son we share in the Son's intimacy with the Father, which is why Jesus instructed his disciples to begin their prayers with the words, "Our Father" (Matt 6:9).

We are, of course, God's adopted sons, and Jesus is his natural Son, that is, the Son is ontologically equal with the Father—he is God. We are mere creatures, mere dust; but we are dust that has been elevated to the status of sons. Jesus is the natural Son of God; we are God's adopted sons (*ST* IIIa, q. 23, arts 1–4, esp. 2 and 4). As God's sons, we can cry out to our heavenly Father in prayer. In the midst of prayer, the Spirit of adoption helps us in our weakness when we do not know how to pray, and the Spirit himself

7. Beale, *Book of Revelation*, 1114–15.

8. Thomas Doolittle, *A Complete Body of Practical Divinity; Being a New Improvement of the Assembly's Catechism* (London: John and Barham Clark, 1723), 214.

9. Barr, "Abba Isn't 'Daddy.'"

intercedes for us with groanings too deep for words (Rom 8:26). The Spirit carries our prayers to heaven and places them into the hands of Christ, who is our advocate before the throne of God in the heavenly holy of holies (Heb 8:1–6).

*Fatherly Care* BECAUSE WE ARE GOD'S SONS in the Son, we can call on him in prayer and know that he will provide for us as a father provides for his children. Jesus taught his disciples, "Which one of you, if his son asks him for bread, will give him a stone? Or if he asks for a fish, will give him a serpent? If you then, who are evil, now how to give good gifts to your children, how much more will your Father who is in heaven give good things to those who ask him!" (Matt 7:9–11). In the words of the Westminster Confession, we "are pitied, protected, provided for" (12.1). All too often in the midst of the Christian life we run hither, thither, and yon trying to find someone to care for us all the while failing to go to our heavenly Father in prayer. We have not because we ask not (Jas 4:2). But we are also "chastened by him, as by a father" (WCF 12.1). The author of Hebrews writes: "For the Lord disciplines the one he loves, and chastises every son whom he receives" (Heb 12:6). The author of Hebrews quotes Proverbs 3:11–12 to remind his readers of God's love for his sons. But he builds the father-son relationship on the work of Christ, who proclaims to the Father: "I will tell of your name to my brothers; in the midst of the congregation I will sing your praise" (Heb 2:12; see Ps 22:22).[10]

Through union with Christ, we share in the status of sonship, which also entails God's fatherly care and discipline. But we must carefully note the difference between God's wrath and fatherly discipline; they are different things. God visits his wrath, curse, and judgment on unrepentant sinners (e.g., Rom 1:18–32). But with his sons,

> God doth continue to forgive the sins of those that are justified; and, although they can never fall from the state of justification, yet they may, by their sins, fall under God's fatherly displeasure, and not have the light of his countenance restored unto them, until they

10. Beale and Carson, *Commentary on the New Testament Use*, 947, 985.

> humble themselves, confess their sins, beg pardon, and renew their faith and repentance. (WCF 11.5)

When believers experience the discipline of God, he treats them as sons, "For what son is there whom his father does not discipline?" (Heb 12:7). God's discipline both is a manifestation of his fatherly love and has the end of conformity to the image of Christ, his only begotten Son: "For the moment all discipline seems painful rather than pleasant, but later it yields the peaceful fruit of righteousness to those who have been trained by it" (Heb 12:11).[11]

*Privileges of Sons* As God's sons there are privileges that estranged, unrepentant children do not enjoy. Jesus, our elder brother, has been appointed as surety within the covenant of redemption (Heb 7:22), and as surety he meets all of the legal demands both in fulfilling covenant obligations and paying penalties for violating the covenant.[12] As those who are in union with Christ, we are no longer under the curse of the law; we are restored sons, and if sons, then heirs (Gal 4:1–7).[13] We must distinguish between the legal and ethical aspects of the doctrine of adoption. The legal aspect of adoption is the basis of the subjective ethical sense of adoption. In the first-century Roman world adoption (υἱοθεσία, Rom 9:4) was a purely legal action and did not bestow on someone the subjective characteristics of a child but simply placed them in the legal category of son. This idea appears in John 1:12, "But to all who did receive him, who believed in his name, he gave the right to become children of God." Immediately following the legal basis of adoption is the transformative work of the Spirit: "Who were born, not of blood nor of the will of the flesh nor of the will of man, but of God" (John 1:13). Paul reveals a similar legal-to-ethical pattern when he writes: "And because you are sons, God has sent the Spirit of his Son into our hearts, crying, 'Abba! Father!'" (Gal 4:6). Because we are first legally God's sons, he sends forth the Spirit

11. Schreiner, *Commentary on Hebrews*, 385–86.

12. Schreiner, *Commentary on Hebrews*, 230–31. Recall, a surety (ἔγγυος) is one who assumes all of the legal responsibilities of a covenant.

13. Vos, *Reformed Dogmatics* 4:156.

to effect our ethical transformation. The legal act is the basis of the believer's subjective possession of the Spirit, the Spirit of adoption.[14]

As Martin Luther observes about the word "Abba": "This is indeed a very short word, but it includes everything. Not the lips but the feelings are speaking here, as though one were to say: 'Even though I am surrounded by anxieties and seem to be deserted and banished from thy presence, nevertheless, I am a child of God on account of Christ; I am beloved on account of the Beloved.'"[15] As God's sons and co-heirs with Christ, we receive the privileges of sons, which include right and title to eternal life because of our justified state.[16] Additionally, as God's sons we are free from the law as a covenant, which requires personal, perpetual, and perfect obedience, because Christ as surety has released us from the bondage of the law. We follow the law as a rule, which informs us of what is pleasing to God and what conduct marks the sons of God (WCF 19.6). But Christian liberty flows from both justification and adoption because Christ has freed us from the guilt of sin, the wrath of God, and the curse of the moral law; moreover, sons of God are also free from the doctrines and commandments of men when contrary to God's word, or beside it in matters of faith or worship (WCF 2.1–2).[17]

## ADOPTION AND THE ORDER OF SALVATION

Adoption comes through union with Christ, but how does it relate to the other benefits of union?[18] Adoption is not effectual calling, by which a person is born again. Effectual calling deals with God's raising us from spiritual death to life by means of his all-powerful word, whereas adoption deals first with our legal status. Adoption is not justification, as justification deals with our legal status vis-à-vis the law, and adoption addresses our legal status concerning God as Father. Justification interfaces with the law, whereas adoption restores

14. Vos, *Reformed Dogmatics* 4:155; also Berkhof, *Systematic Theology*, 516.

15. Luther, *Lectures on Galatians (1535)*, 385.

16. Vos, *Reformed Dogmatics*, IV:156.

17. Turretin, *Institutes of Elenctic Theology* 16.6.9.

18. For what follows, see a similar explanation in Edward Leigh, *A Systeme or Body of Divinity* (London: William Lee, 1662), 707.

our filial relationship. In justification, God is our Judge, whereas in adoption he is our Father. Justification and adoption are linked, however, as adoption comes about as a result of our justification.[19] As Paul writes: "But when the fullness of time had come, God sent forth his Son, born of woman, born under the law, to redeem those who were under the law, so that we might receive adoption as sons" (Gal 4:4–5). Christ frees us from the curse of the law through our justification "so that we might receive adoption as sons" (ἵνα τὴν υἱοθεσίαν ἀπολάβωμεν). To this end, note how the Westminster Confession orders these two benefits: "All those that are justified, God vouchsafeth, in and for his only Son Jesus Christ, to make partakers of the grace of adoption" (12.1). Justification and adoption are not identical, though their objects and causes are the same: *God* justifies and *God* adopts "in and for His only Son Jesus Christ."[20] Adoption is not sanctification. Sanctification is a transformative blessing of union with Christ, whereas adoption is first legal and forensic. Sanctification prepares us for the inheritance we receive as adopted sons of God.[21] While adoption cannot

19. Note that some Reformed theologians such as Heinrich Bullinger, Francis Turretin, Geerhardus Vos, and Louis Berkhof include adoption as a part of justification. See Heinrich Bullinger, *The Decades of Henry Bullinger* (Grand Rapids: Reformation Heritage Books, 2003), 1:104, according to original Parker volume division; Turretin, *Institutes of Elenctic Theology* 16.4.1–13; Vos, *Reformed Dogmatics* 4:155; Berkhof, *Systematic Theology*, 515–16. Others, such as the Westminster Confession of Faith or Edward Leigh, treat it as a distinct element in the *ordo salutis* (Leigh, *Body of Divinity*, 706–9). Note that, whether a theologian places adoption under justification or treats it as a distinct element of the *ordo salutis*, neither contributes to the demise of or misunderstanding of the doctrine (contra Burke, *Adopted into God's Family*, 23–29; similar claims appear in Garner, *Sons in the Son*, 20–34). Theologians who treat adoption under justification do not conflate these two benefits; rather, they recognize they are linked—justification is the cause of the benefits of adoption (*Pace* Douglas F. Kelly, "Adoption: An Underdeveloped Heritage of the Westminster Standards," *Reformed Theological Review* 52, no. 3 [1993]: 110–20, here 112). Another erroneous claim is that adoption has been ignored. These theologians fail to investigate the doctrine under the concepts and terms common to the patristic and Middle Ages, and their exegesis of Scripture, and then mistakenly deem the doctrine absent. For patristic explanations of sonship see, e.g., Walter J. Burghardt, *The Image of God in Man according to Cyril of Alexandria* (Eugene, OR: Wipf & Stock, 2008), 105–25; Augustine, *Sermons on Selected Lessons of the New Testament*, sermon 71, *NPNF* 6:469–70; Origen, *On Prayer* 22.4, in *Origen*, trans. Rowan A. Greer (New York: Paulist Press, 1979), 124–25; Athanasius, *Defense of the Nicene Definition of Homousian* 7.45 and *Three Discourses against the Arians* 22.185, 47, in *Select Treatises of St. Athanasius*, trans. John Henry Newman (London: Longmans, Green, 1888), 1:54, 326, 343; Aquinas, *Summa Theologica* IIIa q. 23 arts. 1–4.

20. R. Michael Allen, *Justification and the Gospel: Understanding Contexts and Controversies* (Grand Rapids: Baker Academic, 2013), 44–45.

21. Berkhof, *Systematic Theology*, 516.

be separated from the other blessings of union with Christ, neither should it be confused with them.

Adoption rests within the *ordo salutis* as a part of our union with Christ, but we should note how the already-but-not-yet colors different elements of the *ordo*. How does adoption relate to other elements of the *ordo*?[22] Predestination is complete already, whereas glorification is entirely not-yet. Effectual calling is complete the moment that God calls a sinner and raises him from death to life, thus is already. Justification is a once-for-all act that God accomplishes immediately upon a profession of faith and is thus already: "There is therefore *now* no condemnation for those who are in Christ Jesus" (Rom 8:1).[23] Similarly, adoption is already, as "adoption is an *act* of the free grace of God" (WLC, q. 74).[24] At the same time, God will later reveal our status as justified sons by means of the resurrection of the dead, just as he did with Christ (Rom 1:3–4).[25] Paul writes: "And not only the creation, but we ourselves, who have the firstfruits of the Spirit, groan inwardly as we wait eagerly for adoption as sons, the redemption of our bodies" (Rom 8:23). For believers, therefore, resurrection is not unto judgment but unto the revelation of sonship. We go to the final judgment as righteous sons in Christ and therefore go to see our heavenly Father, not our Judge: "Beloved, we are God's children now, and what we will be has not yet appeared; but we know that when he appears we shall be like him, because we shall see him as he is" (1 John 3:2).

## CONCLUSION

THE DOCTRINE OF ADOPTION IS ultimately about the reconciliation of God to his estranged, sinful sons, a reversal that the apostle Paul powerfully illustrates through Israel's history of rebellion. Through Hosea and his parabolic marriage to Gomer, a woman of adultery, God declared to Israel that their third child would be called Lo Ammi, "Not My People, for you are not my people, and I am not your God" (Hos 1:9). But in the redemption that comes through union with Christ, Paul rejoices and basks in the mercy of God that was also

22. See Garner, *Sons in the Son*, 12.
23. Contra Burke, *Adopted into God's Family*, 44.
24. See Garner, *Sons in the Son*, 131–45.
25. See Burke, *Adopted into God's Family*, 74.

promised through Hosea: "And in the very place where it was said to them, 'You are not my people,' there they will be called 'sons of the living God'" (Rom 9:26; see Hos 1:10; 2:1 LXX).[26] In the words of Thomas Aquinas, "There they will be called sons of God by divine adoption."[27] Adoption holds out tremendous blessings for those who are in union with Christ. Among Jesus's parables, the prodigal son (Luke 15:11–24) paints a poignant portrait of the doctrine of adoption that John Newton (1725–1807) beautifully captures in poetic verse:

"What have I gain'd by sin, he said
But hunger, shame, and fear;
My father's house abounds with bread,
While I am starving here.

I'll go, and tell him all I've done,
And fall before his face;
Unworthy to be call'd his son,
I'll seek a servant's place."

His father saw him coming back,
He saw, and ran, and smil'd;
And threw his arms around the neck
Of his rebellious child.

"Father," I've sinn'd—but O forgive!"
"I've heard enough," he said,
Rejoice my house, my son's alive,
For whom I mourn'd as dead.

Now let the fatted calf be slain,
And spread the news around;
My son was dead, but lives again,
Was lost, but now is found.

---

26. Beale and Carson, *Commentary on the New Testament Use*, 647–48.

27. Thomas Aquinas, *Commentary on the Letter of Saint Paul to the Romans*, trans. F. R. Larcher, Latin/English Edition of the Works of St. Thomas Aquinas 37 (Lander, WY: Aquinas Institute for the Study of Sacred Doctrine, 2012), §800, on Rom 9:26.

'Tis thus the Lord his love reveals,
To call poor sinners home;
More than a father's love he feels,
And welcomes all that come.[28]

In Christ we are no longer estranged prodigals but welcomed sons of God, heirs, through the redemption that comes through Jesus, our elder brother.

## FURTHER READING

Barr, James. "Abba Isn't 'Daddy.'" *JTS* 39, no. 1 (1988): 28–47. An important essay that shows that "Abba" does not mean "daddy" but was rather a common way that referred to the intimate relationship between a father and his children, even adult children.

Beeke, Joel R. *Heirs with Christ: The Puritans on Adoption.* Grand Rapids: Reformation Heritage Books, 2008. An excellent and brief overview of the doctrine of adoption through the lens of seventeenth-century Puritan works.

Burke, Trevor. *Adopted Into God's Family: Exploring a Pauline Metaphor*. Downers Grove, IL: IVP Academic, 2006. A useful study that surveys the doctrine of adoption through the lens of biblical theology, though Burke overstates issues related to the placement of adoption in relation to justification.

Leigh, Edward. *A Systeme or Body of Divinity*. London: William Lee, 1662. A trove of theological insight though Leigh is little known in our own day. In particular, Leigh treats the doctrine of adoption as a unique element of the order of salvation and might provide some of the backdrop for why the Westminster Assembly made adoption a distinct benefit in the Westminster Confession.

---

28. John Newton, "The Prodigal Son," in *John Newton's Olney Hymns*, ed. Charles J. Doe (Minneapolis: Curiosmith, 2011), 71–72.

VIII

# SANCTIFICATION

## MADE RIGHTEOUS

THE AUTHOR OF THE BOOK of Hebrews exhorted his recipients regarding the need for holiness: "Follow peace with all men, and holiness, without which no man shall see the Lord" (Heb 12:14 KJV). In our justification, God imputes to us the "perfect satisfaction, righteousness, and holiness of Christ, as if I had never sinned nor been a sinner, and as if I had been perfectly obedient as Christ was obedient for me" (HC, q. 60). But salvation is more than justification and Christ's imputed obedience. In justification God declares us righteous by faith alone in Christ alone by his grace alone, and in sanctification God makes us what we have been declared: he makes us righteous and holy. Both justification and sanctification come to us through a Spirit-wrought union with Christ.

Like any doctrine, sanctification finds its roots in the Old Testament, and thus the first part of this chapter explores sanctification in the book of Leviticus in order to understand its nature and goal. Second, the chapter then examines the constituent parts of sanctification, namely, mortification and vivification. Through union with Christ the Spirit puts to death our old man, our former sin-dominated existence in Adam, and he enlivens our new man, our new Spirit-dominated existence in Jesus, the last Adam. Third, the chapter sets forth the differences between justification and sanctification and explains their relationship. In the history of doctrine, some have conflated justification and sanctification, which confuses the legal and transformative aspects of our salvation. In simple terms, if we confuse justification and sanctification, we lose the gospel. To say that God justifies us to some degree on the basis of our own works displaces the obedience of Christ as the sole judicial basis of our salvation. Thus, understanding the differences between justification and sanctification is vital to the preservation of the gospel.

Fourth, the chapter looks at the place of the law in the Christian life. Just because Christ has justified us from the law does not mean that we have no obligation of any kind to the law. Understanding the all-important distinction between the law as a *covenant* versus a *rule* helps Christians navigate between the twin dangers of antinomianism and neonomianism. Fifth and last, the chapter explains how faith works by love and produces good works. If we enter the kingdom of God by the gospel, then we must live the Christian life by the power of the gospel. Good works must arise from the power of the Spirit, from the life-giving union we have with Christ, not by sheer moral effort. The life of sanctification is one marked by both good works and wisdom, a sanctified wisdom that finds its source in Christ.

## OLD TESTAMENT BACKGROUND AND NATURE OF SANCTIFICATION

The doctrine of sanctification begins with the thrice-holy Triune God (Isa 6:3).[1] God requires that his people reflect his holiness: "You shall be holy, for I the Lord your God am holy" (Lev 19:2). In broad brushstrokes, the structure of the book of Leviticus explains how God's people become holy. The first half of Leviticus (1–16) deals with atonement, which segues to the second half (17–27), which explains degrees of holiness. Or in the terms of systematic theology, the book sets forth justification and then sanctification. This is not to say that the first half of Leviticus mentions nothing of sanctification. This division of Leviticus merely gives a bird's-eye view and establishes a framework to understand what informs Paul's explanation of soteriology: "We have *now* been justified by his blood,

1. Allen, *Sanctification*, 23, 33–34, 47–69.

much more shall we be saved by him from the wrath of God" (Rom 5:9).[2] Paul's use of the eschatological νῦν ("now") underscores the already of justification, but his shift to a future passive indicative, σωθησόμεθα ("we shall be saved"), reveals that there is more to salvation than our justification. In this case, the book of Leviticus discloses that we need personal holiness in order to live in communion with God, not merely imputed holiness.

The Levitical sacrifices showcase this pattern (Lev 1:1–6:7). Purification sacrifices bring the *expiation* of sin (Lev 9); fire completely consumes and transforms ascension offerings into smoke, and they impart *consecration* (e.g., Lev 1:9, 17; 2:2); peace offerings involve consuming a meal and denote fellowship, or *communion*. Leviticus 9:22 presents these sacrifices in this order—expiation, consecration, and communion: "Then Aaron lifted up his hands toward the people and blessed them, and he came down from offering the sin offering and the burnt offering and the peace offerings." These offerings correspond to the soteriological categories of justification, sanctification, and communion with God.[3] Another way to order these ideas is to say there is no communion with God apart from dealing with sin and manifesting holiness. Alternatively stated, there is no union with God apart from justification and sanctification. But sinners do not achieve communion with God by their own moral effort—and neither do they atone for their sin or consecrate themselves.

God sent his Son to justify and sanctify his people so that they can have fellowship and communion with him. This salvation comes through union with Christ by means of the Spirit's sovereign work through the gift of faith. Through the Spirit's application of Christ to the believer, God is both justifier and sanctifier—he declares his people righteous on the basis of the imputed righteousness, satisfaction, and holiness of Christ and then makes his people what they have been declared in Christ. Sanctification is therefore "the work of God's free grace, whereby we are renewed in the whole man after the image of God, and are enabled more and more to die unto sin, and live unto righteousness" (WSC q. 35; see also WCF 13.1;

---

2. L. Michael Morales, *Who Shall Ascend the Mountain of the Lord? A Biblical Theology of the Book of Leviticus*, NSBT (Downers Grove, IL: IVP Academic, 2015), 30–31.

3. Morales, *Who Shall Ascend*, 123–24.

BC 24). Redeemed sinners are in union with Christ and thus know a greater degree of intimacy than Adam knew in the garden because they possess the indwelling of the Spirit of Christ, the power of the age to come (Heb 6:5). But the present possession of the Spirit is not the highest degree of possible intimacy. Reformed theologians distinguish between the present mystical and the final eschatological union that believers share with Christ.[4] These are not different unions but terms that delineate the present life of sanctification versus the eschatological state, where believers are fully conformed to the image of Christ. The Westminster Larger Catechism captures these phases of union with Christ when it distinguishes between the unions of grace and glory (qq. 69, 82–83).[5]

Leviticus foreshadows the increased degrees of intimacy and sanctification necessary for communion with God. The wilderness is the haunt of Azazel, demons, unclean gentiles, animals, and birds. Away from the camp are those with persistent uncleanness. Outside the camp are those with temporary uncleanness. Within the camp are the people of God and resident aliens. The court of the tabernacle is for the people of God to draw near for worship. Only the Levites have access to the altar, as the priests are the only ones permitted in the tabernacle, and only the high priest is allowed to enter the holy of holies, where God resides enthroned between the cherubim. The closer one gets to God, the holier he becomes. The same degrees of holiness mark the people of God. The people of God are holy (Exod 19:4–6) and therefore have to live by higher moral standards than their gentile neighbors (Lev 18:2–5, 24–30). They can live in the camp so long as they maintain a state of ritual purity. The priests are holier, and the high priest is the holiest of the people; he has to marry a virgin and cannot contract defilement from anyone's death lest he disqualify himself (Lev 21:10–15).[6] The ongoing sacrificial system facilitated expiation of sin and the holiness of the people, which allowed them to live within the camp and enabled them to draw near to the center of the encampment to worship God, both by their own sacrifices and through the ministrations of the Levites.

---

4. See, e.g., Girolamo Zanchi, *De Religione Christiana Fides—Confession of Christian Religion*, ed. Luca Baschera and Christian Moser (Leiden: Brill, 2007), 12.5 (1:234–35).

5. Allen, *Sanctification*, 158.

6. John Hartley, *Leviticus*, WBC (Grand Rapids: Zondervan, 1992), lvi–lxiii.

In the wake of the ministry of our great high priest, Christ's righteousness constitutes the legal ground that secures the Christian's presence among the people of God. Believers draw near to God not through the sacrificial blood of bulls and goats but through the blood of Jesus Christ. Through union with Christ, they enter into the holy of holies and are seated with him at the right hand of God. The Spirit, moreover, carries their prayers into the holy of holies so they can have a greater degree of intimacy with God than even Adam and Eve knew. But they also draw closer to God as he progressively conforms and transforms his people by increasing degrees of sanctification. Christians engaged in ongoing rebellious sin find their Levitical counterpart in exile outside the camp; they are subject to excommunication. Conversely, those who seek greater conformity to Christ, who regularly pray, worship, and offer the sacrifices of praise, find their Levitical counterpart in the priests who served in the tabernacle.

<table>
<tr><th>Old Testament</th><th>People</th><th>New Testament</th><th>People</th></tr>
<tr><td>holy of holies</td><td>high priest</td><td>heavenly holy of holies</td><td>Jesus Christ</td></tr>
<tr><td>outer tabernacle</td><td>Levitical priests</td><td rowspan="2">visible and invisible church</td><td rowspan="2">believers in union with Christ (invisible church) and nominal Christians (visible church)</td></tr>
<tr><td>camp</td><td>Israelites and resident aliens</td></tr>
<tr><td>outside the camp</td><td>temporary uncleanness</td><td>outside the church</td><td>excommunicated</td></tr>
<tr><td>wilderness</td><td>demons, Azazel, and unclean gentiles</td><td>the world</td><td>unbelievers</td></tr>
</table>

Proximity to God finds its consummation when he removes every vestige of sin in glorification. In a glorified state Christians will know the greatest and highest degree of communion with the Triune God as they dwell eternally in his presence. Union with Christ and its twofold blessing of justification and sanctification therefore ineluctably lead to eternal communion with the Triune God.

## MORTIFICATION AND VIVIFICATION

The process of sanctification involves two principles: putting to death the old man and enlivening the new man, or mortification and vivification. Concerning mortification, Paul writes: "We know that our old man was crucified with him in order that the body of sin might be brought to nothing, so that we would no longer be enslaved to sin" (Rom 6:6, my trans.). Through union with Christ God has crucified our former existence in Adam, our "old man," and set us on a course of conformity to Christ.[7] As John Owen writes: "Set faith at work on Christ for the killing of thy sin. His blood is the great sovereign remedy for sin-sick souls. Live in this, and thou wilt die a conqueror; yea, thou wilt, through the good providence of God, live to see thy lust dead at thy feet."[8] Conversely, concerning vivification Paul writes: "We were buried therefore with him by baptism into death, in order that, just as Christ was raised from the dead by the glory of the Father, we too might walk in the newness of life. For if we have been united with him in a death like his, we shall certainly be united with him in a resurrection like his" (Rom 6:4–5). God has made us alive in Christ by the Spirit.[9] Vivification is to seek to live in the power of the resurrection of Christ and under its tutelage.[10] Romans 6:4–6 sets forth the indicatives of the Christian life—who we are by virtue of the work of Christ through the Spirit and union with him.

On the basis of this indicative, Paul elsewhere sets forth the imperatives of mortification and vivification: "You have put off your old man, which belongs to your former manner of life and is corrupt through deceitful desires, and are being renewed in the spirit of your minds, and have put on the new man, created after the likeness of God in true righteousness and holiness" (Eph 4:22–24, my trans.). The παλαιὸν ἄνθρωπον ("old man") is our former existence in Adam; our καινὸν ἄνθρωπον ("new man") is our new existence in Christ, the last Adam. On the basis of our new existence in Christ, Paul then segues to imperatives: "Therefore [Διὸ], having put away falsehood, let each one of you speak the truth with his neighbor, for

7. Moo, *Letter to the Romans*, 396–400.

8. John Owen, *Of the Mortification of Sin in Believers*, in *Works of John Owen* 6:79.

9. Moo, *Letter to the Romans*, 386–96.

10. John Webster, *Holiness* (Grand Rapids: Eerdmans, 2003), 89.

we are members one of another" (Eph 4:25). Paul's exhortations flow from the fact of union with Christ, not merely from the force of the bald imperatives.[11] In other words, Paul is not saying, "Try harder!" He rests the power to perform the imperatives in the indicative of union with Christ. Human effort does not fuel mortification and vivification, as the power for these sanctifying activities flows from the Spirit of Christ. As the Westminster Larger Catechism explains: "The communion in grace which the members of the invisible church have with Christ, is their partaking of the virtue of his mediation, in their justification, adoption, sanctification, and whatever else, in this life, manifests their union with him" (q. 69). Or the Westminster Confession more succinctly states regarding believers' good works: "Their ability to do good works is not at all of themselves, but wholly from the Spirit of Christ" (16.3).

Mortification and vivification affect the whole person, body and soul, intellect, affections, and will (WCF 13.2). Paul, for example, writes to the Thessalonians, "Now may the God of peace himself sanctify you completely, and may your whole spirit and soul and body be kept blameless at the coming of our Lord Jesus Christ" (1 Thess 5:23). Paul does not say that humans are tripartite (spirit, soul, and body), but rather refers to these different terms to convey the totality of the Spirit's sanctifying work, thus he writes "sanctify you completely."[12] The Spirit's work in the complete sanctification of the redeemed, body and soul, has communion with God as its telos, as believers will be "kept blameless at the coming of our Lord Jesus." Think back to Leviticus and the degrees of intimacy. The more the Spirit sanctifies a believer, the closer his communion with God is—his sanctity allows him to draw nearer to God. To this end, the Spirit transforms the intellect, or understanding.[13] Paul's continual prayer for the church at Colossae is that they will be "filled with the knowledge of God's will in all spiritual wisdom and understanding" (Col 1:9). When the Spirit transforms the intellect, he gives believers the mind of Christ through κοινωνία ("participation" or "fellowship") in the Spirit (Phil 2:1, 5). By transforming the

11. Baugh, *Ephesians*, 368–77.

12. Gordon D. Fee, *The First and Second Letters to the Thessalonians*, NICNT (Grand Rapids: Eerdmans, 2009), 226–33.

13. On the faculty psychology common to both Catholic and Protestant theologians, see *ST* Iae, qq. 79, 82.

intellect, the Spirit enables redeemed sinners to will righteousness and obedience.[14] Paul explains that God is at work in believers "both to will and to work for his good pleasure" (Phil 2:13; see Col 3:1–17).[15] When the Spirit transforms the heart, the natural consequence is a reformation of the affections. The Spirit enables Christians to crucify "the flesh with its passions and desires" (Gal 5:24).[16] If as sinners we set our "mind, will, or affections upon other things, and taking them off from him in whole or in part" (WLC q. 105; see qq. 99, 147–48), then Christ through his Spirit turns our faculties in a Godward direction to reform us and conform us to his holy image. God turns us towards holiness by giving us a new disposition (or *habitus*, "habit"). In justification the habit of faith is passive, as it rests, receives, and accepts the righteousness of Christ. In sanctification faith is active as it works by love.[17]

## THE RELATIONSHIP BETWEEN JUSTIFICATION AND SANCTIFICATION

Understanding the differences between justification and sanctification is vital to the integrity of both doctrines, especially in the wake of the Roman Catholic response to the Reformation at the Council of Trent. Trent formalized the conflation of justification and sanctification:

> If anyone saith that men are justified, either by the sole imputation of the justice of Christ, or by the sole remission of sins, to the exclusion of the grace and *the charity which is poured forth in their hearts by the Holy Ghost*, and is inherent in them; or even that the grace, whereby we are justified, is only the favor of God: let him be anathema.[18]

---

14. Turretin, *Institutes of Elenctic Theology* 15.4.13, 23, 30–31, 49, and 8.7.

15. Peter T. O'Brien, *The Epistle to the Philippians*, NIGTC (Grand Rapids: Eerdmans, 1991), 284–89.

16. Douglas J. Moo, *Galatians*, BECNT (Grand Rapids: Baker Academic, 2013), 367.

17. See, e.g., Robert Rollock, *Treatise of God's Effectual Calling*, in *Select Works of Robert Rollock* (Grand Rapids: Reformation Heritage Books, 2008), 1:200; John Owen, *On Justification*, in *Works of John Owen* 5:63–64; Canons of Dort 3/4:14, also rejection of errors 6.

18. Council of Trent, "Sixth Session, 13 Jan 1547," canon 11, in Schaff, *Creeds of Christendom* 2:112–13.

Justification and sanctification converge in Roman Catholic soteriology because Trent concluded that believers "through the observance of the commandments of God and of the Church, faith co-operating with good works, increase in that justice which they have received through the grace of Christ, and are still further justified."[19] Believers produce good works that contribute and constitute their final, or second, justification (see HC, q. 62; WCF 16). The Reformers, however, distinguished between justification and sanctification.

A succinct statement on the differences between justification and sanctification appears in the Westminster Larger Catechism when it asks, "Wherein do justification and sanctification differ?"

> Although sanctification be inseparably joined with justification, yet they differ, in that God in justification imputeth the righteousness of Christ; in sanctification his Spirit infuseth grace, and enableth to the exercise thereof; in the former, sin is pardoned; in the other, it is subdued: the one doth equally free all believers from the revenging wrath of God, and that perfectly in this life, that they never fall into condemnation; the other is neither equal in all, nor in this life perfect in any, but growing up to perfection. (q. 77)

The catechism explains that justification and sanctification are "inseparably joined," which is because they both come to believers through union with Christ. They can no more be separated than the two natures of Christ can be rent asunder.[20] The links in the golden chain of salvation are unbreakable. But at the same time, the catechism recognizes that the two benefits are distinct.

In justification, God *imputes* the righteousness of Christ: "And to the one who does not work but believes in him who justifies the ungodly, his faith is counted as righteousness" (Rom 4:5).[21] In sanctification God *infuses* grace: "God's love has been poured into our hearts through the Holy Spirit who has been given to us" (Rom 5:5).[22] Justification is a forensic declaration,

---

19. Council of Trent, "Sixth Session, 13 Jan 1547," ch. 10, in Schaff, *Creeds of Christendom* 2:99.

20. Calvin, *Inst.* 3.16.1.

21. Moo, *Letter to the Romans*, 286–88.

22. Moo, *Letter to the Romans*, 332–33.

or judicial act: "Who shall bring any charge against God's elect? It is God who justifies" (Rom 8:33).[23] In sanctification God purifies believers from their sin: "Now may the God of peace himself sanctify you completely" (1 Thess 5:23). Justification is complete the moment God declares a sinner righteous and is irreversible: "There is therefore *now* no condemnation for those who are in Christ Jesus" (Rom 8:1). Paul's νῦν ("now") carries eschatological significance—it is the *now* of the new creation.[24] Correlatively, to say there is "no condemnation" is another way of saying there is *now* justification.[25] Sanctification, on the other hand, varies from person to person: "Surely there is not a righteous man on earth who does good and never sins" (Eccl 7:20). Thus, the Westminster Confession states: "This sanctification is throughout, in the whole man; yet imperfect in this life, there abiding still some remnants of corruption in every part; whence ariseth a continual and irreconcilable war, the flesh lusting against the Spirit, and the Spirit against the flesh" (13.2). In this respect, the Westminster divines rightly distinguish justification from sanctification as an "act" versus a "work of God" (WLC qq. 70, 75). As an *act* God completes justification all at once, whereas sanctification is an *ongoing work*.[26] Given these differences, how then do justification and sanctification relate to each other?

First, justification precedes sanctification. There are two ways this truth appears in Scripture, in the *historia* and the *ordo salutis*. In the *historia salutis* justification precedes sanctification in the covenant of grace, which is the reverse of the covenant of works. In the covenant of works Adam possessed perfect holiness and had to secure his judicial state by his righteousness. The covenant of grace reverses this order. By faith in the last Adam God imputes righteousness to the believer—God irreversibly declares the verdict of the final judgment over the believer in the present. Adam's state vis-à-vis his justification was indeterminate, whereas for the believer in the covenant of grace it is determinate. Following the

23. Moo, *Letter to the Romans*, 563.

24. Moo, *Letter to the Romans*, 495–96.

25. See Moo, *Letter to the Romans*, 97.

26. On the distinction between an act and work, see, e.g., Edwin Hall, *The Shorter Catechism of the Westminster Assembly with Analysis and Scripture Proofs* (Philadelphia: Presbyterian Publication Committee, 1859), 52; Robert Shaw, *An Exposition of the Confession of Faith of the Westminster Assembly of Divines*, 2nd ed. (Edinburgh: John Johnstone, 1845), 143; Hodge, *Systematic Theology* 3:213.

declaration of righteousness, the state of holiness begins to appear through the Spirit's work of sanctification. In this respect, the believer lacks the holiness that Adam possessed before the fall. The justification–sanctification order appears in broad brushstrokes in Paul's Epistle to the Romans: first justification (Rom 3–5), then sanctification (6–8).[27]

The justification–sanctification relationship also appears in the *ordo salutis*, where in the *ordo naturae* ("order of nature") justification comes first. Justification comes first because it is "the legal ground for sanctification" and is "thus in a judicial sense the root of our sanctification."[28] The priority of justification over sanctification is a common staple in classic Reformed theology. John Calvin famously said that justification is "the principal ground on which religion must be supported."[29] Francis Turretin similarly observes: "Justification stands related to sanctification as the means to an end."[30] Wilhelmus à Brakel (1635–1711) writes: "Justification is the fountain of sanctification. … Since justification is the fountain, it therefore defines the proper manifestation of sanctification and its true essence. … He who endeavors to attain to sanctification upon another foundation has gone astray, and will never attain to it, and will never make progress in it."[31]

Preserving the relative order of justification and sanctification is about maintaining Paul's point: "And to the one who does not work but believes in him who justifies the ungodly, his faith is counted as righteousness" (Rom 4:5). God justifies the *ungodly*. Placing justification first ensures that Christ's righteousness and satisfaction are the sole material cause of our justification; good works play no role in our justification. As the Westminster Confession states: "Those whom God effectually calleth, he also freely justifieth: not by infusing righteousness into them, but by pardoning their sins, and by accounting and accepting their persons as righteous; *not for*

---

27. Vos, *Reformed Dogmatics* 4:193.

28. Vos, *Reformed Dogmatics* 4:172, 193; Allen, *Sanctification*, 34, 174, 182–83; Bavinck, *Reformed Dogmatics* 4:249.

29. Calvin, *Inst.* 3.11.1; John Calvin, *Institutio Christianae Religionis* (Geneva: Robert Stephanus, 1559): "praecipuum esse sustinendae religionis cardinem."

30. Turretin, *Institutes of Elenctic Theology* 17.2.4.

31. Wilhelmus à Brakel, *The Christian's Reasonable Service*, trans. Bartel Elshout (Morgan, PA: Soli Deo Gloria, 1992), 2:405–6; also see David VanDrunen, *Divine Covenants and Moral Order: A Biblical Theology of Natural Law* (Grand Rapids: Eerdmans, 2014), 440; Allen, *Sanctification*, 34.

*anything wrought in them, or done by them, but for Christ's sake alone*; nor by imputing faith itself, the act of believing, or any other evangelical obedience to them, as their righteousness" (11.1, emphasis added). Placing justification first also follows the line of Paul's argument in Romans 7:6, "But now we are released from the law, having died to that which held us captive, so that we serve in the new way of the Spirit and not in the old way of the written code." Justification frees believers from the bondage to the law ὥστε ("so that"); note Paul's use of a result clause, "we serve in the new way of the Spirit."[32]

Second, justification is the legal ground for sanctification. Both justification and sanctification come through union with Christ, but the believer's saved state does not rest on the believer's own holiness but on Christ's imputed righteousness, satisfaction, and holiness. Think back to the pattern in Leviticus—expiatory sacrifices precede the purificatory and communion sacrifices. Christ is the covenant surety (Heb 7:22), and thus his imputed righteousness, satisfaction, and holiness completely secure our right and title to eternal life: "For as by the one man's disobedience the many were constituted sinners, so by the one man's obedience the many will be constituted righteous ... so that, as sin reigned in death, grace also might reign through righteousness leading to eternal life through Jesus Christ our Lord" (Rom 5:19–21, my trans.).[33] Sanctification remains completely beyond the legal sphere; our legal standing lies entirely with our justification. Correlatively, justification is *extra nos* ("outside us") and never competes with the distinctive work of sanctification. We must possess the imputed righteousness of Christ, but we must also be holy before God.[34] God, of course, gives both justification and sanctification through our union with Christ.

## THE LAW AND THE CHRISTIAN LIFE

The imputed obedience of Christ justifies the believer from the law (Rom 6:7), but this does not mean the believer is utterly

32. Moo, *Letter to the Romans*, 446.
33. Moo, *Letter to the Romans*, 371.
34. Vos, *Reformed Dogmatics* 4:193–94.

and totally free from it.[35] There is a difference between approaching the law qua covenant versus qua rule. One of the errors that sometimes arises after people hear that Christ has justified them from the law is that they believe they are completely free from it in every sense or that they can engage in sin because they have been forgiven of past, present, and future sins. Paul engages this misunderstanding in his letter to Rome: "What shall we say then? Are we to continue in sin that grace may abound? By no means! How can we who died to sin still live in it?" (Rom 6:1–2).[36] The twin dangers of antinomianism and neonomianism (legalism, or works-righteousness) that threaten the doctrine of justification also threaten sanctification. Antinomians believe that the imputed righteousness of Christ completely and totally frees them from the obligations of the moral law—holiness and good works are unnecessary. Or, in terms of the *ordo salutis*, sanctification is unnecessary. Conversely, neonomians believe that one must perform works of righteousness either to constitute or complete their justification. Neonomianism, or the idea that Christ gives a new law through the grace of the gospel by which sinners may be justified, threatens the place of the all-sufficient work of Christ as the sole material cause of justification, and it destroys the distinct integrity of sanctification by merging it with justification. The gospel, like Christ, is always crucified between two thieves: neonomianism on the one hand and antinomianism on the other. The former robs Christ of the glory of his work for us, and the latter robs him of the glory of his work within us.[37] The truth of the Christian's relationship to the law, therefore, lies between the twin errors of neonomianism and antinomianism.

To sail between the Scylla of neonomianism and the Charybdis of antinomianism, we must carefully parse the law's demands on a sinner both pre- and postjustification. God always administers his law in covenant, whether in the covenant of works with Adam and all his offspring, or the

35. Robert Haldane, *Exposition of the Epistle to the Romans*, 9th ed. (Edinburgh: William Oliphant, 1874), 248–50; Charles Hodge, *A Commentary on the Epistle to the Romans*, 19th ed. (New York: Robert Carter, 1880), 143–44; Allen, *Sanctification*, 186; see also Moo, *Letter to the Romans*, 401.

36. Moo, *Letter to the Romans*, 381–84.

37. James Henley Thornwell, "Antinomianism," in *The Collected Writings of James Henley Thornwell*, ed. John B. Adger (Richmond, VA: Presbyterian Committee of Publication, 1871), 2:383–96, here 385.

Mosaic covenant at Sinai specifically with the Jews. Within the bounds of the covenant there are three key maxims. First, the law is an integral whole: "For whoever keeps the whole law but fails in one point has become guilty of all of it" (Jas 2:10). The law is a mirror, and to break one part shatters the whole.[38] Second, a person must perform the law in order to secure the status of righteous: "And it will be righteousness for us, if we are careful to do all this commandment before the LORD our God, as he has commanded us" (Deut 6:25). Third, anyone who fails to do *all* the law is subject to its curse: "For all who rely on works of the law are under a curse; for it is written, 'Cursed be everyone who does not abide by all things written in the Book of the Law, and do them'" (Gal 3:10; see Deut 27:26).[39] When Paul expounds the justifying significance of Christ's work, he explains that Christ justifies us from the law: "For sin will have no dominion over you, since you are not under law but under grace" (Rom 6:14; see also 5:20; 7:1–6).[40] To state this truth in terms of classic covenant theology: in Christ we are no longer under the covenant of works (or the Mosaic covenant) but under the covenant of grace. But Christ's justifying work does not entirely free Christians from the moral law. Paul specifies: "Christ redeemed us from the curse of the law by becoming a curse for us" (Gal 3:13). Just because Christ justifies us from the *curse* of the law does not mean Christians are utterly free from the moral law.

Paul, for example, instructs the Romans: "Owe no one anything, except to love each other, for the one who loves another has fulfilled the law" (Rom 13:8). He then quotes the sixth, seventh, eighth, and tenth commandments and summarizes them with this biblical quotation from Leviticus: "'You shall love your neighbor as yourself.' Love does no wrong to a neighbor; therefore love is the fulfilling of the law" (Rom 13:9–11; Exod 20:13, 14, 15, 17; Deut 5:17–19, 21; Lev 19:18). Even though justified from the curse of the law, Christians are still obliged to keep the law. But how one attempts to keep the law makes a world of difference. The antinomian completely rejects the moral law and thus does not try to keep it in any sense. Antinomianism is a grievous error and sin. The neonomian tries to keep the law as a means

38. Douglas J. Moo, *The Letter of James*, PNTC (Grand Rapids: Eerdmans, 2000), 113–14.

39. Beale and Carson, *Commentary on the New Testament Use*, 795–800, esp. 796–97.

40. Moo, *Letter to the Romans*, 411–15.

of either his justification (seeking judicial standing through personal obedience) or his sanctification (trying to become holier through his works rather than through union with Christ and the sanctifying power of the Holy Spirit). Neonomianism is as equally dreadful as antinomianism. How, then, should Christians approach the law?

The Westminster Confession offers an important distinction that delineates the sinner's relationship to the law pre- and postjustification. The law as a covenant of works requires "entire, exact, and perpetual obedience," and promises eternal life on its fulfillment (WCF 19.1). This is how all people outside Christ relate to the law—as a covenant of works, whether the protological Adamic or Mosaic law. By way of contrast, "true believers" are "not under the law, as a covenant of works, to be thereby justified, or condemned" because Christ has fulfilled the law qua covenant. The law, consequently, is "of great use to them, as well as to others; in that, as a rule of life informing them of the will of God, and their duty, it directs and binds them to walk accordingly" (WCF 19.6). For those in Christ the law serves qua a rule, not as a covenant requiring perfect, personal, and perpetual obedience. As a *rule*, the law reveals Christians' "sinful pollutions of their nature, hearts, and lives" so they can "come to further conviction of, humiliation for, and hatred against sin" and see their continued need for Christ. As a *rule*, the law restrains a person's corruptions by what it forbids, and its threats show what their sin deserves. Conversely, the law's promises show what blessings Christians might expect if they obey it, "although not as due to them by the law as a covenant of works" (WCF 19.6). Recognizing the law qua covenant versus qua a rule is vital to avoiding the twin errors of antinomianism and neonomianism.[41]

The law as *covenant* versus *rule*, however, is only one part of the Christian life. A second element is that Christians must pursue conformity to Christ by faith. Sanctification is part of the gospel, and thus we do not receive the gift of the gospel by works. Likewise, sanctification comes through union with Christ, and we do not lay hold of Christ by works but by faith in him: "You are in Christ Jesus, who became to us wisdom from God,

---

41. Anthony Burgess, *Vindiciae Legis: or, A Vindication of the Morall Law and the Covenants* (London: Thomas Underhill, 1647), lecture 22, pp. 210–23, esp. 213–14.

righteousness and sanctification and redemption" (1 Cor 1:30).[42] For this reason, the Westminster Confession states: "The principal acts of saving faith are accepting, receiving, and resting upon Christ alone for justification, sanctification, and eternal life, by virtue of the covenant of grace" (14.3). Faith sanctifies because it lays hold of the saving work of Christ for both our legal standing and transformation into the image of Christ. At the same time, in justification faith rests, receives, and accepts Christ and his work, whereas in sanctification faith works through love (Gal 5:6). Sanctification is supernatural—a work of Christ through the Spirit, who works in us "both to will and work for his good pleasure" (Phil 2:13). We do not make ourselves holy; our holiness and growth in grace are not due to our own fidelity, conviction, purpose, watchfulness, or diligence, though all of these virtues are necessary. Rather, the work of the Spirit in sanctification makes us faithful, watchful, and diligent, as the Spirit produces in us the fruit of holiness and righteousness.[43] We must therefore acknowledge our complete dependence on the work of the Spirit. Our activity is enlisted to the fullest extent in the process of sanctification, but we cannot rest on our own strength or resolution or purpose. When we are weak, we are strong: "It is by grace that we are being saved as surely as by grace we have been saved."[44]

## GOOD WORKS

THAT FAITH WORKS BY LOVE means that believers will produce good works because they are in union with Christ. Ezekiel prophesies of this reality when he writes: "And I will put my Spirit within you, and cause you to walk in my statutes and be careful to obey my rules" (Ezek 36:27; see 11:19–20; Jer 31:31, 33).[45] In the New Testament Paul rests his paraenesis on the Old Testament promises of the Spirit. When he calls the Thessalonians to sexual purity, he echoes Ezekiel's prophecy: "For God has not called us for impurity, but in holiness. Therefore whoever disregards this, disregards not man but God, who gives

42. Charles Hodge, *An Exposition of the First Epistle to the Corinthians* (New York: Robert Carter, 1860), 26–28.

43. Hodge, *Systematic Theology* 3:218.

44. Murray, *Redemption Accomplished and Applied*, 147; also Allen, *Sanctification*, 230.

45. Gary Edward Schnittjer, *Old Testament Use of Old Testament: A Book-by-Book Guide* (Grand Rapids: Zondervan, 2021), 334–35.

his Holy Spirit to you" (1 Thess 4:7–8).[46] That Paul speaks of ἀκαθαρσία ("impurity") and ἁγιασμός ("holiness") draws us immediately into the concepts and categories of Leviticus (e.g., Lev 5:3; 7:20–21; 15:3, 24–26, 30–31; 16:16, 19; 18:19; 19:23; 20:21, 25; 22:3–5; Num 19:13; see also Ezek 45:4). In other words, God draws us into his presence by Christ through his Spirit, and the Spirit produces the fruit of holiness and good works in our lives. We do not act as the gentiles who live beyond the sanctified boundaries of God's people but as priests, those who draw nigh to God through Jesus Christ, our great high priest, the head of the body, the church. We are God's workmanship, "created in Christ Jesus for good works, which God prepared beforehand, that we should walk in them" (Eph 2:10). The New Testament repeatedly calls Christians to the performance of good works (Col 1:10; 2 Thess 2:17; 1 Tim 2:10; 5:10, 25; 2 Tim 2:21, 3:17). Believers know what is pleasing to God by using the index of the law as a rule, not as a covenant (WLC qq. 91–115; HC, qq. 86–115, 127); they produce good works as a consequence of their salvation and justification not as a prerequisite.

Through the outpouring of the Spirit, Christ gives us the fruit of love, joy, peace, patience, kindness, goodness, gentleness, faithfulness, and self-control (Gal 5:22–23). As believers live out their sanctification, they ply their priestly position that they share through their union with Christ. In this vein the chief function of the Levitical priests is to distinguish between what is holy versus profane. Ezekiel excoriated the priests of his day for their failed work: "Her priests have done violence to my law and have profaned my holy things. They have made no distinction between the holy and the common, neither have they taught the difference between the unclean and the clean, and they have disregarded my Sabbaths, so that I am profaned among them" (Ezek 22:26).[47] As a royal priesthood and holy nation (1 Pet 2:9), in the new covenant believers distinguish between the sacred and profane, good and evil, righteousness and unrighteousness, and they embrace only what conforms to God's law.

The law as a rule, however, does not address every circumstance in life. There are situations in the Christian life that go beyond the law. Solomon's verdict over the two prostitutes who argued that they were both the mother

46. Beale and Carson, *Commentary on the New Testament Use*, 878.

47. Jacob Milgrom, *Leviticus 1–16*, AB (New York: Doubleday, 1998), 615.

of the same child is a prime example of life exceeding the limits of the law. Both women had newborn sons only days apart, and one of the sons died because one of the women accidentally smothered him in the middle of the night. The woman switched her dead son for the living son, but the robbed woman knew she was the victim of a ruse. When faced with this problem Solomon did not appeal to the law because it does not address such a challenging situation; neither did he employ the Urim and Thummim to seek God's revelation for the answer.[48] Rather, he employed Spirit-given wisdom. He instructed his guards to cleave the child asunder, but the child's true mother did not want harm to come to him, and so she consented to giving the boy to the dishonest woman. Her heartfelt response revealed she was the boy's mother (1 Kgs 3:16–27). The concluding editorial comment reveals how Solomon resolved the thorny issue: "And all Israel heard of the judgment that the king had rendered, and they stood in awe of the king, because they perceived that the wisdom of God was in him to do justice" (1 Kgs 3:28; see Prov 8:22–31). Solomon prayed for wisdom, and God poured out his Spirit on him (1 Kgs 3:1–15).[49] Solomon was a type of Christ, the one "in whom are hidden all the treasures of wisdom and knowledge" (Col 2:3). This means that through union with Christ believers receive the Spirit of both sanctification and wisdom.

Wisdom originates first and foremost with God. The Westminster Confession, for example, recognizes that creation and providence manifest the wisdom of God (1.1; 4.1, 4) and that Christ is the one in whom are "all the treasures of wisdom and knowledge" (8.3). Moreover, God displays his wisdom in redemption and the manner by which he overcomes his enemies (8.8). Believers thus share in God's wisdom through Christ, which they use and apply in the Christian life as they pursue greater sanctification. Although the Westminster Confession does not devote a specific chapter or paragraph to Christian wisdom, there is a sense in which the whole confession and catechisms embody wisdom in the sense that Calvin characterized it: "Our wisdom, in so far as it ought to be deemed true and solid wisdom, consists almost entirely of two parts: the knowledge of God and

48. Cornelis Van Dam, *The Urim and Thummim: A Means of Revelation in Ancient Israel* (Winona Lake, IN: Eisenbrauns, 1997), 269–73.

49. DeVries, *1 Kings*, 50–60.

of ourselves."[50] The Westminster Shorter Catechism captures this wisdom ethos in its familiar answer to its first question, "What is the chief end of man? A. Man's chief end is to glorify God, and to enjoy him forever."

The Shorter Catechism taps into the theology of the patristic church with this unassuming question and answer, yet deep currents of wisdom flow through its simple words. Prior to the Enlightenment, theologians recognized that theology was chiefly about the pursuit of wisdom, about learning who God is. Learning who God is leads to loving him, and loving him leads to fearing him—to wisdom.[51] Such thought informs the notion of enjoying God. In Augustine's *The Trinity*, he distinguishes between *uti* ("use") and *frui* ("enjoyment"), the two processes by which we materially and intellectually appropriate the world:

> For to use is to take up something into the power of the will, but to enjoy is to use with the joy, not of hope, but of the actual thing. Therefore, everyone who enjoys, uses, for he takes up something into the power of the will and finds pleasure in it as an end. But not everyone who uses, enjoys, if he has sought after that which he takes up into the power of the will, not on account of the thing itself, but on account of something else. (10.11.17)

This means that every *frui* ("enjoyment") implies an *uti* ("use"), though not every *uti* is also a *frui*.[52] Sin is the incorrect use of these two forms of appropriation, which means that humans can appropriate the world either correctly or incorrectly. If they appropriate the world incorrectly, then they only arrive at *uti* ("use"). If they appropriate it correctly, then *uti* ("use") gives way to *frui* ("enjoyment"). Augustine elsewhere explains, "To enjoy something is to hold fast to it in love for its own sake. To use something is to apply whatever it may be to the purpose of obtaining what you love—if indeed it is something that ought to be loved" (*On Christian Teaching* 1.8).

Augustine fleshes out the distinction between *uti* and *frui* by pointing to the use of the creation and its ultimate goal:

---

50. Calvin, *Inst.* 1.1.1.

51. Ellen T. Charry, *By the Renewing of Your Minds: The Pastoral Function of Christian Doctrine* (Oxford: Oxford University Press, 1997).

52. Joachim Küpper, "*Uti* and *frui* in Augustine and the Problem of Aesthetic Pleasure in the Western Tradition," *MLN* 127, no. 5 supplement (2012): 126–55, here 127.

> We are like travelers away from our Lord: if we wish to return to the homeland where we can be happy we must use this world, not enjoy it, in order to discern "the invisible attributes of God, which are understood through what has been made" or, in other words, to derive eternal and spiritual value from corporeal and temporal things. The things to be enjoyed are the Father, and the Son and the Holy Spirit, and the Trinity that consists of them. (1.9–10)

If our use of the creation only goes as far as temporal and created things, then we have missed the whole point of the created order, which is to direct us to the Triune God. This brings us full circle to the idea of glorifying God and enjoying him forever. If we approach God only for *uti* ("use"), then we fail to embody true theology and wisdom; we fall short of the *frui* ("enjoyment") of God—loving and praising God chiefly for who he is and secondarily for what he has done. Such an attitude embodies sanctified wisdom.

So, while the Reformed confessions do not contain specific sections dedicated to the topic of wisdom in the Christian life, we must recognize that the theologians who wrote them cast their confessional labors in the mold of wisdom. In the aftermath of the Enlightenment, theologians often pursue theology in terms only of *scientia*, or knowledge. For pre-Enlightenment theologians such as the Westminster divines or St. Augustine, *scientia* was supposed to lead to *sapientia*, or wisdom.[53] Augustine rightly argues that anything in the Scriptures that speaks of wisdom has the Son of God in view, and if the Triune God has made us in his image, then the life of sanctification is the pursuit of the image of God in Christ: "If we are, therefore, to be re-formed to the image of God on account of the example which the Image equal to the Father, gives us, then it should not be wondered at, that the Scripture is referring to the Son when it speaks about wisdom, since we follow Him by living wisely, although the Father Himself is wisdom, as He is light and God" (*Trinity* 7.3.5).

53. Charry, *By the Renewing*, 5–7, 133, 237.

## CONCLUSION

"Holiness implies separation to God as well as separation from the common."[54] Sanctification is the means by which the Triune God separates us to himself by making us what we have been declared in our justification. Resting on the finished work of Christ, we draw nearer to the Triune God through the sanctifying power of the Spirit. Union with Christ and the benefits of justification and sanctification grant us communion with the Triune God. We live out our priestly office as we distinguish between what is sacred versus profane and draw nearer to God through the high-priestly work of Jesus and the sanctifying power of the Holy Spirit. With each step forward in sanctification, we learn to glorify God and enjoy him forever. We manifest the sanctified wisdom of Christ's Spirit in the midst of this sin-darkened world.

## FURTHER READING

Allen, Michael. *Sanctification*. NSD. Grand Rapids: Zondervan, 2017. An edifying account of the doctrine of sanctification that is at the same time exegetical, attentive to redemptive history, theological, and conversant with a wide range of sources, both Reformed and catholic. Readers do well to acquaint themselves with this book.

Charry, Ellen T. *By the Renewing of Your Minds: The Pastoral Function of Christian Doctrine*. Oxford: Oxford University Press, 1997. A fascinating study that explores the nature of doctrine among premodern theologians to show that they saw doctrine as the pursuit of wisdom, not merely knowledge. In the modern period, however, doctrine was recast as the pursuit of knowledge. This is required reading.

Owen, John. *Of the Mortification of Sin in Believers*. In *The Works of John Owen*, vol. 6. London: Johnstone and Hunter, 1851. A classic Reformed study on the doctrine of mortification; well worth the time to work through Owen's arguments.

54. Milgrom, *Leviticus 1–16*, 615.

IX

# THE CHRISTIAN LIFE

## FAITH AND REPENTANCE

THE HEART OF THE COVENANT of grace is Christ and all his benefits, and the Holy Spirit is the lifeblood that conveys these saving benefits to believers. The system that circulates the Spirit's life-giving power is a God-given, Spirit-wrought faith. To change metaphors, faith is the God-given empty hand that lays hold of Christ and all his saving benefits. In the words of the Heidelberg Catechism, "True faith is a sure knowledge whereby I accept as true all that God has revealed to us in his Word. At the same time it is a firm confidence that not only to others, but also to me, God has granted forgiveness of sins, everlasting righteousness, and salvation out of mere grace only for the sake of Christ's merits. This faith the Holy Spirit works in my heart by the gospel" (q. 21; see WLC q. 76). Beyond this description of the nature of true faith, we must have a better understanding of how the gift of faith works as the means by which we lay hold of Christ and his saving work. To that end, this chapter first surveys the relevant biblical terms. Second, it explains the nature of saving faith. Third, the chapter compares and contrasts the biblical doctrine of faith with erroneous conceptions. Fourth and finally, the chapter explains the relationship of faith and repentance, which is one of the initial fruits of saving faith.

## BIBLICAL TERMS

In the Old Testament the *hiphil* form of the verb אמן ("believed") plus the prepositional ב or ל is used in contexts when the latter denotes holding something as true and the former is a trustful resting in an idea or person. For example, "You rebelled against the commandment of the Lord your God and did not believe him" (Deut 9:23; ל is used here). Similarly, "They will not believe me or listen to my voice, for they will say, 'The Lord did not appear to you' " (Exod 4:1). In both of these cases the people either did not or would not believe that something was true. On the other hand, Genesis 15:6 uses a prepositional ב: "And he believed the Lord, and he counted it to him as righteousness." Abraham did not merely believe *that* the promise of God was true, but rather he believed *in* God's promise. Abraham did not acknowledge the veracity of an abstract truth but trusted in the promises of God.[1] In Paul's exegesis of Genesis 15:6 he gives the Greek equivalent of this Old Testament lexeme: "Abraham believed [ἐπίστευσεν] God, and it was counted to him as righteousness" (Rom 4:3). Paul uses the verb πιστεύω, which is typically translated as "believe." In this context, Paul describes Abraham's belief as faith, or πίστις: "For we say that faith was counted to Abraham as righteousness" (Rom 4:9).

When it comes to laying hold of Christ, the terms for faith or belief have three chief things as their object: God, his promises, and Christ. But those who believe in these three things are not trying simultaneously lay hold of three different things. Rather, saving faith lays hold of God's promises in Christ (Gal 3:14, 22; Eph 2:12; 3:6; 2 Tim 1:1; Heb 8:6). In even shorter form, saving faith believes in the gospel. Paul writes that in the gospel "the righteousness of God is revealed from faith to faith, as it is written, 'The righteous shall live by faith'" (Rom 1:17, my trans.; see Hab 2:4).

## NATURE

### *Kinds of Faith*

Taking the biblical data into account, we can define faith as accepting and trusting as true the testimony of another.[2] More specifically, saving faith is trusting in the promises of God, which come through the person and work of Christ by the sovereign work of the Spirit for

1. Vos, *Reformed Dogmatics* 4:72–73.
2. Vos, *Reformed Dogmatics* 4:89.

salvation. The Scriptures, however, also mention other types of faith that stand in contrast to true saving faith. There is a faith of *bare assent* wherein a person acknowledges a known truth, which theologians call *fides historica* ("historical faith"): "You believe that God is one; you do well. Even the demons believe—and shudder!" (Jas 2:19). Demons possess this type of faith. A second type of faith is *temporary faith*, which is when a person assents to the goodness of an object and is filled with delight and joy, but it eventually fades. Christ describes this type of faith in his parable of the sower: "As for what was sown on rocky ground, this is the one who hears the word and immediately receives it with joy, yet he has no root in himself, but endures for a while, and when tribulation or persecution arises on account of the word, immediately he falls away" (Matt 13:20–21). Historical and temporary faith are natural occurrences, and only a fiducial (trusting) apprehension of Christ is the gift of the Holy Spirit. Theologians calls this type of faith *fides iustificans* ("justifying faith").[3]

Though temporary and justifying faith appear similar in their characteristics, they have different sources and foundations. Temporary faith finds its source in natural human capacities—feelings and pleasure—and thus it is entirely subjective. Temporary faith is selfish in nature because as soon as pleasurable or joyful feelings dissipate, it becomes vexed and vanishes. Justifying faith is a supernatural gift of the Holy Spirit and is not motivated by a subjective desire for enjoyment, antinomian impulses, or transitory sympathies. Rather, a love and desire for God's glory, a hunger and thirst for righteousness, motivate the sinner. Saving faith begins with the objective work of the Spirit, which produces subjective changes and desires in the sinner.[4]

### *Acts of Faith*

We must drill down into the specific acts of justifying faith, which are *notitia* ("knowledge"), *assensus* ("assent"), and *fiducia* ("trust").[5] In order to have faith, a person must first possess knowledge of the events and matter of biblical history. We must have a knowledge that Jesus existed as a real person in history, for example. The truth of supernatural revelation, not fiction, is the object of faith,

3. Turretin, *Institutes of Elenctic Theology* 15.7.4; Vos, *Reformed Dogmatics* 4:107.
4. Vos, *Reformed Dogmatics* 4:109.
5. Turretin, *Institutes of Elenctic Theology* 15.8.3; Vos, *Reformed Dogmatics* 4:94–95.

and we must therefore have knowledge of this truth for faith. This knowledge pertains to the content of faith but is neither itself faith nor belongs to its essence.[6] A second act of faith is *assensus*, which is an intellectual assent or agreement with the knowledge of truth. There is a certainty in faith because assent rests on the divine and infallible word of God, but it does not rest on evidence because its foundation is testimony, not human reason. In the use of evidence, we look through it to the one who presents it, in this case God. To this end, the author of Hebrews writes: "Faith is the assurance of things hoped for, the conviction of things not seen" (Heb 11:1).[7] Faith is not merely intellectual assent, but apart from the intellect there is no faith. Faith apart from intellectual assent is merely the faith of demons, or historical faith.[8]

The third act of faith is *fiducia* or trusting in the object of faith, namely, God's promises in Christ. Trust is the essence of faith, a point lost in English but evident in Latin, as *fides* and *fiducia* are etymologically related. *Fiducia* is the crown of faith, the act whereby we judge the gospel to be true and good and therefore worthy of our love and desire. We also judge God's promises in the gospel to be certain for all believers and penitent sinners, and thus whoever trusts in Christ also receives salvation. Paul describes this aspect of faith as being "fully convinced" that God is able to do what he has promised (Rom 4:21). Elsewhere, Paul writes of the "full assurance of understanding and the knowledge of God's mystery, which is Christ" (Col 2:2), and the author of Hebrews similarly writes of the "full assurance of faith" (Heb 10:22).[9] But faith is not merely *fiducia*, or trust, as there must be an object of trust, in this case, an intellectual assent to the truths of God's promises in Christ.[10] Though faith has these three acts (*notitia*, *assensus*, and *fiducia*), they are different aspects of the same act, namely, faith—they are reciprocal and simultaneous.[11] At the same time, establishing the relationship between faith, intellect, and the will is vital to a proper understanding of faith.

---

6. Muller, *Dictionary*, s.v. *fides historica* (236); Turretin, *Institutes of Elenctic Theology* 15.8.5.
7. Turretin, *Institutes of Elenctic Theology* 15.8.6; Muller, *Dictionary*, s.v. *assensus* (42–43).
8. John Owen, "The Strength of Faith," in *Works of John Owen* 9:19–52, here 21.
9. Turretin, *Institutes of Elenctic Theology* 15.8.7; Muller, *Dictionary*, s.v. *fiducia* (123).
10. Owen, "Strength of Faith," 23.
11. Vos, *Reformed Dogmatics* 4:102–3.

Faith is not merely an exercise of the intellect, although faith employs the intellect (or understanding). Reformed confessional documents make a number of statements about the intellect and will. The proper interpretation of Scripture requires a "saving understanding" of those things revealed in the word of God (WCF 1.6) which requires the work of the Spirit to enlighten sinners "in their understandings" (5.6). In the fall, humans have "wholly lost all ability of will to any spiritual good" (9.3), and only through salvation does God enable sinners "freely to will and to do that which is spiritually good" (9.4). God renews sinners' wills through effectual calling (10.1), and by the gift of faith the "elect are enabled to believe to the saving of their souls" (14.1). The Westminster Confession coordinates intellect (understanding), will, and faith, but there are distinct functions to each. The intellect has two inseparable aspects to it, the speculative and practical intellect. The speculative intellect is that which gives consideration to truth, and the practical intellect is that which directs the intellect toward operation, or doing (*ST* Ia, q. 76, art 11). At first glance, the "speculative" in speculative intellect sounds problematic because no one is supposed to say speculative things about God. Speculative statements rest in a cradle of conjecture rather than scriptural exegesis. But in classic theology, "speculative" (*speculativus*) is related to *specula* ("a watchtower"), not *speculum* ("mirror"). Thus, to speculate is to perform a careful observation from a high place. And speculative truths are sought for their value in and of themselves, not for the sake of achieving a goal or end. Seeking knowledge for the sake of a goal is the function of the practical intellect.[12]

We must not forget that faith is the gift of the Holy Spirit, so human natural powers are not in view. But with the gift of faith, the practical intellect judges that the gospel is not only good but true and therefore worthy of our love and desire. The practical intellect directs and leads the will to trust and embrace the promises of God in Christ.[13] That faith employs the practical intellect and the will reveals that faith is not merely knowledge. In other words, faith is not a matter of checking the boxes and assenting to a list of doctrinal propositions. We can and should pursue a speculative

12. Muller, *Dictionary*, s.v. *speculativus* (340).

13. Turretin, *Institutes of Elenctic Theology* 15.8.7; Owen, "Strength of Faith," 24; also see Steven J. Duby, *God in Himself: Scripture, Metaphysics, and the Task of Christian Theology* (Downers Grove, IL: IVP Academic, 2019), 28n58.

knowledge of God and Christ. We can study "and desire to know other things that are excellent and delightful; as both the contemplation of God in creation and the contemplation of God in redemption."[14] But there is also a practical knowledge of God and Christ, which is "not only an acquaintance with God, but a laying up his words in our hearts (Job 22:21–22); which is not a floating knowledge in the head but a knowledge sinking to the heart; not a knowledge in the brain but efficacious to make an union with him (1 John 5:20)."[15] Thus, faith is not only an intellectual assent to the truth, but it involves the practical intellect, the consent of the will, which moves the affections.[16]

*Degrees of Faith* Several places in the Bible reveal that justifying faith has degrees of strength and weakness and that it can also grow and atrophy. Paul says that Abraham "grew strong in his faith" (Rom 4:20), and conversely there are those who are "weak in faith" (Rom 14:1). Stephen was "full of faith and of the Holy Spirit" (Acts 6:5). Similarly, Paul speaks of the faith of the saints "growing abundantly" (2 Thess 1:3), and on the other hand Jesus speaks of those who doubt as being of "little faith" (Matt 14:31). Because faith is a God-given infused habit (disposition), this means that we can strengthen or weaken it depending on our use, misuse, or disuse of the means of grace.[17] As John Owen observes: "Faith, or believing, consists in such an habitual frame of heart, and such actings of the soul, as are capable of degrees of straightening or enlargement, of strength and weakness."[18] The degrees of faith relate differently to the various benefits of union with Christ and require careful parsing. In justification, while faith may be weak or strong, one's justified status is not in peril, because faith is not the ground of justification but the instrument that lays hold of the imputed righteousness of Christ.

---

14. Stephen Charnock, *Discourses on the Knowledge of God*, in *The Works of Stephen Charnock* (Edinburgh: James Nichol, 1865), 4:3–109, here 16.

15. Charnock, *Discourses on the Knowledge*, 17; Duby, *God in Himself*, 28–29.

16. Owen, "Strength of Faith," 21–23.

17. On faith as an infused habit see, e.g., Turretin, *Institutes of Elenctic Theology* 15.4.13; Bavinck, *Reformed Dogmatics* 4:92–95, esp. 94; Wisse, "*Habitus Fidei*"; Christopher Cleveland, "Reformed Theology and Medieval Theology," in *The Oxford Handbook of Reformed Theology*, ed. Scott R. Swain and Michael Allen (Oxford: Oxford University Press, 2020), 24–40, esp. 34–35.

18. Owen, "Strength of Faith," 26; also Canons of Dort 3/4.14.

"A little faith is no less faith than a great faith; yea, a little faith will carry a man as safely to heaven."[19] In other words, in justification the strength of the faith does not matter but rather the strength of its object, namely, the person and work of Christ. As faith pertains to sanctification, a weaker faith will lead to a weaker state of sanctification, and contrariwise a stronger faith is correlative to a stronger state of sanctification. "Others may be more holy than he, but not one in the world is more righteous than he, for he is righteous with the righteousness of Christ."[20]

That God through the Spirit of Christ gives the gift of faith means that our justification always rests secure because while faith may grow or weaken, we cannot lose this gift. The steadfastness of faith is not due to human but divine fidelity to his promises in Christ. So, the chief reason that faith grows or atrophies is due to the use, misuse, or disuse of the means of grace. A correlate of either misusing or disusing the means of grace is being subject to greater and more powerful doubts about the promises of God, which leads to a greater weakening in faith. But receiving the gift of faith does not preclude all external temptations and sources of doubt. A tree can be firmly planted and rooted in good soil, but this does not mean the wind will never blow on it. The house built on the rock does not mean that it will be free from storms.[21] In the end, however, "This faith is different in degrees, weak or strong; may be often and many ways assailed, and weakened, but gets the victory: growing up in many to the attainment of a full assurance, through Christ, who is both the author and finisher of our faith" (WCF 14.3).

## COMPARISON WITH OTHER VIEWS

A COMPARISON WITH OTHER DOCTRINES of faith showcases differences and where they diverge from biblical teaching. Roman Catholicism promotes two errors regarding faith: (1) implicit faith and (2) the function of faith in justification. *Fides implicitas* ("implicit faith") is the Roman Catholic teaching that defines faith as belief without certain knowledge, that is, a faith that accepts the teaching of the church without

19. Owen, "Strength of Faith," 27.
20. Owen, "Strength of Faith," 29.
21. Owen, "Strength of Faith," 27.

knowing the objective contents of faith (*ST* IIa IIae, q. 2, art 6).[22] Early Protestant theologians called implicit faith *fides carbonaria* ("collier's faith"), which is to say that the faith of a collier, or charcoal burner, is sufficient for salvation so long as a person believes in what the church teaches, even if the person does not know what the church teaches.[23] The idea of implicit faith varies among Roman Catholics. Thomas Aquinas writes of it but stipulates that faith cannot consist of blind obedience; a sinner must believe certain articles of faith: "Therefore, as regards the primary points or articles of faith, man is bound to believe them, just as he is bound to have faith; but as to other points of faith, man is not bound to believe them explicitly, but only implicitly, or to be ready to believe them, in so far as he is prepared to believe whatever is contained in the Divine Scriptures."[24]

Aquinas makes the point that a sinner must believe certain things but cannot possibly believe and know everything the Bible teaches. However, the person must be willing to believe whatever Scripture teaches. Thus, the person must possess an implicit faith. Aquinas is not much different from Calvin on this point. Calvin argues that Scripture teaches the idea of implicit faith, such as when the Samaritans believed the woman at the well and her testimony about Jesus (John 4:42): "It is obvious, that even those who are not yet imbued with the first principles, provided they are disposed to obey, are called *believers*, not properly indeed, but inasmuch as God is pleased in kindness so highly to honor their pious feeling. But this docility, with a desire of further progress, is widely different from the gross ignorance in which those sluggishly indulge who are contented with the implicit faith of the Papists."[25] Aquinas and Calvin largely agree that believers need not immediately know everything the Scriptures teach, but they must begin with belief in certain basic truths and be willing ultimately to believe everything that Scripture teaches. Calvin says we can call this

---

22. Muller, *Dictionary*, s.v. *fides implicitas* (122).

23. Petrus Van Mastricht, *Theoretical-Practical Theology*, ed. Joel R. Beeke, trans. Todd M. Rester (Grand Rapids: Reformation Heritage Books, 2019), 1.2.1 (2:17n12); see also Muller, *Dictionary*, s.v. *fides carbonaria* (122).

24. Thomas Aquinas, *Summa Theologica* (repr., Allen, TX: Christian Classics, 1948), IIa IIae q. 2 art. 5.

25. Calvin, *Inst.* 3.2.5.

"implicit faith."[26] That being said, Calvin also derides the papists of his day for a different version of implicit faith.

The likely target of Calvin's criticism was, among others, Roman Catholic theologian Robert Bellarmine (1542–1621). Bellarmine in fact specifically engaged Calvin's arguments (in *Inst.* 3.2) that justifying faith includes knowledge (*notitia*) and assent (*assensus*). Bellarmine appeals to several passages to make this point, such as Isaiah 7:9, "Unless you believe, you will not understand." According to Bellarmine, Isaiah says that faith is not what must be understood but is a path that has degrees of understanding. Bellarmine also appeals to 1 Corinthians 13 and argues that Paul distinguishes between knowledge (*notitia*) and faith (*fide*): "If I understand all mysteries and knowledge, and if I have all faith" (1 Cor 13:2). Paul makes this same distinction when he delineates among God's gifts: "To another the utterance of knowledge according to the same Spirit, to another faith by the same Spirit" (1 Cor 12:8–9). In other words, faith is distinct from knowledge.[27]

Bellarmine's error is fine toothed but an error nonetheless. The specific issue is not whether faith includes *assensus* ("assent"), as both Roman Catholics and Protestants affirm this. Neither is this a matter of whether faith is a full and complete knowledge of the mysteries of God, so that those with faith must believe nothing unless they fully understand. Just as sanctification is imperfect in this life, so faith admits degrees, increases, and grows with respect to knowledge and trust. In this sense, faith can be labeled as implicit for both children and neophytes. Rather, the specific debated issue is whether faith includes knowledge, if not full, at least a true and certain knowledge (*assensus*). The debate is also not a question of knowledge as *scientia*, which has evidence and rests on a foundation of reason. Faith is not founded on reason but on divine testimony. The debated issue is whether faith is blind, devoid of all knowledge, so that it is better defined as ignorance and believing in unknown things. This is the type of implicit faith that Roman Catholicism claims is sufficient for salvation among laypeople—if they believe what the church believes

26. Calvin, *Inst.* 3.2.5.

27. Robert Bellarmine, *De Justificatione* 1.7, in *Opera Omnia* (Naples: Joseph Giuliano, 1858), 4:468–69; Turretin, *Institutes of Elenctic Theology* 15.9.1.

without specifically knowing what the church teaches, then they can be saved. This type of implicit faith must be rejected.[28]

A second error involves the confusion of faith and works in justification, which is common to Roman Catholicism and among some evangelicals. The Scriptures speak of two functions of faith, namely, trusting in the promises of God and faith working through love (Rom 4:1–8; Gal 5:6). Some have therefore erroneously concluded that faith's function is the same for justification and sanctification. That is, because they conflate justification and sanctification, faith and works are necessary for justification. Or, because they define faith as faithfulness rather than chiefly as *fiducia* ("trust"), they conclude that works are a necessary part of faith even if they recognize justification and sanctification are distinct benefits of union with Christ. The Council of Trent declared: "If anyone saith, that men are justified, either by the sole imputation of the justice of Christ, or by the sole remission of sins, to the exclusion of the grace and the charity which is poured forth in their hearts by the Holy Ghost, and is inherent in then; or even that the grace, whereby we are justified, is only the favor of God: let him be anathema."[29] Correlatively, Trent argues that faith must work through love for justification and rejects the idea that it is chiefly a trust (*fiducia*) in God's promises in Christ: "If any one saith, that justifying faith is nothing else but confidence [*fiduciam*] in the divine mercy which remits sins for Christ's sake; or, that this confidence [*fiduciam*] alone is that whereby we are justified: let him be anathema."[30]

Some Reformed and evangelical theologians have defined faith as "faithfulness" or "allegiance," thus proposing that faith must include obedience; consequently, sinners are justified by a combination of faith and works. Norman Shepherd (1933–), for example, writes, "Faith looks away from personal merit to the promises of God. Repentance and obedience flow from faith as the *fullness* of faith. This is faithfulness, and faithfulness is perseverance in faith. A living, active, and abiding faith is the way in which

28. Turretin, *Institutes of Elenctic Theology* 15.9.2–3.

29. Council of Trent, "Sixth Session, 13 Jan 1547," canon 11, in Schaff, *Creeds of Christendom* 2:113.

30. Council of Trent, "Sixth Session, 13 Jan 1547," canon 12, in Schaff, *Creeds of Christendom* 2:114.

the believer enters into eternal life."[31] To write of the *fullness* of faith gives the impression that faith is incomplete unless one adds obedience and repentance to faith in order to secure one's justification. The same ambiguity marks other statements by Shepherd about the nature of justifying faith: "Gospel proclamation calls us to a living faith, that is, to a penitent and obedient faith."[32] Shepherd highlights obedience rather than trust, faithfulness instead of faith. Others such as Matthew Bates reconfigure justifying faith as *allegiance* rather than trust: "The rendering of *pistis* (and its accompanying release from the power of sin) and submission to the law of the Christ amount to nearly the same thing—to give *pistis* means to enact allegiance to the king by obeying his law." Bates concedes that in certain passages, such as Romans 4:1–8, where Paul quotes Genesis 15:6, *pistis* refers to belief or trust but that the English word "allegiance" is a preferable translation because it subsumes faithfulness, or obedience.[33]

The historic Reformed tradition has recognized that "the principal acts of saving faith are accepting, receiving, and resting upon Christ alone for justification, sanctification, and eternal life." But at the same time, faith yields "obedience to the commands, trembling at the threatenings, and embracing the promises of God for this life, and that which is to come" (WCF 14.2). The fruit of justifying faith is obedience, but this obedience does not constitute the principal acts of faith, which are all passive—the God-given open hand to grasp Christ and his saving work: receiving, resting, and accepting. Faith and obedience have distinct roles: "Faith, thus receiving and resting on Christ and his righteousness, is the alone instrument of justification: yet is it not alone in the person justified, but is ever accompanied with all other saving graces, and is no dead faith, but worketh by love" (11.2). Trusting in Christ for justification and salvation by faith leads to faithfulness and obedience, but this faithfulness is neither the foundation nor the material cause of our justification.

---

31. Norman Shepherd, *The Call of Grace: How the Covenant Illuminates Salvation and Evangelism* (Phillipsburg, NJ: P&R, 2000), 50, emphasis added.

32. Norman Shepherd, "Justification by Works in Reformed Theology," in *Backbone of the Bible: Covenant in Contemporary Perspective*, ed. P. Andrew Sandlin (Nacogdoches, LA: Covenant Media Foundation, 2004), 101.

33. Matthew W. Bates, *Salvation by Allegiance Alone: Rethinking Faith, Works, and the Gospel of Jesus the King* (Grand Rapids: Baker Academic, 2017), 87, 90.

A third error is common among some Remonstrant and even Reformed theologians who characterize faith as simply intellectual assent and either eliminate or deemphasize its fiducial character. In the seventeenth century Jacob Arminius prioritized the intellect over trust in his doctrine of faith. When he describes the characteristics of believers, he writes: "For hearing and understanding the word, if approbation of the same is not added, do not constitute a believer." Here Arminius uses the terms *auditio* ("hearing"), *intellectio* ("understanding"), and *approbatio* ("approbation") rather than the more common *notitia*, *assensus*, and *fiducia*.[34] In this case *approbatio* is synonymous with *assensus* ("assent"). In historic Reformed formulations, hearing and understanding do not constitute saving faith, as the fiducial ("trust") element is missing. Hearing and understanding create only *fides historica* ("historical faith"), or the faith of demons. This does not mean that Arminius elides trust from faith but that the intellect takes priority to the will.[35] In other words, there is a rationalizing tendency in Arminius's doctrine of faith.

In the twentieth century Reformed theologian Gordon Clark (1902–1985) made similar claims. He writes that "faith is strictly limited to knowledge."[36] In his criticisms against the Roman Catholic doctrine of implicit faith, he argues that evangelicals reject the idea, but the way he distinguishes between the two views is revealing: "Evangelicalism excludes the Romish doctrine of implicit faith. Hence justification cannot depend on our assent to all revealed truth. Justifying faith must be an assent to some truths, not all."[37] In the end, Clark defines faith as the "assent to understood propositions. Not all cases of assent, even assent to Biblical propositions, are saving faith; but all saving faith is assent to one or more Biblical propositions."[38] Faith is purely an intellectual assent of the mind to doctrinal propositions rather than trusting in Christ.

---

34. Jacob Arminius, *Examination of Dr. Perkins's Pamphlet on Predestination*, in *Works* 3:500; Richard A. Muller, "The Priority of the Intellect," *WTJ* 55 (1993): 55–72, here 57–58.

35. Muller, "Priority of the Intellect," 58; also Jacob Arminius, "Certain Articles, XIX: On Faith," in *Works* 2:500.

36. Gordon Clark, *Faith and Saving Faith* (Jefferson, MA: Trinity Foundation, 1983), 21.

37. Clark, *Faith and Saving Faith*, 55.

38. Clark, *Faith and Saving Faith*, 118.

A fourth error comes from Remonstrant theologians who maintained that faith was the ground of justification rather than the instrumental cause. Arminius writes in a letter to a colleague:

> Faith is imputed to us for righteousness, on account of Christ and his righteousness. In this enunciation, faith is the object of imputation; but Christ and his obedience are the impetratory or meritorious cause of justification. Christ and his obedience are the object of our faith; but not the object of justification or divine imputation, as if God imputes Christ and his righteousness to us for righteousness.[39]

In other words, Arminius believes that a person is not justified on the basis of the imputed righteousness of Christ; instead, God looks on the sinner's *faith* as righteousness. The reason God is willing to do this is Christ's obedience. In short, historically Reformed interpreters have argued that when Paul writes of faith in Romans 4:5 it is a metonym for Christ's righteousness. This interpretive path fits with Paul's statements about the instrumentality of faith. Faith is neither the basis nor the ground of justification but the instrument by which we lay hold of Christ's righteousness.[40] According to Arminius, however, justification is *on the basis* of faith rather than *through* or *by* faith. The Westminster Confession identifies and rejects this error when it states: "God ... freely justifieth: not by infusing righteousness into them ... *nor by imputing faith itself, the act of believing, or any other evangelical obedience to them, as their righteousness*; but by imputing the obedience and satisfaction of Christ unto them, they receiving and resting on him and his righteousness by faith" (11.1, emphasis added).

These errors misconstrue faith because they either confuse, eliminate, or overemphasize one of the three acts of faith, *notitia*, *assensus*, and *fiducia*. Implicit faith wounds or even possibly eliminates *assensus* ("understanding"), whereas Arminius and especially Clark allow *assensus* to swallow *fiducia*. Roman Catholics, Shepherd, and Bates confuse faith and works and thus corrupt the material cause of justification, and Arminius similarly pushes Christ's imputed righteousness to the background and allows

39. Jacob Arminius, "Letter to Hippolytus a Collibus, 8 April 1608," in *Works* 2:702.

40. For a fuller explanation of this interpretive difference, see Fesko, *Arminius and the Reformed Tradition*, 87–106.

faith to become foundational. Regardless of the error, all of them invariably move the center of the gravity of salvation away from Christ over to humanity. To say that one need have only implicit faith elevates the church's magisterium over Christ's revelation. To confuse faith and works makes the work of Christ insufficient for salvation. To prioritize or intellectualize faith diminishes trust in Christ's work and makes faith merely a movement of the mind. And to say that faith saves rather than it saves because it grasps Christ and his righteousness makes Christ a mere enabler rather than a Savior.

## FAITH AND REPENTANCE

One of the regular gospel refrains is, "Repent and believe in the gospel" (Mark 1:15), which gives the impression that sinners must first repent and then believe in Christ in order to be saved. But in order to repent of one's sins, one must first believe that God's word is true, that one is a sinner, that one is incapable of perfect obedience, and that only Christ can save one by faith. How can one therefore believe before one believes? The answer lies in three points. First, rhetoric does not always reveal the *ordo naturae* ("order of nature"), or the way that the different elements of our union with Christ relate to each other. In technical terms, the *ordo docendi* ("order of teaching") does not always reveal the *ordo essendi* ("order of things in themselves"). Second, repentance is an expression or fruit of faith. As Herman Bavinck observes, "Strictly speaking, there are no demands and conditions in the gospel but only promises and gifts. Faith and repentance are as much benefits of the covenant of grace as justification (and so forth). ... Faith and repentance themselves, nevertheless, are components of the gospel, not the workings or fruits of the law." The law can produce neither change nor repentance, and neither can a person repent apart from the sovereign regenerating call of the Holy Spirit.[41] Keeping these things in mind, what is the nature of repentance, and how does it relate to salvation?

### *The Nature of Repentance*

There are several biblical terms that denote repentance, which at its most basic level is a turning

41. Bavinck, *Reformed Dogmatics* 4:454.

away from sin toward God. Ezekiel exhorts Israel: "Repent and turn from all your transgressions, lest iniquity be your ruin" (18:30). Here the prophet employs the term שׁוּב, which means "to turn." The New Testament uses two different terms for repentance: μετανοέω ("to repent") and ἐπιστρέφω ("to turn back"). For example, Peter exhorts Simon Magus: "Repent [μετανόησον], therefore, of this wickedness of yours, and pray to the Lord that, if possible, the intent of your heart may be forgiven you" (Acts 8:22). Peter preaches: "Repent [μετανοήσατε] therefore, and turn back [ἐπιστρέψατε], that your sins may be blotted out" (Acts 3:19). There are two forms of repentance, *false* and *true* repentance. False repentance is when a person temporarily turns from his sin. Rather than a 180-degree turn away from sin, because his repentance stems from only *fides historica*, his turn is ultimately a 360-degree one (Matt 13:20–21). Paul, on the other hand, speaks of true repentance: "For godly grief produces a repentance that leads to salvation without regret, whereas worldly grief produces death" (2 Cor 7:10).

The Westminster Confession offers a description of the nature of true repentance:

> By [repentance], a sinner, out of the sight and sense not only of the danger, but also of the filthiness and odiousness of his sins, as contrary to the holy nature, and righteous law of God; and upon the apprehension of his mercy in Christ to such as are penitent, so grieves for, and hates his sin, as to turn from them all unto God, purposing and endeavoring to walk with him in all the ways of his commandments. (WCF 15.2)

Repentance is a sweeping change of heart and mind followed by an ethical and behavioral change of a sinful life—a sorrowing for sin so as to abandon it altogether.[42] Like the other blessings of union with Christ, repentance is given by the Holy Spirit to the sinner through the gift of faith. Sweeping change of heart, mind, will, and affections means that repentance touches all of the sinner's faculties. David speaks of his change of heart and his deep sorrow for his sin, sin that he recognizes is ultimately against God

42. Thomas C. Oden, *Classic Christianity: A Systematic Theology* (San Francisco: HarperOne, 1992), 567.

(Ps 51:4). Penitent people grieve over their sin and the alienation they have brought between themselves, God, and those in their family or community. Repentance requires a change of the intellect or mind, and the change of mind paves the way for a change of the will.[43]

*Repentance and Salvation*

QUESTIONS ARISE REGARDING THE PRECISE relationship between repentance and salvation. Is repentance a cause of salvation? Reading statements such as Mark 1:15, "Repent and believe," gives the impression that repentance is a cause of salvation. Moreover, Roman Catholic theology takes the doctrine of repentance and externalizes it with its doctrine of penance. In penance a sinner confesses his sin to a priest, who judicially absolves him of sin; the sinner then performs acts of penance: "Raised up from sin, the sinner must still recover his full spiritual health by doing something more to make amends for the sin: he must 'make satisfaction for' or 'expiate' his sins. This satisfaction is also called 'penance.'" At first glance, penance gives the impression that Roman Catholics believe that they can expiate their own sins. Roman Catholics clarify what they mean: "The satisfaction that we make for our sins, however, is not so much ours as though it were not done through Jesus Christ."[44]

Nevertheless, there are at least two problematic elements with these claims. First, the Scriptures know of only one satisfaction for sin, namely, the sacrifice of Christ: We "are justified by his grace as a gift, through the redemption that is in Christ Jesus, whom God put forward as a propitiation by his blood, to be received by faith" (Rom 3:24–25). Scripture is clear: God has canceled "the record of debt that stood against us with its legal demands. This he set aside, nailing it to the cross" (Col 2:14). Likewise, Hebrews 10:12 explains that Christ "offered for all time a single sacrifice for sins." Second, it places repentance in a causal relation to salvation: apart from penance, a person's salvation is in peril. For those who have committed mortal sins and lost their state of grace and justification, penance is

43. Oden, *Classic Christianity*, 568.

44. *Catechism of the Catholic Church*, §1459–60.

the "second plank of salvation."[45] The Roman Catholic doctrine of penance displaces the work of Christ as the sole material cause of our salvation.

There is a difference between Rome's penance and biblical repentance. Repentance is an evangelical grace that all Christians should promote and practice. By God's grace the sinner recognizes his sinfulness and his need to turn from his sin. Repentance, however, is not a cause but a fruit of salvation. Sinners repent because they have been saved, not in order to be saved. In the words of the Westminster Confession, "Although repentance be not to be rested in, as any satisfaction for sin, or any cause of the pardon thereof, which is the act of God's free grace in Christ; yet it is of such necessity to all sinners, that none may expect pardon without it" (15.3). The Heidelberg Catechism explains that no one can be saved who does not repent of his sins: "No unchaste person, no idolater, adulterer, thief, no covetous person, no drunkard, slanderer, robber, or the like will inherit the kingdom of God" (q. 87). Or as John Owen pointedly remarks: "He that would be saved by Christ, and not ruled by him, shall not be saved by him at all."[46]

## CONCLUSION

Faith is the empty God-given hand that enables us to grasp Christ and all of his saving benefits. No one can be saved apart from faith in Christ, apart from trusting in him as Savior and believing that he lived a life of perfect obedience in fulfillment of the law for us. We must believe that he lived a life of suffering, bearing the curse of the law from the moment of his first to his last breath as he hung naked on the cross. We must believe that he has been raised from the dead and now sits in royal session at the right hand of the Father reigning in the midst of his enemies. In the words of the Nicene Creed, "For us and for our salvation he came down from heaven; he became incarnate by the Holy Spirit and the virgin Mary, and was made man. He was crucified for us under Pontius Pilate; he suffered and was buried. The third day he rose again, according to the Scriptures. He ascended to heaven and is seated at the right hand of the Father." When, through the God-given eyes of faith, we realize the great heights from which Christ condescended to us and

45. *Catechism of the Catholic Church*, §1446.

46. Owen, "Strength of Faith," 25.

our utter sinfulness, only then can we mourn and grieve over our sin. Only then do we join with Peter, fall on our knees before Christ, and utter, "Depart from me, for I am a sinful man, O Lord" (Luke 5:8). Blessedly, Christ bids us to rise, binds our wounds, and restores us by his grace.

Before corruption, guilt and fear,
My comforts blasted fell;
And unbelief discover'd near
The dreadful depths of hell.

But Jesus pity'd my distress,
He heard my feeble cry;
Reveal'd his blood and righteousness,
And brought salvation nigh.

Beneath the banner of his love,
I now secure remain;
The tempter frets, but dares not move
To break my peace again.

Lord, since thou thus hast broke my bands,
And set the captive free;
I would devote my tongue, my hands,
My heart, my all to thee.[47]

## FURTHER READING

Bavinck, Herman. *Reformed Dogmatics*, vol. 4, *Holy Spirit, Church, and New Creation*. Translated by John Vriend. Edited by John Bolt. Grand Rapids: Baker Academic, 2008. Treats the doctrine of faith in a thorough fashion in conversation with the history of doctrine and the more recent developments of Bavinck's own nineteenth century. He treats the doctrine of faith on pages 96–175.

Owen, John. "The Strength of Faith." In *The Works of John Owen* 9:19–52. Edinburgh: Banner of Truth, 1998. Originally delivered

47. John Newton, "The Storm Hushed," in *Olney Hymns*, ed. Charles J. Doe (Minneapolis: Curiosmith, 2011), 148.

as two sermons on the doctrine of faith. Owen explains the doctrine in a robustly theological manner with a view to pastoral practicality.

Thompson, Mark. "The Theology of Justification by Faith: The theological Case for Sola Fide." In *The Doctrine on Which the Church Stands or Falls: Justification in Biblical, Theological, Historical, and Pastoral Perspective*, ed. Matthew Barrett, 419–40. Wheaton, IL: Crossway, 2019. An essay that defends the doctrine of *sola fide* in light of recent challenges and debates.

Turretin, Francis. *Institutes of Elenctic Theology*. Vol. 2. Translated by George Musgrave Giger. Edited by James T. Dennison Jr. Phillipsburg, NJ: P&R, 1992–1997. One of the more exegetically, theologically, and historically informed treatments of the doctrine of faith, which Turretin treats in eleven questions on pages 558–623. Careful study of his treatment is well worth the time.

Wisse, Maarten. "*Habitus Fidei*: An Essay on the History of a Concept." *Scottish Journal of Theology* 56, no. 2 (2003): 172–89. An excellent survey of the doctrine of the habit of faith. Some believe that the idea of a habit is Roman Catholic, but this essay shows that it was also a concept employed by Reformed theologians.

X

# ASSURANCE AND PERSEVERANCE

## RESTING IN CHRIST

THE DOCTRINES OF ASSURANCE AND perseverance go hand in hand, as Christians often lack assurance of their salvation because they do not know whether they will persevere. They read Christ's statements that the branches that do not bear fruit will be cut off (John 15:1–3). Some believers fear that they will fall away from Christ. They see their fellow believers commit apostasy and wonder whether they will be next. They read warning passages in Scripture, "For it is impossible, in the case of those who have once been enlightened ... and then have fallen away, to restore them again to repentance" (Heb 6:4, 6).

The key to understanding assurance and perseverance is to recognize that both lie in the cradle of our union with Christ—they are a part of the unbreakable golden chain of salvation. When we lack assurance of the promises of God to save us, we must look to Christ by faith. In the face of besetting sins that generate doubts and vex our hearts, Robert Murray M'Cheyne (1813–1843) advises: "For every look at yourself, take ten looks at Christ. He is altogether lovely. Such infinite majesty, and yet such meekness and grace, and all for sinners, even the chief! Live much in the smiles of God. Bask in His beams. Feel His all-seeing eye settled on you in love, and repose in His almighty arms."[1] In Christ we find the foundation of both our assurance of and perseverance in salvation. The chapter unpacks this truth by examining first the assurance of salvation and second perseverance in salvation.

## ASSURANCE

The Scriptures record many of God's people who suffer from a lack of assurance. The psalmist regularly questions God. Psalm 88 captures heart-aching cries to God: "For my soul is full of troubles, and my life draws near to Sheol. ... But I, O Lord, cry to you; in the morning my prayer comes before you. O Lord, why do you cast my soul away? Why do you hide your face from me?" (Ps 88:3, 13–14). Habakkuk was perplexed and even angry at God because he allowed the Chaldeans to take Israel into exile: "O Lord, how long shall I cry for help, and you will not hear? Or cry to you 'Violence!' and you will not save? Why do you make me see iniquity, and why do you idly look at wrong? Destruction and violence are before me; strife and contention arise" (Hab 1:2–3). John had the privilege of being "Elijah who is to come" (Matt 11:14), the forerunner of the Messiah, the one who baptized the God-man, but doubts poured in like a flood when Jesus seemingly failed to inaugurate his kingdom, to judge the "brood of vipers" (Matt 3:7), and John was incarcerated by Herod. John sent his disciples to Christ with a message: "Are you the one who is to come, or shall we look for another?" (Matt 11:3). These different examples show that God gives the gift of faith to believe in Jesus, but the reception of that gift does not mean there are never struggles with doubt. By faith, we rest on the rock of Christ, but the storm waters may and often rise and lash us. How, then, in the face of the rising waters of doubt can we find assurance of our salvation?

What is assurance? Assurance of salvation is a certain conviction that Christ is all that he professes to be and will do all that he has promised, and that a believer is therefore assured that the believer's sins have been forgiven and that they are in a state of salvation.[2] There are two sides of assurance: objective and subjective. That is, believers who possesses

1. Robert Murray M'Cheyne, *Memoir and Remains of the Rev. R. M. M'Cheyne* (Edinburgh: Oliphant Anderson & Ferrier, 1892), 293.

2. Berkhof, *Systematic Theology*, 507.

assurance of their salvation are objectively certain about Christ's faithfulness to save; conversely, they also have a subjective certainty that they are personally saved. The Scriptures reveal the connection between the objective and subjective sides of assurance. In the light of the objective work of Christ, for example, the author of Hebrews exhorts his recipients to a state of subjective assurance: "Let us draw near with a true heart in full assurance of faith, with our hearts sprinkled clean from an evil conscience and our bodies washed with pure water" (Heb 10:22).[3] The apostle Paul also writes of this connection when he addresses his concern for the Christians at Colossae and Laodicea. He wants them to be "knit together in love, to reach all the riches of full assurance of understanding and the knowledge of God's mystery, which is Christ, in whom are hidden all the treasures of wisdom and knowledge" (Col 2:2–3).[4] Believers' subjective sense of assurance can only rest in their knowledge of the objective work of Christ. The Christian can only access this objective knowledge of Christ through faith. Is assurance of the essence of faith?

The question of whether assurance is of the essence of faith has arisen since the Reformation because of the different opinions among Reformed, Remonstrant, Roman Catholic, and Lutheran theologians.[5] Roman Catholics argue that assurance is not of the essence of faith but that only in certain circumstances God might grant his assurance by an act of special revelation. Roman Catholics do not believe in the assurance of salvation as a regular part of faith because of their view that a person might commit mortal sin and thus lose the grace of justification. The Council of Trent (1547–1563), for example, states: "If anyone saith that he will for certain, of an absolute and infallible certainty, have that great gift of perseverance unto the end,—unless he have learned this by special revelation: let him be anathema."[6] For Roman Catholics, there is no certainty of salvation because only at death do they discover whether they will be saved or damned: "Each man

---

3. William L. Lane, *Hebrews 9–13*, WBC 47b (Dallas: Word Books, 1991), 286.

4. Douglas J. Moo, *The Letters to the Colossians and to Philemon*, PNTC (Grand Rapids: Eerdmans, 2008), 166–68.

5. G. C. Berkouwer, *Faith and Perseverance*, SD (Grand Rapids: Eerdmans, 1979), 17–80; also Jay T. Collier, *Debating Perseverance: The Augustinian Heritage in Post-Reformation England* (Oxford: Oxford University Press, 2018), 59–123. For what structurally follows, see Berkhof, *Systematic Theology*, 545.

6. Council of Trent, "Sixth Session, 13 Jan 1547," in Schaff, *Creeds of Christendom* 2:114.

receives his eternal retribution in his immortal soul at the very moment of his death, in particular judgment that refers his life to Christ: either entrance into the blessedness of heaven—through purification or immediately,—or immediate and everlasting damnation."[7]

Remonstrants took a similar stance on this issue; Jacob Arminius, for example, claimed that if King David had died moments after his sin with Bathsheba he would have gone to hell.[8] Moreover, according to Arminius a person's justification is incomplete until the final judgment. Additionally, a person might lose their salvation by committing apostasy.[9] In the contemporary period theologians such as I. Howard Marshall (1934–2015) have made this same case.[10] Lutheran theologians have historically argued that predestination rests on God's foreknowledge of those who will and will not believe, and correlatively those who will persevere in faith and those who do not persevere. Some fall away into grievous sin and repent, but others fall into unrecoverable sins and perish in apostasy.[11] Lutheran views of perseverance bear similarity to the Remonstrant views of Arminius, though they nevertheless affirm a doctrine of assurance connected with their doctrine of the Lord's Supper.[12]

Given the general rejection of assurance, the Lutheran tradition notwithstanding, Reformed theologians have maintained that faith and assurance go hand in hand, but there has been some confusion regarding the respective positions of John Calvin and the Westminster divines. Calvin appears to claim that assurance is of the essence of faith: "Now we shall possess a right definition of faith if we call it a firm and certain knowledge of God's benevolence toward us."[13] The Westminster divines seemingly state a different opinion: "This infallible assurance doth not so belong to the essence of faith" (WCF 18.3). Does this apparent contradiction mean that

---

7. *Catechism of the Catholic Church*, §1022.

8. Jacob Arminius, *Certain Articles* 20.18, in *Works* 2:725.

9. Arminius, *Private Disputations* 48.12, in *Works* 2:407.

10. I. Howard Marshall, *Kept by the Power of God*, 3rd ed. (Carlisle, UK: Paternoster, 1995).

11. *Formula of Concord* 11:715, in *The Book of Concord; or The Symbolical Books of the Evangelical Lutheran Church*, ed. Henry Eyster Jacobs (Philadelphia: United Lutheran Publication House, 1911), 659.

12. Formula Concord 7:542, 611, 672, 692, in *Book of Concord*, 514, 163, 622, 640.

13. Calvin, *Inst.* 3.2.7.

Calvin took a different view from the Westminster divines? Is assurance of the essence of faith? Answering this question necessitates two caveats.

First, Calvin is neither the doctrinal norm nor the lodestar for the Reformed tradition. Even though the tradition often bears the name "Calvinism," suggesting a normative status, no segment of the Reformed church has ever required subscription to the views of Calvin.[14] Reformed churches have always required subscription to their confessions and catechisms, which are subordinate to the authority of Scripture. Thus, even if Calvin and the Westminster divines were opposed to each other, such opposition would not represent a problem or devolution from a mythical standard. Rather, it would only be evidence of a diversified orthodoxy on one particular doctrinal question. Second, Calvin and the Westminster divines wrote in different theological contexts separated by more than two generations, which explains why they have differing emphases.[15] Calvin wrote before the Arminian controversy, where debate broke out over soteriology, and among the controverted issues were assurance and perseverance.[16] Additionally, debates over antinomianism arose in England, where the topic of assurance was an issue of contention. Antinomians believed that persons should never have subjective doubts about their salvation.[17] The divines therefore addressed a different theological and polemical context from Calvin, which explains their varied emphases. Keeping these two points in mind establishes important contextual reference points. At the same time, despite their diverse emphases, upon closer examination Calvin and the divines agree about the nature of assurance.[18]

In Calvin's sixteenth-century context, he was writing about faith as it was considered abstractly. Note Calvin's definition of faith: "Now we shall

14. Richard A. Muller, "Demoting Calvin: The Issue of Calvin and the Reformed Tradition," in *John Calvin, Myth and Reality: Images and Impact of Geneva's Reformer*, ed. Amy Nelson Burnett (Eugene, OR: Cascade Books, 2011), 3–17.

15. Joel R. Beeke, "Does Assurance Belong to the Essence of Faith? Calvin and the Calvinists," *The Master's Seminary Journal* 5, no. 1 (1994): 43–71, here 48; contra Thomas R. Schreiner and Ardel B. Caneday, *The Race Set before Us: A Biblical Theology of Perseverance and Assurance* (Downers Grove, IL: InterVarsity Press, 2001), 268–76.

16. Keith D. Stanglin, *Arminius on Assurance of Salvation: The Context, Roots, and Shape of the Leiden Debate, 1603–1609* (Leiden: Brill, 2007).

17. Whitney G. Gamble, *Christ and the Law: Antinomianism at the Westminster Assembly* (Grand Rapids: Reformation Heritage Books, 2018), 52–54.

18. Beeke, "Does Assurance Belong," 48–59.

possess a right definition of faith if we call it a firm and certain knowledge of God's benevolence toward us, founded upon the truth of the freely given promise in Christ, both revealed to our minds and sealed upon our hearts through the Holy Spirit."[19] Calvin delineates between the objective promises of Christ and the believer's certainty about them, and the subjective sense of certainty sealed by the testimony of the Holy Spirit. But considered concretely, Calvin qualifies his remarks to account for the vicissitudes of the Christian life: "But it will be said that this differs widely from the experience of believers, who, in recognizing the grace of God toward them, not only feel disquietude (this often happens), but sometimes tremble, overcome with terror, so violent are the temptations which assail their minds. This scarcely seems consistent with certainty of faith."[20] Calvin factors the challenges, doubts, and fears that often assail believers and explains:

> When we say that faith must be certain and secure, we certainly speak not of an assurance which is never affected by doubt, nor a security which anxiety never assails; we rather maintain that believers have a perpetual struggle with their own distrust, and are thus far from thinking that their consciences possess a placid quiet, uninterrupted by perturbation. On the other hand, whatever be the mode in which they are assailed, we deny that they fall off and abandoned that sure confidence which they have formed in the mercy of God.[21]

Calvin acknowledges that believers may struggle with doubts and fears, and therefore in some sense lack assurance of their salvation at times, but these doubts do not erode the "firm and certain knowledge of God's benevolence toward us." There is a difference between objective and subjective assurance. One may have a certain and assured hope because of one's God-given faith in Christ, but this does not extinguish every single subjective doubt.

---

19. Calvin, *Inst.* 3.2.7.
20. Calvin, *Inst.* 3.2.17.
21. Calvin, *Inst.* 3.2.17.

The Westminster divines make similar observations regarding the nature of assurance. Like Calvin, they describe faith as believing "to be true whatsoever is revealed in the Word, for the authority of God himself speaking therein" (WCF 14.2). Moreover, only the "inward illumination of the Spirit of God" can give a person the necessary "understanding of such things as are revealed in the Word" (1.6). This means that those who "truly believe in the Lord Jesus ... may... be certainly assured that they are in the state of grace" (18.1). Like Calvin, the divines affirm the certainty of assurance: "This certainty is not a bare conjectural and probably persuasion grounded upon a fallible hope; but an infallible assurance of faith found upon the divine truth of the promises of salvation" (18.2). But just as Calvin says that believers can be stricken by doubts, the divines also concede: "This infallible assurance doth not so belong to the essence of faith, but that a true believer may wait long, and conflict with many difficulties before he be partaker of it" (18.3). Like Calvin, the divines distinguish between objective and subjective assurance; Calvin and the divines speak with one voice on the nature of assurance, though they lay different degrees of stress on the nature of assurance given their respective historical contexts.

The foregoing survey of the agreement that exists between Calvin and the Westminster divines is not a detour into historical theology, a turn that replaces exegesis with tradition. Calvin and Westminster show that different theologians divided by two generations recognized that certitude about the promises of God in Christ is a part of faith, but that this certitude does not preclude doubts, temptations, or struggles. The Scriptures showcase doubts and struggles with the lack of assurance that the saints at times experienced. At the same time, the psalmist sings dark, forlorn notes of doubt and mourning because it seems as if God has abandoned him, but he almost invariably ends on notes of hope: "When doubts filled my mind, your comfort gave me renewed hope and cheer" (Ps 94:19 NLT). Even though Psalm 88 contains some of the darkest imagery, it too contains hope. The psalmist laments: "You have put me in the depths of the pit, in the regions dark and deep. Your wrath lies heavy upon me, and you overwhelm me with all your waves" (Ps 88:6–7). But in spite of the feelings of doubt the psalmist stubbornly persists, "But I, O Lord, cry to you; in the morning my prayer comes before you" (Ps 88:13). Even Habakkuk's angry, doubt-filled calls to God end on a note of hope and assurance: "Though the fig tree should not blossom, nor fruit be on the vines, the produce of the olive fail and the fields yield no food, the flock be cut off from the fold and there be no herd in the stalls, yet I will rejoice in the LORD; I will take joy in the God of my salvation. GOD, the Lord, is my strength; he makes my feet like the deer's; he makes me tread on my high places" (Hab 3:17–19). Plagued by doubt, these saints nevertheless cried out to God. Their very cries are the fruit of faith and evidence of the assurance of their salvation. A person does not cry out to one who cannot save or who is untrustworthy. They did not rest their faith on the sand of their subjective feelings but on the certainty of God's faithfulness.

## PERSEVERANCE

JUST AS ASSURANCE RESTS ON God's faithfulness to his promises, the Christian's perseverance in salvation has the same foundation.[22] Simply stated, the doctrine of perseverance teaches that those whom God has elected will never fall away from a state of salvation. Or in the words of the apostle Paul: "I am sure of this, that he who began a good work in you will bring it to completion at the day of Jesus Christ" (Phil 1:6). Jesus testified that his sheep knew his voice: "I give them eternal life, and they will never perish, and no one will snatch them out of my hand. My Father, who has given them to me, is greater than all, and no one is able to snatch them out of the Father's hand" (John 10:27–29). What accounts for the perseverance of the saints? Perseverance rests on three key pillars: the immutability of God's decree, the infallibility of Christ's work as covenant surety, and the irreversibility of the eschaton.

First, when the Triune God determines to create and redeem, his decree is immutable and unchanging: "God is not man, that he should lie, or a son of man, that he should change his mind. Has he said, and will he not do it? Or has he spoken, and will he not fulfill it?" (Num 23:19). Coupled with the immutability of the decree is that God has predestined the elect to be in Christ: "Even as he chose us in him before the foundation of the world, that we should be holy and blameless before him. In love he predestined us for adoption to himself as sons through Jesus Christ, according to the purpose of his will" (Eph 1:4–5). The immutability of the decree and being in a

22. Berkouwer, *Faith and Perseverance*, 11.

predestinarian union with Christ undergird Jesus's teaching that none of the elect will perish and that no one can take them out of his hand because the Father has given them to him.

A second factor is the suretyship of Christ. The decree of election unfolds within the context of the pretemporal covenant of redemption—the agreement among Father, Son, and Holy Spirit to create and redeem the elect. God unites the elect to Christ in the decree and appoints his Son to serve as covenant surety. Jesus is the "guarantor of a better covenant," a role given to him by the Father's immutable, sworn covenantal oath. The Son "was made a priest with an oath by the one who said to him: 'The Lord has sworn and will not change his mind, "You are a priest forever" ' " (Heb 7:21–22). A covenant surety undertakes all the legal obligations within a covenant, and in this case, most relevant is Christ's curse-bearing on behalf of his bride: "Christ redeemed us from the curse of the law by becoming a curse for us—for it is written, 'Cursed is everyone who is hanged on a tree' " (Gal 3:13).

The third factor is the finality of the eschaton, the new heavens and earth. Jesus, the last Adam, redeems his people to an indefectible state. When God placed Adam in the garden, he was righteous but in a mutable state; he had *posse mori* ("the ability to die").[23] The last Adam has set us on a path that leads to *non posse non mori* ("the inability to die") because through union with him believers take a step into the new heavens and earth. As Paul writes, "We do not lose heart. Though our outer man is wasting away, our inner man is being renewed day by day" (2 Cor 4:16, my trans.). "If anyone is in Christ, he is new creation. The old has passed away; behold, the new has come" (2 Cor 5:17, my trans.). Paul does not merely say that the one in union with Christ is a new creature, although this is certainly true. Rather, when he invokes the language of καινὴ κτίσις ("new creation"), he alludes to Isaiah's new heavens and earth (Isa 65:17; 66:22).[24] By virtue of their union with Christ, God seats believers in the heavens at the Father's right hand, and they irreversibly, indefectibly, and immutably enter the new creation (Eph 2:4–6; Col 3:1).

---

23. Bavinck, *Reformed Dogmatics* 4:566–67; see Augustine, *City of God*, 2 vols., trans. William Babcock (Hyde Park, NY: New City Press, 2012), 22.30.

24. Beale, "Old Testament Background of Reconciliation."

If Christ merely placed us back where Adam began in the garden with a second chance, freed from sin and unshackled from death, this would undoubtedly be a tremendous blessing. But salvation far exceeds the idea of returning to the garden. In addition to receiving the forgiveness of our sins, invested with the righteousness of Christ, and set free from death and the wrath of God, union with Christ opens a door to the new heavens and earth, a blessing that Adam did not know and had not yet apprehended. Our state and Adam's prefall state are not a matter of a difference of degrees of blessing but rather the difference between two entirely different modes of life—two different worlds. Through our union with Christ, we irreversibly enter the eschaton.[25] We have been raised according to our inner man, and through the power of Christ's resurrection we will be ineluctably raised according to our outer man on the last day (2 Cor 4:16–5:5).

At the same time, some passages of Scripture raise questions in the hearts of Christians about the certainty of perseverance. Christ speaks of cutting away branches from the vine that do not bear fruit, and the author of Hebrews famously writes of those who cannot be restored because they have fallen away (on which see below). At first glance, these passages give the impression that the elect can indeed fall away, but on closer examination they say something different. Jesus told his disciples: "Every branch of mine that does not bear fruit he takes away" (John 15:2). Within the immediate context, Jesus spoke to his twelve disciples, one of whom was Judas, the one whom Jesus identified as a devil: "Did I not chose you, the twelve? And yet one of you is a devil" (John 6:70).[26] This immediately informs us that Christ's group of disciples was a mixed body. We must therefore carefully distinguish between those who are *visibly* united to Christ versus those who are *invisibly* united to Christ. In this vein we should note the differences between the betrayals of Judas and Peter: "Simon, Simon, behold, Satan demanded to have you, that he might sift you like wheat, but I have prayed for you that your faith may not fail. And when you have turned again, strengthen your brothers" (Luke 22:31–32). Not only does Christ

25. Geerhardus Vos, *Grace and Glory: Sermons Preached in the Chapel of Princeton Theological Seminary* (Edinburgh: Banner of Truth, 1994), 166.

26. Carson, *Gospel according to John*, 515; Robert A. Peterson, "Preservation, Perseverance, Assurance, and Apostasy," *Presbyterion* 22, no. 1 (1996): 31–41, here 38.

intercede on Peter's behalf, but he also knows he will repent.[27] This means that anyone who is truly united to Christ will never be cut off the vine, as they rest on the infallible intercessory work of Christ and receive the Spirit as a guarantee, a down payment: "And it is God who establishes us with you in Christ, and has anointed us, and who has also put his zeal on us and given us his Spirit in our hearts as a guarantee [ἀρραβῶνα]" (2 Cor 1:21–22). That Paul says the Spirit is an ἀρραβών means that God has laid his claim on us in Christ through the guarantee of the Spirit, and he will without question complete our redemption.[28] Thus, the NIV translation of this verse says that God has "set his seal of ownership on us, and put his Spirit in our hearts as a deposit, guaranteeing what is to come."[29]

John 15:2 is not the only passage to which some appeal to argue that true believers can lose their salvation. In Hebrews 6, the author writes: "For it is impossible, in the case of those who have once been enlightened, who have tasted the heavenly gift, and have shared in the Holy Spirit, and have tasted the goodness of the word of God and the powers of the age to come, and then have fallen away, to restore them again to repentance, since they are crucifying once again the Son of God to their own harm and holding him up to contempt" (Heb 6:4–6).[30] The immediate and broader canonical contexts point away from any notion that true believers can lose their salvation. In the immediate context the author points his recipients to the unshakable promises of God that secure salvation: "We have this as a sure and steadfast anchor of the soul, a hope that enters into the inner place behind the curtain, where Jesus has gone as forerunner on our behalf, having become a high priest forever after the order of Melchizedek" (Heb 6:19–20).[31] Salvation rests on the foundation of God's promises, not on the shifting sands of our faithfulness.

---

27. Bock, *Luke 9:51–24:53*, 1742–43; Schreiner and Caneday, *Race Set before Us*, 238–43.

28. Murray J. Harris, *The Second Epistle to the Corinthians*, NIGTC (Grand Rapids: Eerdmans, 2005), 207–8.

29. Berkouwer, *Faith and Perseverance*, 208–14.

30. For what follows, see John Calvin, *Hebrews and 1 & 2 Peter*, ed. David W. Torrance and T. F. Torrance, CNTC (Grand Rapids: Eerdmans, 1996), 74–77; John Owen, *An Exposition of the Epistle to the Hebrews*, on Heb 6:4–6, in *Works of John Owen* 21:67–91; Wayne Grudem, "Perseverance of the Saints: A Case Study from Hebrews 6:4–6 and Other Warning Passages of Hebrews," in *The Grace of God and the Bondage of the Will*, ed. Thomas Schreiner and Bruce Ware (Grand Rapids: Baker Books, 1995), 1:133–82.

31. Berkouwer, *Faith and Perseverance*, 116–17.

The wider canonical context of the New Testament is the second piece of evidence that confirms the doctrine of perseverance. In the Gospels Jesus teaches the parable of the sower.[32] The sower cast his seed on four different types of ground. Some seed fell along the path and was eaten by birds, which is symbolic for those who hear the gospel and do not understand it, and the enemy sweeps in and snatches the message away (Matt 13:4, 19). Some seed landed on rocky ground and did not put forth roots, which corresponds to those who hear the word with joy, but then trial comes and they immediately fall away (Matt 13:5–6, 20–21). Other seed fell on thorns and was choked out, which means that some hear the gospel, but the cares and riches of the world drown out the message (Matt 13:7, 22). The final type of seed fell on good soil and produced much fruit, which signifies those who hear the gospel, understand, and believe in it through a God-given faith (Matt 13:8, 23; see 13–17; Eph 2:8–9).

Christ's parable of the sower provides the subtext for Hebrews 6:4–6 because immediately on the heels of giving his warnings, the author invokes the same parabolic imagery: "For land that has drunk the rain that often falls on it, and produces a crop useful to those for whose sake it is cultivated, receives a blessing from God. But if it bears thorns and thistles, it is worthless and near to being cursed, and its end is to be burned" (Heb 6:7–8).[33] The author employs the concepts from Christ's parable of the sower—the good soil produces a harvest, and the bad soil produces thorns and thistles. In Christ's parable, the seed of the gospel grows only in the good soil, which consists of hearts prepared by the Spirit of God and enabled to believe. In other words, good soil does not produce thorns and thistles, which means that no one who truly believes in and is united to Christ falls away. Only those who temporarily receive the gospel but have no root, or whose hearts are overgrown with thorns and thistles, fall away. Theirs, however, is not a true saving faith but merely a *fides historica* ("historical faith"), or the faith of demons. In the words of the apostle John, "They went out from us, but they were not of us; for if they had been of us, they would have continued with us. But they went out, that it might become plain that they all are not of us" (1 John 2:19). Salvation is not the reward for

32. D. A. Carson, "Reflections on Christian Assurance," *WTJ* 54 (1992): 1–29, here 18–19.

33. Carson, "Reflections on Christian Assurance," 19–20.

those who persevere, but rather perseverance is the hallmark of salvation and our union with Christ. Those who fall away were never truly united to Christ and received only a slight taste of the gospel; they experienced only a passing encounter with the Spirit, the power of the age to come.[34]

This means that not all who are visibly united to Christ are truly or invisibly united to Christ. This raises the distinction between the *visible* and *invisible church*. The visible church consists of all of those who *profess* the true religion and their children and is the kingdom of Christ, the house and family of God (WCF 25.2). The invisible church, on the other hand, consists of the whole number of the elect, who are united to Christ by faith and the indwelling of the Holy Spirit (25.1). In redemptive-historical terms, covenant is broader than election. God, for example, chose the nation of Israel as his people, but as Paul explains: "Not all who are descended from Israel belong to Israel" (Rom 9:6). God's election of Israel as a people does not preclude him from saving people from among his people.[35] As Herman Bavinck explains:

> According to the saying of Augustine, there are sheep outside and wolves inside the sheepfold of the church of Christ upon earth. The external and internal sides of the covenant of grace do not correspond fully to each other. There are many who according to our estimate belong within the dispensation of the covenant of grace and nevertheless do not share in the essence and the spiritual blessings of that covenant. In connection with the means of grace, the sign and the thing signified are not always united with each other.[36]

The distinction between the visible and invisible church raises an important aspect regarding the reception of warning statements such as Hebrews 6:4–6.

If the church is a mixed body consisting of believers and nonbelievers, that is, those who truly believe and those who only nominally believe, or who only have a *fides historica*, then we must factor the double-edged nature of divine revelation. We do not have to choose between determining

34. John R. W. Stott, *The Letters of John*, Tyndale New Testament Commentaries (Grand Rapids: Eerdmans, 1988), 110.

35. John Calvin, *Romans and Thessalonians*, on Rom 9:6.

36. Bavinck, *Saved by Grace*, 149; also Peterson, "Preservation, Perseverance," 40.

whether the author of Hebrews wrote to believers or unbelievers. Rather, he wrote to a mixed body—those who truly believed and those who only had a *fides historica*. The author wrote to the visible church. This means that each group received divine revelation but to different ends. Believers received the warning not as an announcement that they could somehow lose their salvation—that Christ would lose his grip on them. Rather, they received such warnings as counsel to cling fast to Christ and to steer clear of the temptations of apostasy. Conversely, those with a mere *fides historica* would either hear the warning and through the effectual calling of the Spirit be drawn into union with Christ by true saving faith, or they would hear the word to their condemnation; they would spurn the word of warning.[37] Or, in the words of Paul: "For we are the aroma of Christ to God among those who are being saved and among those who are perishing, to one a fragrance from death to death, to the other a fragrance from life to life. Who is sufficient for these things?" (2 Cor 2:15–16).

Both the Continental and Presbyterian confessional traditions observe this aspect of the function of warnings. The Canons of Dort state: "God preserves, continues, and completes this work by the hearing and reading of the gospel, by meditation on it, by its exhortations, threats, and promises, and also by the use of the sacraments" (5.14). Likewise, the Westminster Confession says that saving faith believes "to be true whatsoever is revealed in the Word ... yielding obedience to the commands, trembling at the threatenings, and embracing the promises of God for this life, and that which is to come" (14.2). The warnings of God serve to preserve the elect in their faith.[38]

---

37. Owen, *Exposition of Hebrews*, on. Heb 6:4–6 (*Works of John Owen* 21:90); Berkouwer, *Faith and Perseverance*, 110–11, 120–21, 195–96.

38. Schreiner and Caneday claim that their view is historically unprecedented, namely, that the warnings are conducive to the faith of believers (*Race Set before Us*, 38–45). The view that the warnings are a spur to believers, however, has precedent in the Reformed confessional tradition, as noted by the cited passages from the Canons of Dort, Westminster Confession, Owen, and Berkouwer. That being said, Schreiner and Caneday are ambiguous regarding the nature of faith as it relates to perseverance when they argue for the necessity of an obedient faith. For example, Schreiner says that faith and works have a paradoxical relationship (*Race Set before Us*, 98; see also Thomas R. Schreiner, *Run to Win the Prize: Perseverance in the New Testament* [Wheaton, IL: Crossway, 2010], 73; see also 23, 51, 69, 70). At times Schreiner tries to clarify to say that obedience is the fruit of faith (*Race Set before Us*, 71–72, 86).

## CONCLUSION

One of the most important passages of Scripture as it pertains to assurance and perseverance is Peter's threefold denial of Christ. If Peter were left to himself, his faith would have collapsed under the weight of his doubt, but what separated Peter from Judas was Christ's intercession.[39] Blessedly, Jesus not only interceded for Peter, but he also intercedes for his bride: "Holy Father, keep them in your name, which you have given me, that they may be one, even as we are one. … I do not ask for these only, but also for those who will believe in me" (John 17:11, 20).[40] In the words of the Canons of Dort: "Because of these remnants of sin dwelling in them and also because of the temptations of the world and Satan, those who have been converted could not remain standing in this grace if left to their own resources. But God is faithful, mercifully strengthening them in the grace once conferred on them and powerfully preserving them in it to the end" (5.3). The doctrine of perseverance is not simply the conclusion of a logical argument, "I am chosen by God, therefore I will persevere."[41] Rather, perseverance rests on the foundation of the Father's immutable decree of election, the priestly intercession of Christ, and the guarantee and witness of the Spirit. Perseverance rests on the promises and work of the Triune God: "For he has said, 'I will never leave you nor forsake you' " (Heb 13:5). From the faithful promises of God we have a firm foundation for the assurance of salvation: "Neither death nor life, nor angels nor rulers, nor things present nor things to come, nor powers, nor height nor depth, nor anything else in all creation, will be able to separate us from the love of God in Christ Jesus our Lord" (Rom 8:38–39). As we seek to make our calling and election sure (2 Pet 1:10), we must remember that for every one look to self, we take ten looks to Christ. Our assurance and perseverance rest in Christ, not in us.

---

39. Berkouwer, *Faith and Perseverance*, 144–47.

40. Berkouwer, *Faith and Perseverance*, 140.

41. Peterson, "Preservation, Perseverance," 32; Berkouwer, *Faith and Perseverance*, 75, 77.

## FURTHER READING

Beeke, Joel R. "Does Assurance Belong to the Essence of Faith? Calvin and the Calvinists." *The Master's Seminary Journal* 5, no. 1 (1994): 43–71. A study that focuses on the question of whether Calvin and the later "Calvinists" agree or disagree on the nature of assurance. This is a very helpful essay and is recommended reading.

Berkouwer, G. C. *Faith and Perseverance*. SD. Grand Rapids: Eerdmans, 1979. A compact historical, exegetical, and theological treatment of the doctrine of perseverance from a Reformed confessional point of view.

Grudem, Wayne. "Perseverance of the Saints: A Case Study from Hebrews 6:4–6 and Other Warning Passages of Hebrews." In *The Grace of God and the Bondage of the Will*, edited by Thomas Schreiner and Bruce Ware, 1:133–82. Grand Rapids: Baker Books, 1995. A thorough exegetical treatment of the warning passages in Hebrews that persuasively shows that the subtext of these passages is Christ's parable of the sower.

Master, Jonathan. *A Question of Consensus: The Doctrine of Assurance after the Westminster Confession*. Minneapolis: Fortress, 2015. A helpful survey and exploration of the Westminster Confession's doctrine of assurance. One of its highlights is that it shows how the divines had differences of opinion on the doctrine and wrote the confession in such a way as to accommodate a diversified confessional orthodoxy.

XI

# SERVICE IN THE SPIRIT

## GIFTS AND MISSION

THE CULTURE OF THE WEST cuts against the grain of Scripture and has tried to turn the doctrine of salvation into ground and rationale for a manifesto of the individual. In the West's materialistic theology, sinners are saved and receive the gifts of the Spirit for personal gain, notoriety, and upward mobility in the socio-spiritual caste of the church. Self-professed Christians treat theology as design-your-own religion and the church as if it were an optional accessory to their faith.[1] As far removed as the twenty-first century is from the first, similar problems emerged in the early church. Christians were using their spiritual gifts to promote their own standing in the church, and so Paul addressed this problem in his several of his letters to explain the nature of the gifts of the Spirit and their telos: the edification of the church and glory of God.

As the church has reflected on Paul's teaching, it has explained the spiritual gifts under the doctrine of the communion of the saints. The Heidelberg Catechism succinctly summarizes the link between Spirit, gifts, and church with the question, "What do you understand by the 'the communion of the saints'?" The catechism responds: "First, that believers one and all, as members of this community, share in Christ and in all his

---

1. E.g., Tara Isabella Burton, *Strange Rites: New Religions for a Godless World* (New York: Public Affairs, 2020).

treasures and gifts. Second, that each member should consider it a duty to use these gifts readily and joyfully for the service and enrichment of the other members" (q. 55). This chapter therefore first examines Scripture's teaching on the gifts of the Spirit. Second, it explains the doctrine of the communion of the saints. The chapter then concludes with summary observations about the function and goal of the gifts of the Spirit—they are not for the promotion of the individual but for the individual to edify the church and glorify the Triune God.

## GIFTS OF THE SPIRIT

### *Old Testament Background*

ESTABLISHING THE CONTEXT FOR THE gifts of the Spirit is vital for understanding their twin goals: building the church and glorifying God. When God sent Moses to Pharaoh to demand the release of Israel, Moses said: "Thus says the LORD, the God of Israel, 'Let my people go, that they may hold a feast to me in the wilderness'" (Exod 5:1). Moses informed Pharaoh that Israel was supposed to "sacrifice to the LORD" (Exod 5:3). One of the intended goals of the exodus, therefore, was worship—holding a festival and offering sacrifices to God. When God delivered Israel from Egypt, worship was still the goal of their deliverance, and to facilitate this goal God gave Moses instructions for the construction of the desert tabernacle. To facilitate the building of tabernacle, he filled craftsmen with the Spirit:

> The LORD said to Moses, "See, I have called by name Bezalel the son of Uri, son of Hur, of the tribe of Judah, and I have filled him with the Spirit of God, with ability and intelligence, with knowledge and all craftsmanship, to devise artistic designs, to work in gold, silver, and bronze, in cutting stones for setting, and in carving wood, to work in every craft. And behold, I have appointed with him Oholiab, the son of Ahisamach, of the tribe of Dan. And I have given to all able men ability, that they may make all that I have commanded you." (Exod 31:1–6)

God filled both men with the Spirit of God to build the tabernacle, the meeting place between God and his people. But in a subsequent passage, the Scripture reveals another function:

> See, the LORD has called by name Bezalel the son of Uri, son of Hur, of the tribe of Judah; and he has filled him with the Spirit of God, with skill, with intelligence, with knowledge, and with all craftsmanship, to devise artistic designs, to work in gold and silver and bronze, in cutting stones for setting, and in carving wood, for work in every skilled craft. *And he has inspired him to teach*, both him and Oholiab the son of Ahisamach of the tribe of Dan. (Exod 35:30–34)

In this second description, Moses informs the people that God filled both men with the Spirit, gave them gifts, and "inspired him to teach, both him and Oholiab" (Exod 35:34). In other words, Oholiab and Bezalel were supposed to use their Spirit-given gifts to build the tabernacle and to teach others to build the tabernacle.[2] The gifts of the Spirit both are to facilitate worship through the construction of the meeting place for God and his people, and are also to be shared with the rest of the people of God, not used for individual gains or selfishly hoarded. This Old Testament trajectory informs the New Testament's theology of the gifts of the Spirit.

### *The Gifts of the Spirit*

SOMETIMES ONE MUST RESTATE THE obvious because people become too familiar with what they know. In this case, the spiritual gifts come from the Holy Spirit. In the wake of Christ's life, death, resurrection, and ascension, he poured out the Spirit on the church, which occurred at Pentecost (Acts 2:17–18, 33; Joel 2:28–32). The outpouring of the Spirit brought both new life and the sovereign distribution of gifts. A key passage of Scripture in this regard is Paul's appeal to Psalm 68:18, "You ascended on high, leading a host of captives in your train and receiving gifts among men, even among the rebellious, that the LORD God may dwell there." Psalm 68 is one of the more challenging psalms to interpret, as it covers a wide range of events from Israel's history, from the exodus to the formation of the temple on Mount Zion (68:7–18). It speaks of a procession of worshipers praising God (68:24–27) and God's victory over the nations (68:17–18).[3] The ideas of people,

---

2. Jack Levison, *A Boundless God: The Spirit according to the Old Testament* (Grand Rapids: Baker Academic, 2020), 114–15.

3. Beale and Carson, *Commentary on the New Testament Use*, 820.

worship, and temple form the perfect backdrop for Paul's explanation of Christ's gifts to the church through the Spirit.

Paul quotes Psalm 68:18 to make the point that Christ has conquered the nations and distributed gifts to the church through the Spirit: "Therefore it says, 'When he ascended on high he led a host of captives, and he gave gifts to men.' (In saying, 'He ascended,' what does it mean but that he had also descended into the lower regions, the earth? He who descended is the one who also ascended far above all the heavens, that he might fill all things)" (Eph 4:8–10; see Num 8:6, 14; 18:6).[4] In short, Christ's descent to the earth and his finished work inaugurated his reign at the Father's right hand, whence he has poured out the Spirit on the church. The outpouring of the Spirit equipped redeemed sinners to build the church, the meeting place between God and his people.[5] Paul writes: "And he gave some, apostles; and some, prophets; and some, evangelists; and some, pastors and teachers; For the perfecting of the saints, for the work of the ministry, for the edifying of the body of Christ" (Eph 4:11–12 KJV).[6] Notably, the Spirit dispenses word gifts, which are the primary means of building the church. Christ has dispensed the Spirit, who gives gifts to the church, and these gifts are the apostles, prophets, evangelists, pastors, and teachers. Christ through the Spirit gives these gifts for perfecting the saints, for the work of ministry, and for edifying the body of Christ, that is, for building the church. Christ lays the foundation of the church through the apostles and New Testament prophets, and once the foundation has been laid (Eph 2:20), the evangelists, teachers, and pastors continue the work of perfecting the saints, serving and building the church. Like Oholiab and Bezalel teaching others, the evangelists, teachers, and pastors teach others so that they too can contribute to the construction of the church.

Evangelists, teachers, and pastors serve through the ministry of the word; they teach the rest of the church how to put their Spirit-given gifts to use toward building the church. There are two chief passages where Paul lists the gifts of the Spirit:

---

4. On the differences between Ps 68:18 and Paul's quotation in Eph 4:8–10, see Beale and Carson, *Commentary on the New Testament Use*, 822–23.

5. Beale and Carson, *Commentary on the New Testament Use*, 823–24.

6. On the use of the KJV here, see T. David Gordon, "'Equipping' Ministry in Ephesians 4?," *JETS* 37, no. 1 (1994): 69–78.

> Having gifts that differ according to the grace given to us, let us use them: if prophecy, in proportion to our faith; if service, in our serving; the one who teaches, in his teaching; the one who exhorts, in his exhortation; the one who contributes, in generosity; the one who leads, with zeal; the one who does acts of mercy, with cheerfulness. (Rom 12:6–8)

> To each is given the manifestation of the Spirit for the common good. For to one is given through the Spirit the utterance of wisdom, and to another the utterance of knowledge according to the same Spirit, to another faith by the same Spirit, to another gifts of healing by the one Spirit, to another the working of miracles, to another prophecy, to another the ability to distinguish between spirits, to another various kinds of tongues, to another the interpretation of tongues. … And God has appointed in the church first apostles, second prophets, third teachers, then miracles, then gifts of healing, helping, administrating, and various kinds of tongues. (1 Cor 12:7–10, 28)

These two passages list nineteen different spiritual gifts: prophecy, service, teaching, exhortation, giving, leading, acts of mercy, spiritual utterances of wisdom and knowledge, faith, healing, miracles, discernment, speaking in tongues, interpretation of tongues, apostles, prophets, teachers, and administrating. This is not an exhaustive but illustrative list of gifts (see, e.g., 1 Pet 4:10–12). These gifts can be divided into two categories: *extraordinary* gifts, which were used during the foundational stage of the New Testament church, and *ordinary* gifts, which persist from Pentecost through the present day. Among the former are prophecy, healing, miracles, speaking and interpretation of tongues, apostles, and prophets. The latter include service, teaching, exhortation, giving, leading, acts of mercy, spiritual utterances of wisdom and knowledge, faith, discernment, teachers, and administrating.

More specifically, what are these various gifts, and how do they function? The extraordinary gifts fall into three main categories: gifts of divine revelation, the ability to perform miracles, and the gifts of those who hold the office of apostle or New Testament prophet.

- **Prophecy and speaking and interpreting tongues:** Prophecy involved being inspired by the Spirit to utter divine revelation equal to the authority of Scripture. It sometimes involved predicting the future (Acts 11:28; 21:10–12).[7] Speaking in tongues was another form of divine revelation that was performed in a foreign language, and in order for it to be edifying for the church required the gift of interpretation (1 Cor 14:2; see 1 Cor 14:2–25; Acts 2:4–10; Isa 28:11).[8] These gifts expired with the completion of the foundation of the New Testament church and the death of the apostles and prophets (Eph 2:20).

- **Healing and miracles:** The Spirit equipped some first-century Christians such as the apostles with the ability to perform miracles. Peter, for example, healed Aeneas, a paralyzed man who was bedridden for eight years (Acts 9:34–35), and Paul healed the father of Publius from fever and dysentery through prayer and laying hands on him (Acts 28:8); when the people of Malta heard of this, they came to Paul and were healed by him (Acts 28:9).

- **Apostles and prophets:** The Spirit gave the gifts of the apostles and New Testament prophets, both to lead the church in the wake of the ascension of Christ and to speak divine authoritative revelation in the absence of a completed New Testament canon. Given their unique place in redemptive history, the apostles and prophets are extraordinary offices.

The ordinary gifts are as follows:

- **Service:** Also called "ministering," this gift is caring for the material needs of the church to the glory of God; it refers to the specific office of deacon within the church.[9] In the Old Testament, the priests cared for the physical needs of the tabernacle and temple, and in the New Testament deacons

---

7. *Pace* Moo, *Letter to the Romans*, 783.

8. O. Palmer Robertson, "Tongues: Sign of Covenantal Curse and Blessing," *WTJ* 38, no. 1 (1975): 43–53.

9. Moo, *Letter to the Romans*, 785.

care for the physical needs of the church. Paul may also have in view those whom the Spirit enables sacrificially to serve others.

- **Teaching, teachers:** Those who receive the gift of teaching have the ability to pass on the truth of the gospel to the church for its edification. God gives the gift of prophecy to prophets, who speak inspired divine revelation; teachers are able to explain the significance of this divine revelation.[10]
- **Exhortation:** The Spirit enables some within the church to encourage others to live out the truth of the gospel.[11]
- **Giving:** There are some to whom the Spirit gives the ability to share out of their financial and material possessions with others in need.[12] While every Christian should give to the church, some have the gift of giving generously, above and beyond.
- **Leading:** This likely has the elders of the church in view. The Spirit bestows this gift so that church leaders rule in the power of the Spirit: "Let the elders who rule well be considered worthy of double honor" (1 Tim 5:17; see Rom 12:8; 1 Tim 3:4; 5:17; 1 Thess 5:12).[13]
- **Acts of mercy:** This gift includes visiting the sick; caring for those in need, such as the elderly or disabled; and providing for the poor. Those who possess this gift must exercise it with a cheerful, not begrudging, attitude.[14]
- **Utterances of wisdom and knowledge:** All Christians are saved, but not all Christians are wise. As Solomon prayed for the gift of wisdom and knowledge (2 Chr 1:10–12), so the Spirit endows certain people with these gifts. Solomon writes, "The

---

10. Moo, *Letter to the Romans*, 785.
11. Moo, *Letter to the Romans*, 786.
12. Moo, *Letter to the Romans*, 786.
13. Hodge, *Commentary on the Epistle to the Romans*, 293.
14. Moo, *Letter to the Romans*, 787.

fear of the Lord is the beginning of wisdom, and the knowledge of the Holy One is insight" (Prov 9:10). This wisdom and knowledge culminate in Christ, "in whom are hidden all the treasures of wisdom and knowledge" (Col 2:3), and these gifts enable Christians to apply the word of God to the various challenges of the Christian life.

- **Faith:** Paul does not refer to saving faith, that which all believers receive through the sovereign work of the Spirit. Rather, faith as a spiritual gift is the kind of faith that can move mountains (Matt 17:20).[15] In other words, in the face of challenging circumstances, this is a faith that is unflappable and believes in Christ against all odds. Such a gift of faith enables Christians to become martyrs.[16]

- **Discernment:** The Spirit enables a person to discern the difference between the work of the Spirit and false spirits. Pharaoh's sorcerers could duplicate many of the miracles that Moses could perform, and Jesus warned of those who cast out demons in his name but who did not know him (Exod 7:22; 8:7; Matt 17:21–23).[17] The person with the gift of discernment can detect when "Satan disguises himself as an angel of light" (2 Cor 11:14) and warn the church (1 John 4:1).[18]

- **Helping and administration:** There are some individuals within the church whom the Spirit endows with the ability to help those in need with whatever they might require.[19] Administration (κυβερνήσεις) likely invokes for modern readers ideas of organizing, filing, and copying, but this is not what Paul has in mind. Rather, he has in view one whom the Spirit gifts to provide guidance and wise counsel to the church. One

15. D. A. Carson, *Showing the Spirit: A Theological Exposition of 1 Corinthians 12–14* (Grand Rapids: Baker Books, 1987), 38; Hodge, *Exposition of the First Epistle*, 246.

16. Hodge, *Exposition of the First Epistle* , 247.

17. Carson, *Showing the Spirit*, 40.

18. Hodge, *Exposition of the First Epistle*, 248.

19. Carson, *Showing the Spirit*, 40–41; Gordon D. Fee, *God's Empowering Presence: The Holy Spirit in the Letters of Paul* (Peabody, MA: Hendrickson, 1994), 193.

> who administrates through guidance and wise counsel is a person who exercises a form of authority.[20]

There are several important points to note about the variety of gifts and how they function.

First, there are a diversity of gifts within the church, but they all come from the same Holy Spirit. Paul makes this point before he gives a list of gifts: "Now there are varieties of gifts, but the same *Spirit*; and there are varieties of service, but the same *Lord*; and there are varieties of activities, but it is the same *God*" (1 Cor 12:4–6).[21] All the gifts originate with the Spirit, not with the individual Christian. But it is important to note the Trinitarian character of the gifts of the Spirit. The varieties of service come from the Lord, that is, Jesus, and the varieties of activities come from the same God, that is, the Father. Our communion with God and reception of the gifts are through Christ, in the Spirit, and unto the Father.[22]

Second, all the various gifts, however diverse they might be, are for one common end: "To each is given the manifestation of the Spirit for the common good" (1 Cor 12:7). In other words, the gifts are all for the edification of the church. Like Oholiab and Bezalel building the tabernacle, New Testament believers employ their Spirit-given gifts to build the church.

Third, there is no hierarchy among the ordinary gifts. Some might think that teaching, for example, is more important than helping or administrating. But Paul very clearly rejects any notion of hierarchy with his famous body analogy. There is one body, but there are many members. The eye cannot say that it has no need for hearing, and the hand cannot say it has no need of the eye (1 Cor 12:18–26). Paul writes, "God arranged the members in the body, each one of them, as he chose. If all were a single member, where would the body be?" (1 Cor 12:18–19). In other words, think of how the apostolic church would have faltered if they had not appointed deacons to care for the Greek widows who were being passed over in the distribution of food (Acts 6:1–7). The "word of God continued to increase, and the number of the disciples multiplied greatly in Jerusalem, and a great many of the priests became obedient to the faith" (Acts 6:7) because the church

20. Fee, *Empowering Presence*, 193.
21. Carson, *Showing the Spirit*, 32.
22. Owen, *Communion with God*, 10.

appointed deacons to care for the physical needs of the people. Apostolic preaching would have bogged down apart from the appointment of deacons (Acts 6:4). "There are many parts, yet one body" (1 Cor 12:20).

## EMPOWERMENT FOR WITNESS AND MISSION

One of the most important things in understanding the gifts is not losing sight of the Holy Spirit, the source and fount of the gifts. This was and is a pressing perpetual problem for the church. Paul rebukes the Corinthians: "For who sees anything different in you? What do you have that you did not receive? If then you receive it, why do boast as if you did not receive it?" (1 Cor 4:7). A misguided view of the gifts loses sight of the love of God through the outpouring of the Spirit. The Holy Spirit is the bond of love that exists between the Father and Son.[23] The Father through the Son pours out the very bond of love on the church. As explained in chapter 1, God has "sent his only Son into the world, so that we might live through him. In this is love, not that we have loved God but that he loved us and sent his Son to be the propitiation for our sins" (1 John 4:9–10). The "love … from God" does not cease with the Son. As John writes: "Beloved, if God so loved, us, we also ought to love one another. No one has ever seen God; if we love one another, God abides in us and his love is perfected in us" (1 John 4:11–12). By what means does God indwell believers? "By this we know that we abide in him and he in us, because he has given us of his Spirit" (1 John 4:13). The gifts of the Spirit are therefore a manifestation of the love of the Triune God in the church.

"God's love has been poured into our hearts through the Holy Spirit who has been given to us" (Rom 5:5), and because the Spirit indwells us, we "are God's temple" (1 Cor 3:16). Because of the Spirit's presence "within" us (1 Cor 6:19), we enjoy a κοινωνία ("fellowship" or "communion," KJV) with the Holy Spirit (2 Cor 13:14). Given that all believers share in the communion with the Spirit, by virtue of their union with Christ all believers therefore share in a communion with one another through the bond of the Spirit. Augustine illustrates the connection between Spirit and church in terms of the Pauline metaphor of the body of Christ: "What the soul is to the human body, the Holy Spirit is to the body of Christ, which is the Church.

23. Augustine, *Trinity* 15.19.37.

The Holy Spirit does in the whole Church what the soul does in all the parts of one body."[24] Just as the soul unites all of the individual members of the body, the Spirit unites all of the members of the body of Christ, the church. Augustine's insight echoes the Apostles' Creed (ca. 200), which links the Spirit and the communion of believers: "I believe in the Holy Spirit, the holy Catholic church, the communion of saints."[25]

In his exposition of the creed's statement about the communion of the saints, Thomas Aquinas explains:

> Just as in a physical body the operation of one member redounds to the good of the whole body, so it works in a spiritual body, that is to say, in the church. Since all the faithful are one body, the good of one is communicated to another. Paul writes: "Thus, we who are many are one body in Christ," individuals, yet members one of the other [Rom 12:5]. Thus, among other matters which should be believed that the apostles handed down, there remains the communion of goods in the church. This [doctrine] is called "the communion of saints."[26]

The communion of the saints is context for the gifts of the Spirit. Aquinas also uses another analogy for the Spirit's dispensation of gifts to the church, namely, the heart of the church: "The head has a manifest pre-eminence over the other exterior members; but the heart has a certain hidden influence. And hence the Holy Ghost is likened to the heart, since he invisibly quickens and unifies the Church; but Christ is likened to the Head in His visible nature in which man is set over man" (*ST* III, a. 8, art 1, ad. 3) Thus, Christ as head and Spirit as heart and soul are the fount and source of love and communion: a communion between God and his people, and a communion among the church.

The Westminster Confession continues in this catholic path in its articulation of the doctrine of the communion of the saints, though unlike Aquinas, the Reformed tradition emphasizes the ministry of the word, not

---

24. Augustine, *Sermons*, trans. Edmund Hill, The Works of Saint Augustine 7 (New Rochelle, NY: New City Press, 1993), sermon 267, §4 (p. 276); see also Jean-Pierre Torrell, *Saint Thomas Aquinas*, trans. Robert Royal (Washington, DC: Catholic University of America Press, 2003), 2:190n43.

25. Torrell, *Saint Thomas Aquinas* 2:195n52.

26. Thomas Aquinas, *The Sermon Conferences of St. Thomas Aquinas on the Apostles' Creed*, trans. Nicholas Ayo (Notre Dame, IN: University of Notre Dame Press, 1988), 13 (p. 135).

merely the sacraments, as the chief source of grace for the communion of the saints.[27] Moreover, unlike the contemporary Roman Catholic Church, Reformed churches do not enfold the intercession of the saints as part of the communion of the saints.[28] In the Roman view, "the communion of the saints degenerates into mutual veneration that crowds the Mediator of God and humanity into the background."[29] Like Augustine and Aquinas before them, however, the confession explains that believers have union with Christ by the Holy Spirit and "have fellowship with him in his graces, sufferings, death, resurrection, and glory" (WCF 26.1).[30] This is the communion that exists between believers and the Triune God. At the same time, the bond in the Spirit also unites believers to each other: "And, being united to one another in love, they have communion in each other's gifts and graces, and are obliged to the performance of such duties, public and private, as do conduce to their mutual good, both in the inward and outward man" (26.1).[31]

The confession maintains the circle of love between God and his people, as they "maintain an holy fellowship and communion in the worship of God," and conversely perform "other spiritual services as tend to their mutual edification" as they serve "each other in outward things" (WCF 26.2). In other words, as they receive the love of God and return it to him in worship, they also return God's love by using their spiritual gifts to love one another as they care for each other's spiritual and practical needs: "Truly, I say to you, as you did it to one of the least of these my brothers, you did it to me" (Matt 25:40). The outpoured love of the Father through the Son and by the Spirit dispenses gifts to the church to empower their love, service, and witness as they extend God's love "unto all those who, in every place, call upon the name of the Lord Jesus" (WCF 26.2). The communion of the saints is the means by which Christ gathers his elect from the beginning

27. See Aquinas, *Sermon Conferences* 13 (pp. 135–41.); Bavinck, *Reformed Dogmatics* 4:287–88. For an early modern Reformed treatment of the doctrine, see Henry Ainsworth, *The Communion of the Saints* (London: John Bellamie, 1641).

28. E.g., *Catechism of the Catholic Church*, §956.

29. Bavinck, *Reformed Dogmatics* 4:627; see also à Brakel, *Christian's Reasonable Service* 2:99–100.

30. E.g., à Brakel, *Christian's Reasonable Service* 2:87–97.

31. E.g., à Brakel, *Christian's Reasonable Service* 2:97–106.

to the end of the world.[32] The communion of the saints is the "womb of the believing community."[33]

## CONCLUSION

THE GIFTS OF THE SPIRIT are not merely about how individual Christians have been blessed by the Spirit. The gifts of the Spirit are all about communion with the Triune God and communion with the saints—the gifts are about receiving the love of God and sharing that love among the body of Christ for its edification. All the gifts are grounded in the inseparable operations of Father, Son, and Holy Spirit. The psalmist provides a typological picture of the gifts of the Spirit within the context of union and communion with Christ:

> Behold, how good and pleasant it is
>   when brothers dwell in unity!
> It is like the precious oil on the head,
>   running down on the beard,
> on the beard of Aaron,
>   running down on the collar of his robes!
> It is like the dew of Hermon,
>   which falls on the mountains of Zion!
> For there the LORD has commanded the blessing,
>   life forevermore. (Ps 133)

God the Father anointed the Son with the Spirit so that he was "thoroughly furnished to execute the office of a mediator, and surety" (WCF 8.3). As Christ, the head of the church, received the outpouring of the Father's love in the Spirit, so too the Spirit runs down from the head on the rest of the body to furnish the church with the necessary gifts so it can carry out its divine commission. The church receives the outpoured love of God through Christ and the Spirit and shares this love among one another. The gifts are from the Triune God for the church, and as believers use them one for another, they return God's love and bring glory to him.

32. Bavinck, *Reformed Dogmatics* 4:447.
33. Bavinck, *Reformed Dogmatics* 4:332.

## FURTHER READING

Carson, D. A. *Showing the Spirit: A Theological Exposition of 1 Corinthians 12–14*. Grand Rapids: Baker Books, 1987. A good exegetical and theological treatment of the gifts of the Sprit that is worth careful study, though Carson writes from a continuationist perspective.

Gordon, T. David. "'Equipping' Ministry in Ephesians 4?" *JETS* 37, no. 1 (1994): 69–78. Exegetically demonstrates that Paul does not speak of an "every-member ministry" in Ephesians 4 and persuasively argues that the KJV translation of Ephesians 4:11–12 is preferable to more recent translations. Required reading.

Owen, John. *Of Communion with God the Father, Son, and Holy Ghost*. In *The Works of John Owen*, vol. 2, edited by William H. Goold. Edinburgh: Banner of Truth, 1997. A Reformed classic on the doctrine of communion; this is required reading.

Robertson, O. Palmer. "Tongues: Sign of Covenantal Curse and Blessing." *WTJ* 38, no. 1 (1975): 43–53. An insightful essay that explains the Old Testament background for New Testament tongues, which thus illuminates their function, especially as pertains to God's judgment against unbelief.

Vos, Geerhardus. "Paul's Eschatological Concept of the Spirit." In *Redemptive History and Biblical Interpretation: The Shorter Writings of Geerhardus Vos*, edited by Richard B. Gaffin Jr., 91–125. Phillipsburg, NJ: P&R, 1980. An essay that discusses the links between the outpouring of the Spirit and eschatology. Vos's writing is sometimes dense and challenging, but he definitely shines much-needed light on these topics.

PART 3

# TRUTH FOR WORSHIP, LIFE, AND MISSION

XII

# TRUE CONVERSION

## COUNTERFEIT VS. GENUINE FAITH

THE TWIN THREATS OF ANTINOMIANISM and legalism have continually challenged the church's doctrine of salvation. On the one hand, the church has combated those who promote a nominal faith and engage in some form of antinomianism. In other words, a Christian's immoral conduct is of no concern so long as the Christian professes faith in Christ. On the other hand, an equally destructive error has come in the form of legalism, wherein professing Christians claim that their adherence to the law is a material cause of their salvation. Legalism often comes in the form of "second blessing" theology, namely that one's justification is about past sins but that a person must experience the second blessing of sanctification in order to be saved, a blessing that stands at a temporal distance from the first blessing of justification. Both ideas are unscriptural, and so this chapter briefly examines the origins and nature of these errors, then states the biblical position. The chapter first examines true versus counterfeit faith and then explores second blessing or higher-life doctrines of sanctification.

### TRUE AND COUNTERFEIT FAITH

COUNTERFEIT FAITH IS A PERSISTENT threat that the church has battled since the Old Testament, when Cain and Abel both worshiped God—both brought sacrifices, both worshiped, yet God rejected Cain's offering but accepted Abel's. The author of Hebrews explains that the difference between the two acts of worship was a true versus a counterfeit faith: "By faith Abel offered to God a more acceptable sacrifice than Cain, through which he was commended as righteous, God commending him by accepting his gifts. And through his faith, though he died, he still speaks" (Heb 11:4). The interesting fact about Hebrews's explanation is that the Genesis text (Gen 4:3–5) mentions nothing of Abel's faith, though it does say that "Cain brought to the LORD an offering of the fruit of the ground, and Abel also brought the firstborn of his flock and of their fat portions" (Gen 4:3–4). In Abel's worship the author of Hebrews detects an act of obedience, and all obedience flows from a Spirit-wrought gift of faith (Eph 2:8–10).[1] The author of Hebrews does not say that God regarded Abel righteous because of his offering but because of his *faith*: "By faith Abel offered to God a more acceptable sacrifice than Cain, through which he was commended as righteous" (Heb 11:4). The author of Hebrews matches Paul's teaching on the relationship between faith and justification (Rom 4:1–8).[2]

The book of James addresses similar issues when it rebukes the letter's recipients for a false faith: "You believe that God is one; you do well. Even the demons believe—and shudder!" (Jas 2:19).[3] James was dealing with Christians who claimed to have faith, but their lives were barren of the fruit of good works. James counters this claim by showing that true faith produces good works: "Show me your faith apart from your works, and I will show you my faith by my works" (Jas 2:18).[4] Distinguishing between true and counterfeit faith, therefore, is a perennial challenge to the church. How is one to proceed? How does one distinguish genuine from counterfeit faith?

The first step comes in acknowledging the scriptural principle that one of the characteristics of true faith is that it produces good works. Abel offered a God-honoring sacrifice, and James says that "faith apart from works is dead" (Jas 2:26).[5] At the same time, we must distinguish between

1. Schreiner, *Commentary on Hebrews*, 344.
2. Schreiner, *Commentary on Hebrews*, 344.
3. Peter H. Davids, *The Epistle of James*, NIGTC (Grand Rapids: Eerdmans, 1982), 125.
4. Davids, *Epistle of James*, 123–24.
5. Davids, *Epistle of James*, 133–34.

the *role* of faith in justification and the *fruit* of faith, which is works; to confound the role and fruit of faith jeopardizes the integrity of the gospel and the doctrine of justification.[6] Paul emphasizes that faith *alone* justifies sinners: "For we hold that one is justified by faith apart from works of the law" (Rom 3:28).[7] Paul makes this point abundantly clear when he writes: "And to the one who does not work but believes in him who justifies the ungodly, his faith is counted as righteousness" (Rom 4:5).[8] When Paul gives a generalized statement of salvation, he gives works no role: "For by grace you have been saved through faith. And this is not your own doing; it is the gift of God, not a result of works, so that no one may boast" (Eph 2:8–9). The Westminster Confession takes these Pauline teachings and distills them into a concise statement on the nature of justification: "Those whom God effectually called, he also freely justified: not by infusing righteousness into them, but by pardoning their sins, and by accounting and accepting their persons as righteous; *not for anything wrought in them, or done by them, but for Christ's sake alone; nor by imputing faith itself, the act of believing, or any other evangelical obedience to them, as their righteousness*" (1.1, emphasis added). The confession also notes, "The principal acts of saving faith are accepting, receiving, and resting upon Christ alone for justification, sanctification, and eternal life" (14.3). Such is the nature of saving faith as it relates to the sinner's justification.

The fruit of faith is another important aspect of true faith. Just as James recognizes that "faith apart from works is dead" (Jas 2:26), Paul also teaches the same principle. Even though he says that we are "saved through faith ... not a result of works," he specifies that we are God's "workmanship, created in Christ Jesus for good works, which God prepared beforehand, that we should walk in them" (Eph 2:10).[9] Paul and James speak with one voice. However, Paul and James deal with different theological problems, which accounts for their respective emphases, the former on justification and the latter on sanctification. Paul addresses the false teaching of legalism, or

6. This is the problem with the recent work of John Piper, who rejects the distinction between what faith is versus what faith does. E.g., contra John Piper, *What Is Saving Faith? Reflections on Receiving Christ as Treasure* (Wheaton, IL: Crossway, 2022), 62n9.

7. Moo, *Letter to the Romans*, 271–72.

8. Moo, *Letter to the Romans*, 286.

9. Baugh, *Ephesians*, 163–64.

works-righteousness—the claim that sinners can be justified only by faith *and* works. James, however, deals with the false teaching of antinomianism, namely that so long as one professes faith in Jesus, one's conduct is irrelevant—sanctification is unnecessary.[10] Thus, Paul states that we are "saved through faith ... not a result of works" (Eph 2:8–9), and James conversely writes, "A person is justified by works and not by faith alone" (Jas 2:24). The key to seeing the harmony between James and Paul is to recognize that both use the terms "faith" and "justification" but with different meanings.

When Paul writes of faith, he has genuine trust and belief in the promises of God in view: "Abraham believed God, and it was counted to him as righteousness" (Rom 4:3). Here the statement from Hebrews aptly describes what Paul means by faith: "Now faith is the assurance of things hoped for, the conviction of things not seen" (Heb 11:1). James, on the other hand, does not mean the same thing when he writes of faith: "You believe that God is one; you do well. Even the demons believe—and shudder!" (Jas 2:19). Does Paul have the faith of demons in view when he writes that "Abraham believed God"? No. As J. Gresham Machen (1881–1937) keenly observes: "The faith that James is condemning is not the faith that Paul is commending."[11] Conversely, one can say that the works Paul condemns are not the works James commends. In other words, Paul condemns the works of legalism. whereas James commends good works as the fruit of faith.

James and Paul speak of justification in different senses. When Paul speaks of justification, he has in view the legal-forensic verdict that God declares over sinners who place their faith in Christ for salvation. Paul writes, "For by works of the law no human being will be justified in his sight, since through the law comes knowledge of sin" (Rom 3:20). James, however, speaks of justification in a different sense: "Was not Abraham our father justified by works when he offered up his son Isaac on the altar?" (Jas 2:21).[12] James does not have a legal verdict in view, but writes of justification in terms of *vindication* or *confirmation*. This is the manner in which Christ uses the term when he says: "Wisdom is justified by her deeds" (Matt 11:19);

---

10. Turretin, *Institutes of Elenctic Theology* 16.9.22; also, e.g., Luke Timothy Johnson, *The Letter of James*, AB 37a (New York: Doubleday, 1995), 64.

11. J. Gresham Machen, *The New Testament: An Introduction to Its Literature and History* (Edinburgh: Banner of Truth, 1986), 238–39.

12. Davids, *Epistle of James*, 127–28; see also Moo, *Letter of James*, 132–36.

in other words, wisdom will be proven right by her deeds in comparison to the deeds of foolishness.[13] This means that according to Paul, God justifies the *believer* by faith alone in Christ alone, and according to James God justifies the believer's *faith* by the believer's works.[14]

Faith "is the alone instrument of justification: yet is it not alone in the person justified, but is every accompanied with all other saving graces, and is no dead faith, but worketh by love" (WCF 11.2). This means that one of the ways to distinguish genuine from counterfeit faith is whether professing Christians have the fruit of good works in their lives. There are various statements in Scripture that point to the role of works confirming the genuineness of faith. Beyond James's epistle, Jesus teaches:

> Beware of false prophets, who come to you in sheep's clothing but inwardly are ravenous wolves. You will recognize them by their fruits. Are grapes gathered from thornbushes, or figs from thistles? So, every healthy tree bears good fruit, but the diseased tree bears bad fruit. A healthy tree cannot bear bad fruit, nor can a diseased tree bear good fruit. Every tree that does not bear good fruit is cut down and thrown into the fire. Thus you will recognize them by their fruits. (Matt 7:15–20)[15]

Genuine faith produces the fruit of works, which is a point that Jesus also makes in the parable of the sower. The seed that the sower cast on the good soil produced "grain, growing up and increasing and yielding thirtyfold and sixtyfold and a hundredfold" (Mark 4:8), whereas the seed that "fell among thorns ... yielded no grain" (Mark 4:7). To this end Paul exhorts the Corinthians, "Examine yourselves, to see whether you are in the faith. Test yourselves. Or do you not realize this about yourselves, that Jesus Christ is in you?" (2 Cor 13:5).[16] Likewise, Peter writes: "Be all the more diligent to confirm your calling and election, for if you practice these qualities you

13. Donald A. Hagner, *Matthew 1–13*, WBC 33a (Dallas: Word, 1993), 311.
14. Turretin, *Institutes of Elenctic Theology* 16.8.4–6.
15. Hagner, *Matthew 1–13*, 183–84.
16. Charles Hodge, *1 & 2 Corinthians* (Edinburgh: Banner of Truth, 1994), 681–82.

will never fall" (2 Pet 1:10).[17] John also writes: "And by this we know that we have come to know him, if we keep his commandments" (1 John 2:3).[18]

Historically, Reformed theologians have explained the relationship between faith, its fruit, and self-examination under the idea of the *syllogismus practicus* ("the practical syllogism"). William Perkins gives a common version of the syllogism:

> Major premise: Only those who have genuine faith produce good works.
>
> Minor premise: By the grace of God, I produce good works.
>
> Conclusion: Therefore, I possess a genuine faith.[19]

Some have criticized Perkins and claim that John Calvin never taught the syllogism on the grounds that it averts the Christian's eyes from Christ and turns the gaze faith within.[20] The historical claim of Calvin versus the so-called Calvinists is both erroneous and beyond the scope of this section.[21] Nevertheless, it is important to observe that Perkins characterizes the syllogism as "an application of the promises of the gospel in the form of a practical syllogism."[22] The practical syllogism is a secondary means of assurance that rests on the primary means, which is the sovereign grace of the Father, the saving work of Christ, and the applicatory work of the Spirit.[23]

Based on the various passages of Scripture that exhort making one's calling and election sure, the historic Reformed tradition has taught that believers can receive assurance of their salvation "not by inquisitive searching into the hidden and deep things of God, but by noticing within

---

17. Calvin, *Hebrews and 1 & 2 Peter*, 334.

18. Stott, *Letters of John*, 95.

19. William Perkins, *An Exposition of the Creed*, in *The Works of William Perkins*, ed. Joel R. Beeke and Derek W. H. Thomas (Grand Rapids: Reformation Heritage Books, 2014–20), 5:337.

20. E.g., R. T. Kendall, *Calvin and English Calvinism to 1649* (Milton Keyes, UK: Paternoster, 1997), 8–9, 33–34, 69–74.

21. On the historical question see Richard A. Muller, *Calvin and the Reformed Tradition: On the Work of Christ and the Order of Salvation* (Grand Rapids: Baker Academic, 2012), 244–76.

22. Perkins, *Exposition of the Creed*, 337.

23. Joel R. Beeke and Mark Jones, *A Puritan Theology: Doctrine for Life* (Grand Rapids: Reformation Heritage Books, 2012), 593.

themselves, with spiritual joy and holy delight, the unmistakable fruits of election pointed out in God's Word—such as true faith in Christ, a childlike fear of God, a godly sorrow for their sins, a hunger and thirst for righteousness, and so on" (Canons of Dort 1.12).[24] Likewise, the Westminster Confession states that good works, "done in obedience to God's commandments, are the fruits and evidences of a true and lively faith" (16.2). And like Perkins, who characterized the practical syllogism as a secondary means of assurance, the confession explains that the certainty of salvation is "an infallible assurance of faith founded upon the divine truth of the promises of salvation, the inward evidence of those graces unto which these promises are made, [and] the testimony of the Spirit of adoption witnessing with our spirits that we are children of God" (18.2). The Westminster divines sandwich the "inward evidence" (i.e., the result of the practical syllogism) between the "promises of salvation" and the "testimony of the Spirit."[25] In short, one of the ways to distinguish true from counterfeit faith is to examine whether there are fruits and evidences of a lively faith or whether a person's faith is merely a nominal profession barren of any fruit. As Christ teaches, "Beware of false prophets, who come to you in sheep's clothing but inwardly are ravenous wolves. You will recognize them by their fruits" (Matt 7:15–16).

## SECOND-BLESSING THEOLOGY

If counterfeit faith is a manifestation of the spirit of antinomianism, then second-blessing theology (aka perfectionism, higher-life, and Keswick views) is a symptom of legalism.[26] While there are a number of different branches in the second-blessing tree, they all

24. G. C. Berkouwer, *Divine Election*, trans. Hugo Bekker, SD (Grand Rapids: Eerdmans, 1960), 285–86.

25. Joel R. Beeke, "The Assurance Debate: Six Key Questions," in *Drawn into Controversie: Reformed Theological Diversity and Debates within Seventeenth-Century British Puritanism*, ed. Michael A. G. Haykin and Mark Jones (Göttingen: Vandenhoeck & Ruprecht, 2011), 263–83, here 274; Jonathan Master, *A Question of Consensus: The Doctrine of Assurance after the Westminster Confession* (Minneapolis: Fortress, 2015), 130–36.

26. The most extensive examination of perfectionism comes from B. B. Warfield's two volumes of collected studies. See Warfield, *Perfectionism*, 2 vols., in *The Works of B. B. Warfield* 7–8 (Grand Rapids: Baker Books, 1981), esp. 7:345–99 and 8:463–611.

arguably originate with the theology of John Wesley (1703–1791).[27] Wesley promoted his notion of perfection as the idea that Christians could be wholly devoted to God in thought, word, and deed. He argues that Christians can cease from sinning—they can attain a state of perfection. Achieving perfection means attaining a higher state of salvation than those who are initially saved. By perfection, however, Wesley means that a Christian is wholly devoted to God, both inwardly and outwardly. This state of perfection does not mean that a Christian might never sin. Wesley stipulates that a Christian will cease from voluntary sin but might nevertheless commit involuntary sins—transgressions performed out of ignorance or mistakes. Wesley conceives of justification and sanctification occurring in two distinct phases. When a person professes faith in Christ, God immediately justifies that person. However, ordinarily there is a considerable amount of time before a person's complete sanctification begins.[28] The perfection of sanctification constitutes the higher life or second blessing; this is Wesley's chief contribution to higher-life views that separate justification from sanctification.[29]

One of the key players in higher-life theology is William E. Boardman (1810–1886), who published *The Higher Christian Life*.[30] Like Wesley, Boardman divided his doctrine of salvation into two distinct phases, initial conversion (or justification) and a second higher state (or sanctification), which both constitute full salvation. This second stage, or second conversion, sometimes occurs years after the first. In the second conversion the Christian enters a more profound union with Christ through a deeper work of grace. In the first conversion Christians receive Christ for their justification, and in their second they receive him for their sanctification. In the second conversion Christians enter into a state of perfection.

---

27. B. B. Warfield, "The German Higher Life Movement in Its Chief Exponent," in *Works of B. B. Warfield* 7:345–99, here 369; Andrew David Naselli, "Keswick Theology: A Survey and Analysis of the Doctrine of Sanctification in the Early Keswick Movement," *Detroit Baptist Seminary Journal* 13 (2008): 17–67, here 18–20. For an overview of second-blessing theology, see Andrew David Naselli, *No Quick Fix: Where Higher Life Theology Came From, What It Is, and Why It's Harmful* (Bellingham, WA: Lexham Press, 2017).

28. John Wesley, *A Plain Account of Christian Perfection*, 5th ed. (London: J. Paramore, 1785), 3, 16–17, 26, 29, 37, 39–40, 67, 72–73.

29. Naselli, "Keswick Theology," 20.

30. For a biographical and theological overview of Boardman's life, see B. B. Warfield, "The 'Higher Life' Movement," in *Works of B. B. Warfield* 8:463–558, here 466–91.

Even though believers receive justification and sanctification by faith in Christ, faith initially lays hold of Christ for only justification in the first conversion experience. But only when Christians fully trust Christ do they experience the second conversion and receive Christ for their sanctification. There is a radical difference between the pardon of sins (justification) and the purging of sins (sanctification); this second work of Christ occurs well after the first.[31]

The second conversion creates the perfected state, which is also marked by an "obedient and trustful" faith. Boardman believes that the Bible reveals these two phases of salvation in Old Testament Israel's redemption from Egypt. Their initial conversion occurred in the Red Sea crossing, but their second conversion transpired when they actually entered the promised land: "Like them we have the two stages, and the two works, and both by faith, and both to learn." There are many Christians who willingly accept the first conversion but struggle to enter the second because they are unwilling to be wholly conformed to Christ. The second conversion coincides with the baptism of the Spirit, which is the "higher experience." This means that there are two types of Christians in the world: those who are in the first phase of conversion and those who are in the second phase. Those in the first phase have come to a realization that they are sinners, whereas those at the second have made the transition from Romans 7 to Romans 8. Second-blessing Christians have moved from the struggle with sin to complete salvation in Christ; second-conversion Christians no longer have a Savior far off in heaven but one near to them on earth. The way a person enters the second stage of salvation is to look beyond ministers of the gospel and their preaching and go straight to the teaching of Jesus.[32]

Wesley's and Boardman's views appear in the theology of other second-blessing theologians and denominations, such as A. B. Simpson (1843–1919), founder of the Christian and Missionary Alliance; Evan Henry Hopkins (1837–1918), a founder of the Keswick conference movement in England; and Dwight Lyman Moody (1837–1899). Similar two-stage views of salvation appear among dispensational theologians Lewis Sperry Chafer

31. W. E. Boardman, *The Higher Christian Life* (Boston: Henry Hoyt, 1858), 45, 47–48, 51, 53, 63, 66–67, 94, 98–99, 116.

32. Boardman, *Higher Christian Life*, 138, 141, 149, 198, 237, 265–69, 281, 320.

(1871–1952) and John F. Walvoord (1910–2002).[33] Wesleyan higher-life and Keswick views of salvation still have contemporary advocates within broader evangelicalism.[34]

There are several problematic elements concerning higher-life views of salvation, including (1) subjectivism, (2) separating justification from sanctification, and (3) legalism. The first problem with higher-life views of salvation is that they are marked by a pronounced emphasis on experiential subjectivism. A subjective reception of salvation is unquestionably a mark of the Christian life, but not to the point that it becomes the defining characteristic. In his book on the higher life, for example, Boardman repeatedly stresses the experience of second conversion, and rather than rest his arguments on exegesis, he highlights the experiences of various prominent figures from church and biblical history who supposedly experienced a second conversion. While frequency statistics do not reveal everything about a book, Boardman uses the term "experience" 158 times in a book that is 344 pages long, whereas "sanctification" only occurs 49 times and "justification" only 14 times. The higher-life movement is part of a larger subjectivist trend that was fed by mysticism, Romanticism, and revivalism, wherein experience rather than Scripture shaped theological conviction.[35] This trend continues among contemporary advocates of higher-life theology who make repeated appeals to "experience" and a necessary "crisis moment" of sanctification.[36]

The second error is separating justification from sanctification. Second-blessing theologians do not rend justification and sanctification asunder, as if to say that a person could be justified but never sanctified.[37] Nevertheless,

---

33. Naselli, "Keswick Theology," 23, 25, 27; Randall Gleason, "B. B. Warfield and Lewis S. Chafer on Sanctification," *JETS* 40, no. 2 (1997): 241–58; John F. Walvoord, "The Augustinian-Dispensational Perspective," in *Five Views on Sanctification*, ed. Melvin E. Dieter (Grand Rapids: Zondervan, 1987), 197–226.

34. Melvin E. Dieter, "The Wesleyan Perspective," in Dieter, *Five Views*, 9–46, J. Robertson McQuilkin, "The Keswick Perspective," in Dieter, *Five Views*, 149–83.

35. E.g., Michael Gladwin, "Mission and Colonialism," in *The Oxford Handbook of Nineteenth-Century Christian Thought* (Oxford: Oxford University Press, 2017), 282–304, here 293–94; also Simeon Zahl, "Experience," in *Oxford Handbook of Nineteenth-Century Christian Thought*, 177–95; Sydney E. Ahlstrom, *A Religious History of the American People* (New Haven: Yale University Press, 1972), 415–54.

36. E.g., Dieter, "Wesleyan Perspective," 12, 13, 17, 18, 19, 20, 38, 40, 41, 42, 43.

37. E.g., Dieter, "Wesleyan Perspective," 20.

they stretch the relationship between the two benefits of union with Christ to say that there is typically a time delay between the reception of them. There is, however, no indication in Scripture that justification and sanctification are in any way separated by a time delay. The same Spirit of Christ who gives the gift of justifying faith is also the Spirit of sanctification. In the words of Edward Fisher's (1627–1655) *Marrow of Modern Divinity*: "Believe it then, I beseech you, that Christ Jesus will either be a whole Saviour or no Saviour, he will either save you alone, or not save you at all."[38] As Paul writes: "We were buried therefore with him by baptism into death, in order that [ἵνα], just as Christ was raised from the dead by the glory of the Father, we too might walk in newness of life" (Rom 6:4; also see 7:6).[39] Paul's use of a ἵνα clause shows that the point of salvation is to walk in the newness of life. Justified Christians walk in the newness of life because they "walk not according to the flesh but according to the Spirit" (Rom 8:4). Believers in union with Christ receive the imputed "satisfaction, righteousness, and holiness of Christ," which renders them positionally holy in him through their justification (HC, q. 60).[40] At the same time, the moment of the Christian's union with Christ is also the alpha point of his sanctification. Correlatively, the Scriptures do not speak of two classes of Christians, those who are justified and those who are justified *and* sanctified. Paul, for example, only speaks of the natural man (ψυχικὸς ἄνθρωπος) and spiritual man (πνευματικὸς); there is no tertium quid (1 Cor 2:14).[41] When the Spirit regenerates a sinner, the person is "born again," by nature a child of wrath but made alive with Christ, raised according to his inner man, and "being renewed day by day" (John 3:3, 7; 1 Pet 1:3, 23; Eph 2:1–3;

38. Edward Fisher, *The Marrow of Modern Divinity*, 16th ed., ed. Thomas Boston (Glasgow: John Bryce, 1796), 101.

39. Moo, *Letter to the Romans*, 391–92.

40. Note that the historic Reformed tradition has not appealed to the concept of definitive sanctification, a novel category created by John Murray (1898–1975), who was influenced by Keswick higher-life views of sanctification. See John Murray, "Definitive Sanctification," in *Select Lectures in Systematic Theology*, Collected Writings 2 (Edinburgh: Banner of Truth, 2009), 277–84, and Murray, "The Agency in Definitive Sanctification," in *Select Lectures in Systematic Theology*, 277–84, 285–93. For the connections between the Keswick view of sanctification and Murray's view, see David D. Cho, *The Ground of Holy Life: A Reformed Response to the Holiness Movement in America with Progressive and Definitive Sanctification* (Eugene, OR: Resource, 2021), esp. 147–81; see also McQuilkin, "Keswick Perspective," 158–60.

41. Contra, e.g., Dieter, "Wesleyan Perspective," 32–33.

2 Cor 4:16). Those who are justified begin the process of sanctification the moment they are in union with Christ. They receive the whole Christ and the double grace of justification and sanctification.

The third error is that higher-life theology is often marked by legalism, or works-righteousness.[42] When Wesley, for example, claims that Christians can achieve a level of perfection, he can make this claim only by redefining sin as voluntary and willful acts of sin; he passes by sins done in ignorance.[43] Yet the Bible clearly presents violations of God's law, even done in ignorance, as sin (Lev 5:17), and to violate part of the law is to break the whole law (Jas 2:10). If there were ever a highly sanctified saint, it was the apostle Paul, one who was willing to be cut off from Christ for his fellow Israelites that they might embrace the gospel (Rom 9:1–5). Yet Paul nevertheless writes: "Not that I have already obtained this or am already perfect, but I press on to make it my own, because Christ Jesus has made me his own" (Phil 3:12). Paul prays for the total sanctification of the Philippians, but he also knows that this will not occur until "the day of Christ" (Phil 1:10), which is why he acknowledges that he is imperfect. He reminds the Philippians, "He who began a good work in you will bring it to completion at the day of Jesus Christ" (Phil 1:6).[44]

The Bible teaches that the Spirit begins his transforming work of sanctification and that it touches on the whole person—every faculty—intellect, will, and affections (1 Thess 5:23). At the same time, until the Christian's glorification there is an ongoing struggle. This is why John explains: "If we say we have no sin, we deceive ourselves, and the truth is not in us. If we confess ours sins, he is faithful and just to forgive us our sins and to cleanse us from all unrighteousness" (1 John 1:8–9).[45] Paul describes sanctification

---

42. There are legalistic statements among some proponents: "The law in this sense becomes a gospel" (Dieter, "Wesleyan Perspective," 26). Or, "Faith is a choice to commit all of oneself unconditionally to the person of God" (McQuilkin, "Keswick Perspective," 169). There are outright explicit works-salvation statements among historic perfectionist theologians such as Charles Finney, who writes: "Some theologians have made justification a condition of sanctification instead of making sanctification a condition of justification. But this we shall see is an erroneous view of the subject" (Finney, *Lectures on Systematic Theology* [Oberlin, OH: James M. Fitch, 1847], 106). See also Warfield, "'Higher Life' Movement," 493, 555.

43. For sin as only voluntary action, see also McQuilkin, "Keswick Perspective," 171–72.

44. Moises Silva, *Philippians*, 2nd ed., BECNT (Grand Rapids: Baker Academic, 2005), 52–53.

45. Stott, *Letters of John*, 81–82.

in terms of a battle: "For the desires of the flesh are against the Spirit, and the desires of the Spirit are against the flesh, for these are opposed to each other, to keep you from doing the things you want to do" (Gal 5:17).[46] But in the end, he holds out hope: "For sin will have no dominion over you, since you are not under law but under grace" (Rom 6:14).[47] Thus, the Westminster Confession states: "In which war, although the remaining corruption, for a time, may much prevail; yet, through the continual supply of strength from the sanctifying Spirit of Christ, the regenerate part doth overcome; and so, the saints grow in grace, perfecting holiness in the fear of God" (13.3).

## CONCLUSION

ANTINOMIANISM AND LEGALISM ARE THREATS to the church and the gospel. Both errors turn the Christian's gaze away from Christ. Antinomians turn away from Christ's word and his Spirit of sanctification; they turn away from union with Christ and foolishly believe a counterfeit faith will survive divine scrutiny. Legalists turn away from Christ by looking within and believe they can achieve a state of perfection. The remedy for both errors is holding the law and gospel up to our hearts. The law shows us how far we fall short and that Christ is our only hope. The gospel is the balm to our guilt-stricken consciences in the face of the law's demands and imparts to us unending peace, joy, and sinless perfection when Christ glorifies us through the Spirit. Maranatha, come quickly, Lord Jesus.

### FURTHER READING

Beeke, Joel R. "The Assurance Debate: Six Key Questions." In *Drawn into Controversie: Reformed Theological Diversity and Debates within Seventeenth-Century British Puritanism*, edited by Michael A. G. Haykin and Mark Jones, 263–83. Göttingen: Vandenhoeck & Ruprecht, 2011. An excellent survey of the key issues that have been discussed in the debates over the doctrine of assurance within the Reformed churches.

46. Moo, *Galatians*, 354.
47. Moo, *Letter to the Romans*, 410–15.

Naselli, Andrew David. *No Quick Fix: Where Higher Life Theology Came From, What It Is, and Why It's Harmful*. Bellingham, WA: Lexham Press, 2017. A helpful and brief survey of the origins and errors of the higher life movement; recommended reading.

Warfield, B. B. *The Works of B. B. Warfield*. Volumes 7–8. Grand Rapids: Baker Books, 1981. Volumes on the history and theology of the various forms of perfectionism. Warfield's volumes are required reading for anyone who wants thorough studies on this topic.

XIII

# LIFE IN THE SPIRIT

## ENJOYING GOD FOREVER

THE ANSWER TO THE OPENING question of the Westminster Shorter Catechism gives an important framework for understanding life in the Spirit: "Man's chief end is to glorify God, and to enjoy him forever" (q. 1). Even though this question was aimed at children and novitiates in the faith, it has deep currents of theological truth that set forth the twin goals of life in the Spirit. This chapter therefore explains the nature of the Shorter Catechism's answer in two parts. First, what it means to enjoy God and how enjoying him creates the framework for living the Christian life. Second, life in the Spirit consists in faith and repentance, prayer, seeking Christian maturity, and bearing fruit, which are the means by which we glorify God. The chapter concludes with some brief observations about glorifying God and enjoying him forever—the twin foci of life in the Spirit.

### ENJOYING GOD

ST. AUGUSTINE PROVIDES AN IMPORTANT distinction between using versus enjoying something in his work *On Christian Teaching*: "There are some things which are to be enjoyed, some which are to be used, and some whose function is both to enjoy and to use." "To enjoy something," writes Augustine, "is to hold fast to it in love for its own sake," whereas "to use something is to apply whatever it may be to the purpose of obtaining what you love." Augustine applies these ideas to the Christian life by showing how we are like pilgrims on a journey far from the Lord. If we desire to return to our homeland, where we can be happy, we must use this world, but we must not enjoy it. Rather, as we use the world, we must discern how it points beyond itself to God's "invisible attributes, namely, his eternal power and divine nature" (Rom 1:20). Or, in other words, we "derive eternal and spiritual value from corporeal and temporal things." If we merely use the creation but fail to turn our gaze to God, then we have misused it. God made the world to point us to him, not as an end in and of itself. Only when we use the creation as God intended can we truly enjoy it because it turns our attention to God through faith and worship. Thus, Augustine writes: "The things which are to be enjoyed, then, are the Father and the Son and the Holy Spirit, and the Trinity." What lies at the heart of enjoying God, according to Augustine, is love: "By love I mean the impulse of one's mind to enjoy God on his own account and to enjoy oneself and one's neighbor on account of God."[1]

The use-and-enjoyment dynamic appears in numerous places throughout the Scriptures. Augustine rightly points to Paul's statements in Romans 1 and how the creation points beyond itself to God. If we rightly use the creation, it leads us to worship God, not turning the creation into an object of worship. Similarly, God enabled the Israelites to plunder the Egyptians (Exod 11:2–3; 12:35–36). They received gold, silver, jewelry, and fine clothing. God intended Israel to use this wealth as a means to create the desert tabernacle, which would have enabled them to use it and, more importantly, enjoy God by worshiping him. Instead, they misused the wealth to create the golden calf—they did not use the wealth as God intended, and thus they neither rightly used it nor enjoyed God (Exod 32). God gives his people many gifts, but they are not ends in themselves. Paul rebukes the Corinthians for taking the gifts of the Spirit and using them for personal aggrandizement rather than edifying the church. He presses the question, "What do you have that you did not receive? If then you receive it, why do you boast as if you did not receive it?" (1 Cor 4:7). The Corinthians were supposed to use the gifts to point others to the Triune God, not themselves, and by so doing enjoy the gifts and glorify God. In this vein, properly used, everything in this creation leads to the enjoyment and glory

1. Augustine, *On Christian Teaching* 1.7–10, 3.37 (pp. 9–10, 76).

of God: "So, whether you eat or drink, or whatever you do, do all to the glory of God" (1 Cor 10:31).

Even in our love for one another, we must recognize the divine telos. God commands us to love one another (John 13:34; 15:12, 17), but are we supposed to love people for their own sake or for some other reason? If we love people purely for themselves, then we enjoy them; but if we love them for another reason, then we use them, not in the sense of exploiting someone but rather "using them" in the manner God intended. "For if something is to be loved on its own account, it is made to constitute the happy life, even if it is not as yet the reality but hope of it which consoles us at this time. But 'cursed is he who puts his hope in a man' [Jer 17:5]."[2] Thus, in our love for one another the telos of our love must be the Triune God, not the person, lest we turn the person into an idol and seek enjoyment not in God but in humanity.[3] As divine image-bearers, the capability to enjoy God is a unique gift, an ability not found in animals, who only act according to natural instinct (*ST* Ia IIae, q. 16, arts 2–3). The Christian life is therefore the pursuit of the love of God, glorifying and enjoying him forever, a goal we will find at the consummation as we behold the beatific vision in Christ (*ST* Ia IIae, q. 16, art 3).[4]

## LIFE IN THE SPIRIT

Glorifying God and enjoying him forever is both the road and destination of the Christian life—it is not something that awaits the eschaton but is a present reality. At the same time, given that our salvation is incomplete and we struggle with abiding sin, life in the Spirit is one wherein we repent of our sins, seek the power of Christ's Spirit through prayer, and strive to grow in grace that we might bear the fruit of holiness.

### *Faith and Repentance*

The Westminster Shorter Catechism defines sin as "any want of conformity unto, or transgression of,

2. Augustine, *On Christian Teaching* 1.40 (pp. 16–17).

3. Matthew Levering, *The Theology of Augustine: An Introductory Guide to His Most Important Works* (Grand Rapids: Baker Academic, 2013), 3–8; Peter Lombard, *The Sentences*, trans. Giulio Silano (Toronto: PIMS, 2007), 1.3.4.

4. Michael Allen, *Grounded in Heaven: Recentering Christian Hope and Life on God* (Grand Rapids: Eerdmans, 2018).

the law of God" (q. 14). Violations of God's law are more than transgressing a moral standard—breaking a rule. The Scriptures regularly pair obedience and love (Deut 6:4–6; 11:13; 30:16; Matt 22:37–39). This is why John writes, "By this we know that we love the children of God, when we love God and obey his commandments" (1 John 5:2). When we sin, we fall short of the goals of the Christian life—we fail to glorify and enjoy God. We take the blessings of salvation and merely use them, or we outright violate God's commands. By God's grace he convicts us when we sin through the work of the Spirit, and he opens a door to repentance, to turning away from our sin. Repentance is not merely for the entry point to the Christian life, something unbelievers do when they embrace Christ by the gift of faith; rather, repentance should characterize life in the Spirit (e.g., WSC, q. 87).

When we repent, we must intellectually grasp the nature of our sin, as Paul explains that the law reveals the "knowledge of sin" (Rom 3:20). Sin is not merely a subjective state wherein we feel bad but the objective violation of God's moral law, a transgression we must understand. The sinner must recognize the "filthiness and odiousness of his sins, as contrary to the holy nature, and righteous law of God" (WCF 15.2). When we repent, we should have a change of feeling, which becomes manifest in sorrow for the sin we have committed against our holy God. David's heartfelt cries when he repented of his sins against God, Uriah the Hittite, and Bathsheba revealed his sorrow: "Have mercy on me, O God, according to your steadfast love. ... Against you, you only, have I sinned and done what is evil in your sight" (Ps 51:1, 4). The sinner "grieves for, and hates his sins" (WCF 15.2).

When we repent there is a volitional element, which is manifest in willing to turn away from sin. As David writes: "Create in me a clean heart, O God, and renew a right spirit within me" (Ps 51:10).[5] The sinner turns from his sins and "unto God, purposing and endeavoring to walk with him in all the ways of his commandments" (WCF 15.2). When we repent, we must "endeavor to repent of ... particular sins, particularly" (15.5). That is, we should not throw a generic blanket of repentance over our actions—"Forgive me of my sins, whatever they are"—but rather we should seek

---

5. Berkhof, *Systematic Theology*, 486; Andre Rivet et al., *Synopsis Purioris Theologiae/Synopsis of a Purer Theology*, ed. Henk van den Belt et al. (Leiden: Brill, 2016), 33.16–24 (2:282–89).

to repent of specific sins. We can do so privately for sins committed in private but also publicly for sins we commit in public (15.6). We belong to the church, and when we sin against others, we have a moral obligation to seek the forgiveness of those whom we have offended.

*Prayer* REPENTANCE IN THE CHRISTIAN LIFE is not something that comes from the natural abilities of the believer but is a work of the Spirit—repentance comes from our union with Christ: "I am the vine; you are the branches. Whoever abides in me and I in him, he it is that bears much fruit, for apart from me you can do nothing" (John 15:5). For this reason the "Spirit helps us in our weakness" when "we do not know what to pray" (Rom 8:26).[6] C. S. Lewis (1898–1963) beautifully expresses the Spirit's work: "Take not, oh Lord, our literal sense. Lord, in thy great, unbroken speech our limping metaphor translate."[7] The Spirit intercedes in our prayers because we are in union with Christ and have our high priest and covenant surety, who sits at the right hand of the Father in the heavenly holy of holies. In prayer we do not come to God in an effort to bend the divine will in an earthly direction but rather to seek to have our will conformed to God's will (*ST* IIa IIae q. 83 art. 2).[8] We must ask whether we are merely using prayer or enjoying God in prayer. Are we using prayer in the manner that God intended, which is to seek conformity to Christ, or do we seek the fulfillment of our will? The words of the Book of Common Prayer capture the penitent confession where one turns away from self and to God: "Almighty and most merciful Father, we have erred and strayed from thy ways like lost sheep, we have followed too much the devices and desires of our own hearts."[9]

As John Calvin explains: "For [God] ordained it not so much for his own sake as for ours."[10] Again, Lewis has a helpful observation in this regard:

---

6. Rivet et al., *Synopsis Purioris* 33.25 (2:288–91).

7. C. S. Lewis, *Poems*, ed. Walter Hooper (New York: Harcourt Brace Jovanovich, 1965), 129.

8. See also Karl Barth, *Prayer: 50th Anniversary Edition*, ed. Don E. Saliers, trans. Sara F. Terrien (Louisville: Westminster John Knox, 2002), 19.

9. "Morning Prayer I," in *Book of Common Prayer* (1979), 41.

10. Calvin, *Inst.* 3.20.3.

> There are, no doubt, passages in the New Testament which may seem at first sight to promise an invariable granting of our prayers. But that cannot be what they really mean. For in the very heart of the story we meet a glaring instance to the contrary. In Gethsemane the holiest of all petitioners prayed three times that a certain cup might pass from Him. It did not. After that the idea that prayer is recommended to us as a sort of infallible gimmick may be dismissed.[11]

Prayer is the arena into which believers enter to present their desires before God but at the same time to seek conformity to God's will.[12] Like Christ in the garden of Gethsemane, who prayed, "Not my will but thine be done," in prayer we glorify God and enjoy him. The only way Christians can discover God's will, so they can pray according to it, is to immerse themselves in his word. Prayer is a grand cathedral whose architecture bears the marks of Scripture and is where God and humans meet in holy communion.

### *Maturity and Fruit*

Prayer is a part of the means of grace (word, sacraments, and prayer)—the means by which we can receive the grace of the gospel to fuel our growth in the Christian life. Christians often struggle with their sanctification because they do not live for the twin foci of glorifying God and enjoying him forever. Augustine confesses that his chief problem prior to his conversion was that he tried to find fulfillment in earthly things when only God would suffice: "My sin consisted in this, that I sought pleasure, sublimity, and truth not in God but in his creatures, in myself and other created beings. So it was that I plunged into miseries, confusions, and errors."[13] Augustine's statement describes his preconversion sin, but this same pattern continues after conversion. Christians sin—they seek pleasure in themselves and creatures rather than in God. The apostle Paul provides a catalog of vices in his epistle to the Galatian churches: "The works of the flesh are evident: sexual

---

11. C. S. Lewis, "The Efficacy of Prayer," in *The World's Last Night and Other Essays* (New York: Harcourt Brace Jovanovich, 1959), 5.

12. Herman Witsius, *Lord's Prayer*, trans. William Pringle (Phillipsburg, NJ: P&R, 1994), 46.

13. Augustine, *Confessions*, trans. Henry Chadwick (Oxford: Oxford University Press, 1991), 1.20.31 (pp. 22–23); see Rebecca Konyndyk DeYoung, *Glittering Vices: A New Look at the Seven Deadly Sins and Their Remedies* (Grand Rapids: Brazos, 2009), 38.

immorality, impurity, sensuality, idolatry, sorcery, enmity, strife, jealousy, fits of anger, rivalries, dissensions, divisions, envy, drunkenness, orgies, and things like these" (Gal 5:19–21). Conversely, Paul lists the fruit of the Spirit as love, joy, peace, patience, kindness, goodness, faithfulness, gentleness, and self-control (Gal 5:22–23). The pursuit of the Christian life is to live in the power of the Spirit rather than according to the desires of the flesh.

But pursuit of life in the Spirit is not about pulling yourself up by your moral bootstraps and trying harder to be holy. Peter explains that God's "divine power has granted to us all things that pertain to life and godliness, through the knowledge of him who called us to his own glory and excellence, by which he has granted to us his precious and very great promises, so that through them you may become partakers of the divine nature, having escaped from the corruption that is in the world because of sinful desire" (2 Pet 1:3–4). Peter underscores the indicatives of the Christian life by laying a foundation in God's power, his promises, and our participation in the divine nature, our union with Christ, as the source of our holiness. On the basis of these indicatives, Peter gives imperatives: "For this very reason, make every effort to supplement your faith with virtue, and virtue with knowledge, and knowledge with self-control, and self-control with steadfastness, and steadfastness with godliness, and godliness with brotherly affection, and brotherly affection with love" (2 Pet 1:5–7).[14] We must make every effort to supplement our faith with godly virtue but do so by drawing on the power of the Spirit of Christ.

Key to growth in grace, Christian maturity, and producing the fruit of holiness is developing the habit of virtue. "Virtue," writes William Ames (1576–1633), "is a condition or habit by which the will is inclined to do well."[15] Or, according to Augustine, "I hold that virtue is nothing other than the perfect love of God."[16] In order to act in a holy manner, to love God, Christians must practice holiness and love: "Solid food is for the mature,

---

14. DeYoung, *Glittering Vices*, 87–88.

15. William Ames, *The Marrow of Theology*, trans. John Dykstra Eusden (Grand Rapids: Baker Books, 1968), 2.2.4 (p. 224). For what follows, see Luca Baschera, "Ethics in Reformed Orthodoxy," in *A Companion to Reformed Orthodoxy*, ed. Herman J. Selderhuis (Leiden: Brill, 2013), 519–52, here esp. 527–30.

16. Augustine, *On the Morals of the Catholic Church* 15.25, in *NPNF*[1] 4:48; DeYoung, *Glittering Vices*, 27.

for those who have their powers of discernment trained [ἕξιν] by constant practice to distinguish good from evil" (Heb 5:14).[17] Here the author says that mature Christians have developed a ἕξις ("habit") to discern between good and evil.[18] According to Paul, the way that Christians develop a habit for holiness is by setting the mind on "whatsoever things are true, whatsoever things are honest, whatsoever things are just, whatsoever things are pure, whatsoever things are lovely, whatsoever things are of good report; if there be any virtue [ἀρετὴ], and if there be any praise, think on these things" (Phil 4:8 KJV).[19] The chief place where Christians find virtue is in Christ and his word, the revealed will of God (*ST* IIIa, prologue).[20] As Ames rightly observes, "There can be no other teaching of the virtues than theology which brings the whole revealed will of God to the directing of our reason, will, and life."[21]

Developing Christian virtue amounts to resting in the power and promises of the gospel of Christ by drawing nigh to him through the means of grace. By entering into the presence of Christ, we share and enjoy a communion with the Triune God, a communion of holiness, love, and virtue in which simply by being in his presence God transforms us into his image. Like Moses, whose face shone the glory of God simply by being in his presence, so too we more and more reflect the glory of Christ by being in his presence through word, sacrament, and prayer. As we rest in the presence of Christ, he works in us to "will and to work for his good pleasure" (Phil 2:13). God's grace in Christ empowers us to grow in grace, to develop a habit of Christian virtues.[22] These virtues, of course, are the long-promised fulfillment of the eschatological outpouring of the Spirit. In the face of Israel's disobedience and absence of love for God, he promised to pour out his Spirit on the house of Israel from on high so that streams of living water would soak the dry ground, the wilderness would become a fruitful field, and he would cause his people to walk in his statutes—obey his law (Isa 32:15; 44:3; Ezek 36:27; 39:29). In short, the Son's outpouring of the

---

17. Ames, *Marrow of Theology* 2.2.6 (p. 224).
18. Schreiner, *Commentary on Hebrews*, 172.
19. Ames, *Marrow of Theology* 2.2.7 (p. 225).
20. See also Ames, *Marrow of Theology* 2.2.13 (p. 225); DeYoung, *Glittering Vices*, 17.
21. Ames, *Marrow of Theology* 2.2.16 (p. 226).
22. Ames, *Marrow of Theology* 2.2.42 (p. 231).

Spirit is the means by which God enables his people to obey his commandments by loving him with all of their hearts, souls, minds, and strength and loving their neighbors as themselves (Deut 10:16; 30:6; Matt 22:37–39).

## CONCLUSION

LOVE FOR GOD AND NEIGHBOR lie at the heart of life in the Spirit, a love that empowers repentance, prayer, and growth in grace. But our love for God and neighbor must keep the twin teloi of glorifying God and enjoying him forever in view. If we merely pursue moderation, courage, justice, and wisdom for the sake of self-love or earthly ends, we have missed the point of loving God and neighbor entirely. All of our virtues must keep the glory and enjoyment of God as their goal. Moderation is keeping one's self pure for God; courage is bearing hardship for God; justice is love only serving God, and wisdom is seeking that which points us to God (Augustine, *On the Morals of the Catholic Church* 15.25). The selfish use of the things of God's creation has led droves of people away from enjoying God. Augustine famously observed that the love for self and the love of God have created two cities:

> Love of self, even to the point of contempt for God, made the earthly city, and love of God, even to the point of contempt for self, made the heavenly city. Thus the former glories in itself, and the latter glories in the Lord. The former seeks its glory from men, but the latter finds its highest glory in God, the witness of our conscience. The former lifts up its head in its own glory; the latter says to its God, *My glory, and the one who lifts up my head* (Ps. 3:3). In the former the lust for domination dominates both its princes and the nations that it subjugates; in the latter both leaders and followers serve one another in love, the leaders by their counsel, the followers by their obedience. The former loves its own strength, displayed in its men of power; the latter says to its God, *I love you, O Lord, my strength* (Ps. 18:1).[23]

Godliness and holiness rest first in God's love for fallen sinners: "We love because he first loved us" (1 John 4:19). "What is man that you are mindful of him, and the son of man that you care for him?" (Ps 8:4). God takes a "little

23. Augustine, *City of God*, 2 vols., trans. William Babcock, The Works of Saint Augustine (Hyde Park, NY: New City Press, 2012), 14.28; DeYoung, *Glittering Vices*, 68.

piece" of his creation and raises us up from the mire of sin and the bondage to death so that we can love him.[24] But our love for God and neighbor will stay true only if we seek to love him by glorifying and enjoying him forever.

## FURTHER READING

Allen, Michael. *Grounded in Heaven: Recentering Christian Hope and Life on God*. Grand Rapids: Eerdmans, 2018. A study on the beatific vision, the goal of the Christian life—how believers will find fulfillment in beholding the face of God in the face of Christ. This is a relatively brief treatment but covers a lot of ground and is worthwhile reading.

Augustine. *City of God*. 2 vols. Translated by William Babcock. The Works of Saint Augustine. Hyde Park, NY: New City, 2012. A foundational text in the Western theological canon, sweeping in its scope. Among other topics, Augustine explains how Christians can live in the midst of the city of man while at the same time living as citizens in the city of God.

———. *On Christian Teaching*. Oxford: Oxford University Press, 2008. Another foundational text in the Western theological canon and thus worthwhile reading. Augustine explains how to read and teach Scripture in this work.

DeYoung, Rebecca Konyndyk. *Glittering Vices: A New Look at the Seven Deadly Sins and Their Remedies*. Grand Rapids: Brazos, 2009. An insightful book on the seven deadly sins. This work dissects the seven deadly sins and explains how pervasive they are, but at the same time offers remedies for addressing them. This book explores these sins from the perspective of Scripture and the history of the church. Well worth the investment of time to read it.

24. Augustine, *Confessions* 1.1 (Chadwick, p. 3).

XIV

# WITNESS AND MISSION

## CONTINUATION OR CESSATION?

Before Christ ascended to his royal session at his Father's right hand, he commissioned his church to preach the gospel to the ends of the earth: "All authority in heaven and on earth has been given to me. Go therefore and make disciples of all nations, baptizing them in the name of the Father and of the Son and of the Holy Spirit, teaching them to observe all that I have commanded you" (Matt 28:18–20). Christ's actions were that of the victorious Son of Man, one like Adam, who would now restore God's reign throughout the creation (Gen 1:28; Ps 8; Dan 7; Luke 22:69–71). God's chosen means of gathering the bride of Christ, the elect from every nation, is the foolishness of preaching (1 Cor 1:21). The word of God is the chief means by which the church testifies to the world—God's revelation empowers the church's mission to extend the kingdom of Christ to every tribe, tongue, and nation (Rev 14:6). Virtually all Christians recognize this truth, but not all agree on whether the written word of God is the sole instrument at God's disposal to gather the church.

In addition to Scripture, some maintain that extra-scriptural divine revelation and the spiritual gifts of miracles and speaking in tongues continue into the present day. This chapter briefly considers the question of whether revelation, the gift of miracles, and speaking in tongues continue. The short answer to this question is, no. These gifts have ceased, and word and sacraments are the sole means by which God gathers his elect. But arguing for the cessation of revelation, miraculous gifts, and speaking in tongues does not mean that the Reformed tradition tries to confine the sovereign work of the Spirit. Nor does it mean that the Reformed tradition has succumbed to an Enlightenment worldview, a devotion to modern scientific discovery, and unbridled arrogance that casually dismisses Scripture's claims.[1]

Rather, the historic Reformed tradition teaches the cessation of revelation and miraculous gifts because this is what the Bible teaches (WCF 1.1).[2] The chapter therefore first presents the claims of those who argue for the continuation of revelation, miraculous gifts, and tongues. Second, it explains where Scripture teaches cessationism. Third, it explains that the ceasing of revelation, tongues, and the gift of miracles does not strip the church of the prophetic word of God; this third section therefore unpacks the prophetic nature of the church's mission. The chapter concludes with summary observations about the absolute necessity for the word of God in the church's witness and mission.

## CONTINUATION

### *Revelation?*

Among the proponents of the continuation of revelation and miraculous gifts, Wayne Grudem presents one of the more detailed arguments.[3] Grudem identifies 1 Corinthians 14:37–38 as one of the most significant Pauline passages regarding the question of continuing prophecy in the New Testament period.[4] Paul writes: "Or was it from you that the word of God came? Or are you the only ones it has reached? If anyone thinks that he is a prophet, or spiritual, he should acknowledge that the things I am writing to you are a command of the Lord" (1 Cor 14:36–37). Grudem argues that Paul here distinguishes between

1. Contra Fee, *God's Empowering Presence*, 887–88.

2. On the meaning of "private spirits" (1.10), see Garnet H. Milen, "'Private Spirits' in the Westminster Confession of Faith and in Protestant-Catholic Debates: A Response to Byron Curtis," *WTJ* 61 (1999): 101–10; see also Bryon Curtis, "'Private Spirits' in the Westminster Confession of Faith 1.10 and in Catholic-Protestant Debate (1588–1652)," *WTJ* 58 (1996): 257–66.

3. For a discussion of the gifts of the Spirit, see ch. 11.

4. Wayne Grudem, *The Gift of Prophecy in 1 Corinthians* (Eugene, OR: Wipf & Stock, 1999), 50.

his own apostolic authority and the subordinate authority of New Testament prophets; in other words, there are two tiers of prophecy, apostolic and prophetic. New Testament prophets uttered divine revelation, but it might have been mixed with truth and error; thus the church had to weigh and evaluate it. The subordinate type of prophecy was different from the prophecy of the Old Testament or what appears in the book of Revelation. To delineate divine revelation from this subordinate type of revelation, Grudem places quotes around the term "revelation." The function of these New Testament prophets and their "revelation" was to edify the church, and this type of prophecy continues until Christ returns (1 Cor 13:10). Those who had the gift of prophecy were allowed to use their gift, but no one prophesied at will.[5]

*Tongues?* In addition to Grudem, other scholars argue that the gift of tongues continues into the present day. D. A. Carson did an extensive study on the work of the Spirit in 1 Corinthians 12–14 and comes to several conclusions regarding tongues. First, tongues is a gift of real cognitive languages, whether of angels or people. When the Spirit gave to a believer the gift of tongues, it meant the person had the ability to speak in a language that the believer had never previously learned or studied. Correlatively, the gift of interpretation is the ability to interpret a cognitive language that the person had never previously learned or studied (1 Cor 14:1–13). Like Grudem, Carson argues that 1 Corinthians 13:9–10 indicates that the gifts of tongues and interpretation continue: "For we know in part and we prophesy in part, but when the perfect comes, the partial will pass away" (1 Cor 13:9–10). In this case, τὸ τέλειον ("the perfect") refers not to the church's maturity, or the completed canon of Scripture, but to the return of Christ.[6]

*Gifts of Miracles?* In an essay that is representative of classical Pentecostalism, Douglas Oss argues for the continuation of the miraculous gifts. Oss frames the continuation of the miraculous gifts under the second blessing of the Spirit, where the Spirit

5. Grudem, *Gift of Prophecy*, 54, 66, 74, 179–80, 229, 239.

6. Carson, *Showing the Spirit*, 66–70, 83.

empowers believers in "charismatic" ways. Given that the Spirit can and does empower Christians in two distinct ways (regeneration and gifting), every believer should desire both experiences. Oss argues that all of the gifts of the Spirit in passages such as 1 Corinthians 12–14 appear to be not temporary or abnormal. This means, in addition to prophecy, tongues, and the interpretation of tongues, that "healing by the one Spirit" (1 Cor 12:10) is a continuing gift that believers can seek. Those beyond the apostolic band performed miracles, which were used to confirm the message of the gospel and were a common side effect of the advent of Christ's kingdom. Oss rejects the distinction between miraculous (e.g., healing) and nonmiraculous (e.g., acts of mercy) gifts, as he believes all of the gifts of the Spirit are miraculous. Therefore, signs and wonders accompany the preaching of the gospel in areas that are evangelized for the first time. Exorcisms are more common in areas dominated by Satan. Like Grudem and Carson, Oss believes that 1 Corinthians 13:8–10 refers to the return of Christ, and thus the gifts continue until the parousia.[7]

## THE CASE FOR CESSATIONISM

The claims that revelation, speaking in tongues, and the gift of miracles continue into the present hinge on the assumption that their first-century existence is normative for the entire inter-advental period, from Christ's ascension to his return. However, as Carson observes, the apostles are identified as gifts of the Spirit, yet few would argue that there are still apostles in the church. Thus, there is a prima facie case that at least one of the Spirit's gifts ceased to exist with the death of the apostles. Asking whether other gifts also expire is consequently not an unreasonable question.[8]

Moving forward, there are three parts of the cessationist argument: (1) there is only one type of prophecy in Scripture; there is no such thing as revelation versus "revelation"; (2) speaking in tongues is a form of divine

---

7. Douglas Oss, "A Pentecostal/Charismatic View," in *Are Miraculous Gifts for Today? Four Views*, ed. Wayne A. Grudem (Grand Rapids: Zondervan, 1996), 237–83, here 240, 242, 274, 277–78, 281, 274.

8. Carson, *Showing the Spirit*, 88; also Richard B. Gaffin Jr., "A Cessationist View," in Grudem, *Are Miraculous Gifts for Today?*, 23–64, here 45. For a historical survey of cessationism, see B. B. Warfield, *Counterfeit Miracles* (New York: Charles Scribner's Sons, 1918).

revelation; and (3) miracles accompany divine revelation to attest to its legitimacy, and thus with the cessation of revelation there is also cessation of the gift of miracles.

*Prophecy* KEY TO THE CLAIM OF ongoing prophecy and revelation is that there are two types, revelation and "revelation," or canonical versus congregational revelation. Proponents of this understanding base this on the fact that Paul instructed the Corinthians to test and verify the message of the prophets: "Let two or three prophets speak, and let the others weigh what is said" (1 Cor 14:29; see 1 Thess 5:20–21).[9] Yet, evaluating and weighing prophecy is something that God instructs his people to do in both the Old and New Testaments. God instructed the Israelites to see whether a prophet's words came true, and if they did not, they could ignore him (Deut 18:22).[10] Likewise, when Paul taught the Bereans, they too evaluated his teaching: "They received the word with all eagerness, examining the Scriptures daily to see if these things were so" (Acts 17:11).[11] In these instances, both prophet and prophecy merited evaluation. In the words of John, "Do not believe every spirit, but test the spirits to see whether they are from God, for many false prophets have gone out into the world" (1 John 4:1).[12] Testing therefore does not reveal two types of revelation; there is only one type of divine revelation, that which is given by God through the Spirit that testifies to the unfolding plan of redemption, which culminates in Christ, though not all prophecy was intended for inclusion in the canon.[13]

If there is only one type of divine revelation, then who in the New Testament were the bearers of prophecy? The New Testament reveals that there were two classes: the apostles and prophets. Fundamental to the cessationist case is what Paul says about the apostles and prophets: "You are fellow citizens with the saints and members of the household of God, built on the foundation of the apostles and prophets" (Eph 2:19–20). Paul says

9. Grudem, *Gift of Prophecy*, 66; see also Carson, *Showing the Spirit*, 94–100.

10. Peter C. Craigie, *The Book of Deuteronomy*, NICOT (Grand Rapids: 1976), 262–64.

11. Bock, *Acts*, 556.

12. Stott, *Letters of John*, 156–57.

13. Richard B. Gaffin Jr., *Perspectives on Pentecost: New Testament Teaching on the Gifts of the Holy Spirit* (Phillipsburg, NJ: P&R, 1979), 99–100.

that the apostles and prophets are part of the foundation of the church. Are we still in the foundation period of the church? No. If the gift of the apostles has passed with their death, and they were part of the foundation of the church, then it stands to reason that the prophets have also passed, since they too are part of the church's foundation.

Continuationist proponents such as Grudem argue that "built on the foundation of the apostles and prophets" is not the proper translation of the underlying Greek. Rather, he claims that Paul says, "built on the foundation of the apostles who are also prophets." Grudem bases his case on the lexeme τῶν ἀποστόλων καὶ προφητῶν and concludes that, since there is only one definite article, the anarthrous προφητῶν means that the reference is to one distinct group, not two.[14] Grudem concedes that there are occurrences of one group with two distinct components governed by one definite article (Acts 13:50; 15:2; Rom 1:20; 2 Cor 6:7; 7:3, 13, 11; Phil 1:19, 25; 2 Thess 1:4; 2:2).[15] Grudem's candor is welcome but ultimately undermines his claim, especially in light of the fact that no English translation renders Ephesians 2:20 in this manner (so ESV, KJV, NKJ, NLT-SE, NET, NIV, Weymouth, NAS, Young's, NRSV, TNIV; see also Eph 3:5).[16] Furthermore, had Paul written of the "prophets and the apostles," one might argue that he intended to refer to the Old Testament prophets and New Testament apostles, which would mean that the New Testament prophets were no longer consigned to the foundation. Yet, that Paul writes of "apostles and prophets" means that he refers to the New Testament rather than Old Testament prophets. Thus, the New Testament prophets were part of the foundation and passed with the apostles; there are no longer prophets in the postapostolic church.[17]

### *Speaking in Tongues*

THE GIFT OF TONGUES AND their interpretation is a form of divine revelation, of prophecy, evident when Paul writes: "For one who speaks in a tongue speaks not to men

---

14. Grudem, *Gift of Prophecy*, 82–105.

15. Grudem, *Gift of Prophecy*, 100; see also Carson, *Showing the Spirit*, 96–97.

16. Gaffin, "Cessationist View," 48; also Fee, *God's Empowering Presence*, 687n97; Daniel B. Wallace, "The Semantic Range of the Article-Noun-Kai-Noun Plural Construction in the New Testament," *GTJ* 4 (1983): 59–84; Baugh, *Ephesians*, 201–2.

17. Gaffin, "Cessationist View," 43–44; Gaffin, *Perspectives on Pentecost*, 95.

but to God; for no one understands him, but he utters mysteries in the Spirit" (1 Cor 14:2). That Paul says that the tongue-speaker utters divine revelation is apparent because the person πνεύματι δὲ λαλεῖ μυστήρια ("speaks mysteries by the Spirit").[18] Mysteries are something once hidden but now revealed, as Paul intimates: "Now to him who is able to strengthen you according to my gospel and the preaching of Jesus Christ, according to the revelation of the mystery that was kept secret for long ages but has now been disclosed and through the prophetic writings has been made known to all nations" (Rom 16:25–26).[19]

The question of whether the tongue-revelation was blessing or judgment on the church hinged on whether there was someone present with the gift of interpretation: "The one who prophesies is greater than the one who speaks in tongues, unless someone interprets, so that the church may be built up" (1 Cor 14:5). With interpretation, tongue-revelation was a means of blessing to the church. But apart from interpretation, tongue-revelation was means of judgment: "By people of strange tongues and by the lips of foreigners will I speak to this people, and even then they will not listen to me, says the Lord" (1 Cor 14:21; Isa 28:11).[20] The church would hear the word of God but not understand it, which is why Paul writes: "Tongues are a sign not for believers but for unbelievers, while prophecy is a sign not for unbelievers but for believers" (1 Cor 14:22). Tongue-revelation is therefore a form of prophecy and expired with the gift of prophets, since they were part of the foundation of the church.

### *The Gift of Miracles*

GIVEN THE PASSING OF THE apostles and prophets, the attending authenticating miracles have also expired with them. To be clear, the Reformed tradition does not claim that miracles have ceased or that God cannot or does not miraculously heal those who are ill. As the Westminster Confession observes, "God, in his ordinary providence, maketh use of means, yet is free to work without, above, and against them, at his pleasure" (5.3). Christians can and should pray for the miraculous healing of those who are ill: "The prayer of faith

18. Gaffin, *Perspectives on Pentecost*, 57.

19. *Pace* Fee, *God's Empowering Presence*, 218.

20. Gaffin, *Perspectives on Pentecost*, 103–9; also Robertson, "Tongues."

will save the one who is sick" (Jas 5:15). Similarly, the tradition does not say that demonic exorcism is impossible. Jesus, for example, told his disciples that some demons could only be exorcized by prayer (Mark 9:29).[21] Rather, to say that the gift of healing has expired means that those individuals who had the power directly and immediately to heal or cast out demons are no longer present in the church; the gift of healing expired with the passing of the generation of apostles and prophets because miracles that authenticate their message are longer required (2 Cor 12:12).[22]

In more technical terms, God gives revelation in both words and acts. In this case, the apostolic and prophetic word-revelation was confirmed by the act-revelation of miracles. With the cessation of word-revelation, there was a corresponding cessation of the accompanying act-revelation.[23] When Jesus, for example, forgave the paralytic of his sins (Mark 2:5), he followed this word-revelation with the act-revelation of healing: "'But that you may know that the Son of Man has authority on earth to forgive sins'—he said to the paralytic—'I say to you, rise, pick up your bed, and go home'" (Mark 2:10–11). The miraculous act-revelation of healing the paralytic authenticated Christ's word-revelation. The same pattern appears with the miracle of Jesus raising Lazarus from the dead. Jesus spoke his word-revelation: "I am the resurrection and the life. Whoever believes in me, though he die, yet shall he live, and everyone who lives and believes in me shall never die" (John 11:25–26). To confirm his word-revelation, he raised Lazarus through his miraculous act-revelation.[24]

### *1 Corinthians 13 and the Perfect?*

Appealing to 1 Corinthians 13:8–12 as evidence that prophecy, the gift of miracles, and tongues continue until the parousia is understandable but ultimately inconclusive. Paul does not say that these gifts persist until Christ's return: "Love never ends. As for prophecies, they will pass away; as for tongues, they will cease; as for knowledge, it will pass away. For we know

21. E.g., John Livingston Nevius, *Demon Possessions and Allied Themes: Being an Inductive Study of Phenomena of Our Own Times*, 2nd ed. (Chicago: Revell, 1896).

22. Gaffin, "Cessationist View," 41–60.

23. Geerhardus Vos, *Biblical Theology: Old and New Testaments* (Edinburgh: Banner of Truth, 1996), 7; Gaffin, "Cessationist View," 44; Gaffin, *Perspectives on Pentecost*, 52.

24. Gaffin, "Cessationist View," 57.

in part and we prophesy in part, but when the perfect comes, the partial will pass away. ... For now we see in a mirror dimly, but then face to face" (1 Cor 13:8–10, 12). Rather, Paul contrasts the quality of the believer's present knowledge with the specific means by which God reveals it: prophecy and tongues versus seeing Christ face to face. Paul addresses a similar dynamic in Ephesians 4:11–13, where he lists the gifts of "apostles, the prophets, the evangelists, the shepherds and teachers" as those who "perfect the saints" "until we all attain to the unity of the faith and the knowledge of the Son of God" at his return. Paul does not specify here that the gift of apostles, for example, expires prior to Christ's return.[25] Moreover, Paul's Greek construction ὅταν δὲ ("but when," 1 Cor 13:10), followed by τότε δὲ ("but then," 1 Cor 13:12), suggests that τὸ τέλειον ("the perfect," 1 Cor 13:12) refers to seeing Christ πρόσωπον πρὸς πρόσωπον ("face to face," 1 Cor 13:12).

## THE CHURCH'S PROPHETIC WITNESS

The cessation of prophecy, the gift of miracles, and tongues does not mean that the church's prophetic witness has withered with the passing of time. On the contrary, if we recognize that Pentecost is part of the *historia* rather than the *ordo salutis*, part of the unfolding of the work of Christ rather than part of the believer's personal salvation experience, then we can recognize that Christ poured out the Spirit on the church to empower its witness to the world.[26] Jesus told his disciples: "But you will receive power when the Holy Spirit has come upon you, and you will be my witnesses in Jerusalem and in all Judea and Samaria, and to the end of the earth" (Acts 1:8).[27] Note the connection between the empowerment of the Spirit and witnessing to the ends of the earth. The primary means by which the Spirit empowers the church is through the gift of pastors, those who have been called and gifted to herald the gospel.[28]

---

25. Gaffin, "Cessationist View," 55–56; also Gaffin, *Perspectives on Pentecost*, 109–12. See also R. F. White, "Richard Gaffin and Wayne Grudem on 1 Corinthians 13:10: A Comparison of Cessationist and Noncessationist Argumentation," *JETS* 25 (1992): 173–81.

26. Gaffin, "Cessationist View," 30–41.

27. Bock, *Acts*, 63–67.

28. In the apostolic church there was a transition from extraordinary offices (apostle and prophets) to ordinary and perpetual offices (pastors and elders; Acts 14:23; Titus 1:5). In this transition the apostles were commissioned by Christ to bear witness on the basis of

Paul draws the connection between the outpouring of the Spirit and preaching when he quotes the words of Joel's prophecy, "For 'everyone who calls on the name of the Lord will be saved'" (Rom 10:13; see Joel 2:32). How will they call on Christ unless preachers are sent (Rom 10:14–15)? Then Paul quotes from Isaiah, "How beautiful are the feet of those who preach the good news!" (Rom 10:15; see Isa 52:7; Nah 1:15). Within the original Isaianic context, the prophet refers to the fact that God will directly address his people: "Therefore my people shall know my name. Therefore in that day they shall know that it is I who speak; here I am" (Isa 52:6).[29] The import of Paul's quotation from Isaiah is that God speaks to his people through the Spirit-empowered preaching of the gospel.

Preachers are "stewards of the mysteries of God" (1 Cor 4:1), stewards of his prophetic revelation.[30] As they preach the word of God, they prophetically herald the message of salvation to the world (Rev 11:1–10).[31] They have been commissioned by Christ, who has all authority in heaven and on earth to gather his bride (Matt 28:18–19). This is why the Reformed tradition has placed such a high premium on preaching. The Second Helvetic Confession (1566), written by Heinrich Bullinger (1504–1575), for example, states:

> Wherefore when this Word of God is now preached in the church by preachers lawfully called, we believe the very Word of God is proclaimed, and received by the faithful; and that neither any other Word of God is to be invented nor is to be expected from heaven: and that now the Word itself which is preached is to be regarded, not the minister that preaches; for even if he be evil and a sinner, nevertheless the Word of God remains still true and good. (1)

Likewise, the Westminster Larger Catechism asks, "How is the word made effectual to salvation?" The catechism responds:

> The Spirit of God maketh the reading, but especially the preaching of the word, an effectual means of enlightening, convincing, and

---

their own personal eyewitness testimony (1 John 1:1–5), whereas pastors and elders testify on the basis of apostolic testimony, or Scripture.

29. Beale and Carson, *Commentary on the New Testament Use*, 661.

30. Gaffin, *Perspectives on Pentecost*, 72; Hodge, *1 & 2 Corinthians*, 64. Note the distinction between the stewardship of the apostles versus postapostolic preachers (see nXX above).

31. Beale, *Book of Revelation*, 557–96, esp. 573.

> humbling sinners; of driving them out of themselves, and drawing them unto Christ; of conforming them to his image, and subduing them to his will; of strengthening them against temptations and corruptions; of building them up in grace, and establishing their hearts in holiness and comfort through faith unto salvation. (q. 155)

The divines believed there was power in preaching because within the pages of holy writ is "no other but the Holy Spirit speaking in the Scripture" (WCF 1.10).

## CONCLUSION

Do miracles still happen today? Yes, they do. But too many people within the church have domesticated or ignored the preaching of God's word. They come to church, listen to the sermon, check their phones, think about the week's tasks, and do not realize that the Spirit of God is speaking to them through the reading and preaching of Scripture. To borrow lines from C. S. Lewis's description of his titular Christ-figure, Aslan, in his *The Lion, the Witch, and the Wardrobe*, the word of God is neither safe nor tame, but it is good.[32] When preachers mount pulpits and herald the gospel, the message is "the aroma of Christ to God among those who are being saved and among those who are perishing, to one a fragrance from death to death, to the other a fragrance from life to life" (2 Cor 2:14–16). Beneath the weight of such a burden, Paul cried out, "Who is sufficient for these things?" (2 Cor 2:16). By the grace of God in Christ through the Spirit, preachers and the whole church give witness to the gospel of Christ as they gather the bride of Christ from the four corners of the earth for the great wedding feast of the lamb (Rev 19:1–10). Until that great feast, the words of Isaac Watts's (1674–1748) hymn "How Sweet and Awful Is the Place" beautifully capture the church's prophetic mission and witness:

> Pity the nations, O our God,
> constrain the earth to come;
> send your victorious Word abroad,
> and bring the strangers home.

---

32. C. S. Lewis, *The Lion, the Witch and the Wardrobe* (New York: Collier Books, 1970), 75–77, 180.

We long to see your churches full,
that all the chosen race
may, with one voice and heart and soul,
sing your redeeming grace.

## FURTHER READING

Gaffin, Richard B. *Perspectives on Pentecost: New Testament Teaching on the Gifts of the Holy Spirit*. Phillipsburg, NJ: P&R, 1979. A brief but excellent study on the nature of Pentecost, namely, that it is part of the *historia*, not *ordo* salutis. Therefore, continuing revelation and speaking in tongues is not a normative part of the Christian life but a part of the once-for-all unfolding plan of redemption.

Wallace, Daniel B. "The Semantic Range of the Article-Noun-Kai-Noun Plural Construction in the New Testament." *GTJ* 4 (1983): 59–84. Explains the grammar of single articles governing two plural nouns, which is the form of lexeme in Ephesians 2:20. This is a very helpful study and well worth reading.

Warfield, B. B. *Counterfeit Miracles*. New York: Charles Scribner's Sons, 1918. A study of the history of the claims of the continuation of miraculous gifts. There are few books written on this topic, and thus Warfield's work is most welcome.

CONCLUSION

# TWELVE THESES ON SOTERIOLOGY

THE ENTIRE AIM OF THE Christian life is to glorify God and enjoy him forever, whether in this world or the next. Until faith gives way to sight and this mortal frame dons immortality, our prayer should be that we would live the glory and enjoyment of our Triune God in the present. In the words of George Herbert (1593–1633):

> LORD, Who hast form'd me out of mud,
> And hast redeem'd me through Thy bloud,
> And sanctifi'd me to do good.
>
> Purge all my sinnes done heretofore;
> For I confesse my heavie score,
> And I will strive to sinne no more.
>
> Enrich my heart, mouth, hands in me,
> With faith, with hope, with charitie,
> That I may runne, rise, rest with Thee.[1]

Herbert's words beautifully express the blessings of redemption, and this book has plumbed the depths of God's grace. However, lest we merely wonder without understanding, the following twelve theses summarize the salient points of this rich salvation from God by Christ through the Spirit:

1. George Herbert, "Trinitie Sunday," in *The Poems of George Herbert* (London: Oxford University Press, 1913), 68.

1. The new heavens and earth unfold in the same manner as the original creation, by the Father creating through the agency of the Son and the Spirit.

2. In the pretemporal covenant of redemption (*pactum salutis*), the Father appoints the Son as covenant surety and mediator, and the Father and Son determine to send the Spirit to apply the Son's work of redemption to the elect.

3. The Father promises to equip the Son for his work of redemption by anointing him with the Holy Spirit, and the Son in turn anoints the church with the Spirit to redeem them.

4. The Triune God executes the covenant of redemption through the covenant of grace.

5. In the covenant of redemption God unites the elect to Christ their covenant surety and fulfills this decree in the covenant of grace, whereby God effectually calls the elect by the sovereign work of the Spirit.

6. The Spirit unites the elect to Christ through the effectual call and gives them the salvific blessings of union with Christ, which are distinguished in the *ordo salutis*.

7. God declares righteous those in union with Christ on the sole basis of the imputed satisfaction and obedience of Christ received by grace alone through faith alone in Christ alone.

8. God adopts those who are united to Christ as his sons, and therefore they are treated and receive all the privileges of sons.

9. Those united to Christ also receive the gift of sanctification, whereby the Spirit progressively conforms the redeemed to the image of Christ.

10. The believer's assurance of and perseverance in salvation rests in the immutable decree of God, the all-sufficient intercession of the Son, and the seal and guarantee of the Holy Spirit.

11. The Holy Spirit equips believers through his gifts, which enables the church to carry out its mission of witness and ministry.

12. Christ's outpouring of the Spirit brings about the new heavens and earth, and at the second coming of Christ he raises the dead in Christ and glorifies them.

## TWELVE THESES

*1. The new heavens and earth unfold in the same manner as the original creation, by the Father creating through the agency of the Son and the Spirit.*

The Triune God creates and redeems in parallel fashion, with the new heavens and earth coming into existence by the Father creating through the work of the Son and the Holy Spirit. The difference between creation and redemption is that God creates *ex nihilo* ("out of nothing") by the power of his spoken word, and redemption unfolds in the midst of the present creation. Just as God formed Adam from the dust of the earth and breathed life into him by the Holy Spirit, so the Holy Spirit hovered over Mary and miraculously conceived the incarnate Son of God, the last Adam. The last Adam brings about the new heavens and earth through his work and unleashing of the Holy Spirit.

*2. In the pretemporal covenant of redemption (*pactum salutis*), the Father appoints the Son as covenant surety and mediator, and the Father and Son determine to send the Spirit to apply the Son's work of redemption to the elect.*

The Triune God covenants in eternity to appoint the Son as covenant mediator and surety, which means that he takes on himself all covenantal obligations and responsibilities on behalf of the elect, fulfilling the law and suffering the penalty for its fracture. The Father anoints the Son with the Spirit to carry out his work as mediator and surety, and then the Father and the Son in turn pour out the Spirit on the people of God to apply the Son's work of redemption to their salvation.

*3. The Father promises to equip the Son for his work of redemption by anointing him with the Holy Spirit, and the Son in turn anoints the church with the Spirit to redeem them.*

The Father promises to equip the Son for his work of redemption by giving him the Spirit, who gives him a spirit of wisdom, understanding, knowledge, and fear of the Lord (Isa 11:1–3), the Spirit by whom he will "bring forth justice to the nations" (Isa 42:1), bring good news to the poor, and proclaim freedom to the captives (Isa 61:1–2). The Son receives the Spirit at his baptism and pivots to baptize the creation with the Spirit upon the completion of his labors (Matt 3:11; Luke 3:16; Acts 2:32–35).

*4. The Triune God executes the covenant of redemption through the covenant of grace.*

The eternal foundation of the temporal covenant of grace is the covenant of redemption. God first reveals the saving work of Christ in Genesis 3:15 to Adam and Eve with the promised redemption that will come through the seed of the woman. God progressively unfolds and reveals this redemption in the covenant of grace through Old Testament shadows and types, which find their fulfillment in New Testament antitypes. As God dwelled amid his people in the Old Testament tabernacle through the presence of the Spirit, so God now dwells in his people by means of the work of Christ and through the outpoured presence of the Holy Spirit.

*5. In the covenant of redemption God unites the elect to Christ their covenant surety and fulfills this decree in the covenant of grace, whereby God effectually calls the elect by the sovereign work of the Spirit.*

The Father appoints the Son covenant mediator and surety (Heb 7:22) and unites the elect to him, as he predestines them for adoption as sons through Jesus (Eph 1:4–5). God's election of the saints in the decree becomes reality in the covenant of grace through the sovereign work of the Holy Spirit.

*6. The Spirit unites the elect to Christ through the effectual call and gives them the salvific blessings of union with Christ, which are distinguished in the* ordo salutis*.*

The Holy Spirit unites elect sinners to Christ by means of his effectual call. There are multiple blessings of union with Christ that are distinguished in the *ordo salutis* ("the order of salvation"): election, effectual calling, faith, justification, adoption, sanctification, perseverance, and glorification. Union with Christ and the *ordo salutis* are not competing ideas. Rather, the *ordo salutis* explains the nature of union with Christ. Union with Christ is the forest, and the *ordo salutis* points out the individual trees that comprise the forest. The benefits of salvation come through union with Christ, but to conflate or confuse them compromises the gospel and the doctrine of salvation. Effectual calling, for example, is not faith, and justification is not sanctification, but all of these are benefits of union with Christ.

*7. God declares righteous those in union with Christ on the sole basis of the imputed satisfaction and obedience of Christ received by grace alone through faith alone in Christ alone.*

Justification is the divine verdict by which God declares a sinner righteous in his sight by means of the imputed (not infused) satisfaction and obedience of Christ. Christ's obedience is his active fulfillment of the whole law on behalf of the believer, and his satisfaction is his passive (suffering) obedience in bearing the penalty and curse for the violation of the law on behalf of the believer. Believers receive the imputed active and passive obedience of Christ by grace alone through faith alone. Christ's satisfaction and obedience are the sole material cause of the believer's justification.

*8. God adopts those who are united to Christ as his sons, and therefore they are treated and receive all the privileges of sons.*

As a consequence of the verdict of justification, God adopts redeemed sinners as his sons, which includes both male and female believers because they are all "one in Christ" (Gal 3:28).

In a word, they are sons in the Son, and therefore they receive the right and title to eternal life and are co-heirs with Christ. As God's sons, believers also receive God's fatherly care, provision, discipline, and the corroborating testimony of the Spirit, by which they can cry out to God, "Abba! Father!"

*9. Those united to Christ also receive the gift of sanctification, whereby the Spirit progressively conforms the redeemed to the image of Christ.*

In justification God declares sinners righteous by grace alone through faith alone in Christ alone, and in sanctification he makes them what they have been declared. Saving faith rests, receives, and accepts Christ alone for justification, sanctification, and eternal life. In sanctification God transforms sinners as they put to death their old man, their former existence in Adam, and enlivens sinners in their new man, their new existence in Christ, the last Adam. Believers' sanctification affects their whole being and all their faculties, intellect, will, and affections, but will not be complete until their glorification at the return of Christ.

*10. The believer's assurance of and perseverance in salvation rests in the immutable decree of God, the all-sufficient intercession of the Son, and the seal and guarantee of the Holy Spirit.*

The doctrines of assurance and perseverance do not rest in the subjective feelings or efforts of the believer but on the work of the Triune God in salvation. Believers can be assured of their salvation because of the immutability of God's decree—he does not change his mind. They can rest assured because of the completed all-sufficient work of Christ—his satisfaction and obedience constitute the sole, unbreakable foundation of our salvation. God has given us the guarantee of the Holy Spirit, who testifies in our hearts that we are indeed sons of the living God. These three things also assure us that we will persevere to the end, not because of our fidelity, but because of God's faithfulness to his promises.

*11. The Holy Spirit equips believers through his gifts, which enables the church to carry out its mission of witness and ministry.*

Not only does the Holy Spirit unite sinners to Christ in order to save them, but also Christ dispenses gifts to the church through the Holy Spirit for the church's edification—building the final temple. During the foundational apostolic phase of the church, the Spirit gave the extraordinary gifts of prophecy, speaking in and interpreting tongues (known languages), healing, miracles, and the offices of apostle and prophet. In the postapostolic age, the Spirit still gives gifts to the church. The ordinary gifts of the Spirit are service, teaching, exhorting, giving, leading, acts of mercy, utterances of wisdom and knowledge, faith, discernment, helping, and administration. All these gifts are for the edification of the church, not the elevation of the status of the individual who possesses the gift.

*12. Christ's outpouring of the Spirit brings about the new heavens and earth, and at the second coming of Christ he raises the dead in Christ and glorifies them.*

Christ pours out the Spirit on the whole creation to bring about the new heavens and earth. The Spirit's renewal of the creation has the transformation and glorification of the saints as its centerpiece; as the last blast of the trumpet sounds, the Spirit raises the dead in Christ, and he finalizes their sanctification by removing every last vestige of sin and fully conforming them to the image of the last Adam, Jesus, the Son of God.

The Triune God, Father, Son, and Holy Spirit, made a covenant to create and save a people—for the Father to send the Son to redeem his bride, and win her to himself by the work of the Spirit. This plan slowly and progressively unfolded in redemptive history. The Old Testament hinted and whispered the nature of the Son's kingdom—that he would come in the power of the Spirit and then pour out the Spirit on the church—to gather his bride from the four corners of the earth. The eternal Son came as the eschatological Adam, and unlike the protological Adam, he was obedient to the point of death, even death on a cross. So, the Father exalted him to his right hand to reign in the midst of his enemies. From the Father's right hand, the last Adam poured out on the creation the Spirit, the "Lord and giver of life." Through the prophetic preaching of the word, the Spirit effectually calls sinners and raises them from death to life, and by grace alone through faith alone in Christ alone the Father declares risen sinners righteous because of the Son's imputed righteousness, satisfaction, and holiness. The Father, through the Son, by the Spirit then makes these sinners what they have been declared—he makes them righteous and holy.

But the sanctified life is not one in which Christians sit idly awaiting their transformation and glorification. Rather, as pilgrims on the way, we live in the power of the Spirit. Christians no longer walk in the flesh but draw on the Spirit's power to overcome temptation and sin knowing that, though they struggle, their justification ensures that they will never fall out of favor with their heavenly Father. He may and does discipline his children, but their sanctification, not punishment, is the goal of his fatherly care. Assured of the Father's love, Christians can know that they often fail but that he never has, does, or will. Christians do not live for themselves but have been united to Christ their head and to his body, the "one holy catholic and apostolic church." As Christians draw nigh to Christ through the means of grace, they inevitably draw nigh to one another as the Spirit knits the body of Christ together in an ever-growing ecclesial union. Believers employ the gifts of the Spirit for the mutual edification of the body all the while looking forward to the resurrection of the dead and the life of the world to come.

# GLOSSARY

**adoption**: an act of God's free grace wherein he adopts believers as his sons and grants them all of the rights and privileges due to an heir of God.

**antinomianism**: the erroneous belief that Christ frees believers from the duties of the moral law, and thus their moral conduct is irrelevant.

**Aqedah**: the binding of Isaac in Genesis 22.

***assensus***: "assent," or an intellectual recognition and agreement with the claims of Scripture and the gospel.

**assurance**: a conviction that Christ is all that he professes to be and will do all that he has promised, which means a believer knows they are in a state of salvation.

**biblical theology**: the progressive and organic unfolding of God's supernatural revelation throughout preredemptive and redemptive history, Genesis to Revelation.

**common grace**: the favor of the Triune God to the entire creation and to all people, irrespective of whether they are believers.

**common operations of the Spirit**: the Holy Spirit's work in upholding the cosmos.

**covenant**: at its most fundamental level, an agreement between two or more persons that creates a relationship with attending blessings and responsibilities. Depending on the context and parties, a covenant can take on different characteristics that stress either its promissory or obligatory character.

**covenant of grace**: the covenant between God and the elect sinner in Christ, which promises salvation from sin by grace alone through faith alone in Christ alone.

**covenant of redemption**: the intra-Trinitarian covenant among Father, Son, and Holy Spirit to appoint the Son as covenant surety and mediator and to send the Spirit to gather the elect.

**covenant of works**: the covenant between God and Adam to give him eternal life on the condition of his obedience to both the dominion mandate (Gen 1:28) and the prohibition against eating from the tree of knowledge (Gen 2:16–17).

**eschatological**: related to the study of the end of creation, the last things, which began with the first advent of Christ, the last days.

**eschaton**: the age of the new heavens and earth, the age of the last Adam, Jesus.

***ex nihilo***: "out of nothing," used in reference to *creation* out of nothing. Namely, God did not use any preexisting matter when he created the cosmos.

***ex opere operato***: "by the work performed," a Latin term that describes the Roman Catholic view of sacramental efficacy. Namely, apart from faith the sacrament imparts grace to the recipient.

**extraordinary gifts**: those gifts of the Spirit that existed during the foundational stage of the church, such as apostles, prophets, prophecy, speaking in tongues, and interpreting tongues. With the expiration of the first generation and completion of the church's foundation, those gifts ceased to exist.

***fides carbonaria***: "collier's faith," or the faith of a collier, or charcoal burner. That is, a faith that believes all that the church teaches even if the person does not know what the church teaches.

***fides historica***: "historical faith," or a bare intellectual ascent to the revealed truth—the faith of demons (Jas 2:19).

***fides implicitas***: "implicit faith," a teaching of the Roman Catholic Church that defines faith as belief without certain knowledge. That is, a faith that accepts the teaching of the church without knowing the objective contents of faith.

***fides iustificans***: "justifying faith," a Spirit-wrought gift of trusting in the person and work of Christ for salvation.

***fiducia***: "trust" in the promises of the gospel, the essence of faith, and works in concert with *notitia* ("knowledge") and *assensus* ("assent").

***filioque***: "and from the Son," a phrase from the Latin translation of the Niceno-Constantinopolitan Creed (381) that the Holy Spirit proceeds from the Father "and the Son" (*filoque*).

**firstfruits**: the very best portion of the harvest, which the Israelites brought to God to offer as thanks for a bountiful harvest (Lev 23:1–2, 9–14), a representative portion of the harvest to come. Paul applies this term to Jesus—the firstfruits of the resurrection harvest (1 Cor 15:20–28).

***frui***: "enjoyment."

***habit***: a disposition or inclination toward a certain thing. An infused habit is a God-given disposition toward spiritual good and stands in contrast to an acquired habit, which is something that is natural to human beings that they acquire through practice.

***historia salutis***: redemptive history, which is the unfolding of God's plan of redemption.

***hypostasis***: the Greek term that is translated as "person" in reference to the persons of the Trinity, Father, Son, and Holy Spirit.

**inseparable operations**: refers to how the Triune God, Father, Son, and Holy Spirit, always works in concert in both creation and redemption.

***insitio in Christum***: "inserted in Christ"; see also *unio cum Christo* ("union with Christ").

**invisible church**: the elect from every age in Christ who are united to him by faith and the indwelling of the Holy Spirit.

**justification**: an act of God's free grace wherein he forgives us of our sins and declares us righteous on the basis of the imputed, alien righteousness of Christ.

**legalism**: see *neonomianism*.

**lexeme**: a basic unit of a written text, a biblical phrase.

**mission(s)**: the respective undivided work of the Triune God as specifically pertains to each member of the Godhead: the Father sending, the Son and Spirit being sent.

**neonomianism**: the erroneous belief that the believer's good works are necessary to supplement Christ's works for salvation. Also known as legalism, or works-righteousness.

***non posse non mori***: "the inability to die," applied to believers in the new heavens and earth at the consummation of all things.

**notion**: the proper idea whereby we know a divine person of the Trinity, which are the Father's *innascibility* (unbegottenness) or *paternity*, the Son's *filiation*, and the Spirit's *procession* or *spiration*. Thus there are five notions: innascibility, paternity, filiation, spiration, and procession.

***notitia***: "knowledge," such as that Jesus existed and that supernatural revelation is not fiction.

***nuda verbum***: the "naked word," or the word of God apart from the applicatory work of the Holy Spirit.

***opera trinitatis ad extra indivisa sunt***: "the external works of the Trinity are indivisible."

**ordinary gifts**: the gifts of the Spirit that perpetually exist in the church, such as service, teaching, exhortation, giving, leading, acts of mercy, and so on.

***ordo docendi***: "the order of teaching," or the order in which something is taught, which does not reflect the *ordo essendi* ("order of things in themselves"), or the order in which they exist.

**order of nature**: refers to a logical, not temporal, moment in an otherwise indivisible thing, such as God's decree or the order of salvation. Faith, for example, logically precedes justification in the order of nature because one cannot be justified apart from faith even if the sinner receives both faith and justification in the same temporal moment.

***ordo salutis***: "the order of salvation," which is commonly predestination, effectual calling, faith, justification, adoption, sanctification, perseverance, and glorification, which are all benefits of the believer's union with Christ.

***opera ad extra***: "the external work" of the Trinity, which is the works of creation and redemption.

***opera ad intra***: "the internal work" of the Trinity, which is the Father's filiation, or eternal begetting, of the Son, and the Spirit eternally proceeding from Father and Son, or the eternal spiration of the Spirit.

***pactum salutis***: see *covenant of redemption*.

**Pentateuch**: the first five books of the Bible: Genesis, Exodus, Leviticus, Numbers, and Deuteronomy.

**pneumatology**: the study of the person and work of the Holy Spirit.

***posse mori***: "the ability to die," applied to Adam's prefall state in the garden of Eden.

**practical intellect**: that which directs the intellect toward operation, or doing.

**procession(s)**: the filiation of the Son and the spiration of the Holy Spirit.

**propitiation**: a sacrifice that averts the wrath of God.

**protological**: refers to the study of the beginnings of the creation, in contrast to "eschatological," namely, that which deals with the end of creation, or last things.

**proton**: the age of the original creation, the age of Adam.

**Remonstrants**: the disciples of Jacob Arminius who lodged their remonstrance with the States General in Holland and submitted the Five Points of Remonstrance, otherwise known as the Arminian Articles.

**sanctification**: a work of God's free grace wherein he progressively makes us more like Christ where believers put to death their old existence in Adam and seek their new existence in Christ.

***sedes doctrinae***: the "chair" passage of a doctrine, that is, one of the more common passages for a particular doctrine.

**special operations of the Spirit**: the Holy Spirit's work in applying the work of Christ to the elect for their salvation.

**special revelation**: the knowledge of God that the Spirit discloses chiefly through the written word that focuses on Christ and the gospel.

**speculative intellect**: that which gives consideration to truth.

**subsistence**: an existing relation within the Triune God, or a person within the Godhead, that is, the Father, Son, or Holy Spirit.

***syllogismus practicus***: "the practical syllogism," namely that only those who have genuine faith produce good works. By the grace of God, I produce good works. Therefore, I possess a genuine faith. This is a secondary means of assurance that rests on the primary means of God's grace in Christ through the testimony of the Spirit.

***temporary faith***: when a person temporarily assents to the truths of the gospel and then eventually falters and ceases to believe in the gospel.

***unio cum Christo***: "union with Christ."

**union of application**: when the Spirit unites elect sinners to Christ by means of effectual calling and faith.

**union of the decree**: the predestinarian "in him" or "in Christ."

***uti***: "use."

***verbum efficax***: "effectual word" or "call."

**visible church**: those who profess the true religion and their children who participate in the church.

***vocatio externa***: the "external call," that is, the preaching of the gospel apart from the *vocatio interna* (the "internal call") of the Holy Spirit.

***vocatio interna***: the "internal call," or effectual call of the Holy Spirit as he applies the *vocatio externa* ("external call") of the word of God.

**word-act-word revelation**: in Scripture God discloses his word, gives a revelatory deed, and then follows the deed with an interpretive word. God is his own interpreter.

**works-righteousness**: see *neonomianism*.

# BIBLIOGRAPHY


Adhinarta, Yuzo. *The Doctrine of the Holy Spirit in the Major Reformed Confessions and Catechisms of the Sixteenth and Seventeenth Centuries*. Cambridge, UK: Langham Press, 2012.

Ahlstrom, Sydney E. *A Religious History of the American People*. New Haven: Yale University Press, 1972.

Ainsworth, Henry. *The Communion of the Saints*. London: John Bellamie, 1641.

Alexander, Joseph Addison. *The Acts of the Apostles Explained*. Vol. 2. London: James Nisbet and Co., 1857.

Allen, Michael. *The Christ's Faith: A Dogmatic Account*. London: T&T Clark, 2009.

———. *Grounded in Heaven: Recentering Christian Hope and Life on God*. Grand Rapids: Eerdmans, 2018.

———. *Justification and the Gospel: Understanding Contexts and Controversies*. Grand Rapids: Baker Academic, 2013.

———. *Sanctification, New Studies in Dogmatics*. Grand Rapids: Zondervan, 2017.

Allen, Michael, and Scott Swain. *Christian Dogmatics: Reformed Theology for the Church Catholic*. Grand Rapids: Baker Academic, 2016.

Allison, Gregg R., and Andreas J. Köstenberger. *The Holy Spirit, Theology for the People of God*. Nashville: B&H Academic, 2020.

Alsted, Johann Heinrich. *Theologia Scholastica Didactica: Exhibens Locos Communes Theologicos Methodo Scholastica*. Hanau: Eifridus, 1618.

Ambrose. *Exposition of the Christian Faith*. Vol. 10 of *Nicene and Post-Nicene Fathers*, Series 2. Edited by Phillip Schaff. 14 vols. Peabody, MA: Hendrickson, 1994.

Ames, William. *A Fresh Suit Against Human Ceremonies in God's Worship*. Amsterdam: Giles Thorp, 1633.

——. *The Marrow of Theology*. Translated by John Dykstra Eusden. Grand Rapids: Baker Books, 1968.

Anselm. *Anselm of Canterbury: The Major Works*. Edited by Brian Davies and G. R. Evans. Oxford: Oxford University Press, 1998.

Aquinas, Thomas. *Commentary on the Letter of Saint Paul to the Romans*. Vol. 37 of Latin/English Edition of the Works of St. Thomas Aquinas. Translated by F. R. Larcher. Lander, WY: The Aquinas Institute for the Study of Sacred Doctrine, 2012.

——. *The Sermon Conferences of St. Thomas Aquinas on the Apostles' Creed*. Translated by Nicholas Ayo Notre Dame, IN: University of Notre Dame Press, 1988.

——. *Summa Theologica*. Repr., Allen, TX: Christian Classics, 1948.

Arminius, Jacob. *The Works of James Arminius*. Edited by James Nichols. 3 vols. 1825; 1828; 1875. Repr., Grand Rapids: Baker Books, 1996.

Augustine. *On Christian Teaching*. Translated R. P. H. Green. Oxford: Oxford University Press, 1997.

——. *City of God*. Translated by William Babcock. 2 vols. Hyde Park, NY: New City Press, 2012.

——. *Confessions*. Translated by Henry Chadwick. Oxford: Oxford University Press, 1991.

——. *On the Holy Trinity*. Vol. 3 of *Nicene and Post-Nicene Fathers*, Series 1. Edited by Phillip Schaff. 1887. Repr., Grand Rapids: Eerdmans, 1991.

——. *On the Morals of the Catholic Church*. Vol. 4 of *Nicene and Post-Nicene Fathers*, Series 1. Edited by Phillip Schaff. 1887. Repr., Grand Rapids: Eerdmans, 1991.

——. *Reply to Faustus the Manichean*. Vol. 1 of *Nicene and Post-Nicene Fathers*, Series 1. Edited by Phillip Schaff. 1887. Grand Rapids: Eerdmans, 1991.

——. *Sermons on Selected Lessons of the New Testament*. Sermon LXXI. Vol. 6 of *Nicene and Post-Nicene Fathers*, Series 1. Edited by Phillip Schaff. 1887. Grand Rapids: Eerdmans, 1991.

——. *The Trinity*. The Fathers of the Church. Translated by Stephen McKenna. Washington, D. C: The Catholic University Press of America, 1963.

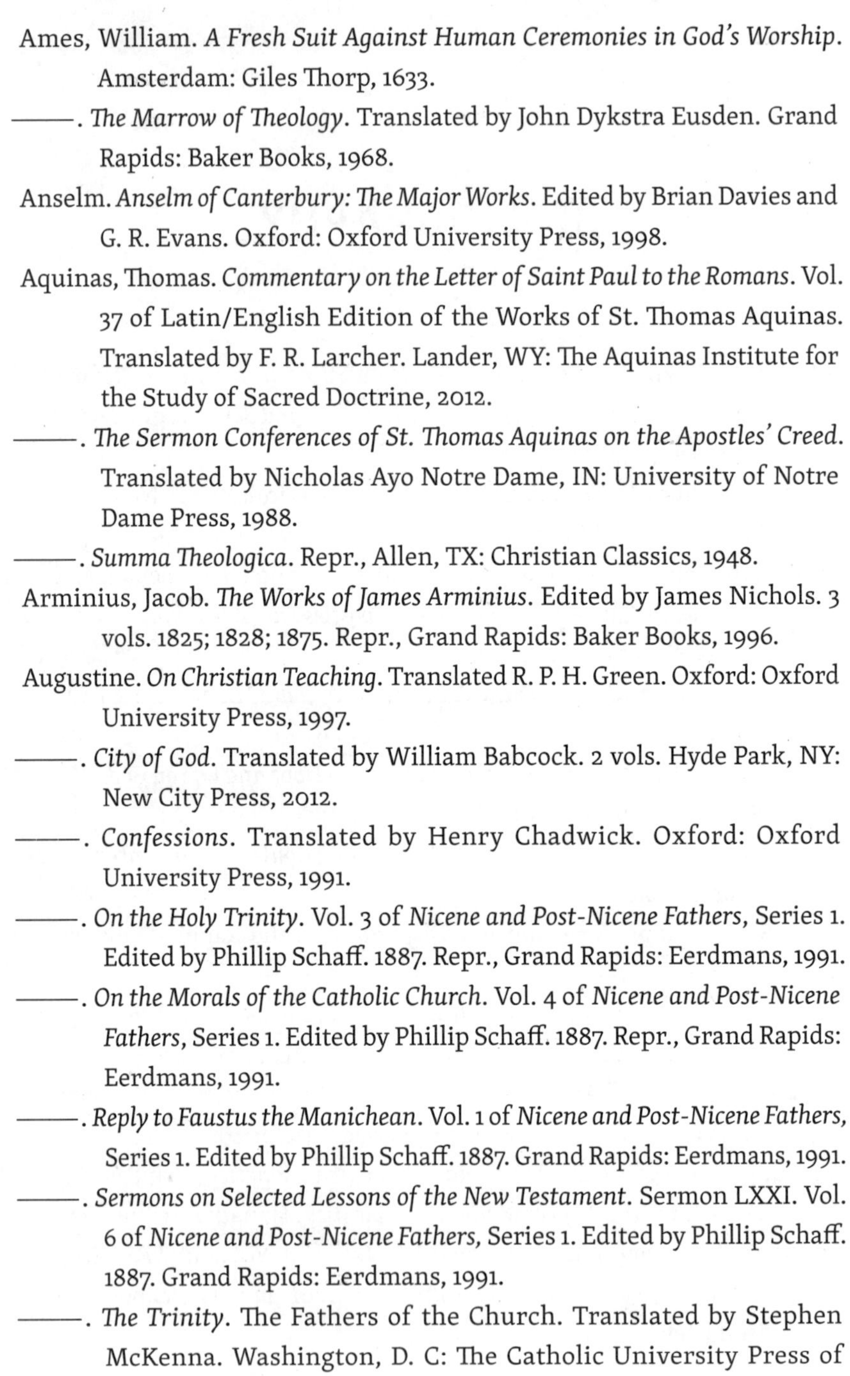

Barr, James. "Abba Isn't 'Daddy.' " *Journal of Theological Studies* 39/1 (1988): 28–47.

Barth, Karl. *Prayer: 50th Anniversary Edition*. Edited by Don E. Saliers. Translated by Sara F. Terrien. 1952. Repr., Louisville, KY: Westminster John Knox, 2002.

———. *Theology of the Reformed Confessions*. Translated by Darrell L. Guder and Judith J. Guder. Louisville, KY: Westminster John Knox, 2002.

Baschera, Luca. "Ethics in Reformed Orthodoxy." Pages 519–52 in *A Companion to Reformed Orthodoxy*. Edited by Herman J. Selderhuis. Leiden: Brill, 2013.

Bates, Matthew W. *Salvation by Allegiance Alone: Rethinking Faith, Works, and the Gospel of Jesus the King*. Grand Rapids: Baker Academic, 2017.

Baugh, S. M. *Ephesians*. Evangelical Exegetical Commentary. Bellingham, WA: Lexham Press, 2016.

Bavinck, Herman. "Common Grace." Translated by Raymond C. Van Leeuwen. *Calvin Theological Journal* 24 (1989): 35–65.

———. *Reformed Dogmatics*. Edited by John Bolt. Translated by John Vriend. 4 vols. Grand Rapids: Baker Academic, 2003–2008.

———. *Saved by Grace: The Holy Spirit's Work in Calling and Regeneration*. Translated by Nelson D. Kloosterman. Grand Rapids: Reformation Heritage Books, 2012.

Baxter, Richard. *Confession of His Faith: Especially Concerning the Interest of Repentance and Sincere Obedience to Christ, in our Justification and Salvation*. London: 1654.

Beale, G. K. *The Book of Revelation*. New International Greek Testament Commentary. Grand Rapids: Eerdmans, 1999.

———. "The Descent of the Eschatological Temple in the Form of the Spirit at Pentecost. Part I: The Clearest Evidence," *Tyndale Bulletin* 56/1 (2005): 73–102.

———. *A New Testament Biblical Theology: The Unfolding of the Old Testament in the New*. Grand Rapids: Baker Academic, 2011.

———. "The Old Testament Background of Paul's Reference to the 'Fruit of the Spirit' in Galatians 5:22." *Bulletin for Biblical Research* 15 (2005): 1–38.

———. "The Old Testament Background of Reconciliation in 2 Cor 5–7 and its Bearing on the Literary Problem of 2 Corinthians 6:14–7:1." *New Testament Studies* 35 (1989): 550–81.

———. *The Temple and the Church's Mission: A Biblical Theology of the Dwelling Place of God*. New Studies in Biblical Theology. Downers Grove, IL: IVP Academic, 2004.

Beale, G. K., and D. A. Carson, eds. *The New Testament Commentary on the Use of the Old Testament*. Grand Rapids: Baker Academic, 2007.

Beeke, Joel R. "The Assurance Debate: Six Key Questions." Pages 263–83 in *Drawn Into Controversie: Reformed Theological Diversity and Debates Within Seventeenth-Century British Puritanism*. Edited by Michael A. G. Haykin and Mark Jones. Göttingen: Vandenhoeck & Ruprecht, 2011.

———. "Does Assurance Belong to the Essence of Faith? Calvin and the Calvinists." *The Master's Seminary Journal* 5/1 (1994): 43–71.

———. *Heirs with Christ: the Puritans on Adoption*. Grand Rapids: Reformation Heritage Books, 2008.

Beeke, Joel R. and Mark Jones. *A Puritan Theology: Doctrine for Life*. Grand Rapids: Reformation Heritage Books, 2012.

Bellarmine, Robert. *De Justificatione*. Pages 460–635 in vol. 4 of *Opera Omnia*. Naples: Joseph Giuliano, 1858.

Berkhof, Louis. *Systematic Theology: New Combined Edition*. Grand Rapids: Eerdmans, 1996.

Berkouwer, G. C. *Divine Election*. Translated by Hugo Bekker. Studies in Dogmatics. Grand Rapids: Eerdmans, 1960.

———. *Faith and Justification*. Studies in Dogmatics. Grand Rapids: Eerdmans, 1954.

———. *Faith and Perseverance*. Studies in Dogmatics. Grand Rapids: Eerdmans, 1979.

Billings, J. Todd. *Union with Christ: Reframing Theology and Ministry for the Church*. Grand Rapids: Baker Academic, 2011.

Bird, Michael. *Jesus the Eternal Son: Answering Adoptionist Christology*. Grand Rapids: Eerdmans, 2017.

Block, Daniel I. *The Book of Ezekiel: Chapters 25–48*. New International Commentary on the Old Testament. Grand Rapids: Eerdmans, 1998.

Boardman, W. E. *The Higher Christian Life*. Boston: Henry Hoyt, 1858.

Bock, Darrell L. *Acts*. Baker Exegetical Commentary on the New Testament. Grand Rapids: Baker Academic, 2007.

———. *Luke 9:51–24:53*. Baker Exegetical Commentary on the New Testament. Grand Rapids: Baker Academic, 1996.

Brakel, Wilhelmus à. *The Christian's Reasonable Service*. Translated by Bartel Elshout. 4 vols. Morgan, PA: Soli Deo Gloria, 1992.

Brooks, Thomas. *Paradise Opened*. Pages 265–85 in vol. 5 of *The Complete Works of Thomas Brooks*. Edinburgh: James Nichol, 1867.

Brown, Sherri. *Gift Upon Gift: Covenant Through Word in the Gospel of John*. Eugene, OR: Pickwick, 2010.

Bruce, F. F. *The Book of Acts*. New International Commentary on the New Testament. Grand Rapids: Eerdmans, 1988.

Brunner, Emil. *The Christian Doctrine of Creation and Redemption*. Vol. 2 of *Dogmatics*. Translated by Olive Wyon. Philadelphia, PA: Westminster, 1952.

Buchanan, James. *The Doctrine of Justification: An Outline of Its History in the Church, and of Its Exposition from Scripture*. Edinburgh: T&T Clark, 1867.

———. *The Office and Work of the Holy Spirit*. New York: Robert Carter, 1847.

Bullinger, Heinrich. *The Decades of Henry Bullinger*. 2 vols. 1849–52. Grand Rapids: Reformation Heritage Books, 2003.

Burgess, Anthony. *Vindiciae Legis: or, A Vindication of the Morall Law and the Covenants*. London: Thomas Underhill, 1647.

Burghardt, Walter J. *The Image of God in Man According to Cyril of Alexandria*. 1957. Repr., Eugene, OR: Wipf & Stock, 2008.

Burke, Trevor J. *Adopted into God's Family: Exploring a Pauline Metaphor*. Downers Grove, IL: InterVarsity Press, 2006.

Burton, Tara Isabella. *Strange Rites: New Religions for a Godless World*. New York: Public Affairs, 2020.

Buzenitz, Nathan. *Long Before Luther: Tracing the Heart of the Gospel from Christ to the Reformation*. Chicago: Moody Publishers, 2017.

Calvin, John. *Commentary on Genesis*. Calvin Translation Society. Translated by James Anderson. 1849. Repr., Grand Rapids: Baker, 1993.

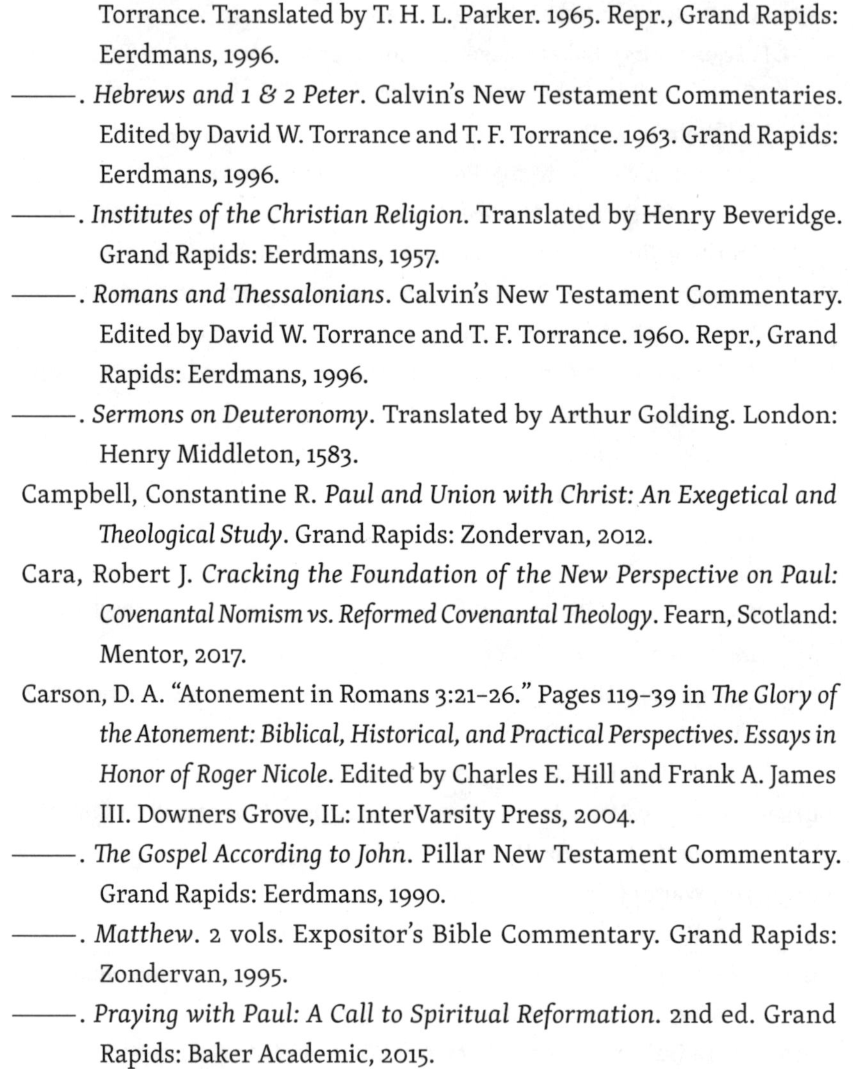

———. *Galatians, Ephesians, Philippians, and Colossians*. Calvin's New Testament Commentaries. Edited by David W. Torrance and T. F. Torrance. Translated by T. H. L. Parker. 1965. Repr., Grand Rapids: Eerdmans, 1996.

———. *Hebrews and 1 & 2 Peter*. Calvin's New Testament Commentaries. Edited by David W. Torrance and T. F. Torrance. 1963. Grand Rapids: Eerdmans, 1996.

———. *Institutes of the Christian Religion*. Translated by Henry Beveridge. Grand Rapids: Eerdmans, 1957.

———. *Romans and Thessalonians*. Calvin's New Testament Commentary. Edited by David W. Torrance and T. F. Torrance. 1960. Repr., Grand Rapids: Eerdmans, 1996.

———. *Sermons on Deuteronomy*. Translated by Arthur Golding. London: Henry Middleton, 1583.

Campbell, Constantine R. *Paul and Union with Christ: An Exegetical and Theological Study*. Grand Rapids: Zondervan, 2012.

Cara, Robert J. *Cracking the Foundation of the New Perspective on Paul: Covenantal Nomism vs. Reformed Covenantal Theology*. Fearn, Scotland: Mentor, 2017.

Carson, D. A. "Atonement in Romans 3:21–26." Pages 119–39 in *The Glory of the Atonement: Biblical, Historical, and Practical Perspectives. Essays in Honor of Roger Nicole*. Edited by Charles E. Hill and Frank A. James III. Downers Grove, IL: InterVarsity Press, 2004.

———. *The Gospel According to John*. Pillar New Testament Commentary. Grand Rapids: Eerdmans, 1990.

———. *Matthew*. 2 vols. Expositor's Bible Commentary. Grand Rapids: Zondervan, 1995.

———. *Praying with Paul: A Call to Spiritual Reformation*. 2nd ed. Grand Rapids: Baker Academic, 2015.

———. "Reflections on Christian Assurance," *Westminster Theological Journal* 54 (1992): 1–29.

———. *Showing the Spirit: A Theological Exposition of 1 Corinthians 12–14*. Grand Rapids: Baker Books, 1987.

Carson, D. A., Peter T. O'Brien, and Mark A. Seifrid, eds. *Justification and Variegated Nomism*. 2 vols. Grand Rapids: Baker Academic, 2001, 2004.

Cartwright, Thomas. *Christian Religion, Substantially, Methodicallie, Plainlie, and Profitablie Treatised*. London: Felix Man, 1611.

Casselli, Stephen J. "The Threefold Division of the Law in the Thought of Aquinas," *Westminster Theological Journal* 61/2 (1999): 175–207.

*Catechism of the Catholic Church*. 2nd ed. New York, NY: Doubleday, 2003.

Charnock, Stephen. *Discourses on the Knowledge of God*. Vol. 4 of *The Works of Stephen Charnock*. Edinburgh: James Nichol, 1865.

Charry, Ellen T. *By the Renewing of Your Minds: The Pastoral Function of Christian Doctrine*. Oxford: Oxford University Press, 1997.

Chesterton, G. K. "The Toy Theatre." Pages 141–46 in *On Lying in Bed and Other Essays*. Edited by Alberto Manguel. Calgary, Alberta: Bayeux Arts, 2004.

Cho, David D. *The Ground of Holy Life: A Reformed Response to the Holiness Movement in America with Progressive and Definitive Sanctification*. Eugene, OR: Resource Publications, 2021.

Clark, Gordon. *Faith and Saving Faith*. Jefferson, MA: The Trinity Foundation, 1983.

———. *The Word Hesed in the Hebrew Bible*. Sheffield: JSOT Press, 1993.

Cleveland, Christopher. "Reformed Theology and Medieval Theology." Pages 24–40 in *The Oxford Handbook of Reformed Theology*. Edited by Scott R. Swain and Michael Allen. Oxford: Oxford University Press, 2020.

Collier, Jay T. *Debating Perseverance: The Augustinian Heritage in Post-Reformation England*. Oxford: Oxford University Press, 2018.

Collins, C. John. "Echoes of Aristotle in Romans 2:14–15: Or, Maybe Abimelech Was Not So Bad After All." *Journal of Markets and Morality* 13/1 (2010): 123–73.

Craigie, Peter C. *The Book of Deuteronomy*. New International Commentary on the Old Testament. Grand Rapids: 1976.

Crowe, Brandon D. Last Adam: A Theology of the Obedient Life of Jesus in the Gospels. Grand Rapids: Baker Academic, 2017.

———. "The Passive *and* Active Obedience of Christ: Retrieving a Biblical Distinction." Pages 441–68 in *The Doctrine on Which the Church Stands or Falls*. Edited by Matthew Barrett. Wheaton, IL: Crossway, 2019.

Curtis, Byron. "'Private Spirits' in the Westminster Confession of Faith 1.10 and in Catholic-Protestant Debate (1588–1652)." *Westminster Theological Journal* 58 (1996): 257–66.

Davids, Peter H. *The Epistle of James*. New International Greek Testament Commentary. Grand Rapids: Eerdmans, 1982.

Davies, J. A. "'Discerning Between Good and Evil': Solomon as a New Adam." *Westminster Theological Journal* 73 (2011): 39–57.

Davies, W. D. and D. C. Allison. *Matthew 1–7*. International Critical Commentary. London: T&T Clark, 1988.

De Campos, Heber Carlos. *Doctrine in Development: Johannes Piscator and Debates over Christ's Active Obedience*. Grand Rapids: Reformation Heritage Books, 2017.

Dempster, Stephen G. *Dominion and Dynasty: A Theology of the Hebrew Bible*. Downers Grove, IL: InterVarsity Press, 2003.

DeVries, Simon J. *1 Kings*. Word Biblical Commentary. Waco, TX: Word Books, 1985.

DeYoung, Rebecca Konyndyk. *Glittering Vices: A New Look at the Seven Deadly Sins and Their Remedies*. Grand Rapids: Brazos, 2009.

Dickson, David. *A Brief Explication of the Last Fifty Psalmes, from Ps. 100 to the End*. London: T. R. and E. M., 1654.

Dieter, Melvin E., ed. *Five Views on Sanctification*. Grand Rapids: Zondervan, 1987.

Dillard, Raymond B. "Intrabiblical Exegesis and the Effusion of the Spirit in Joel." Pages 87–94 in *Creator, Redeemer, Consummator: Festschrift for Meredith G. Kline*. Edited by Howard Griffith and John R. Muether. Greenville, SC: Reformed Academic Press, 2000.

Doolittle, Thomas. *A Complete Body of Practical Divinity; Being a New Improvement of the Assembly's Catechism*. London: John and Barham Clark, 1723.

Duby, Steven J. *God in Himself: Scripture, Metaphysics, and the Task of Christian Theology*. Downers Grove, IL: IVP Academic, 2019.

Dumbrell, William. *Covenant and Creation: A Theology of the Old Testament Covenants*. 2nd ed. Milton Keynes, UK: Authentic Media, 2002.

Dunn, James D. G. *Baptism in the Holy Spirit*. Louisville: Westminster John Knox, 1970.

———. *Jesus, Paul, and the Law: Studies in Mark and Galatians*. Louisville: Westminster John Knox, 1990.

———. *The New Perspective on Paul*. 2nd ed. Grand Rapids: Eerdmans, 2007.

———. *The Theology of Paul the Apostle*. Grand Rapids: Eerdmans, 1998.

Dunson, Ben C. *Individual and Community in Paul's Letter to the Romans*. Tübingen: Mohr Siebeck, 2012.

Durham, John I. *Exodus*. Vol. 3. Word Biblical Commentary. Nashville: Thomas Nelson, 1987.

Emery, Giles. *The Trinitarian Theology of St. Thomas Aquinas*. Oxford: Oxford University Press, 2010.

———. *The Trinity: An Introduction to the Catholic Doctrine of the Triune God*. Washington, DC: The Catholic University of America Press, 2011.

Evans, William B. *Imputation and Impartation: Union with Christ in American Reformed Theology*. Milton Keynes: Paternoster, 2008.

Farrow, Douglas B. *Ascension and Ecclesia: On the Significance of the Doctrine of Ascension*. Edinburgh: T&T Clark, 1999.

Fee, Gordon D. *The First and Second Letters to the Thessalonians*. New International Commentary on the New Testament. Grand Rapids: Eerdmans, 2009.

———. *God's Empowering Presence: The Holy Spirit in the Letters of Paul*. Peabody, MA: Hendrickson, 1994.

Ferguson, Sinclair. *The Holy Spirit*. Contours of Christian Theology. Downers Grove, IL: IVP Academic, 1997.

Fesko, J. V. "Aquinas's Doctrine of Justification and Infused Habits in Reformed Soteriology." Pages 249–66 in *Aquinas Among the Protestants*. Edited by Manfred Svenson and David VanDrunen. Oxford: Wiley-Blackwell, 2018.

———. *Arminius and the Reformed Tradition: Grace and the Doctrine of Salvation*. Grand Rapids: Reformation Heritage Books, 2022.

———. *Justification: Understanding the Classic Reformed Doctrine*. Phillipsburg, NJ: P&R Publishing, 2007.

———. *Last Things First: Unlocking Genesis with the Christ of Eschatology*. Fearn: Mentor, 2007.

———. "Romans 8.29–30 and the Question of the *Ordo Salutis*." *Journal of Reformed Theology* 8 (2014): 35–60.

———. *The Rule of Love: Broken, Fulfilled, and Applied*. Grand Rapids: Reformation Heritage Books, 2009.

———. *The Trinity and the Covenant of Redemption*. Fearn: Mentor, 2016.

———. *Where Wisdom is Found: Christ in Ecclesiastes*. Grand Rapids: Reformation Heritage Books, 2010.

Finney, Charles G. *Finney's Systematic Theology: The Complete and Newly Expanded 1878 Edition*. Edited by Dennis Carroll, Bill Nicely, and L. G. Parkhurst Jr. 1878. Repr., Minneapolis: Bethany House, 1994.

———. *Lectures on Revivals of Religion*. Edited by William G. McLoughlin. 1835. Repr., Cambridge, MA: Harvard University Press, 1960.

Fisher, Edward. *The Marrow of Modern Divinity*. 16th ed. Edited by Thomas Boston. Glasgow: John Bryce, 1796.

France, R. T. *The Gospel of Mark*. New International Greek Testament Commentary. Grand Rapids: Eerdmans, 2002.

Gaffin Jr., Richard B. "A Cessationist View." Pages 23–64 in *Are Miraculous Gifts for Today? Four Views*. Edited by Wayne A. Grudem. Grand Rapids: Zondervan, 1996.

———. *Perspectives on Pentecost: New Testament Teaching on the Gifts of the Holy Spirit*. Phillipsburg, NJ: P&R, 1979.

Gamble, Whitney G. *Christ and the Law: Antinomianism at the Westminster Assembly*. Grand Rapids: Reformation Heritage Books, 2018.

Garlington, Don. *In Defense of the New Perspective on Paul: Essays and Reviews*. Eugene, OR: Wipf & Stock, 2005.

Garner, David B. *Sons in the Son: The Riches and Reach of Adoption in Christ*. Phillipsburg, NJ: P&R, 2016.

Gathercole, S. J. "A Law Unto Themselves: The Gentiles in Romans 2.14–15 Revisited." *Journal for the Study of the New Testament* 85 (2002): 27–49.

Gladwin, Michael. "Mission and Colonialism." Pages 282–304 in *The Oxford Handbook of Nineteenth-Century Christian Thought*. Oxford: Oxford University Press, 2017.

Gleason, Randall. "B. B. Warfield and Lewis S. Chafer on Sanctification." *Journal of the Evangelical Theological Society* 40/2 (1997): 241–56.

Glueck, Nelson. *Hesed in the Bible*. New York: Ktav Publishing House, 1975.

Goldingay, John. *The Message of Isaiah 40–55: A Literary-Theological Commentary*. London: T&T Clark, 2005.

Goodwin, Thomas. *Of the Work of the Holy Ghost*. In vol. 6 of *The Works of Thomas Goodwin D. D.* Edinburgh: James Nichol, 1863.

———. *The Work of the Holy Ghost in Our Salvation*. Vol. 6 of *The Works of Thomas Goodwin*. 10 vols. 1861–66. Repr., Eureka, CA: Tanski Publications, 1996.

Gootjes, Albert. *Claude Pajon (1626–1685) and the Academy of Saumur: The First Controversy over Grace*. Leiden: Brill, 2013.

Gordon, T. David. "'Equipping' Ministry in Ephesians 4?" *Journal of the Evangelical Theological Society* 37/1 (1994): 69–78.

Gregory of Nazianzus. "Against Apollinarius; The Second Letter to Cledonius (Ep. CII)." Pages 443-45 in vol. 7 of *Nicene and Post-Nicene Fathers*, Series 2. Edited by Phillip Schaff. 1887. Peabody, MA: Hendrickson, 1994.

———. *On God and Christ: The Five Theological Orations and Two Letters to Cleodonius*. Yonkers, NY: St. Vladimir's Seminary Press, 2002.

Gregory of Nyssa. "On 'Not Three Gods' to Ablabius." Pages 332–36 in vol. 5 of *Nicene and Post-Nicene Fathers*, Series 2. Edited by Phillip Schaff. 1887. Peabody, MA: Hendrickson, 1994.

Grindheim, Sigurd. "A Theology of Glory: Paul's use of *Doxa* Terminology in Romans." *Journal of Biblical Literature* 136/2 (2017): 451–65.

Grudem, Wayne. *The Gift of Prophecy in 1 Corinthians*. Eugene, OR: Wipf & Stock, 1999.

———. "Perseverance of the Saints: A Case Study from Hebrews 6:4–6 and Other Warning Passages of Hebrews." Pages 133–82 in vol. 1 of *The Grace of God and the Bondage of the Will*. Edited by Thomas Schreiner and Bruce Ware. Grand Rapids: Baker Books, 1995.

Grundke, Christopher L. K. "A Tempest in a Teapot? Genesis III 8 Again." *Vetus Testamentum* 51/4 (2001): 548–51.

Hagner, Donald A. *Matthew 1–13*. Word Biblical Commentary 33a. Dallas: Word, 1993.

Hahn, Scott. *Kinship by Covenant: A Canonical Approach to the Fulfillment of God's Saving Promises*. New Haven: Yale University Press, 2009.

Haldane, Robert. *Exposition of the Epistle to the Romans*. 9th ed. Edinburgh: William Oliphant and Co., 1874.

Hall, Edwin. *The Shorter Catechism of the Westminster Assembly with Analysis and Scripture Proofs*. Philadelphia, PA: Presbyterian Publication Committee, 1859.

Halyburton, Thomas. *The Works of the Rev. Thomas Halyburton*.London: Thomas Tegg & Son, 1835.

Harris, Murray J. *The Second Epistle to the Corinthians*. New International Greek Testament Commentary. Grand Rapids: Eerdmans, 2005.

Hartley, John. *Leviticus*. Word Biblical Commentary. Grand Rapids: Zondervan, 1992.

Heppe, Heinrich. *Reformed Dogmatics: Set Out and Illustrated from the Sources*. Edited by Ernst Bizer. Translated by G. T. Thomson. London: George and Unwin Ltd., 1950.

Herbert, George. *The Poems of George Herbert*. London: Oxford University Press, 1913.

Hillers, Delbert R. *The History of a Biblical Idea*. Baltimore: The Johns Hopkins University Press, 1969.

Hodge, Charles. *1 & 2 Corinthians*. 1857, 1859. Repr., Edinburgh: Banner of Truth, 1994.

———. *A Commentary on the Epistle to the Romans*. 19th ed. New York: Robert Carter & Bros., 1880.

———. *An Exposition of the First Epistle to the Corinthians*. New York: Robert Carter & Bros., 1860.

———. *An Exposition of the Second Epistle to the Corinthians*. New York: Robert Carter & Bros., 1866.

———. *Romans*. 1835. Edinburgh: Banner of Truth, 1989.

———. *Systematic Theology*. 3 vols. New York: Scribner, Armstrong, and Co., 1876.

Hofius, Otfried. "The Fourth Servant Song in the New Testament Letters." Pages 163–68 in *The Suffering Servant: Isaiah 53 in Jewish and Christian Sources*. Edited by Bernd Janowski and Peter Stuhlmacher. Grand Rapids: Eerdmans, 2004.

Hoglund, Jonathan. *Called by Triune Grace: Divine Rhetoric and the Effectual Call*. Studies in Christian Doctrine and Scripture. Downers Grove, IL: IVP Academic, 2016.

Holmes, Christopher R. J. *The Holy Spirit*. New Studies in Dogmatics. Grand Rapids: Zondervan, 2015.

Holmes, Michael W., J. B. Lightfoot, and J. R. Harmer ed. and trans. *The Apostolic Fathers: Greek Texts and English Translation*. 3rd ed. 1891. Repr., Grand Rapids: Baker Academic, 2007.

Horton, Michael S. *The Christian Faith: A Systematic Theology for Pilgrims on the Way*. Grand Rapids: Zondervan, 2011.

———. *Covenant and Salvation: Union with Christ*. Louisville: Westminster John Knox, 2007.

Irenaeus. *Against Heresies*. Pages 315–567 in vol. 1 of *Ante-Nicene Fathers*. Edited by Phillip Schaff. Peabody, MA: Hendrickson, 1996.

Irons, Charles Lee. *The Righteousness of God: A Lexical Examination of the Covenant-Faithfulness Interpretation*. Tübingen: Mohr Siebeck, 2015.

Jeremias, Joachim. *The Prayers of Jesus*. Philadelphia: Fortress, 1967.

Jobes, Karen H. *1 Peter*. Baker Exegetical Commentary on the New Testament. Grand Rapids: Baker Academic, 2005.

John of Chrysostom. *Homilies on Genesis 1–17*. Fathers of the Church. Translated by Robert C. Hill. Washington, DC: The Catholic University of America Press, 1999.

John of Damascus. *An Exact Exposition of the Orthodox Faith*. Pages 165–406 in *Saint John of Damascus: Writings*. Vol. 37 of The Fathers of the Church. Translated by Frederic H. Chase, Jr. Washington, D.C.: The Catholic University of America Press, 1958.

Johnson, Luke Timothy. *The Letter of James*. Anchor Bible 37a. New York: Doubleday, 1995.

Kaufman, Stephen A. "The Structure of the Deuteronomic Law," *MAARAV* 1/2 (1979): 105–58.

Kearney, Peter J. "Creation and Liturgy: The P Redaction of Ex 25–40." *Zeitschrift für die alttestamentliche Wissenschaft* 89 (1977): 375–87.

Kelly, Douglas F. "Adoption: an Underdeveloped Heritage of the Westminster Standards." *Reformed Theological Review* 52/3 (1993): 110–20.

Kendall, R. T. *Calvin and English Calvinism to 1649*. Milton Keyes: Paternoster, 1997.

Kidner, Derek. *Psalms 73–150*. Tyndale Old Testament Commentary. Downers Grove, IL: IVP Academic, 1981.

Klein, Ralph W. *1 Samuel*. Word Biblical Commentary. Nashville: Thomas Nelson, 2000.

Kline, Meredith G. *By Oath Consigned: A Reinterpretation of the Covenant Signs of Circumcision and Baptism*. Grand Rapids: Eerdmans, 1968.

———. *God, Heaven, and Har Magedon: A Covenantal Tale of Cosmos and Telos*. Eugene, OR: Wipf & Stock, 2006.

———. *Images of the Spirit*. 1980. Repr., Eugene, OR: Wipf & Stock, 1999.

———. *Kingdom Prologue: Genesis Foundations for a Covenantal Worldview*. Eugene, OR: Wipf & Stock, 2006.

———. *The Structure of Biblical Authority*. 1989. Repr., Eugene, OR: Wipf & Stock, 1997.

Küpper, Joachim. "*Uti* and *frui* in Augustine and the Problem of Aesthetic Pleasure in the Western Tradition." *MLN* 127/5 Supplement (2012): 126–55.

Kuyper, Abraham. *Common Grace*. 3 vols. Bellingham, WA: Lexham Press, 2015–20.

———. *The Work of the Holy Spirit*. Translated by Henri De Vries. New York: Funk & Wagnalls, 1900. Repr., Chattanooga, TN: AMG Publishers, 1995.

Lane, William L. *Hebrews 9–13*. Word Biblical Commentary 47b. Dallas: Word Books, 1991.

Ladd, George Eldon. *A Theology of the New Testament: Revised Edition*. Edited by Donald A. Hagner. 1974. Repr., Grand Rapids: Eerdmans, 1993.

LaRondelle, Hans K. *The Israel of God in Prophecy: Principles of Prophetic Interpretation*. Berrien Springs, MI: Andrews University Press, 1983.

Leigh, Edward. *A Systeme or Body of Divinity*. London: William Lee, 1662.

Letham, Robert. *The Holy Trinity: In Scripture, History, Theology, and Worship*. Phillipsburg: NJ: P&R, 2004.

Levering, Matthew. *Engaging the Doctrine of the Holy Spirit: Love and Gift in the Trinity and the Church*. Grand Rapids: Baker Academic, 2016.

———. *The Theology of Augustine: An Introductory Guide to His Most Important Works*. Grand Rapids: Baker Academic, 2013.

Levison, Jack. *A Boundless God: The Spirit According to the Old Testament*. Grand Rapids: Baker Academic, 2020.

Lewis, C. S. "The Efficacy of Prayer." Pages 3–12 in *The World's Last Night and Other Essays*. New York: Harcourt Brace Jovanovich, 1959.

———. *The Lion, the Witch and the Wardrobe*. 1950. Repr., New York: Collier Books, 1970.

———. *Poems*. Edited by Walter Hooper. New York: Harcourt Brace Jovanovich, 1965.

Lombard, Peter. *The Sentences*. 4 vols. Translated by Giulio Silano. Toronto, Canada: PIMS, 2007.

Longman III, Tremper. *Proverbs*. Baker Commentary on the Old Testament Wisdom and Psalms. Grand Rapids: Baker Academic, 2006.

Luther, Martin. *Lectures on Galatians (1535): Chapters 1–4*. Vol. 26 of *Luther's Works*. Edited by Jaroslav Pelikan. St. Louis: Concordia, 1963.

———. "Sermon on Matt. 3:13–17." Pages 313–30 in vol. 51 of *Luther's Works*. Edited by Jaroslav Pelikan. Philadelphia: Fortress, 1959.

Machen, J. Gresham. *The New Testament: An Introduction to its Literature and History*. Edinburgh: Banner of Truth, 1986.

Malatesta, Edward. *Interiority and Covenant: A Study of* εἶναι ἐν *and* μένειν *In the First Letter of Saint John*. Rome: Biblical Institute Press, 1978.

Marshall, I. Howard. *The Epistles of John*. New International Commentary on the New Testament. Grand Rapids: Eerdmans, 1978.

———. *Kept by the Power of God*. 3rd ed. 1969. Repr., Carlisle, UK: Paternoster, 1995.

Master, Jonathan. *A Question of Consensus: The Doctrine of Assurance after the Westminster Confession*. Minneapolis: Fortress, 2015.

McCaskill, Grant. *Living in Union with Christ: Paul's Gospel and Christian Moral Identity*. Grand Rapids: Baker Academic, 2019.

M'Cheyne, Robert Murray. *Memoir and Remains of the Rev. R. M. M'Cheyne*. Edinburgh: Oliphant Anderson & Ferrier, 1892.

McComisky, Thomas Edward. *The Minor Prophets*. 1992. Repr., Grand Rapids: Baker Academic, 2009.

McFadden, Kevin W. *Faith in the Son of God: The Place of Christ-Oriented Faith Within Pauline Theology*. Wheaton, IL: Crossway, 2021.

McGrath, Alister. *Iustitia Dei: A History of the Christian Doctrine of Justification*. 2nd ed. 1986. Repr., Cambridge: Cambridge University Press, 1998.

Michaels, J. Ramsey. "Atonement in John's Gospel and Epistles." Pages 106–18 in *The Glory of the Atonement: Essays in Honor of Roger Nicole*. Downers Grove, IL: InterVarsity Press, 2004.

Milen, Garnet H. "'Private Spirits' in the Westminster Confession of Faith and in Protestant-Catholic Debates: A Response to Byron Curtis." *Westminster Theological Journal* 61 (1999): 101–10.

Milgrom, Jacob. *Leviticus*. Anchor Bible. New Haven: Yale University Press, 1991.

———. *Leviticus 1–16*. Anchor Bible. New York: Doubleday, 1998.

Moo, Douglas. *The Epistle to the Romans*. New International Commentary on the New Testament. Grand Rapids: Eerdmans, 1996.

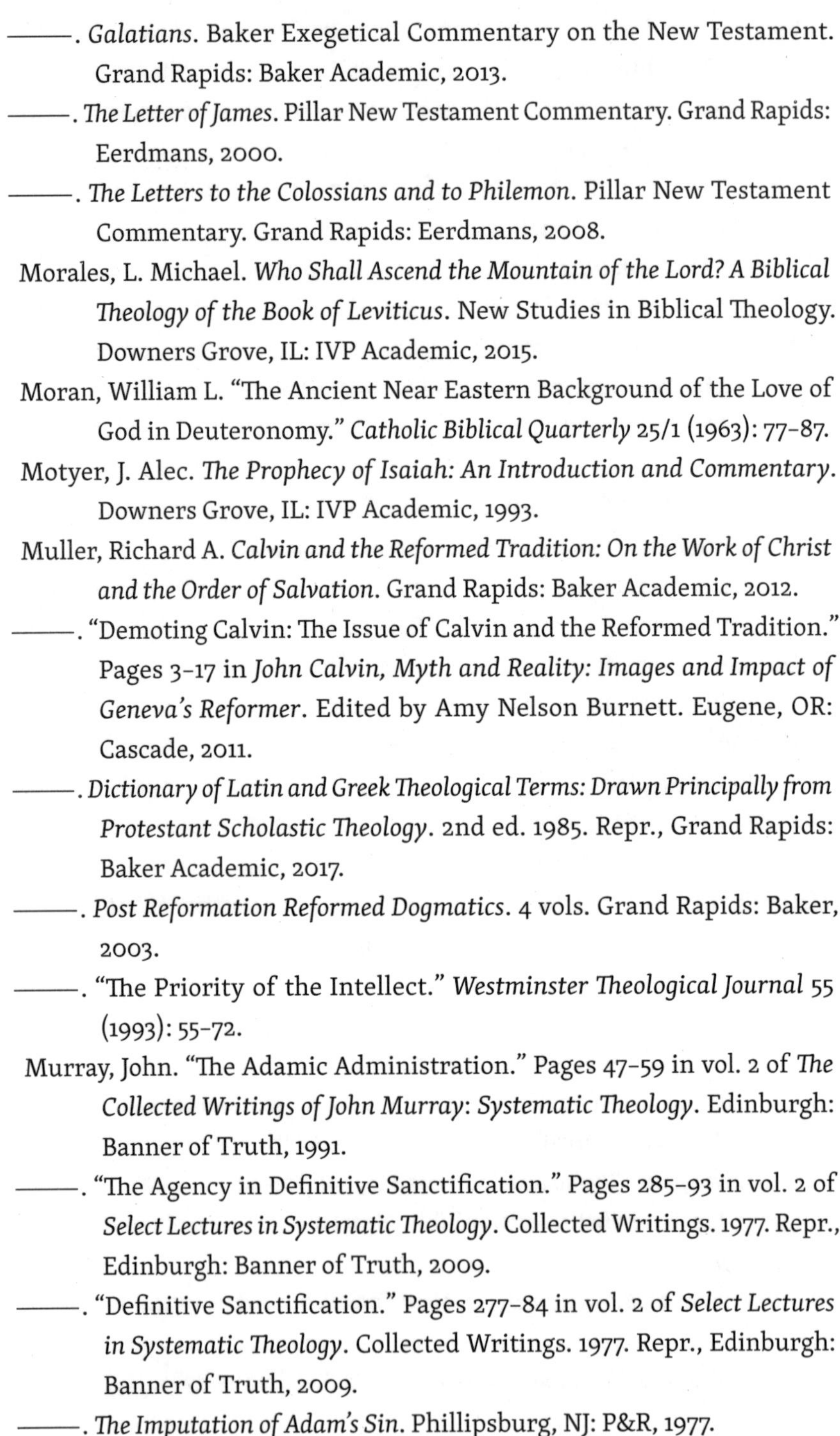

———. *Galatians*. Baker Exegetical Commentary on the New Testament. Grand Rapids: Baker Academic, 2013.

———. *The Letter of James*. Pillar New Testament Commentary. Grand Rapids: Eerdmans, 2000.

———. *The Letters to the Colossians and to Philemon*. Pillar New Testament Commentary. Grand Rapids: Eerdmans, 2008.

Morales, L. Michael. *Who Shall Ascend the Mountain of the Lord? A Biblical Theology of the Book of Leviticus*. New Studies in Biblical Theology. Downers Grove, IL: IVP Academic, 2015.

Moran, William L. "The Ancient Near Eastern Background of the Love of God in Deuteronomy." *Catholic Biblical Quarterly* 25/1 (1963): 77–87.

Motyer, J. Alec. *The Prophecy of Isaiah: An Introduction and Commentary*. Downers Grove, IL: IVP Academic, 1993.

Muller, Richard A. *Calvin and the Reformed Tradition: On the Work of Christ and the Order of Salvation*. Grand Rapids: Baker Academic, 2012.

———. "Demoting Calvin: The Issue of Calvin and the Reformed Tradition." Pages 3–17 in *John Calvin, Myth and Reality: Images and Impact of Geneva's Reformer*. Edited by Amy Nelson Burnett. Eugene, OR: Cascade, 2011.

———. *Dictionary of Latin and Greek Theological Terms: Drawn Principally from Protestant Scholastic Theology*. 2nd ed. 1985. Repr., Grand Rapids: Baker Academic, 2017.

———. *Post Reformation Reformed Dogmatics*. 4 vols. Grand Rapids: Baker, 2003.

———. "The Priority of the Intellect." *Westminster Theological Journal* 55 (1993): 55–72.

Murray, John. "The Adamic Administration." Pages 47–59 in vol. 2 of *The Collected Writings of John Murray: Systematic Theology*. Edinburgh: Banner of Truth, 1991.

———. "The Agency in Definitive Sanctification." Pages 285–93 in vol. 2 of *Select Lectures in Systematic Theology*. Collected Writings. 1977. Repr., Edinburgh: Banner of Truth, 2009.

———. "Definitive Sanctification." Pages 277–84 in vol. 2 of *Select Lectures in Systematic Theology*. Collected Writings. 1977. Repr., Edinburgh: Banner of Truth, 2009.

———. *The Imputation of Adam's Sin*. Phillipsburg, NJ: P&R, 1977.

———. *Redemption Accomplished and Applied*. Grand Rapids: Eerdmans, 1955.

Naselli, Andrew David. "Keswick Theology: A Survey and Analysis of the Doctrine of Sanctification in the Early Keswick Movement." *Detroit Baptist Seminary Journal* 13 (2008): 17–67.

———. *No Quick Fix: Where Higher Life Theology Came From, What It Is, and Why It's Harmful*. Bellingham, WA: Lexham Press, 2017.

Neusner, Jacob. *First-Century Judaism in Crisis: Yohanan ben Zakkai and the Renaissance of Torah*. 1975. Repr., Eugene, OR: Wipf & Stock, 2006.

Nevius, John Livingston. *Demon Possessions and Allied Themes: Being an Inductive Study of Phenomena of Our Own Times*. 2nd ed. Chicago, IL: Revell, 1896.

Niehaus, Jeffery. "In the Wind of the Storm: Another Look at Genesis 3:8." *Vetus Testamentum* 44/2 (1994): 263–67.

O'Brien, Peter T. *The Epistle to the Philippians*. New International Greek Testament Commentary. Grand Rapids: Eerdmans, 1991.

Oden, Thomas C. *Classic Christianity: A Systematic Theology*. San Francisco, CA: Harper One, 1992.

Old, Hughes Oliphant. *The Reading and Preaching of the Scriptures in the Worship of the Christian Church*. 7 vols. Grand Rapids: Eerdmans, 1998.

Ortlund, Dane. "What Does It Mean to Fall Short of the Glory of God? Romans 3:23 in Biblical-Theological Perspective." *Westminster Theological Journal* 80 (2018): 121–40.

Oss, Douglas. "A Pentecostal / Charismatic View." Pages 237–83 in *Are Miraculous Gifts for Today? Four Views*. Edited by Wayne A. Grudem. Grand Rapids: Zondervan, 1996.

Owen, John. *The Works of John Owen*. 24 vols. Edited by William H. Goold. 1851–1862. Repr., Edinburgh: Banner of Truth, 1966.

Pelagius. *The Letters of Pelagius and His Followers*. Translated by B. R. Rees. Rochester, NY: Boydell & Brewer, 1991.

Perkins, William. *A Golden Chaine, or The Description of Theologie, Containing the Order of the Causes of Salvation and Damnation, According to Gods Word*. Cambridge: John Legate, 1597.

———. *The Works of William Perkins*. 10 vols. Edited by Joel R. Beeke and Derek W. H. Thomas. Grand Rapids: Reformation Heritage Books, 2014–2020.

Peterson, Robert A. "Preservation, Perseverance, Assurance, and Apostasy." *Presbyterion* 22/1 (1996): 31–41.

Pierce, Timothy M. *Enthroned on Our Praise: An Old Testament Theology of Worship*. Nashville: B&H Academic, 2008.

Piper, John. *What Is Saving Faith? Reflections on Receiving Christ as Treasure*. Wheaton, IL: Crossway, 2022.

Piscator, Johannes. *A Learned and Profitable Treatise on Man's Justification*. London: 1599.

Pitre, Brant. "The Lord's Prayer and the New Exodus." *Letter & Spirit* 2 (2006): 69–96.

Polyander, Johannes et al. *Synopsis Purioris Theologiae / Synopsis of a Purer Theology*. 3 vols. Edited by Dolf te Velde, et al. Leiden: Brill, 2014–2020.

Pugliese, Marc A. "How Important Is the Filioque for Reformed Orthodoxy?" *Westminster Theological Journal* 66/1 (2004): 159–77.

Robertson, O. Palmer. *The Books of Nahum, Habakkuk, and Zephaniah*. New International Commentary on the Old Testament. Grand Rapids: Eerdmans, 1990.

———. *The Israel of God: Yesterday, Today, and Tomorrow*. Phillipsburg, NJ: P&R, 2000.

———. "Tongues: Sign of Covenantal Curse and Blessing." *Westminster Theological Journal* 38/1 (1975): 43–53.

Rollock, Robert. *A Treatise of Our Effectual Calling*. Pages 29–288 in *Select Works of Robert Rollock*. Edited by William M. Gunn. Edinburgh: Wodrow Society, 1844.

Rutherford, Samuel. *The Covenant of Life Opened*. Edinburgh: Robert Broun, 1654.

Sailhamer, John. *The Pentateuch as Narrative: A Biblical-Theological Commentary*. Grand Rapids: Zondervan, 1992.

Sakenfeld, Katherine Doob. *The Meaning of Hesed in the Hebrew Bible*. Missoula, MT: Scholars Press, 1978.

Sarna, Nahum M. *Genesis*. JPS Torah Commentary. Philadelphia: Jewish Publication Society, 1989.

Schaff, Phillip, ed. *The Creeds of Christendom*. 3 vols. 6th ed. Repr., Grand Rapids: Baker Books, 1990.

Schmid, Heinrich. *The Doctrinal Theology of the Evangelical Lutheran Church.* Translated by Charles A. Hay and Henry E. Jacobs. Philadelphia: Lutheran Publication Society, 1876.

Schnittjer, Gary Edward. *Old Testament Use of Old Testament: A Book-by-Book Guide*. Grand Rapids: Zondervan, 2021.

Schreiner, Thomas R. *Commentary on Hebrews*. Biblical Theology for Christian Proclamation. Nashville: Holman Reference, 2015.

———. *Romans*. 2nd ed. Baker Exegetical Commentary on the New Testament. Grand Rapids: Baker Academic, 2018.

———. *Run to Win the Prize: Perseverance in the New Testament*. Wheaton, IL: Crossway, 2010.

Schreiner, Thomas R., and Ardel B. Caneday. *The Race Set Before Us: A Biblical Theology of Perseverance and Assurance*. Downers Grove, IL: InterVarsity Press, 2001.

Scott, James. *Adoption as Sons of God: An Exegetical Investigation into the Background in the Pauline Corpus*. Tübingen: Mohr Siebeck, 1992.

Shaw, Robert. *An Exposition of the Confession of Faith of the Westminster Assembly of Divines*. 2nd ed. Edinburgh: John Johnstone, 1845.

Shelton, Sally J. "Overshadowed by the Spirit: Mary, Mother of Our Lord, Prototype of Spirit-Baptized Humanity." PhD Diss., Regent University, 2016.

Shepherd, Norman. *The Call of Grace: How the Covenant Illuminates Salvation and Evangelism*. Phillipsburg, NJ: P&R, 2000.

———. "Justification by Works in Reformed Theology." In *Backbone of the Bible: Covenant in Contemporary Perspective*. Edited by P. Andrew Sandlin. Nacogdoches, LA: Covenant Media Foundation, 2004.

Siecienski, A. Edward. *The Filioque: History of a Doctrinal Controversy*. Oxford: Oxford University Press, 2010.

Silva, Moisés. "Faith Versus Works of Law in Galatians." Pages 217–48 in vol. 2 of *Justification and Variegated Nomism*. Edited by D. A. Carson, Peter T. O'Brien, and Mark Seifrid. Grand Rapids: Baker Academic, 2004.

———. *Philippians*. 2nd ed. Baker Exegetical Commentary on the New Testament. 1992. Repr., Grand Rapids: Baker Academic, 2005.

Smeaton, George. *The Doctrine of the Holy Spirit*. Edinburgh: T&T Clark, 1882.

Smith, M. J. "God's Righteousness, Christ's Faith/fulness, and 'Justification by Faith Alone' (Rom. 3:21–26)." Pages 181–254 in *Romans and the*

*Legacy of St. Paul: Historical, Theological, and Social Perspectives*. Edited P. G. Bold and J. R. Harrison. Macquarie Park: SCD Press, 2019.

———. "Paul in the Twenty-First Century." Pages 1–33 in *All Things to All Cultures: Paul among Jews, Greeks and Romans*. Edited by M. Harding and A. Nobbs. Grand Rapids: Eerdmans, 2013.

Snodgrass, Kline R. *Stories with Intent: A Comprehensive Guide to the Parables*. 2nd ed. 2008. Repr., Grand Rapids: Eerdmans, 2018.

Speiser, E. A. *Genesis*. Anchor Bible. New York: Doubleday, 1962.

Stanglin, Keith D. *Arminius on Assurance of Salvation: The Context, Roots, and Shape of the Leiden Debate, 1603–1609*. Leiden: Brill, 2007.

Stott, John W. *The Letters of John*. Tyndale New Testament Commentaries. Grand Rapids: Eerdmans, 1988.

Swain, Scott "Covenant of Redemption," Pages 78–106 in *Christian Dogmatics: Reformed Theology for the Church Catholic*. Edited by Michael Allen and Scott Swain. Grand Rapids: Baker Academic, 2016.

Jacobs, Henry Eyster, ed. *The Book of Concord; or The Symbolical Books of the Evangelical Lutheran Church*. Philadelphia: The United Lutheran Publication House, 1911.

Thiselton, Anthony C. *The Holy Spirit—In Biblical Teaching, through the Centuries, and Today*. Grand Rapids: Eerdmans, 2013.

Thompson, Mark, "The Theology of Justification by Faith: The theological case for Sola Fide." Pages 419–40 in *The Doctrine on Which the Church Stands or Falls: Justification in Biblical, Theological, Historical, and Pastoral Perspective*. Edited by Matthew Barrett. Wheaton, IL: Crossway, 2019.

Thompson, J. S. *Deuteronomy*. Tyndale Old Testament Commentary. Downers Grove, IL: InterVarsity Press, 1974.

Thornwell, James Henley. "Antinomianism." Pages 238–96 in vol. 2 of *The Collected Writings of James Henley Thornwell*. Edited by John B. Adger. Richmond, VA: Presbyterian Committee of Publication, 1871.

Torrell, Jean-Pierre. *Saint Thomas Aquinas*. 2 vols. Translated by Robert Royal. Washington, DC: The Catholic University of America Press, 2003.

Trumper, Tim J. R. "The Theological History of Adoption I: An Account." *Scottish Bulletin of Evangelical Theology* 20/1 (2002): 4–28.

———. "The Theological History of Adoption II: A Rationale." *Scottish Bulletin of Evangelical Theology* 20/2 (2002): 177–202.

Turretin, Francis. *Institutes of Elenctic Theology*. Edited by James T. Dennison, Jr. Translated by George Musgrave Giger. Phillipsburg, NJ: P&R, 1992–1997.

Ursinus, Zacharias. *Corpus Doctrinae Orthodoxae, sive Catecheticarum Explicationum*. Heidelberg: Ionas Rhodius, 1616.

———. *Larger Catechism*. Pages 168–69 in *An Introduction to the Heidelberg Catechism: Sources, History and Theology*. Edited by Lyle D. Bierma, et al. Grand Rapids: Baker Academic, 2005.

Van Dam, Cornelis. *The Urim and Thummim: A Means of Revelation in Ancient Israel*. Winona Lake, IN: Eisenbrauns, 1997.

Van der Kooi, Cornelis and Gijsbert van den Brink. *Christian Dogmatics: An Introduction*. Translated by Reinder Bruinsma and James D. Bratt. Grand Rapids: Eerdmans, 2017.

VanDrunen, David. *Divine Covenants and Moral Order: A Biblical Theology of Natural Law*. Grand Rapids: Eerdmans, 2014.

———. "To Obey Is Better Than Sacrifice: A Defense of the Active Obedience of Christ in the Light of Recent Criticism." Pages 127–46 in *By Faith Alone: Answering the Challenges to the Doctrine of Justification*. Edited by Gary L. W. Johnson and Guy P. Waters. Wheaton, IL: Crossway, 2006.

VanGemeren, Willem A. *Interpreting the Prophetic Word: An Introduction to the Prophetic Literature of the Old Testament*. Grand Rapids: Zondervan, 1990.

Van Mastricht, Petrus. *Theoretical-Practical Theology*. Edited by Joel R. Beeke. Translated by Todd M. Rester. 2 vols. Grand Rapids: Reformation Heritage Books, 2019.

———. *A Treatise on Regeneration*. Edited by Brandon Withrow. Morgan, PA: Soli Deo Gloria, 2002.

Vickers, Brian. *Jesus' Blood and Righteousness: Paul's Theology of Imputation*. Wheaton, IL: Crossway, 2006.

———. *Justification by Grace Through Faith: Finding Freedom from Legalism, Lawlessness, Pride, and Despair*. Explorations in Biblical Theology. Phillipsburg, NJ: P&R, 2013.

Vidu, Adonis. *The Same God Who Works All Things: Inseparable Operations in Trinitarian Theology*. Grand Rapids: Eerdmans, 2021.

Von Rad, Gerhard. *Genesis*. Old Testament Library. 1961. Repr., Philadelphia: Westminster, 1972.

Vos, Geerhardus. *Biblical Theology*. 1985. Repr., Edinburgh: Banner of Truth, 2014.

———. "The Doctrine of the Covenant in Reformed Theology." Pages 234–67 in *Redemptive History and Biblical Interpretation: The Shorter Writings of Geerhardus Vos*. Edited by Richard B. Gaffin, Jr. Phillipsburg, NJ: P&R, 1980.

———. "Eschatology and the Spirit in Paul." Pages 211–59 in *Biblical and Theological Studies*. New York: Scribner's Sons, 1912.

———. *Grace and Glory: Sermons Preached in the Chapel of Princeton Theological Seminary*. 1922. Repr., Edinburgh: Banner of Truth, 1994.

———. "The Idea of Biblical Theology." Pages 3–24 in *Redemptive History and Biblical Interpretation: The Shorter Writings of Geerhardus Vos*. Edited by Richard B. Gaffin, Jr. Phillipsburg, NJ: P&R, 1980.

———. *The Pauline Eschatology*. 1930. Repr., Phillipsburg, NJ: P&R, 1994.

———. *Reformed Dogmatics*. 5 vols. Edited by Richard B. Gaffin, Jr. Bellingham, WA: Lexham Press, 2014–2016.

———. *The Self-Disclosure of Jesus: The Modern Debate About the Messianic Consciousness*. 2nd ed. Edited by J. G. Vos. 1926; 1953. Repr., Phillipsburg, NJ: P & R, 2002.

Wallace, Daniel B. "The Semantic Range of the Article-Noun-Kai-Noun Plural Construction in the New Testament." *Grace Theological Journal* 4 (1983): 59–84.

Walvoord, John F. "The Augustinian-Dispensational Perspective." Pages 197–226 in *Five Views on Sanctification*. Edited by Melvin E. Dieter. Grand Rapids: Zondervan, 1987.

Warfield, B. B. *Counterfeit Miracles*. New York: Scribner's Sons, 1918.

———. *The Works of B. B. Warfield*. 10 vols. Grand Rapids: Baker Books, 1981.

Waters, Guy Prentiss. *Justification and the New Perspectives on Paul: A Review and Response*. Phillipsburg, NJ: P&R, 2004.

Weber, Otto. *Foundations for Dogmatics*. 2 vols. Translated by Darrell L. Guder. Grand Rapids: Eerdmans, 1983.

Webster, John. *Holiness*. Grand Rapids: Eerdmans, 2003.

Weinandy, Thomas. *Jesus Becoming Jesus: A Theological Interpretation of the Synoptic Gospels*. Washington DC: The Catholic University of America Press, 2018.

Wellum, Stephen. *God the Son Incarnate: The Doctrine of Christ*. Foundations of Evangelical Theology. Wheaton, IL: Crossway, 2016.

Wenham, Gordon J. "Sanctuary Symbolism in the Garden of Eden Story." Pages 399–404 in *I Studied Inscriptions from Before the Flood: Ancient Near Eastern, Literary, and Linguistic Approaches to Genesis 1-11*. Edited by Richard S. Hess and David Toshio Tsumura. Winona Lake, IN: Eisenbrauns, 1994.

Wesley, John. *A Plain Account of Christian Perfection*. 5th ed. London: J. Paramore, 1785.

Westerholm, Stephen. *Perspectives Old and New on Paul: The 'Lutheran' Paul and His Critics*. Grand Rapids: Eerdmans, 2003.

White, R. F. "Richard Gaffin and Wayne Grudem on 1 Corinthians 13:10: A Comparison of Cessationist and Noncessationist Argumentation." *Journal of the Evangelical Theological Society* 25 (1992): 173–81.

Wilder, William N. *Echoes of the Exodus Narrative in the Context and Background of Galatians 5:18*. New York: Lang, 2001.

———. "Illumination and Investiture: The Royal Significance of the Tree of Wisdom." *Westminster Theological Journal* 68 (2006): 56–69.

Wisse, Maarten. "*Habitus Fidei*: an Essay on the History of a Concept." *Scottish Journal of Theology* 56/2 (2003): 172–89.

Witsius, Herman. *Conciliatory, or Irenical Animadversions on the Controversies Agitated in Britain, Under the Unhappy Names of Antinomians and Neonomians*. Translated by Thomas Bell. Glasgow, Scotland: Lang, 1807.

———. *Lord's Prayer*. Translated by William Pringle. 1839. Repr., Phillipsburg, NJ: P&R, 1994.

Wollebius, Johannes. *Christiana Theologia Compendium*. Amsterdam: Johannes Jansonius, 1633.

Wright, Christopher J. H. *Knowing the Holy Spirit Through the Old Testament*. Downers Grove, IL: 2006.

Wright, N. T. *Jesus and the Victory of God*. Minneapolis: Fortress, 1996.

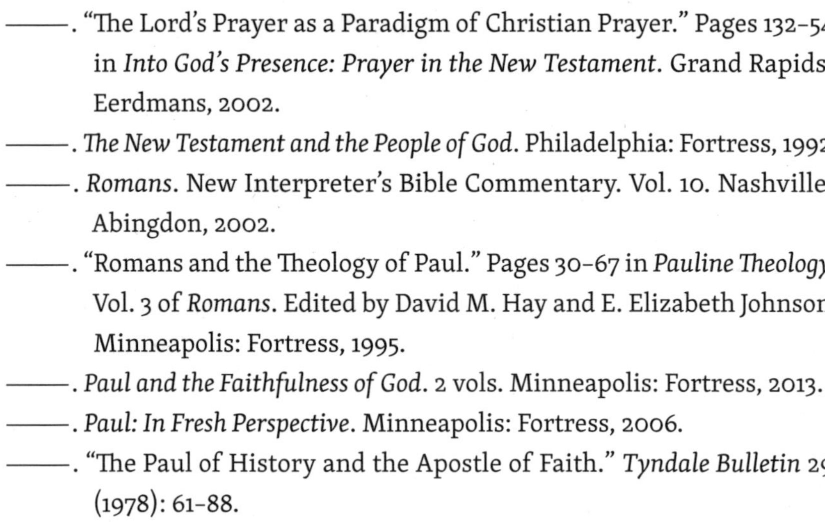

———. "The Lord's Prayer as a Paradigm of Christian Prayer." Pages 132–54 in *Into God's Presence: Prayer in the New Testament*. Grand Rapids: Eerdmans, 2002.

———. *The New Testament and the People of God*. Philadelphia: Fortress, 1992.

———. *Romans*. New Interpreter's Bible Commentary. Vol. 10. Nashville: Abingdon, 2002.

———. "Romans and the Theology of Paul." Pages 30–67 in *Pauline Theology*. Vol. 3 of *Romans*. Edited by David M. Hay and E. Elizabeth Johnson. Minneapolis: Fortress, 1995.

———. *Paul and the Faithfulness of God*. 2 vols. Minneapolis: Fortress, 2013.

———. *Paul: In Fresh Perspective*. Minneapolis: Fortress, 2006.

———. "The Paul of History and the Apostle of Faith." *Tyndale Bulletin* 29 (1978): 61–88.

Wuellner, Bernard. *Dictionary of Scholastic Philosophy*. Fitzwilliam, NH: Loreto Publications, 2012.

Yinger, Kent. *The New Perspective: An Introduction*. Eugene, OR: Cascade Books, 2011.

Young, E. J. *The Book of Isaiah*. 3 vols. Grand Rapids: Eerdmans, 1972.

Zahl, Simeon. "Experience," Pages 177–95 in *Oxford Handbook of Nineteenth-Century Christian Thought*. Oxford: Oxford University Press, 2017.

Zanchi, Girolamo. *De Religione Christiana Fides—Confession of Christian Religion*. 2 vols. Edited by Luca Baschera and Christian Moser. Leiden: Brill, 2007.

———. *The Spiritual Marriage Between Christ and His Church and Every One of the Faithful*. Translated by Patrick O'Banion. Grand Rapids: Reformation Heritage Books, 2021.

# SUBJECT INDEX

# AUTHOR INDEX

# SCRIPTURE INDEX

## Old Testament

Leviticus

## New Testament

The
LORD
JESUS
CHRIST
WE BELIEVE · WE BELIEVE · WE
The
BIBLICAL
DOCTRINE
of the
PERSON
AND
WORK
of CHRIST
Volume Three
BRANDON D.
CROWE
Series Editors
JOHN McCLEAN &
MURRAY J. SMITH